From Racism to Genocide

From Racism to Genocide

Anthropology in the Third Reich

Gretchen E. Schafft

University of Illinois Press
Urbana and Chicago

Library of Congress Cataloging-in-Publication Data
Schafft, Gretchen Engle.
From racism to genocide : anthropology in the Third Reich / Gretchen
E. Schafft.
p.   cm.
Includes bibliographical references and index.
ISBN 0-252-02930-5 (cloth : alk. paper)
1. Anthropology—Germany—History—20th century.
2. Racism in anthropology—Germany—History—20th century.
3. Anthropometry—Germany—History—20th century.
4. Eugenics—Germany—History—20th century. 5. Anthropological
ethics—Germany—History—20th century. 6. National socialism—
Germany—History. 7. National Anthropological Archives—History—
Sources. 8. Institut für Deutsche Ostarbeit (Krakow, Poland)—
History—Sources. 9. Germany—History—1933–1945. 10. Germany—
Politics and government—1933–1945. 11. World War, 1939–1945—
Collaborationists—Germany. I. Title.
GN17.3.G3S33   2004
301.'0943'0904—dc22   2003024634

For my grandmother,
Bertha Nehlsen Wade,
who made Germany seem so interesting;
and for my parents,
Margaretta Wade Engle and Orville Engle,
who recognized racism when they saw it
and did what they could

Contents

Preface

I have always considered myself a social anthropologist. My training included exposure to the four fields of anthropology: physical anthropology, archaeology, linguistics, and social anthropology; but I was drawn to social anthropology and linguistics.

Each of the variety of fields and topics touched on in this book could support scholarship from its own particular point of view. Any of the four fields of anthropology could have been an appropriate focus, as could history or biology. Emphasis could have been placed on World War II history, biological anthropology, or sociology as well.

The goals I had in writing this book were quite different. Foremost, I wanted to expose, analyze, and critique the actions of anthropologists in the Third Reich in order to break the silence on their extensive participation in racist decision making and destruction of human lives. The victims of Nazi anthropology were not only, or even primarily, Jews, for most of the Jews living during the years of the Third Reich were identified on the basis of civil records about which there was little debate. Usually, but not always, it was in individual cases of verification of "Jewishness" or in instances in which particular people were brought before racial courts that anthropologists played a large role. More often, their advice and research was sought by the bureaucracies of the Third Reich in questions of mixed identities and unclear ethnicities. Poles, Ukrainians, Roma ("Gypsies"), and even the handicapped were more likely to fall into these ambiguous groups. Thus, while this book explains in broad strokes what happened to the Jews and looks at one case (Tarnów) in which the Jews were targeted for anthropological study, it explores more thoroughly aspects of the Third Reich that have been addressed less often in the literature: the overall drive of the Hitler regime to exploit all resources while building what they hoped would be a flawlessly homogeneous society.

I also wanted to show the connections between issues that we identify with the Third Reich and issues that confront us today, such as scientism, racism, and civic and professional denial. Unethical research on human subjects—objectifying those who are the focus of research in ways that dehumanize them, essentializing groups ethnically different from us—all reflect both the hierarchical placement of humans in the political economy and a widening of the us/them gap that exists among all human groups. We must continue to face these problems, not as problems that occurred at another time, but as issues that are human in nature and that will always need to be identified and dealt with.

Finally, I wrote this book as a beginning of the exploration of the role of anthropologists in the genocidal history of the last century, not as the final word. It sketches the outline of the history of the times, repeats some common knowledge of events and personages in the Third Reich in order to place the anthropological activities in context, and then explicates the deeds that have too often been shrouded in a convenient silence. If a tone of moral outrage creeps in here and there, so be it.

*   *   *

I want to thank many who contributed to my thoughts and ideas about this topic, but the book certainly would not have been written without the participation and support of four particular people. Gerhard Zeidler has been my dedicated colleague and friend for more than a dozen years. He has a relentless enthusiasm for research and has participated with utter enthusiasm in every step of this investigation. Harry Schafft, my husband of more than forty years, never faltered in his support of this project. He is the essence of integrity, and that quality alone made his substantive comments and suggestions on the content of the book invaluable. Hilda Wenner, my irreplaceable sister and friend, has shared my profound interest in the period and constantly alerted me to materials that would be useful. She also provided significant editorial assistance. Robert Garrison, my employer during much of the time spent on this book, without a complaint allowed me to have a work schedule that accommodated my trips to Europe for archival research. His kindness and constant cheer kept my spirits up when the material itself seemed almost too much to bear.

William Leap suggested the University of Illinois Press and helped to "wordsmith" the language I used in preparing materials for them, just as he has since the time when I was his graduate student. Adrian Wenner and Bettina Arnold offered extensive commentaries that were very focused and helpful. Erika Falkenreck read parts of the original draft and faithfully provided me with translations of difficult phrases and articles from the German press on topics covered in this book. Adam Bartosz offered information and support on issues concerning the Roma and the Jews of Tarnów. Michael Zeidler contributed commentary from Germany. Teresa Ulewicz provided several valuable materials not available to me elsewhere. Elizabeth Mahoney helped produce the initial copy for publication review, and Carol Godley helped in the final production of the manuscript with great skill and energy. Michael Neufeld, Norig Asbed, Jeannette Asbed, Daniel Wade, Kay Johnson, and Barbara Rosing offered comments on all or part of the manuscript.

John Homiak, director of the National Anthropological Archives at the Smithsonian Institution, gave me and Gerhard Zeidler the rare privilege of shelving the Institut für Deutsche Ostarbeit materials and rewriting the documentation that described them. Alan Bain, Vyrtis Thomas, and Robert Leopold of the anthropological archive staff were particularly supportive and offered valuable assistance. Archivists in Europe often were extremely helpful, and as an added bonus, some of them had a real excitement about the project. In that regard, a special thanks to Gregor Pickro of the Bundesarchiv Koblenz, Adam Cieslak of the Uniwersytet Jagiellonski Archiwum, Marion Kazemi of the Max Planck Gesellschaft Archiv, and Julien Baranowski of the Archiwum Państwowe in Łódź. Of course, I appreciated the assistance of all of the archive staffs whom we met during our research. Uwe Hossfeld discussed the materials in the Universitätsarchiv Jena with me and was very candid about many of the issues that have impacted anthropology in Germany.

Karl-Otto Henseling and his wife, Ria Henseling, opened his personal photo albums and documentation about his father to me, and they were willing to discuss what they knew of the elder Henselings' roles in the Institut für Deutsche Ostarbeit. Dr. Henseling not only elucidated the position of his father and the later development of his mother's beliefs and values but broke my own facile stereotype of perpetrators to show me a much more complicated picture.

Other friends, such as Barbara Lenkerd, Mauricio Cortina, Ruth Cernea, Muriel Crespi, Karen Levenback, Gail Perry, Austin Perry, Terry Katz, Jonathan Katz, Kyle Whitley, Helisa Whitley, Marion Pelny, and Berthold Schmidt, listened and discussed aspects of the book, offered suggestions, and sometimes even housed me during trips to archives away from the Washington area. Sharon Scanlan, Gene Mirkin, and Jerry Haller, in their own ways, kept me going.

My thanks also go to the University of Illinois Press and especially Elizabeth Dulany, who believed in this book, and John K. Wilson, who edited it with great care.

I owe a great deal to survivors of the Third Reich who shared their stories with me and allowed me the privilege of working with them in their groups and organizations. Particularly, my thanks go to Yves Béon, who has been a friend and colleague for more than a decade and opened many doors to me; and Martin Adler, whose generous spirit and brave intelligence sought reconciliation when it was possible. The victims of the Third Reich were very much with me as I wrote this book.

Abbreviations

AA	Państwowe Muzeum, Auschwitz-Birkenau, Oświęcim, Poland
AAA	American Anthropological Association
BAK	Bundesarchiv Koblenz, Koblenz, Germany
BAL	Bundesarchiv Lichterfelde, Berlin, Germany
BDC	Berlin Document Center
DAF	Deutsche Arbeitsfront
DFG	Deutsche Forschungsgemeinschaft
DVL	Deutsche Volksliste
FDRL	Franklin Delano Roosevelt Library, Hyde Park, New York
FRG	Federal Republic of Germany
GDR	German Democratic Republic
GG	Generalgouvernement
IDO	Institut für Deutsche Ostarbeit
IMT	International Military Tribunal, Nuremberg, Germany
KWG	Kaiser-Wilhelm-Gesellschaft
KWI	Kaiser-Wilhelm-Institut, Berlin, Germany (with branches in other cities)
KWIA	Kaiser-Wilhelm-Institut für Anthropologie, menschliche Erblehre und Eugenik, Berlin, Germany
LA	Archiwum Państwowe, Łódź, Poland
MPGA	Archiv zur Geschichte der Max-Planck-Gesellschaft, Berlin, Germany
NA	National Archives, Washington, D.C.
NAA-SI	National Anthropological Archives, Smithsonian Institution, Washington, D.C.
NDW	Notgemeinschaft der Deutschen Wissenschaft
NSDAP	Nationalsozialistische Deutsche Arbeiter Partei
PA	Archiwum Państwowe, Poznań, Poland
RAC	Rockefeller Archive Center, Sleepy Hollow, New York

RKF	Reichskommissar für die Festigung deutschen Volkstums
RSHA	Reichssicherheitshauptamt
RuSHA	SS-Rasse- und Siedlungshauptamt
SA	Sturmabteilungen
SD	Sicherheitsdienst
SPD	Sozialdemokratische Partei Deutschlands
SRV	Sektion Rassen- und Volkstumsforschung
SS	Schutzstaffeln
UJA	Uniwersytet Jagiellonski Archiwum, Kraków, Poland
WA	Archiwum Państwowe, Warsaw, Poland
WVHA	SS-Wirtschafts-Verwaltungshauptamt

From Racism to Genocide

Introduction

A Professional Dilemma

The phone rang one evening about a year after my colleague and I had finished archiving papers and artifacts collected by Nazi anthropologists working in Poland during the Second World War. The caller introduced himself as a physical anthropologist. He had heard of the materials we had rediscovered in packing crates at the Smithsonian's National Anthropological Archives (NAA-SI) and had described in an archival "finding" aid.[1] He wanted to discuss with me a dilemma he was having. He wanted to do a thorough analysis of these measurements and the physical data made of various population groups during Poland's occupation in the war, now available at the Smithsonian. A colleague with whom he had discussed his plans accused him of being unethical, for he would be following the Nazi agenda in this pursuit. He assured me that he only wanted to discover similarities and differences among population groups whose data had been recorded. What did I think?

He may have expected a short answer, but I had just spent the year pondering the imponderable. How could the anthropologists in Germany have conducted research on people in camps and ghettos slated for death or slave labor? How could they have been so callous toward the human suffering they witnessed and helped to cause? I had concluded that a large part of their involvement in the Third Reich and its wide-reaching evils had been a zeal for "scientism," the urge to follow lines of inquiry to their ultimate conclusion regardless of human consequences and without respect for standards of scientific thought and process. These anthropologists wanted above all to build their own careers.

The caller continued, asserting that he was really upset and troubled by the disparity between his "scientific" interests and the implication that he was insensitive to issues of human research. Did I think it would be wrong to reopen these research data and explore them for the light they might shed on past populations of Poland and parts of Eastern Europe?

The forty-two morphological measurements, collected on printed forms from many population groups in occupied Poland, were not gathered in a benign fashion. They were taken from people brought to data collection centers by force and at gunpoint. Interpretations of the measurements could mean life or death for the subject: those individuals labeled "Jewish" or "Gypsy" could be sent to a death camp. Even those identified as having German ethnic traits might be sent to the Russian front as the least valued among the "German" troops. For those thought to be "Serb-Oriental," a fate in occupied Poland or the Ukraine would be devised.

I had to answer the caller's questions with some of my own. "Why do you want to explore these measurements? What is the purpose of the studies you want to do?" Bypassing these questions, my caller told me how it was *possible* to do these studies, that *today* gathering such a large variety of measurements is no longer possible: therefore, these data should not be wasted.

"But, for what purpose?" I asked again.

"To show patterns of migration and population settlement," he answered.

I could not understand what other measurements exist with which these could be compared. How could a single set of measurements show a time-sequence of movement of these groups of people? With what data would the NAA-SI data be compared? The caller could give no specific answers but became more and more agitated. "I don't want to do what the Nazis did," he said. "I want to use scientific materials to do meaningful research." The physical anthropologist could now analyze the measurements taken in 1942 and 1943 with computer programs that could scan the data, reveal interrelationships among the indices, and discover patterns of physical characteristics. The conversation continued for another quarter of an hour, but I could not discover what sort of scientific questions the caller wanted to answer or his purpose for further investigation using these materials.

I was disturbed by the conversation. It seemed to me that, lacking any real research agenda, these materials were best left alone as relics of an age of terror. Even if one put aside the deadly nature of the Nazi enterprise, the anthropologists' arrogant assumption in the 1940s of their *right* as part of the German occupation of Poland to ask scientific questions without reflection was wrong then and wrong now.

The caller's tone reminded me of the mind-set of those earlier German and Austrian anthropologists, who were too careless in their assumptions about the basic necessity for conducting research on human variation that they hoped would define human races. As they cut locks of hair from their research subjects, as they fingerprinted them, as they measured the length of their noses or the circumference of their heads, these researchers had no plan for analysis of these data. They only knew that these data would be useful in "racial hygiene," the effort to "cleanse the fatherland" and newly conquered territory of imagined "others," defined by physical characteristics thought to be non-Aryan. In the process, they would build their own careers.

The hallmark of this misbegotten enterprise was, at the very least, a lack of attention to the ultimate uses of the research. More than that, however, some of the scientists may not ever seriously have considered the ideological suppositions that made up the context into which the research was placed. In fact, today we still hear physical scientists of this previous age excused for their lack of attention to human concerns by expressions such as "they were scientists and didn't think about what was going on around them" or "they weren't interested in the political situation; they only wanted to advance their research." The anthropologists and racial hygienists had no unified or consistent research agenda with a well-defined need for the collection of each data element. They merely collected data on humans, examined physical specimens, or conducted experiments, with no consideration of the human costs and benefits.

On the other hand, perhaps many of the Nazi anthropologists had a very accurate idea of the ultimate use of the research and believed that no human cost would have been too high. If that were the case, the only part of their scheme that was inconsistent was the lack of a plan for analyzing the outcome of the various measurements. Implications of the imperceptible slide from scientific interest into a prurient and inane pursuit of "racial" identification will become more explicit as this book proceeds.

Scientists in this country now have stringent research reviews. However, we continually need to examine our own complicity in creating an aura of scientism. Scientism is fostered when we pursue data for its own sake and have no motive other than exploring spurious topics of questionable validity to enhance our professional reputations, framing the results of such inquiries in language that provides the appearance of learned endeavors.[2] Scientism also becomes more prevalent when we tailor research to match government agency agendas without offering clear statements about the limitations such funding and policy influences place upon the scientific enterprise and when we believe in our own objectivity without appropriate skepticism.

This book explores how ordinary German social scientists became involved in genocide through exactly this process. They meshed their scientism to radical and deadly racial schemes and policies that they had also helped to develop and support. The personal fates of the people they studied were viewed as outside their purview, as they worked in lockstep with a national agenda to produce a race of individuals that exhibited pseudo-purity and physical and intellectual homogeneity.

I told the physical anthropologist on the phone that given his lack of a clear research agenda, I could not think of any reason why he should do a further analysis of the Nazi anthropological materials. The caller was clearly abashed at my lack of support for his plans, and I never heard from him again. He almost certainly had no nefarious intent in his interest to use the Nazi data, but he also had not thought through the implications of increasing his own store of data by using research that, at best, was gathered and reported in ways that could only be called immoral. Most anthropologists know little about the Nazi anthropological research, for until now details of its purpose and methods and how its subjects were engaged in the venture have not been published.

The Growth of Personal Interest

The growing public and private endeavors that explain, illustrate, define, and use the Holocaust in more tangential ways to reach other goals indicate that there is a widespread fascination in this brief time period. Many of us find ourselves unable to describe the nature of our own interest or the extent to which this singular epoch has captured us.

My own memory of how this interest came into my life has emerged slowly through the years. Often, in the midst of teaching my class on the Holocaust, I remember a particular link that deepens my commitment to, curiosity about, or compassion for the subject matter. For instance, showing a film to my students of newsreel footage of the liberation of concentration camps suddenly brought back a memory of going to the movies with my mother when I was seven or eight years old. Mother had grabbed me by the hair during the newsreel and thrust my head into her lap. The last glimpse I had before my eyes were shrouded was of bodies on a cart, naked, scarcely recognizable as human. And for a moment in the classroom, I felt a visceral reaction to an image that I now recognize and even know well but that, at age seven or eight, could not have understood. I also could not forget.

My sister and I would lie in bed at night about that time, and she would ask me, "If you had to choose between being killed or being saved by sacrificing me, what would you do?" We had a premonition of "Sophie's choice" long before Styron's book was written.[3] Perhaps part of the response of the public to that novel is the reality of these imagined choices that came to us through listening to the news immediately after the war as the horrors of genocide became ever clearer.

In the 1950s and 1960s, those postwar notions rarely came to my mind. There were other things to be concerned about: starting a family, returning to graduate school, being politically active. In the 1970s, with two children at home, one of whom should have been reading but was stymied by dyslexia, I sought to show him how exciting books are and to share with him the joys of reading. We looked for children's books about adventure, heroism, and tricksters, and he was denied none of the thrill of reading, even if it was my voice he was hearing. Among those books I read aloud were Holocaust stories relevant to children: *The Upstairs Room, The Diary of Anne Frank,* and many others.[4] At the same time, I began to read more of the Holocaust literature myself, authors such as Primo Levi, Eli Wiesel, Bruno Bettelheim, and Hannah Arendt.

Throughout these years, my in-laws were part of our lives. Both born in Germany, they had a group of friends and family who had lived in the United States since before World War II. They spoke and read German more than English. As each died, we took the books and personal papers that no one else wanted to keep. I had been introduced to German as a young child by my maternal grandmother and then studied German in college and made up my mind that I would read primarily in German when I read for pleasure. I needed an intellectual challenge and found this decision opened for me a new range of literature from working-class novels to early twentieth-century German social critics. My thoughts often were immersed in this period, and I came to understand well the point of view, the vocabularies, and physical surroundings of that time.

My husband's family had come to New York City in the 1920s and settled into a kind of working-class liberalism, expressed primarily through unionism. When they spoke of Germany, it was to recount specific memories— funny, sad, tragic, or fearful. When they spoke of the Nazi era, which they had not experienced firsthand, it was with disgust and hatred. They mentioned in this context a certain Kurt Bangemann, my mother-in-law's first cousin, who joined the French Resistance when he had to leave Germany in 1933. He died in a concentration camp eleven years later. The statements were ritualized. Kurt was the family hero: the "good" German. He fought until "they" killed him. His mother had written grief-filled letters after the war. These letters were discussed but not shown to us. If anyone went beyond the standard stories to reveal a little more of the time period, he or she was given the family admonition: "You talk too much."

In 1989, the last family member of that German immigrant group died. He left a peculiar message along with his books and papers. Kurt Bangemann had been married and had a wife and family in France—and there was an address! Why had no one told us before?

We wrote, arranged to take the pictures and materials to the French Bange-mann family, and left for Provence. To our surprise, Kurt's son, who met us at the train station, was dark-complected, with curly hair. We soon learned that his mother was French-African. Over a period of time, we also learned that the American immigrants had not helped their cousin or his family, be-cause they did not know what to do with the African wife and her child. When they could have helped Kurt and his family to escape from France in the 1930s, they did nothing. Kurt's own efforts did not suffice to find him an exit visa, so he was sent back to the land of his birth, where he died a Resistance fighter, leaving a wife and child in France. This information touched us deeply. As in many families, Holocaust denial was exhibited through a misappropria-tion and selection of facts to simplify complex events. It was personal and immediate.

We traveled to Germany within days of our stay in France and tried to find out the rest of the story. We found a great deal. Kurt Bangemann had been sent to Buchenwald, then Mittelbau-Dora, and then Ellrich, each an outer camp of the previous one. In the summer of 1944, it was murderous in the camps located in central Germany, where "wonder" weapons were being developed and produced. Ellrich was certainly one of the worst, with pris-oners blasting and digging tunnels into the Harz Mountains to make space for more V-1 and V-2 production. The life expectancy from arrival in camp to death was only a few weeks. Kurt died, or was murdered, six weeks after being sent to Ellrich.

I wanted to write a book about Kurt but turned my focus instead to the more immediate question of memorializing concentration camps. The me-morials seemed endangered with the unification of the two Germanies and, concomitantly, subject to a new interpretation of and approach to history. However, the memorials survived the decade, and the book outlining the history and function of the camps and their memorials served to deepen my interest in the Third Reich.[5]

As far as I know, I was the first to offer a course on the Holocaust from within an anthropology department at a university. It was a way for me to bring my ideas together with a classroom of students. At the same time, I became quite active with survivors of the Buchenwald–Mittelbau-Dora com-plex and became the representative of a European survivor group in the United States, gathering information and bringing them together, if only on paper.

Gathering Evidence on Anthropology in the Third Reich

As I increased my reading, I came upon more and more references to anthropology in the Third Reich. I became familiar with the venues in which anthropologists in the Third Reich worked. In the summer of 1997, I went to Berlin and worked in the Max Planck Society Archives (*Archiv zur Geschichte der Max-Planck-Gesellschaft*, or MPGA), reading the records of the Kaiser Wilhelm Institute for Anthropology, Human Genetics, and Eugenics (*Kaiser-Wilhelm-Institut für Anthropologie, menschliche Erblehre und Eugenik*, or KWIA). Much of the material was shocking. Clearly, anthropologists had been in leadership roles in the development and implementation of the Third Reich's racial policies. Organizing a system of affidavits for family "racial" background checks, they also served on racial courts and had even been key figures in concentration camp medical experiments.

In the fall of 1997, while preparing a paper to present at the American Anthropological Association meetings, I looked in the NAA-SI intending to find out what American anthropologists had known of the work of their German colleagues. I noticed a reference to materials from the "IDO," which I knew was the Institute for German Work in the East (*Institut für Deutsche Ostarbeit*) and asked the archivist if I could see them.[6] "Actually, they are still in the large crates that they came in from Germany after the war. They have never been shelved," she explained. I told her that if the archive staff ever uncrated them, I would like to be there. A few hours later, she came in with a cart on which were piled small boxes. She said, "I opened one of the crates and brought you a few of the boxes that are in it." I thanked her, and we both waited with bated breath while I untied the original string and opened the box. There were more than one hundred envelopes, each numbered and stamped with a swastika. I opened the first envelope, and inside it there was a lock of human hair. We both gasped, and I closed the box. "I don't know if we should look at that," the archivist said. "Those are human remains."

Over a period of time, the staff of the NAA-SI asked if I would try to make sense of the collection and shelve the materials in the three crates. Thus, I could see that it contained not only the raw data from the investigations of anthropologists sent to Poland by the German occupying government but also the accumulation of information about the involvement of anthropologists from the first to the last. Presenting this in book form became a necessity.

The information that became available through the discovery at the Smithsonian came at the turn of the millennium. I began to see this book as a bridge between the twentieth and the twenty-first centuries. In the last century, people learned about the Holocaust and the Nazi era from their personal experience, from personal accounts, from both indirect references and images they heard and saw. Increasingly, they read the literature for themselves. Toward the end of the century, Holocaust museums had been erected in various cities, primarily in America, and memorials had been erected in Germany and Central Europe, as well as in England. In this century, public history will display the Holocaust memories differently.[7]

Learning about the Holocaust in the Twentieth Century

In the twentieth century, there were several lenses through which people viewed the Holocaust. If one lived the last half of the century in the Soviet-controlled bloc, one spoke not of the Holocaust but of the fight against fascism, which was defined as a particular kind of militaristic capitalism. The Soviets attributed this rise of fascism and the establishment of the Third Reich to the race for profits through the production of armaments, whereby money brokers in collusion with governments sped toward war in order to create an ever-growing demand for their products. The victims, identified in the literature, were portrayed first of all as the myriad numbers of nonpolitical Soviet citizens, communists, and those killed for racist motives, by which was meant Jews and Gypsies. Under this interpretation of historical events, the heroism of the Soviet Army and communists throughout Europe brought the slaughter to an end, creating a blanket of unquestionable legitimacy for Soviet bloc rule for the next fifty years. Noticeable from this perspective is the absence of any internalization of a Jewish Holocaust, which is the center of the Western understanding of the tragedy of Nazi rule. In a similar vein, in the West there was little serious examination of the role of international capital in the growth of fascism in Germany or the deadly nature of slave labor in the Third Reich.[8] Only recently has international capital been explored as having played a major part in the development of the Nazi system and the fate of German industrialists following the war.[9]

The American, and to a large extent, the Western European view of the Holocaust is that it was a tragic, almost inexplicable phenomenon, the center of which was European Jewry.[10] Soviet losses, usually estimated at thirty million people, were understood to mean Jews and Soviet troops. There was virtually no public understanding of the Nazi system of racial sorting and separation of people according to ethnic or physical characteristics into groups that each had its assigned fate. Nor was there much understanding of slave labor, a well-oiled machine that brought millions of Soviet, Polish, Czech, and other citizens of occupied countries into Germany, where they were forced to work on farms or in munitions plants or to clear unexploded bombs from cities. Some were murdered forthwith in concentration camps such as Buchenwald, Sachsenhausen, and Bergen-Belsen. Hundreds of thousands of Jews and non-Jews died in these prisoner-of-war camps, labor camps, and labor battalions. Cemeteries in which they are buried dot the German landscape, and ashes from crematoria fill marshlands and create sediments in the bottoms of lakes throughout the country. Yet, the non-Jewish victims of the Third Reich are seldom, or only parenthetically, mentioned in the United States.

Why are there such radically different views of the Holocaust in different parts of the world? Most likely, the explanation is in the nature of twentieth-century historiography. Following liberation of the camps, the slave laborers were sent home or to receiving countries. Those who went back to the Soviet Union and Soviet bloc countries and had the chance to write or tell their stories were often venerated. The political forces in power used the sanctioned oral and written histories to strengthen their grip on their satellites. Others, through no fault of their own, were punished by the state for not resisting the Nazi machine and placed in gulags for years. A "conspiracy of silence" shrouded the history of the Third Reich in the Federal Republic of Germany (FRG) following the war, until the early 1960s.[11] A combination of court trials and the publication of exposés by the German Democratic Republic (GDR) of Nazi perpetrators still active in the FRG's political and commercial life caused considerable commentary and controversy.

In the United States, the immigration of Jewish refugees brought their stories closer to the American public. Our accounts of the Holocaust stressed the almost complete annihilation of European Jewry but for many decades tended to omit the implication of capital in the underlying causes of the war and the many targeted groups who suffered dislocation, imprisonment, and death. The McCarthy era, following close after the end of World War II, diminished the likelihood that Americans would come to understand the contribution of communist forces to the downfall of the Nazi empire. Losses the Soviet Union had endured and the sacrifices of its people to bringing about the end of the war became subsumed by a great hatred and fear of the "red menace."

What both sides had in common was a view of history based on survivor accounts and a national-political perspective influenced by a cold war agenda. Neither used *all* of the information available cross-nationally to validate an inclusive view of the Holocaust. Each version of history was based within the political currency of the time, stressed its own perspective, and spoke of "other losses."

The Holocaust Interpreted in the Twenty-first Century

Interpretation is already changing. While fewer survivors are left each year to add to our first-person knowledge of what happened under the Nazis, vast resources of historical documentation are increasingly available to scholars and others with interest in the topic. Nuances of previous accounts can be exhaustively explored. The Internet can facilitate not only the spread of written information but can put individuals, including scholars, in touch with one another in the pursuit of common themes. The vast accumulation of data is now available in archives as well as in the print media that publishes documentation for others to use in new and imaginative ways. One can hope that there will be increasing debate on the value and ethical use of these sources and interpretations and that this debate will not evolve into a ritualized, academic discourse.[12]

For example, instead of time-specific and geographic-specific studies, themes increasingly will be examined across the years and geographic perspectives. What were the logistics of moving the masses of people out of the Ukraine? How did the slave labor battalions move into the smallest of German towns? What general information was available to the German public? What niches of the population had access to information about the extermination camps? Was the reaction of these people with information different in Poland than in Austria or Germany?

As the public comes to know its country's image of the Holocaust and that image becomes part of the general information one has, decisions will be made at local levels about how to commemorate the events. The content of museums and memorials will have the input of larger numbers of people with a concern and a stake in the history. There will be more debate about details.

Theory will also play a larger role in discussions of the Holocaust. Addressed both directly and indirectly, questions of why it happened will enter into the debate. Comparisons of the Holocaust to other genocidal events will serve not only to explain but also will be fashioned to give information that might serve to prevent future horrors.[13]

With the vast array of materials at hand, the picture that any country has of the Holocaust will be more complete, including its own responsibility as a place where perpetrators, victims, and bystanders found a home. Saturating the public, for example, with a single account of a victim group and with horrifying, but ultimately uninformative, visual images will not be sufficient. The packaged presentation will be a thing of the past, and failure to link the Holocaust with policy, or linking it inappropriately and too often to relatively unimportant events, will be called into question. Instead, there will be more emphasis placed on the relevance of the Holocaust to the terror experienced in the twenty-first century, in which once again ideologues and zealots justify the murder of innocents as a necessary act in order to kill their culture, their history, and their values.

Linking the Centuries in Holocaust Literature

All knowledge is personal. We know because we care to know or must know or cannot avoid knowing. Energy spent denying, reconfiguring, or bounding our knowledge robs us of valuable time that we could spend in understanding and analyzing information that is available to us. My interest grew out of personal links to the material but came to encompass new analyses of old, deeply moving, and relevant data. It took me to cities in Germany and Poland where I spent days and weeks poring over dusty papers that only a handful of readers had leafed through before me. Often, I had simultaneous feelings of awe and horror.

This study takes the responsibility for the human annihilation of the Nazi era, which is often assigned to a band of culprits within an evil empire, and places it not only with the German political and military forces but broadly among *people who thought themselves scientists*.[14] These scientists used an evil national agenda to support their careerist goals. They ignored human misery and found pleasure in unfettered research conducted without restraint.

This book will show, through the focus on a single profession, the growth of racist ideas to the point where genocide and mass murder could become accepted as a matter of course. It would be a mistake, however, to believe that anthropology is the only discipline for which this book is relevant. The Third Reich was a conflicted modern and technologically advanced era.[15] The nature of science reflected that and was interdisciplinary, as the structures of the two major institutes, the IDO and the KWIA, described herein, will illustrate. Certainly, scientism was not limited only to the anthropologists nor only to those who considered themselves biological anthropologists.

In this book, you will follow the research process that I used. I followed the leads that opened to me. I traveled back and forth across Europe, searching for clues to a history that is buried in euphemism and denial. I met amazing people. Survivors told me hundreds of their stories. Informants in Germany, France, and Poland shared their views of events that occurred during the Third Reich and the way these events were remembered in the varying postwar political climates.

The primary resource used in this book, however, is archival data. The leads I followed often were provided by excellent and dedicated archivists in Germany, America, and Poland. It continually surprised me how much material exists but how a full understanding of the material depends upon first learning the context from which it emerges and in which it must be placed. Going back repeatedly to the material over time revealed more and more information that I had not understood or fully grasped earlier. Like working a crossword puzzle, working with archival data often means gathering enough information to make sense of another part of the data. Archival documents give the researcher snippets of information but not a clear narrative, which can only emerge from the author's own thought processes and conclusions. It is, indeed, a heavy responsibility to interpret accurately the materials gathered in this way.

Notes

1. Schafft and Zeidler, *Register to the Materials of the Institut für Deutsche Ostarbeit.*
2. See Sokal and Bricmont, *Fashionable Nonsense.*
3. Styron, *Sophie's Choice.*
4. Frank, *Diary of Anne Frank;* Reiss, *Upstairs Room.*
5. Schafft and Zeidler, *Die KZ-Mahn- und Gedenkstätten in Deutschland.*
6. The original acquisition note to the collection was written in 1947 by F. H. Setzler: "The anthropometric data, of most interest to us, were apparently secured with traditional German thoroughness, and are tied in with excellent photos and negatives, hair samples, contour tracings of the head and nasal region, personal and medical information for each subject." Obviously, the larger meaning of the collection was not ascertained at that time.
7. The Holocaust, of course, occurred during the Third Reich. The word "Holocaust" generally refers to the willful genocide of the Jewish population in Nazi Germany and occupied territory. It often includes the willful attempt to annihilate the Roma population of these areas as well. There is no single word that expresses the broader losses caused by Nazi human rights abuses and destruction, many of which will be discussed in this book. It is difficult, therefore, to distinguish the breadth of the subject matter that is discussed here. Unless the topic is specifically designated with the word "Holocaust," the author is referring to crimes of the Third Reich against all population groups.
8. Edward Homze, Ulrich Herbert, and Benjamin Ferenz were the best-known authors who explored issues of Nazi slave labor at the end of the twentieth century.
9. See, for example, Simpson, *Splendid Blond Beast;* Black, *IBM and the Holocaust;* and Borkin, *Crime and Punishment of I. G. Farben.*
10. This is not to suggest that professional historians and their readers do not have a more sophisticated view of the Holocaust. The author refers here to general, less informed, public perceptions.
11. Herbert, "Extermination Policy," 5.

12. Goldhagen, *Hitler's Willing Executioners,* 10–14.

13. See Hinton, *Annihilation of Difference;* and Levi and Rothberg, *Holocaust.*

14. The author does not consider this book to be a venue to discuss Holocaust theory. The reader is referred to works by Yehuda Bauer, Steven T. Katz, Michael Marrus, and other Holocaust scholars for a thorough discussion of issues of the Holocaust, its uniqueness, and its place among other genocides.

15. For a discussion of the issues of modernity and the Third Reich, see Bauman, *Modernity and the Holocaust;* and Herf, *Reactionary Modernism.*

CHAPTER ONE

The Jews of the Tarnów Ghetto

Preparations

From the University of Vienna came a letter from an anthropologist ready to serve the Third Reich in a most critical mission, addressed to Dr. Anton Plügel in Kraków, Poland. Plügel, head of the Section on Race and Ethnicity Research (*Sektion Rassen- und Volkstumsforschung,* or SRV) of the IDO, must have read it with satisfaction.

> November 3, 1941
>
> Dear Herr Doktor!
>
> Many thanks for your letter. I want to make a suggestion for photographing the Jews. Because none of us can spare more time, I have turned to a fellow worker, who, like others is in the military. He serves, however, in the *Hilfspolizei* [a civil, auxiliary police force] and it appears it is easier to get a leave of absence there. I think that this colleague, under the guidance of Dr. Fliethmann who is already used to doing the photography, could perform the necessary investigations [body and face measurements, finger printing, and sketches of the structure of the irises]. You have already suggested people [SS?] for the photography and also for the blood group investigations. The finger and hand prints can, if necessary, also be done by the [Polish] assistants who can be trained beforehand. Perhaps you can take photos of 100 families in this way so that we have at least saved something of the material if any kind of measures should be taken. I could then come in summer and make any further studies there and if possible carry out the research in other villages. . . . I hope that this time you are satisfied with me!
>
> Best regards and Heil Hitler!
>
> Your Dora Kahlich[1]

"Material" was the common term used by Nazi scientists for what we now call research subjects. In speaking or writing about the number of subjects needed, they used the word "pieces." Certainly, Plügel recognized the need to save this material from the soon-to-be-enacted "measures," but not for humanitarian reasons or out of concern for their continued existence as human beings. No, Plügel and Kahlich were concerned about data; measurements, photographs, and fingerprints would be lost if the Jews were removed before the anthropologists reached them. Speed was of the essence, and the Jews were the first population in occupied Poland to be targeted for anthropological research.

The urge to save something of the Jewish culture and memory, as well as descriptions of their physical characteristics, was widespread among anthropologists in the Third Reich, many of whom knew that the extermination of Jews was imminent. Many collected and stored religious artwork and silver confiscated from synagogues for later use in German museums and gathered books from public and private libraries. Of immediate interest, however, were the *physical* remains of murdered Jews. For example, professors from the University of Strasburg requested of the *Reichsführer,* Heinrich Himmler, chief of all the SS (*Schutzstaffeln*) police, security police, Gestapo, and concentration camps, that they be allowed a major role in the preservation of Jewish physical remains.[2] They described their competence as follows:

> In regard to the security of the material . . . the person in charge has been able to make a series of photographs and anthropological measurements, [and] as far as possible . . . record genealogies, birth dates, and other personal data. After the Jews are killed, these heads must not be damaged, so he separates the head from the torso and sends it in a preserving liquid, beds it in a tin container that closes tightly and is made for this purpose, and sends it to the designated place. . . . The new Reich University in Strasburg, in its arrangements and its mission, is made to order for the preservation and research of this skull material.[3]

As early as October 4, 1938, the University of Vienna was given the order to remove all monuments and other materials and religious spaces that were related to Jews. Busts of noteworthy people, if they were Jewish, were ordered removed, as was their written work in book or manuscript form. Immediately, the anthropology department wrote to the authorities and requested assistance:

> I have learned through the *Gauleitung* [local party leadership] that there is a plan to turn the Eisenstädter cemetery into a park and there is, therefore, the upcoming opportunity to uncover valuable and useful Jewish skeletons. I beg your friendship in telling me as soon as this plan is carried out, for I have a lively interest in this—as you will understand—out of pure scientific motivation, and the

Anthropological Institute has a large involvement in the Jewish question. At the same time, I have written a letter to the mayor of Eisenstadt in which I expressed my interest.

Heil Hitler

E. Geyer[4]

Kahlich had already corresponded with Plügel for some time about their plans to conduct research on living Polish Jews. They knew each other from Vienna, where both had ties to the university. Plügel recruited many of his staff through the recommendations of Dr. Robert Routil, a docent in the Anthropological Institute of the University of Vienna (*Anthropologisches Institut der Universität Wien*), who had done studies of Russian prisoners during World War I. In June of 1941, Plügel had hired Elfriede Fliethmann, an assistant in the Viennese institute, to serve in a research capacity in the SRV.[5] The word *Volkstumsforschung* in the section's name meant more than research into questions of ethnicity. *Volkstum* was a newly coined word in the Third Reich, not appearing in the dictionaries of the time. It implied finding homogeneous groups of people and identifying their ethnicities. Volkstum research could then be applied in making political decisions about how to handle each group.

Plügel and Kahlich had hoped to find a tight, isolated community in eastern Galicia in which to conduct inquiries, but the Germans had herded the Jews into ghettos too quickly, and these Jewish communities (*shtetls*) were no longer in existence.[6] The ghetto at Tarnów, Poland, seemed to be the best location for the research. Tarnów was intimately tied to Vienna, where the Anthropological Institute "often had the opportunity to examine Viennese Jews in the course of providing affidavits of parentage and kinship."[7] The plan was to investigate Jews in the land to which, the anthropologists believed, most of the Viennese Jews could trace their origin. This would provide comparative material for the Viennese data.

The Anthropological Institute of Vienna was heavily involved in providing certificates (*Gutachten*) of racial heredity. Beginning with the Austrian law enacted in 1938, the Removal of Jews from Public Life (*Entjudung des Öffentlichen Lebens*), every public employee had to swear that he or she was not Jewish as defined by the Nuremberg Laws (*Nürnberger Gesetze*). This provided anthropological institutes and anthropology departments in universities a critical role in carrying out the racial agenda of the state. It also provided income to the public institutions. In the case of the Anthropological Institute of Vienna, providing these certificates brought in an income of 4504.94 reichsmarks (RM) in the few months between March and November 1938.[8] Kahlich was involved in doing the racial investigations necessary in providing these certificates.

In the early summer, Kahlich had written to Plügel about using her husband as a researcher at the IDO, for Dr. Herbert Kahlich was in a student military battalion and, with his friend Herbert Walkerstorfer, was ready to take photos and produce "genetic-racial" pictures. Dora Kahlich saw the research as providing "the basis for relocation and new settlements; as the basis of racial science, race biology, and race psychology of the Jewish people; and not least important, the solution to problems of mixed race individuals with both Jewish and non-Jewish kin [Mischlinge]."[9] This she expressed to the command post in which her husband served, but the officers there were required to send the request further up the line of command with a cover letter from the IDO.

Kahlich asked that Plügel make this request indicating that the two men were needed for scientific work assignments that could be done during their vacation.[10] Plügel wasted no time after being told of the need for this letter by Dora Kahlich, and on June 19, 1941, he sent a letter to the men's commander requesting the two Herberts: Kahlich and Walkerstorfer. He used the exact words that Dora Kahlich had suggested and added, "it would also serve to foster progress of this work, as well as the scientific quality of very valuable research, if they were worked into the research during their vacation as both practical and theoretical anthropologists."[11]

However, by September no permission had been granted, and the work faltered. Plügel asked Dora Kahlich to check again and in the meantime to lend him photographs that had been taken by her mentor, Dr. Routil, of prisoners of war during World War I.[12] He was on to a new line of inquiry. In thanking her for the pictures, Plügel again reminded her that "we don't know what measures about the expulsion of the Jewish people are planned in the next months, which under certain circumstances, if we wait too long, could deprive us of valuable material."[13]

Auschwitz had been built in the summer of 1940. By 1942, all Jews in Poland, about 1.2 million, were living in ghettos. Some were murdered on the streets of the ghettos by the occupying soldiers, and transports were sending others to their death in extermination centers, but more Jews arrived every day from Austria and Germany as well as from the other occupied countries of Europe. The mobile death squads, or Einsatzgruppen, as they were called, had murdered hundreds of thousands of Jews along with some partisans and communists in the forests and towns in the Baltic and the Ukraine before April 1942.[14] The Holocaust was in full swing, and the Jews were indeed about to disappear from the ranks of the living.

On March 22, 1942, Dora Kahlich with two assistants arrived in Kraków, bringing measurement instruments and the photographic supplies with them. She immediately changed trains and went on to Tarnów, where she and at least one of her assistants, Fräulein Marianne Pevny, met Plügel, Elfriede Fliethmann, and their Polish assistants. She had only twelve days to spare between semesters. Dr. Fliethmann brought the paperwork and ration cards for food with her. Plügel handled the coordination with the SS.[15]

Plügel assured the Viennese contingent that Tarnów had the "best working conditions" and, in addition, the Jewish intelligentsia as well as workers and craftspeople were represented among the ghetto inhabitants. According to Plügel, most of the Jews in Vienna traced their ancestry to Tarnów.[16] Undoubtedly, many of the Jews who found themselves in Tarnów in 1942 had made their residence in Vienna only a short time before their deportation.

When the German Army entered Tarnów on September 8, 1939, they found 25,000 Jews living in poverty.[17] Their economic fortunes had diminished under Polish independence following World War I, and they were restricted in their communal affairs by a Polish commissariat. Tarnów had once been the home of flourishing enterprises, largely in the clothing and hat manufacturing trades. It had been one of the most wealthy and influential Jewish settlements in Europe in previous centuries.[18] Now, it had become a place where the Jewish community spent more on social welfare to support their people than they collected in their communal income.

In February 1942, the occupying Germans established the Tarnów Ghetto by decree.[19] Soon, prominent members of the community were deported to Auschwitz and were among the first Polish Jews to be killed there. The leadership of the community now became the *Judenrat* (Jewish council), which was directly under the thumb of the Gestapo. The Judenrat appointed its own police force, called the *Ordnungsdienst,* which had the job of carrying out all the orders of the SS within the ghetto. Tarnów's ghetto reduced the living space for Jews to about a dozen streets. There, about 40,000 Jews who had lived in Tarnów and its environs, and Jews who had been delivered there in transports from Germany, Austria, and Czechoslovakia, were crowded together, starving and suffering from a number of contagious diseases including tuberculosis and typhus. One of the features of the Tarnów Ghetto that made it suitable for the anthropological inquiry was that it was divided into two parts, a forced labor camp and a family camp. It was the latter that interested the anthropological researchers.

Indeed, most families in the ghetto were desperate to stay together.[20] Selections of those healthy and strong enough for work and those doomed to death were regular occurrences, and families tried many ploys to save their members. Those older than sixty or too young to join a workforce were denied identity cards and lived illegally in the ghetto until they were caught.[21] For those with identity and food ration cards, only a few hundred calories were allotted per day. Inhabitants of the ghetto were starving and being shot on the streets daily at the time that the anthropologists were ready to conduct their research in Tarnów.

The *Stadtkommissar* (city commissioner), Dr. Hein, made the security and logistic arrangements for the anthropological team. He was responsible for the workspace, food, and sleeping quarters for the staff. The Judenrat "stood ready with the [Jewish] police and assistants at all times so that our work was made easier in every way."[22] These arrangements were very satisfactory to the anthropologists, who were able to examine and question a large number of informants in the less than two weeks allotted to their visit. The concern that the Austrian contingent had had about lice and the danger of contacting typhus were allayed through careful disinfection routines undertaken by the ghetto administration for all of the people selected to be interviewed and examined.

The Research

The research centered on families with two or more children. Dr. Kahlich made eighteen different measurements of the subjects' heads using a lead cable and supervised the assistants as they measured both the sagittal and horizontal circumference of the skull. Dr. Fliethmann made thirteen measurements of their bodies. The eye colors of the subjects were noted according to a chart designed by Martin and Schultz and the hair color according to a chart developed by Fischer and Saller.[23] Fräulein Pevny drew a sketch of the irises of each subject, for "according to our experience in providing affidavits, the iris structure of the eyes has a great meaning in assigning the inheritance."[24] Photos of the men were taken by a Herr Dodenhoff of the Central Film and Picture Department of the administration of the General Government (*Generalgouvernement,* or GG), the German administration of a large section of occupied Poland. Dr. Fliethmann took the pictures of the women. Two different cameras were used, a Contax 18 cm Sonnar for head shots of each person, and a Contax 13.5 cm Sonnar for shots of the naked bodies.

The unit of analysis of the study was intended to be the family, so the team made few measurements of single persons, except for noting their complexion and height. Colored photos, instead of the black-and-white used for the main subjects, were taken to record this information. This film was also used for members of family groups whose complexions were of particular interest.

In order to emphasize the social structure and the ethnic background of the Jews, only a small amount of personal data was collected. These included name, age, place of birth, citizenship, mother tongue, religion, education, occupation, place of residence, military service, sport activities, travel abroad, and illnesses they or their family members had had. For every respondent, information about their four grandparents was included, particularly their names, occupations, and causes of death.

Fliethmann's Reports

The responsibility for writing the report lay with Dr. Fliethmann, but she depended on her Polish assistants for much of the analysis. "Anyway, I do not know the exact formulas for determining the average and sigma etc. and assign these things to a very talented Polish girl who learned it from Dr. Plügel."[25] She reported that, in all, 106 families were examined, which included 565 members and 13 unrelated singles. They were primarily orthodox Jews, because these were the people with the most children. The families in the survey had an average of 3.96 children. However, Dr. Fliethmann pointed out in her report that the policies of the last three years had had their effect:

> [T]he Judenrat informs me that the Jews of Tarnów's joy in having children has changed in the last three years:

Year	Births	Deaths	Surplus Births
1939	426	293	133
1941	236	540	−304

> During the year 1939, for every 100 births there were 68 deaths, while in 1941 there were 288 or twice as many as were born. . . . The number of children measured per family is somewhat smaller [than expected], for some had died and others are no longer here.[26]

The demographics of the ghetto were more complicated than that, as the women anthropologists confided in their correspondence. They knew that families were not able to stay together and probably did not know what had become of one another. There was no way to accurately assess who was still alive or where they might be living or might have died. Fliethmann asked the commander of the Security Police in Tarnów for help in clarifying numbers, but he wrote, "It is not possible [to ascertain] a conclusive number of children among living Jewish families in Tarnów. In case you absolutely need these numbers, you must tell me again. This work would take a long time."[27]

Nor did Plügel have any better luck. "As the men of the Security Police have told me, it is totally futile to get information about relocated Jews, for they are no longer recorded by name [when transported out of the ghetto], so no one can find out their further destination. One must let fate take its course in these matters."[28]

Fliethmann and Kahlich knew enough about data to realize that what they had gathered could not be correctly analyzed. "We did not ask our research families whether the number of children reported was correct or whether some had been sent off, etc. We also have no idea if the number of children we recorded really is the total number of children in the family who are living. The dead ones we have recorded accurately."[29] In other words, in every family some of the children already might have been sent out to labor camps or been selected for extermination, leaving the families to report only those living with them at the time. In other cases, children may have been hidden or may have left the German reign of terror through emigration while it was still possible. The women anthropologists undoubtedly knew of these possibilities but, as was usually the case in correspondence under the Nazis, disguised this knowledge through the use of a kind of shorthand. Had they written openly about the number of ways to account for missing family members, they would have faced serious repercussions, possibly imprisonment in a concentration camp.

In her report, Fliethmann expressed regrets that it was not possible to restrict the study exclusively to Jewish families native to Tarnów. The reason was that "during the war many families fled to foreign countries, and many Jewish families came into the ghetto as a result of closing other ghettos and resettling Jews from the *Reichsgebiet* [Germany as it had existed under prewar boundaries]." Only eight families represented those in which both the parents were natives of Tarnów. An additional twenty-seven families represented those in which one parent was a native of Tarnów. All but one of the remaining families came from surrounding areas in Poland.

Fliethmann reported on the occupations of the Jews of Tarnów. The majority of men listed their occupation as salesman or tailor. Women who worked reported that they were either typists or seamstresses. Thirty-six of the research subjects reported that they had owned either a house or a business prior to the German invasion. However, Fliethmann noted that the middle class was very weak in Tarnów, not only among the Jews but among the non-Jewish Polish population as well.[30]

Fliethmann found, counterintuitively, that the respondents reported having been more active in sports than she would have expected since, as she said, "seen from the religious perspective, [the Jewish religion] like the Catholic fosters a deadening of the body." This strange finding, she believed, could only be explained in racial terms by attributing it to the influence of the European component that had worked its way into the genetic mix and by the Jews' "strong urge to survive."[31]

The health of the subjects was surprisingly good, thought Fliethmann. One child was mentally and physically retarded, and another had spent time in a mental institution. Still another boy had a clubfoot. These were the only genetic problems that the team observed. Many more of the respondents appeared to have a tendency to spinal problems and poor posture or gait. She speculated that this could be due to incipient illness, occupational illness, a lifetime of environmental inadequacies, or the constitutional predisposition to such problems within the Jewish population. She decided that the greatest probable cause was the constitutional one, but when she observed the poor development of the children aged six to eight, she felt one might conclude it had to do with the "weak living conditions of the Jews."[32]

The team saw little infectious disease, such as typhus, which Fliethmann attributed to the outstanding job of Tarnów's Jewish Sanitary Service, which was responsible for delousing and disinfection. While the informants reported many cases of tuberculosis, there were none observed by the researchers, although a certain weakness of the respiratory system was seen. This, she felt, could again be blamed on the weak Jewish constitution.

In summary, Fliethmann put forth her "anthropological observations." She found, based on personal experience, a stronger influence of the Near Eastern–Oriental race in the Viennese Jews than in the Jews examined at Tarnów, who showed the influence of the "European race, and especially the Eastern–East Baltic races."[33] However, she was not so sure and stated that it could later prove to be just the opposite. As if to guarantee that no one would misunderstand her political position, however, she stated: "The Jewish people are comprised of such a mix of various races that each has had its influence on the development of the people's character. It probably is the Near Eastern–Asian race that gives the Jews, particularly those in east Europe, their physical and mental condition, their typical and strange aggressive tendency. It is exactly their strong business and entrepreneurial sense and their lack of scruples in many things that characterize the Near Eastern race and that is also seen in certain non-Jewish, Near Eastern people [*Volk*], such as the Armenians."[34]

Fliethmann reported further that there were few "athletic types" in her sample but, much to her surprise, a number of individuals with light-colored or blue eyes. (She removed this observation from her later reports.) Characteristics she described that were more in line with the racist ideology were the Jews' "thick, hanging lower lip and the large protruding ears."[35] She concluded that, contrary to the beliefs of some writers, one can always tell a Jew by appearance.

Nonsense as Science

The purpose of the anthropological investigation in Tarnów was to record characteristics of Jews before the extermination took place. The anthropological team was in constant communication with and under the supervision of the SS. Fliethmann and Kahlich must have been aware that their efforts to preserve the physical measurements and social/medical data on the Jews tied neatly with the exhumation of Jewish corpses from graves in other parts of Europe and the robbery of Jewish artifacts from synagogues, museums, and libraries. All of these measures would leave a kind of data in the future for researchers to analyze when discussing this extinct population.

The women did not take into account one major factor in conducting the research, however. The context of the study had *everything* to do with virtually all of the answers they received from their subjects. "How many children did you have, and how many have died?" left out the most crucial possibility, which they thought of later: Some of the children had already been "relocated," exterminated without their parents' knowledge, or lost to their parents during transport. It would have been unlikely that the Jewish subjects would have asked the researchers for clarification, "Do you mean those who were born but sent away or killed, as well as those whom I know are living now?" At the end of the study, the researchers realized that the reported numbers of people in the family did not provide accurate data for analysis. Yet, the family unit had been the topic around which the research was meant to revolve.

Similarly, Fliethmann was surprised that there were so few infectious diseases among the interviewees. Yet, all of the people who came in to see the anthropologists had been screened for disease. The Germans were not about to expose themselves to the epidemics that raced through the ghettos. The Jews only showed a lack of physical fitness because of the starvation and deprivation they had encountered. Yet, this was also a topic about which Fliethmann could not comment.

The anthropologists did not seem to have had second thoughts about their inquiry into work occupations, although they should have recognized what factors would have influenced the answers. Camp inmates were constantly asked for their occupations by authorities. Their answers often determined their chances for survival. This was such a loaded question that it would have been impossible for the Jews of Tarnów to answer accurately. No resident of the ghetto was free to choose a work placement in 1942, yet they all needed to work in order to get food rations. The ghetto inhabitants soon determined what occupations were valued and claimed adherence to them as a way to extend life for a few more days, weeks, or months.

The anthropological questionnaire did not indicate time frames. Did the researchers supply one? When they asked about those who had owned homes or shops, to what year were they referring? In stating that the middle class was "weak," did Fliethmann ever think of the decimation of merchants and shop owners over the course of the previous years? It must also be taken into account that the research subjects had to weigh their answers to the anthropologists' questions with a view to the possible positive or negative influence those answers would have on their own chances for survival, and perhaps they feared that being perceived as "middle class" would only infuriate the Nazis more.

The questions about health appear to be the most bizarre. Few children among those interviewed had disabilities. Did it not occur to Fliethmann and Kahlich that many children had already been murdered in various euthanasia actions or selected for deportation? Perhaps the Judenrat or the Jewish police had been able to prescreen the subjects so that those with obvious illnesses would not be executed on the spot. The respondents had every motivation to tell the anthropologists that they were active in sports and were in good physical condition. That information might also prolong their lives. The crooked spines and the weak constitutions might also have been the result of beatings, endless days of hard labor, and lack of nutrition, but the women anthropologists did not seem to take that into account.

The anthropologists put nothing in context and accepted the false information they had collected as valuable research data. They then set about analyzing it.

The Aftermath

Only a few weeks after the stay in Tarnów, Dora Kahlich was back in Vienna and well along in the data analysis. She complained that she was working from eight in the morning until eight at night, with barely enough time for lunch. "The library is a pig pen."[36]

The Security Police in Tarnów helped the anthropological team finish its data collection. After the fieldwork had been completed, they provided correct birth dates for children and marriage dates for the couples for whom genealogical data had been gathered. For this service, they wanted something in return. "The office asks you for a report on the success of your work in Tarnów. Above all else, whether there is German blood in the Jewish families you investigated. The experiences you had in doing the racial investigations here in Tarnów are also interesting [to us]."[37] Fliethmann answered in a way that contradicted Nazi ideology, for Hitler spoke endlessly of "German blood." She claimed that it could be said that the Jews showed the influence of the European races, but it would be impossible to say which nationality that represented. Indeed, she said, race does not indicate nationality. She promised to explain more in her publications.[38]

The difficulties of writing the reports and manipulating the data from the study of the Tarnów Jews were offset by the personal relationship that developed between the two women. An unexpected pleasure for Dr. Kahlich was the comradeship she experienced with Dr. Fliethmann, with whom she began a correspondence that lasted for the length of their engagement with the IDO. "It makes me really happy that there are still people for whom money and position are not the most important things," she wrote. In return for Fliethmann's hospitality, Kahlich had taken packages back to Vienna for her new friend's mother. Fliethmann also had generously provided a large bottle of schnapps for Kahlich's father-in-law, who was suitably impressed.[39]

However, Kahlich was not totally happy with Fliethmann's characterization of their work in her research report. "I ask you really urgently: change the first paragraph or I will be eaten up by the people here."[40] The offending paragraph read:

> The Anthropological Institute in Vienna has often had the opportunity while producing certificates of fatherhood and kinship to conduct detailed anthropological examinations of Viennese Jews. It occurred to us, therefore, to examine a large number of Jews in the land from which most Viennese Jews originated, former Poland, in order to obtain comparative material for the Viennese data. The Section on Race and Ethnicity Research in the Institute for German Work in the East, in addition to the pure racial interest in all the population groups living in the General Government and Eastern Europe, also had an interest in getting a very broad selection of subjects from large families of genetic and constitutional types for research. It is exactly the Jews, who through their strong race mixing and inbreeding provide such a rich material for investigation.[41]

Kahlich said that she would be more cautious about the assignment of races to the Jews if she were doing the writing. "[That] has to do with the practical application [of my work here], for I am constantly in contact with Jews, and the Jews of Tarnów look to me like typical Jews in every aspect."[42] She closes her letter with the admonition: "Use my remarks [on the draft paper] in the right places. You know my point of view: show that women too can do something!"[43]

In response to the criticism, Fliethmann changed the first sentence of her publication to read, "In the Anthropological Institute of the University of Vienna, in the context of twin and family investigations, paternity and kinship information has been collected on about 1,000 Jews and Jewish mixtures [*Mischlinge*]."[44] The alteration was slight but significant. Instead of saying that the work in Vienna was done in order to provide individuals with certificates of their "race" and "racial heritage," she placed the work in the context of *research,* indicating that the work was of a serious academic nature. In fact, the university's anthropological institute was being paid to do routine examinations of people to serve political and social purposes and probably sought to find a way to make that task more academic and seemingly scientific while they were at it.

Perhaps Fliethmann did not take the criticism too well. At any rate, she did not answer this letter until the thirteenth of May. In her reply, she complained that her stomach was tied in knots because "every day I get to hear another complaint." She confessed that she had no idea how to do the statistics required for the analysis of the data and knew only that it has to do "with arithmetic."[45]

Fliethmann urged Kahlich once again to come to the GG: "Furthermore, we could easily drive to Tarnów for a few days and complete the material. The stipend for you is still running. Couldn't you let your very honorable Herr professors [docents] stew in their own juice for eight days and appear here again? At any case, if it is possible, one should make use of all possible research subjects. Leave your interns and other things and also your worthy husband in the lurch for eight days and come. You too have to lick out the flesh pots of Tarnów."[46] Fliethmann assured her friend that she would take her suggestions on the draft report and use them. "In my naïveté, I didn't intend to harm the institute."[47]

On June 6, Kahlich continued the correspondence. She did not mention coming back to Tarnów but voiced her intention of working with Fliethmann in the summer. Again, she complained about the men:

> One can only say: Oh these men! Terrible! Our's is as moody as an old maid. I also am eating gall, quiet and composed, and wait for the right minute to talk back. I will move to Kraków when Geyer returns. Pevny will go along. I look forward to summer! Hearty greetings until then.
>
> Your Dora Kahlich[48]

As she prepared for the next research trip that summer, Kahlich looked fondly back on the time in Tarnów.

[T]o a happy reunion and good work. I am thinking of the really nice days in Tarnów and we all are looking forward to a new adventure. Many greetings and love

Your Dora Kahlich[49]

The Case of Blau

Dora Kahlich had another responsibility to fulfill on her trip to Poland. She was asked to examine the Blau family imprisoned in the concentration camp Lagow near Kielce. There is no specific information about the nature of the investigation except that it was relevant to a court case. The content of the following letters indicates that the nature of the inquiry was to determine the racial classification of Blau and his children. Kahlich conducted this racial certification exercise during or after the trip to Tarnów. She was then called to appear in court. She wrote on October 29, 1942, to Fliethmann:

> Now here is an interesting thing. I was ordered yesterday by telephone to appear at a hearing in the case of Blau. This is what I learned today, that the case is before the appeals judge and today was the final hearing. I, the expert witness, had to make a big deal of being in favor. In this case the judgment would be given immediately, in contrast to usual procedure, and the outcome was that the decision was delayed. The case of Blau is therefore settled in a satisfactory way, for he is a half-Jew and the children quarter-Jews.[50] But now there's another complication. At the hearing, Blau's mother-in-law, thus the grandmother of the children, said that the last letter and package were returned with the note "relocated." Now there is the danger of course that Blau and his nine children no longer live. A tragic fate! I would like to ask you if it would be possible to find out about the deportation of Blau at the Lagow Concentration Camp. You are near and we are far from the mark. I am, as before, not interested in the matter further, but if possible I would like to contact the caretaker of the children as I know the circumstances, and in this case you are closer than I am to Lagow.[51]

Kahlich's assertion that she was not interested in the case is contradicted by her potentially dangerous request that Fliethmann get specific information about a person who was under investigation. Fliethmann wrote back to Kahlich some time later to tell her that Blau had contacted her by letter. She did not say from where the letter had originated. He had asked for Kahlich's address in order to "thank her for the money." He had not heard about the court hearing. Fliethmann asked Kahlich about it in a tone of reproach and by using the word "still" indicated that she believed that Kahlich had provided funds to Blau:

Do you still think that it makes sense to support them? They are never going to get away from there, or at least only further east, for at this time it is being thoroughly cleaned up here again. I cannot investigate any Jews in Galicia anymore. Of the Tarnówer, there are only 8,000 left, but as Bernhardt said, almost none of ours [are left]. Our material has, therefore, a rare value.

I am sending along to you the sketch of the work on the Jews. Enjoy it!

Many greetings and Heil Hitler! Fl.[52]

Usually in their correspondence the women did not use the signature greeting "Heil Hitler." Fliethmann used it this time, perhaps as an extra precaution in asserting her loyalty to the dictates of the regime.

Kahlich was not happy with this news from Fliethmann. It made her very nervous:

Thank you very much for your dear letter. I have to answer right away, for the business about Blau seems very suspicious to me. I never sent him money and was never in contact with him. The conclusion of his affidavit must never have been settled, or he would have heard something. I also don't believe that he will return to Vienna with his children. I believe also that it would be better for you to give up the business [of trying to find out the fate of the Blau children]. If it hasn't happened already, then please don't send him my address. I cannot correspond with people who are in the court process and also do not have any interest in doing so. It is enough when I have to listen to all the crying in my office hours in Vienna.[53]

On October 21, Fliethmann was able to assure Kahlich that the matter had come to an end. "You can breathe easy about Blau; I cautiously never answered him because it didn't look quite right to me either. I will simply ignore any possible future letter from him."[54] It appears, however, that Fliethmann continued to search for Blau. She wrote to Kahlich on November 20, 1942, echoing Plügel's earlier point: "Somewhat late, I am getting around to giving you clear information about the thing. As the man from the Security Police told me, it is totally pointless to get information about deported Jews, for they aren't even dealt with individually anymore. Therefore, one can't ask where they are by name. In these cases, one has to let fate take its course."[55]

Further Investigations of Jews

Fliethmann wanted to continue to conduct research on Jews, particularly those who had owned farmland. She gathered information, compiled by a Jewish anthropologist, Dr. Salomon Czortkower, born June 6, 1903, in Lvov, called Lemberg by the Germans. His great-grandfather was a Russian "Aryan," according to the commander of the Security Police in Galicia. There had been 30,000 Jewish families engaged in agriculture, although "through events of war, this number has been greatly reduced."[56]

The commander, however, could only regret to inform Fliethmann that "the conditions in the Galician District make research impossible."[57] He continued:

> I would like to know your interest in [devising] a division of ethnicity among the people in this district that is [currently] racially and biologically unclear, to the point that questions of how they should be handled, politically and socially, are not clear. It concerns the town Halitsch where the Karaimen or Karatiz people live. They number about 1,500 in the district. According to all the anthropological and historical information, they are of Turkish origin, originally from Palestine, but have lived without reference to Judaism and also are not mixed with them through bloodlines. I suggest this line of inquiry to you, not only out of scientific interest, but from the point of view of political practice, it is very important. I would be very grateful to you if, when you finish your studies of Jews in September or the beginning of October, you could take on this assignment.[58]

Fliethmann responded enthusiastically that she would indeed look forward to working on the Karaimen problem, for the institute's Department of Jewish Research was addressing the same issue at this time. She exclaimed, "and so from the historical and ethnological side, as well as the anthropological side, we can make a contribution to the solution of this problem."[59] She explained that she would need a group of at least one hundred adults between the ages of twenty and fifty. She urged the SS *Hauptsturmführer,* Captain Schenk, to write to Herr Niemann, head of the IDO branch in Lemberg (Lvov), to set up the logistics.

This investigation did not take place either, for the necessary number of subjects was not available. They had already been sent to a larger ghetto or to their deaths.[60] The possibility of studying further populations of Jews was growing dimmer.

Life and Death of the Tarnów Ghetto

A few survivor accounts exist that report a different view of the Tarnów Ghetto from that given in the anthropologists' accounts. The Jews had never lived comfortably with their Polish neighbors in Tarnów, according to survivors' memoirs. Local priests often stirred their parishioners into a hatred of their Jewish neighbors by referring to "Christ killers" in their sermons. The Polish nobility, who lived in grand style, were satisfied to have a scapegoat on which Polish peasants could vent their rage. However, there was interaction among the population groups in schools, businesses, and community markets, and many Poles and Jews got on well together.[61]

When the Germans arrived in Tarnów in the fall of 1939, events took a different turn. It became dangerous for Jews to be on the streets. Schools were no longer open to Jews, and gentiles no longer used the Jewish hospital. Many Jews who had an alternative left Tarnów, and the population decreased. Executions began on a regular basis. One of the first executions was the mass shooting of Polish intellectuals and resistance fighters. Then came executions of well-known Jews. The German troops marched through Tarnów on their way to the war in the east, and food was in short supply.

At the same time that the anthropologists were examining their subjects in Tarnów, the Jewish inhabitants were charged a tax of 300,000 zlotys. On June 10, 1942, the first mass deportation from the ghetto began. From June 11 to June 13, ghetto inhabitants were deported to the Belzec death camp, where they were exterminated. Thousands more were shot in the Jewish Cemetery of Tarnów and in the center of the ghetto. From that time until the ghetto's demise in December 1943, deportations occurred periodically to Belzec, Auschwitz, and Plaszow, accompanied by mass shootings.[62]

An eyewitness recounts the end of the Tarnów Ghetto.

> On October 23, 1943, after a second departure of prisoners, there were only three hundred Jews left in the Ghetto, along with four members of the Judenrat. A few days later, Mother, Tusia, and I received the order to join a group of 150 Jews who were leaving for Shebnie. This exit would leave behind in the Ghetto only half the Jews that had made it so far. Father, having lost all hope by now, appealed once again to Goet, saying that he did not wish to be separated from his immediate family, that he would rather take his own chances along with his wife and children. Goet listened to him and did not keep him from joining us, despite the fact that Father was a member of the Judenrat. The other three members stayed behind in the Ghetto, only to be hanged in the middle of the square two days later. Such was the fate of those who had witnessed, one way or another, the atrocities committed by the Nazis in those days. The remaining 150 men were taken to the camp at Plashow [Plaszow] in February of 1944, being the very last Jews to leave Tarnów.[63]

Scientism in the Holocaust

The anthropologists who worked in the ghetto of Tarnów refused to recognize the true conditions of the subjects of their study. They completely objectified these persons, slanting all their conclusions to fit the political picture that would help them gain more access and be more successful in their careers.

Fliethmann referred to Tarnów as a "flesh pot" to be "licked out."[64] In terms of the wages that the women anthropologists earned, this was certainly an apt description. Elfriede Fliethmann received 10,252.74 zlotys a year in 1941–42,[65] or a little more than 500 RM a month gross, and after taxes, 420 RM net.[66] Her counterpart in Vienna received about one-third as much, perhaps because the cost of living was higher in the GG.[67] There is no indication of the location where the anthropologists actually came into contact with their subjects, or whether they were at any time inside the ghetto itself. It could be that the Jews were brought outside the ghetto for their examinations and that the anthropologists did not personally experience the horrors of the place.

The research of the anthropologists at the IDO was totally meaningless. For all the measurements taken and the villages studied, there was little analysis, nor could there be. There were no standards by which to judge Jewishness, so no conclusions ever could have been drawn from the morphological measurements. Even had it been possible from the data, the anthropologists themselves did not know how to do the simplest statistical procedures.

Had the anthropologists not been willing participants in the racist state, they might have recognized the horror of which they were a part. As it was, any cognitive dissonance that they might have experienced was not disturbing enough to them to cause them to leave this land of terror, slavery, and death until late in the game. They left no real information about the conditions under which people in the Tarnów Ghetto lived but only a trail of damning documentation of their own inhumanity, banality, and egocentric perspectives.

There is no indication here that the women heard complaints from their research subjects that would have enlightened their view of the reality of the ghetto and its prospective annihilation. The research subjects certainly must have been terrified, brought to the examining room by police, who most likely stayed at hand during the examination. However, the two women presented a great deal of evidence in their correspondence that they were indeed aware of the overall threat to the existence of the Jews. The Anthropological Institute of Vienna, where both of them had professional connections, was collecting skeletons in view of the future dearth of Jews in Europe and was involved in various kinds of research that could further the cause of the Reich.

In the case of the family Blau, it was Kahlich who had the responsibility to determine the extent to which he and his children were Jewish. She obviously knew the consequences of deciding that they were Jews, for she stated clearly that the possibility existed that "they no longer live" and called it a "tragic fate." Yet, she herself produced that fate on a regular basis for other

Jews! Her heartstrings were tugged only by the possibility that Blau and his children were *not* (sufficiently) Jewish.

However, even these "mistakes" had to be overlooked in order to get on with the research and to protect oneself in this political climate, Fliethmann implied. The women were aware of the destiny of the Jews in Europe and were privy to information about the fate of Jews and non-Jews through their SS contacts. They exhibited no humane reaction to this news of annihilation of a total population, but as "scientists" they were disappointed that their research would be curtailed. As women off on an adventure, they were even more disappointed, for this was their chance to make a name for themselves while enjoying their local status and importance.

Nor did they indicate any personal empathy with their colleagues. One wonders what they felt about the Polish assistants, aside from valuing their willingness to work and their skill. They expressed disdain for the male leadership in their respective workplaces. Kahlich, who was married, showed no concern for her husband's safety or fate in the military, and both were positively elated as their colleagues were sent to the front and their own careers advanced. Fliethmann suddenly married while in the employ of the IDO but had never mentioned her intended during the course of the correspondence with her friend. The man she married, Robert Henseling, was a well-known astronomer working directly for Hans Frank, general governor of the GG. Henseling was twice her age and took her to the outskirts of Berlin in the last months of the war instead of back to Vienna. Files indicate that Henseling had not been a Nazi, nor was he even an enthusiast of the ideology. He was in trouble almost from the start of his work with Frank and under constant suspicion.[68] How he reconciled these views with those of his wife is not recorded. There is no indication that Fliethmann and Kahlich were intimate friends, in the German sense of the word, for they never abandoned the formal German address in their correspondence. There was definitely a trust between them, however, for they wrote about their personal opinions with a remarkable ease and a candor that ignored the possibility that others, then or now, would read their letters.

Thanks to the work of a few dedicated journalists and social and natural scientists, the role of *Schreibtischtäter,* literally "desk perpetrators," or those who facilitated the Holocaust through policy and implementation without dirtying their hands, has become well known in Germany and recognized in the United States.[69] The anthropologists of the IDO fall clearly into this category, although their complicity has seldom been reported. All that is left of their work are a few pictures of unidentified men and women and hundreds of forms on which unusable data are recorded. The clearest outcome of the anthropologists' work in the Tarnów Ghetto is a damning picture of pseudoscience in the Third Reich.

Notes

1. UJA, IDO Collection, Folder 70, Letter from Kahlich to Plügel, Nov. 3, 1941. (All UJA citations are to the IDO Collection.)

2. Professor Hirt and Dr. Anton Kiesselbach of the University of Strasburg also conducted mustard gas experiments on concentration camp prisoners. See Kater, *Doctors under Hitler.*

3. Quoted in Seidler and Rett, *Rassenhygiene,* 231.

4. Quoted in ibid.

5. BAL, R53 IV, 169, 20.

6. UJA, Folder 104, Draft of Report about the Tarnów Jews by Elfriede Fliethmann, "Vorläufiger Bericht über anthropologische Aufnahmen an Judenfamilien in Tarnów." This report was later published under the same title in *Deutsche Forschung im Osten* 2:3 (1942): 92–111. See also Pohl, *Nationalsozialistische Judenverfolgung in Ostgalizien 1941–1944.*

7. UJA, Folder 104, Draft Report.

8. Seidler and Rett, *Rassenhygiene,* 254.

9. UJA, Folder 70, Letter from Kahlich to Plügel, June 6, 1941.

10. Ibid.

11. UJA, Folder 70, Letter from Plügel to Wehrkreiskommando XVII, June 19, 1941.

12. Ibid., Letter from Plügel to Kahlich, Sept. 19, 1941.

13. Ibid., Letter from Plügel to Kahlich, Oct. 22, 1941.

14. Weinmann, *Das nationalsozialistische Lagersystem,* xxvii.

15. UJA, Folder 70, Letter from Kahlich to Plügel, Mar. 4, 1942.

16. Ibid., Letter from Plügel to Kahlich, Mar. 13, 1942.

17. Gutman, *Encyclopedia of the Holocaust,* 1452.

18. See Bartosz, *Tarnowskie Judaica.*

19. Mogilanski, *Ghetto Anthology,* 298.

20. See Kornbluth, *Sentenced to Remember.*

21. Frankel, *I Survived Hell,* 54.

22. UJA, Folder 104, Draft Report, 2.

23. Ibid.

24. Ibid.

25. UJA, Folder 70, Letter from Fliethmann to Kahlich, May 13, 1942. Fliethmann's description of a Polish woman who could carry out analyses that she herself did not know how to perform is interesting. At that time, the German government had decided that Poles would only be educated enough to read and write, as they were *Untermenschen* whom, the Germans wanted to believe, were not intelligent enough to do more.

26. UJA, Folder 104, Draft Report, 7–8.

27. UJA, Folder 70, Letter from Kommandeur der Sicherheitspolizei und des SD im Distrikt Krakau, SD-Aussenkommando Tarnów to Fliethmann, Apr. 28, 1942.

28. Ibid., Letter from Fliethmann to Kahlich, Nov. 20, 1942.

29. Ibid., Letter from Kahlich to Fliethmann, Apr. 21, 1942.

30. UJA, Folder 104, Draft Report, 15.

31. Ibid., 16.

32. Ibid.

33. Ibid., 18.

34. Ibid., 19.

35. Ibid., 22.

36. UJA, Folder 70, Letter from Kahlich to Fliethmann, Apr. 21, 1942.

37. Ibid., Letter from Kommandeur der Sicherheitspolizei und des SD to Fliethmann, Apr. 28, 1942.

38. Ibid., Letter from Fliethmann to Kommandeur der Sicherheitspolizei und des SD, May 12, 1942.

39. Ibid., Letter from Kahlich to Fliethmann, Apr. 8, 1942.

40. Ibid., Letter from Kahlich to Fliethmann, May 4, 1942.

41. UJA, Folder 104, Draft Report, 1.

42. UJA, Folder 70, Letter from Kahlich to Fliethmann, May 4, 1942. The work Kahlich refers to is the examinations she was conducting for certificates of the presence or absence of "Jewish" heritage.

43. Ibid.

44. UJA, Folder 104, Draft Report, 92.

45. UJA, Folder 70, Letter from Fliethmann to Kahlich, May 13, 1942.

46. Ibid.

47. Ibid.

48. Ibid., Letter from Kahlich to Fliethmann, June 4, 1942.

49. Ibid., Letter from Kahlich to Fliethmann, July 9, 1942.

50. From the context, one can assume that "satisfactory" meant that Blau was judged part Jewish and, thus, should not be in a concentration camp or, for that matter, in the GG.

51. UJA, Folder 70, Letter from Kahlich to Fliethmann, Oct. 29, 1942.

52. Ibid., Letter from Fliethmann to Kahlich, no discernible date (perhaps early October 1942).

53. Ibid., Letter from Kahlich to Fliethmann, Oct. 10, 1942.

54. Ibid., Letter from Fliethmann to Kahlich, Oct. 21, 1942.

55. Ibid., Letter from Fliethmann to Kahlich, Nov. 20, 1942.

56. Ibid., Letter from Kommandeur der Sicherheitspolizei und des SD to Fliethmann, May 22, 1942.

57. Ibid. A complete discussion of the situation with the Jews of Galicia is found in Pohl, *Nationalsozialistische Judenverfolgung in Ostgalizien 1941–1944*. See also Stein-

bacher, "In the Shadow of Auschwitz"; and Sandkühler, "Anti-Jewish Policy and the Murder of the Jews in the District of Galicia, 1941–43." Mass shootings had occurred in Galicia since the fall and winter of 1941. By May 1942, a chaotic situation reigned throughout the region as Jews were "sorted" for labor battalions, death camps, ghettos, and immediate execution.

58. UJA, Folder 70, Letter from Kommandeur der Sicherheitspolizei und des SD to Fliethmann, Sept. 16, 1942.

59. Ibid., Letter from Fliethmann to Kommandeur der Sicherheitspolizei und des SD, Sept. 30, 1942.

60. According to one source, the Karaimen, or Karäer, were a kind of Jewish sect but were not necessarily considered by the Nazis to be racially Jewish. There were 300 members of the group in Halicz and Zalukiew who are reported to have been exempt from persecution. Pohl, *Nationalsozialistische Judenverfolgung in Ostgalizien 1941– 1944,* 102.

61. See, for example, Kornbluth, *Sentenced to Remember;* and Frankel, *I Survived Hell.*

62. See Mogilanski, *Encyclopedia Judaica;* and Bartosz, *Tarnowskie Judaica,* 298.

63. Frankel, *I Survived Hell,* 68–69.

64. *Fleischtopf* is the word that Fliethmann used. It was a common expression used as a symbol of good living.

65. UJA, Folder 38, "Zusammenstellung der Gehälter für die deutschen Gefolgschaftsmitglieder," Rechnungsjahr 1941/1942.

66. UJA, Folder 70, Letter from Plügel to Fliethmann, May 25, 1941.

67. Seidler and Rett, *Rassenhygiene,* 257.

68. WA, Signatur. 1452/47, "Generalgouvernement, Robert Henseling Acta."

69. Among these must be counted Götz Aly, Ernst Klee, Benno Müller-Hill, and others.

CHAPTER TWO

Anthropology in Germany before the Second World War: The Kaiser Wilhelm Institute

The popular idea that Nazi pursuits sprang up spontaneously in the Hitler era is simply wrong. Elfriede Fliethmann, Dora Kahlich, and other anthropologists holding responsible academic or applied positions in the German Reich were not outside the mainstream. Nor were the ideas and methods they took into the field new. Virtually all of the theories and methods of the anthropologists in the 1930s and 1940s were reinventions of much earlier attempts to study humankind. Many of the actions Nazis engaged in were suggested half a century earlier.

A description of the development of anthropology in Europe until the beginning of the Second World War covers a period of almost two hundred years. An overview of this particular history of a developing discipline and its applied field is necessary if we are to understand German anthropologists' participation in the later disintegration of virtually every humanistic inclination. Many of the early anthropologists became figures in the Nazi era either as gray eminences or as pioneer racist philosophers for the Holocaust. Their theoretical positions make it clear that there was nothing new under the sun in Nazi orders for the geographic and social segregation, and even in some cases the elimination, of various population groups.

That some ethnic groups should flourish and others disappear forever was not merely an outcome of Hitlerism but also an outcome of philosophies that had found an accepted place in the literature and in the hearts of men and women for more than a hundred years. Other prominent early German anthropologists, representing philosophies and methodologies that promised a tolerant and inclusive society, deserve to have their names known as well. They show us what might have been and how much might *not* have been lost if their voices had maintained dominance among the intelligentsia during a decisive era.

The Development of Anthropology in Europe before Darwin

What is the nature of humankind? This philosophical question has been with us since the beginning of the written word. The early Greeks addressed this fundamental question of anthropology in terms of the nature of the human mind and spirit. Anthropology professors have asked their students for generations to reflect on how we humans are alike and how we differ from one group to another. This interest in human variation has always concentrated on both the physical and the sociocultural nature of humanity, but in Europe more emphasis was placed on the physical. It is not surprising that at its inception as a discipline, anthropology was interdisciplinary and closely aligned to anatomy and biology.

The French nobility undertook anthropological pursuits in the beginning of the eighteenth century, although it was not until the nineteenth century that the word "anthropology" was used. This early philosophical work, as well as the work of those in other countries, was based on armchair ruminations of the tales of travelers to exotic places. It was easy to use the descriptions of aboriginal peoples, often referred to as savages, to provide a justification for the developing schemes that differentiated among groups of humans. It was only a small step to justify further the privileges enjoyed by the few, even in their own countries, based on this differentiation. Certainly, it was argued, not only were there differences among people, but these differences indicated that some people *deserved* more than others. Industrialization and the concomitant growth of a middle class made this line of reasoning resonate among landholders. A century later, however, these ideas stood in sharp contrast to the egalitarian and democratic ideas and ideals of the French Revolution.[1]

Anthropology as an academic discipline began in France in the mid-nineteenth century with the dedication of a chair at the University of Paris that formerly had been in the anatomy department. Only a few years later, the Société d'Anthropologie de Paris was founded. Germany was not far behind France in its anthropological interests. A German professor in 1824 published a book entitled *Vorlesungen über Anthropologie für den Selbstunterricht* (Lectures about Anthropology for Self-Study).[2] This book was a purely anatomical discussion of prehistoric finds with comparisons of skulls across geographic areas and time periods.

Measurement of skulls taken from old graveyards began the focus on craniology that marked anthropology for many decades to come.[3] There was no single way of making measurements, and much confusion arose from the various published scientific papers. Thus, in 1861, a meeting was held in Göttingen in which efforts were made to unify methods of measuring skulls and bones and to develop standards for such measurements. This led to professionalizing the discipline, and five years later, the first journal of anthropology appeared in Germany. The *Archiv für Anthropologie* concentrated on comparisons of anatomical measurements in prehistoric and more recent skeletal and cranial remains and provided a forum for these early anthropologists.

Interests in the physical differences among people went hand-in-hand with a more generalized view of human differentiation, usually with an emphasis on the hierarchical placement of human groups. The superiority of the "northern races" was first presented by Count Joseph Arthur de Gobineau, a cultural historian and diplomat from the German kaiser's government. He published his theories in the late 1800s and warned of the dangers of race mixing.[4] He wrote that the races of the German people, the Indo-Germanic and the Aryan, were those from which all culture evolved; only members of these races could rule others. To this end, he urged that these racial groups must remain pure. Gobineau's theories found great acceptance in Germany, and copies of his books sold well. One nationalist organization later distributed translations of Gobineau's works to soldiers in World War I.[5] His ideas were planted in German society and resonated among anthropologists such as Alfred Ploetz, the founder of the eugenics movement.[6]

For those who perceived a danger in racial variation, it was important to explore all the ways in which this danger could be manifested in society. Ludwig Gumplowicz foresaw a negative outcome emerging from human variation in the nature of future racial wars. He introduced the idea of danger (*Gefahr*) into the discussion of human variation and popularized the idea that those in "superior" racial groups needed to *protect* their own interests in racial matters.

Gumplowicz introduced the term *Rassenkunde,* which has no exact English translation. Frank Spencer acknowledged this semantic problem in his article on the terms *Rassenhygiene* and *Rassenkunde* in the encyclopedic *History of Physical Anthropology* and decided it could best be translated as "racial lore."[7] It is questionable, however, whether Gumplowicz would have thought of this as lore rather than knowledge or information about races.[8] What he wanted to convey was the accumulated knowledge that, he believed, existed at the time on the nature of race and the divisions among *Homo sapiens* of variations that could be described and valued differentially.

In Europe the very word "anthropology" came to mean what we in America would think of as physical or biological anthropology. This does not imply that there was no overlap with social anthropology. Indeed, the Berlin Society for Anthropology, Ethnology, and Prehistory (*Berliner Gesellschaft für Anthropologie, Ethnologie und Urgeschichte*) was the most important anthropological association in Germany in 1869, with branches in ten other German cities.[9] In practice, anthropologists became engaged in both the physical and cultural side of human diversity, as we shall see.

Darwin and the Evolution of Anthropological Theory

Darwin's publication *On the Origin of Species* brought about a great tidal wave of interest in speciation. If animals of other species had varieties within them, why not look for such variation in humans as well? Perhaps all humankind had not evolved from the same sources. Two different theses arose about human origins: monogenesis and polygenesis. The monogeneticists believed that humans evolved from a single source, while polygeneticists believed they evolved through various prehominid species, resulting in different "kinds" of people. The debate was a precursor to the discussion of race, and interest in this controversy ran high within the burgeoning field of anthropology. Darwin had created a new vocabulary and a new way of looking at existing anthropological questions about human remains and about living human groups.

One author summarized Darwin's influence on anthropology in the following way. Anthropologists began to link prehominid remains with evidence of current human variation, trying to establish lines of heredity. They also tried to develop a kind of "culture-anatomy" and to find common cultural roots in the past. In looking at human heredity and culture in an evolutionary framework, anthropology became a strong force in secularizing society against the power of the church.[10]

Anthropologists had collected remains of human varieties throughout the world, and archaeologists continued to dig at new sites. Collections of such artifacts became a central measure of a museum's or a university's prestige, and efforts to systematize racial history and contemporary groupings became a dominant theme in the anthropological literature. Ethnographic museums sprang up throughout Germany and were the envy of museum people throughout the world. Far from presenting a pedagogical point of view, most were anxious to show their collections per se.[11]

In England, at about the same time, Sir Francis Galton transposed Darwinian ideas into the theory of social Darwinism, which held that genetic characteristics determined the social and economic place one found in life, one's social value. According to this point of view, one could not change the outcome of genetic predisposition through environmental intervention. Social classes were simply genetically determined. They could only be improved upon by consciously selecting the best individuals for reproduction and inhibiting the worst from having offspring. Thus, the field of eugenics was developed. This field fostered a groundswell of support for social engineering to encourage goal-directed procreation. Social Darwinism and eugenics came together and stimulated further discussion and theorizing about human variation, posited hierarchical valuation of different human groups, and suggested guidelines on how to improve the human species by using the principles of Mendelian genetics.

Another Englishman, Houston Stewart Chamberlain, added to the mix. He moved to Germany for his health and felt at home with the racial discussions taking place there and the idea of German superiority. Chamberlain suggested that the intellect of human beings was connected with their racial identity; thus, the great humanists of the Renaissance were really of Germanic origin. He even believed that Jesus could not have been a Jew but rather was the illegitimate son of a Germanic warrior who happened to be in the region at the time.

Not all anthropologists in Germany in the mid to late 1800s were followers of social Darwinism. Rudolph Virchow and W. Koner, who in 1869 founded the Berlin Society for Anthropology, Ethnology, and Prehistory, which later became the German Society for Anthropology, Ethnology, and Prehistory, employed a wide range of approaches and points of view to examine the nature of humankind. Indeed, the society's journal was entitled *Zeitschrift für Ethnologie* (Journal for Ethnology). Still, for many, the study of anthropology meant measurements of living and nonliving craniums and, thus, many attempted to improve upon the measurement techniques and enlarge the scope of taxonomic development in the study of humans. The development of species, subspecies, and races was a strong theme among anthropologists until the end of the 1800s.

An opponent of Virchow, the biologist Ernst Heinrich Haeckel was a major supporter of Darwin in Germany and the person in that country most responsible for Darwin's popularization.[12] Haeckel was influenced by the idealistic and somewhat spiritual German writers like Goethe. Haeckel believed that humans could be divided into twelve distinct species and that, of them all, the Germans were superior.[13]

Haeckel wanted Darwinism taught in the public schools. Virchow objected to this, for he believed that Darwinism as a theory was subject to a literal interpretation based on conclusions drawn from too few specimens of early humans, particularly the Neanderthal remains.[14] Perhaps he foresaw the damage that social Darwinism would do to the German nation and those it sought to conquer.[15]

In a book he wrote in 1900, Josephe Deniker, a French anthropologist, engaged the German anthropologists in a debate when he broadened, as well as demarcated, the concept of human races. Following the Darwinian debate, he claimed that the concept of "species" could never be tested in humankind, for it depended on two definitive criteria: similarities in appearance and structure, as well as the ability to procreate with one another. The latter criterion could never be proved conclusively among humans, for one could never experiment with the most disparate of human beings from vastly different areas of the world. Thus, he believed, one must depend on physical appearance to determine definitive varieties of humankind, and these differences could be inclusively described within six races. However, within every ethnic group, several races would be represented because of the nature of human migration. In general, he was not convinced of the usefulness of the term "race" in regard to the human species and felt it should be reserved for other animals.[16] He believed that language, culture, and religion were the important factors that differentiated people.

Virchow and many other prominent German anthropologists accepted Deniker's conclusions for the most part, disregarding the need for strict taxonomic schemes of human variation. They saw the human race as immensely variable and believed that definitive groupings within the species probably were not to be found. After measuring the skulls of almost seven million school children, Virchow reported that, "If one wants to have a [single] German type, one has to exclude a large part of south and west Germany." Virchow was a German Jew, and he included in this study a large percentage of Jewish children whom he considered to be part of a heterogeneous German population, as he did himself.[17]

At the turn of the nineteenth century and beginning of the twentieth, strong influences to give up the quest for classification of human variation into rigid groups existed in Germany. A good example of this position was that of Felix von Luschan in his book *Völker, Rassen, Sprachen* (People, Races, Languages). "All efforts to divide humans into artificial groups based on skin color, the length or breadth of their skulls, or type of hair are fully in error. As often as this kind of schematic division is tried, one comes to inconclusive results. . . . Yes, one can even say, that the future attempts of this kind . . . will never come to factual conclusions and will always produce fruitless games."[18]

The history of anthropology in the late 1800s and early 1900s would not be complete without mention of the role it played in open-air displays of "exotic" peoples for the enjoyment of the big-city crowds. Contracting with natives of the colonized African countries, anthropologists acted as the certifiers of authenticity of the popular exhibits. They used the exhibited people as subjects for anthropometric measurements and descriptions, despite the obvious lack of enthusiasm from their objectified subjects. The Africans were also brought to anthropological meetings for display and discussion, dehumanizing them further.[19]

This was not the only position, however. Other anthropologists at the turn of the century represented a tradition more in line with Gobineau and Gumplowicz. Anthropologists such as Alfred Ploetz could still find an audience. Ploetz took from Galton's work the idea of actively advocating the improvement of the race through selective breeding and sterilization. This concept he termed "racial hygiene," and he developed his ideas within the German context. He proposed that those who were weaker should be discouraged or even prohibited from having children. Ploetz advocated the institution of measures similar to those used in mating animals. For his forum, he founded the German Society for Racial Hygiene (*Deutsche Gesellschaft für Rassenhygiene*), which was generously supported by the kaiser's government as well as industry.

Ploetz defined the purpose of his new society in 1905, describing the members as "Knights of Life" who must return to a "healthy and blooming, strong and beautiful life that gushes a bounty of earthly happiness." That could be accomplished only by reclaiming the future from the past.[20] His writings over the years spelled out that the way to do this was through selective reproduction and sterilization, returning the Nordic race to a purity it had lost through "degeneration."

Ploetz had spent four years in the United States before beginning his medical and anthropological studies. His knowledge of English undoubtedly helped him to understand Francis Galton, and a year after attending a lecture titled "Eugenics, Its Definition, Scope, and Aims," Ploetz founded the German Society for Racial Hygiene on June 22, 1905. No other country had a eugenics society at that time, and with his thirty-one members he made history. He had ambitions to spread his philosophy much further than Germany. He therefore renamed it the International Society for Racial Hygiene and formed branches in Berlin, Munich, Freiburg, and, in 1910, Stuttgart. Sweden, England, Holland, and the United States formed their own societies in the early 1900s. The society was so active in proselytizing and carrying out its philosophy that by 1930 it had become a movement.

Otto Ammon, the first to use the term "social anthropology," like Ploetz, was determined to be an activist in racial questions. His popular text, published in 1900, advocated sterilization of "beggars and hoboes" and expressed regret that they could not be eliminated like animals.[21] At the turn of the century, he and Ludwig Wilser initiated perhaps the first physical anthropological examination of a large group of somewhat randomly selected adults.[22] They gained permission to measure and question army inductees in Baden, an enterprise that cost the government 12,000 RM.[23] Their purpose was to determine the racial characteristics of Germans, a lasting motive in German anthropology that continued for almost fifty years. This pioneering study had enormous implications for the future of anthropological investigations.[24]

In August 1903, an anthropological congress met in Worms. Here, the young anatomist and anthropologist Eugen Fischer, the president of the International Society for Racial Hygiene in Freiburg, presented his findings based on work in South Africa and his collection of various bones from both prehistoric and current sources. He had found a gap in the literature that he sought to fill with an analysis of measurements of bones from the arms of black Africans, Egyptians, Australians, New Zealanders, and others. He stated that between the similar bones of Neanderthals and those of these other groups, no clear differences could be determined. Thus, the evolutionary line from Neanderthals to modern humans could be established. For this work, Fischer won the highest honor awarded in anthropology at the time, the Broca-Medallion of the Ecole d'Anthropologie de Paris.[25]

At this meeting, a radical idea was proposed: the initiation of the largest anthropological investigation to date, based on the initial study of Ammon and Wilser. It would be a physical-anthropological investigation of the total population in the German Reich. As in the previous study, they would examine a cohort of military recruits throughout the Reich at their induction. The anthropological congress established a commission composed of members of the German Society of Anthropologists (*Deutsche Gesellschaft für Anthropologie*) to approach the state ministry with their proposal. The most renowned anthropologists in the field sat on the commission: Gustav Schwalbe from Strasburg, Wilhelm Waldeyer and Felix von Luschan from Berlin, Georg Thilenius from Breslau, Rudolf Martin from Zurich, and Eugen Fischer from Freiburg.[26] For the examination, they planned to use existing measurement instruments, such as the skin color chart of Luschan, the eye color chart of Martin and Schultz, and the hair color chart developed by Fischer and Saller.

The plan was not put into effect, although permissions had been granted to study population groups in the army and the marines as well as certain schools and hospitals. The commission's own budget called for an expenditure of

360,000 RM and possibly as much as 500,000 RM. With the beginning of the First World War on the horizon, such expenditures were simply not thinkable.[27]

European Anthropology and the First World War

By the time the First World War started, German anthropology was established in many universities, with six anthropological journals published regularly. Two different directions were being followed: Some anthropologists leaned toward a descriptive analysis of the ways of life of peoples, and others were committed to the development of a taxonomy of human types, with hierarchical implications.

Professors began moving away from the mandarin style of academics. Rather than looking at discrete problems, they began to prefer big, overarching problems that required integrative or "synthetic" solutions. Scientists were rewarded for the breadth of their knowledge, not their specialization.[28] Industry needed answers to problems of production and military readiness if profits were to be gained and victories won on the battlefield. Many professors began to embrace applied science and began looking for solutions to these problems in industry and government. Academic expertise at this time in the physical and natural sciences could lead to success on many fronts. The social scientists, like those of the anthropological commission, also had new ideas about how to pursue their research and careerist agendas in cooperation with the government.

A new role as "expert" emerged for learned people. The university was not the only venue for academic work; the development of industrial laboratories and institutes for research was on the horizon. Industrialists hired experts from universities and institutes to help them in many areas as advisers. Thus, the intellectual, no longer confined to the ivory tower, became a part of the production and consumption of knowledge in the world of capital.[29]

The Development of the Kaiser Wilhelm Institute

As academics became more tied to industry and the state during and after the First World War, they developed an organizational acumen that led them to protect and foster their own research interests through cooperative ventures. The Emergency Society for German Science (*Notgemeinschaft der Deutschen Wissenschaft,* or NDW) was such a venture. Founded with the help of a noted German scientist, the Nobel prizewinner Fritz Haber, the NDW became a major funding source for research.[30]

The Kaiser Wilhelm Society (*Kaiser-Wilhelm-Gesellschaft,* or KWG) was another such organization for the support of scientific ventures and research. Dedicated on October 10, 1910, the hundredth anniversary of the founding of the University of Berlin, the KWG set out to provide an environment in which German science would have the support it needed to be the best in the world. Its purpose was not to support random scientific ventures but to build a national science center in which the KWG would support the most advanced technological and intellectual progress through a system of institutes. Thus, a short time later, in 1912, the KWG, working through a steering committee comprised of representatives from the state, from academe, and from industry and banking, founded the Kaiser Wilhelm Institute (*Kaiser-Wilhelm-Institut,* or KWI), a collection of laboratories of various natural, physical, and social scientific disciplines. In only a few months after the KWI was established, sixteen million RM had come into its coffers from "industries, banking corporations, commercial enterprises, and private persons."[31] Despite the fact that Germany entered into war in 1914, or perhaps *because* of it, more money was made available every year, enabling the KWI to add institutes. The KWG remained active as an oversight and funding entity.

The KWI, located in Berlin-Dahlem, functioned as Germany's equivalent to a national institute of science. According to the plan, within the various institutes of the KWI, scientists who were all acknowledged experts in their fields would not have teaching assignments or any other duties to distract them from their research. Within several years, the KWI had gained distinction through the extraordinary number of Nobel prizes that had been awarded to its scientists, including Albert Einstein (for physics in 1921), and for the advances it had made in all areas of science.

From its inception, the KWI was bound by considerations of the relationship among science, the state, and its citizens. Its board of directors, or Senate, as it was called, was comprised of representatives of each of these groups. The KWI Senate, consisting of forty-three members, was designed to help raise the necessary money for the work of the scientists in the KWI. By design, the KWI intended to allow scientists to work without the usual roadblocks to progress. New, interdisciplinary ways of cooperating would be developed and fostered. Scientists from other countries would work in labs beside German scientists. International funding sources would be identified and exploited. Fund-raising would be aided by the advantages that the KWI would afford to industry and government through the applied nature of the work and its application to the solution of long-term and pressing problems. Links between the theoretical scientists and those needing practical applications of those theories would be strengthened through every means possible. All of these goals were largely accomplished.

In 1922, the Prussian State Health Commission for Racial Hygiene (*Preussischer Landesgesundheitsrat für Rassenhygiene*) proposed a central institution for further research and practical applications of racial hygiene, eugenics, and anthropology.[32] By this time, anthropology was widely viewed in Germany as a discipline with applications that could vastly improve the physical and moral conditions of the people. Stung by the defeat of World War I and entranced by the flowery promises of a future that could build upon a glorious, if distant, past—not to speak of an improved race—anthropology seemed to hold many promises. This glorified optimism led to support for the development of the Kaiser Wilhelm Institute for Anthropology, Human Genetics, and Eugenics (KWIA) in Berlin.

By 1933, there were thirty-one institutes within the KWI. There were institutes for inorganic and organic chemistry, physical chemistry, electric chemistry, and physics and for research in coal, iron, fiber chemistry, leather, hydroengineering, and meteorology. Leading scientific figures, such as Albert Einstein and Max Planck, led some of these institutes. There were institutes of biology, biochemistry, physiology, microbiology, anthropology, plant nutrition, brain research, psychiatry, labor physiology, entomology, and even a bird observatory. Under the heading "Institutes of the Arts and Literature," there were institutes of German history, foreign public law, foreign and international private law, and a medical institute in Heidelberg.

In keeping with its policy of inclusiveness, the KWG accepted "memberships" (financial support) from cities, provinces, industries, banks, scientific and cultural associations, and private persons. Its directors wanted the KWG to be a national organization representing the entire citizenry. Nor was that support limited to German entities. In a voice of optimism, the director of the KWG, Adolf Morsbach, stated:

> I have learned here that the Americans are just as eager as the European scientists to do all in their power towards cultivating and furthering the cause of international scientific development by the cooperation of the scholars of the world. They have realized the importance of such an institution dedicated to the interests of every nation and its tremendous value in promoting international peace and good will. We sincerely hope this house will serve as a span to bridge oceans and to bring the nations of the world more closely together.[33]

And, indeed, "the Americans," namely the Rockefeller Foundation, provided money for many of the institutes, bought land and built facilities for them, and, in general, were enthusiastic supporters of many of the KWI institutes until shortly before the war broke out in 1939. For example, when the Institute for Cell Physiology and Physics found itself in financial trouble, Professor Otto Warburg, its director and a Nobel prizewinner, suggested to the Paris staff of the Rockefeller Foundation that they take over the funding, in exchange for which it would become known as the Rockefeller Institute. The general director of the KWG, however, wrote to the Rockefeller Foundation with a request to handle the correspondence secretly, saying that such a change would be impossible. After all, he explained, it had only been an idea of Dr. Warburg and did not represent the wishes of the KWG.[34] This interchange did not preclude further massive spending by the Rockefeller Foundation for these institutes and others.

Rockefeller Foundation Support for the KWIA

The KWIA was established in 1927 as one of six medical institutes administered and supported by the KWG. The president of the KWG, Adolf von Harnack, officiated at its opening and officially put the institute into the care of Eugen Fischer, who had continued to distinguish himself in the combined fields of anatomy and anthropology. Born on the border of Switzerland and Germany, Fischer had spent the first part of his career in the University of Freiburg as a lecturer. He gained his reputation by studying race among South Africans, particularly the case of mixed-race people. The publication of his work on the "Rehobath Bastards" struck the right chord with the anthropological community, and he rose in influence. Between the world wars, he was called in to help with the problem of another "bastard" population: the "Rhineland Bastards," a group of French African–German children fathered by troops stationed in the Rhineland after World War I. Many of these children were sterilized, a fate not known or publicized at the time.

The KWIA had a well-defined program to address research agendas in the fields of physical and social anthropology, human heredity, and genetics. In addition, according to the plan, the KWIA would study social problems with a "method of approach which distinguishes it from other institutes concerned especially with the study of the individual."[35] The new institute attracted the attention of staff members of the Rockefeller Foundation stationed in Paris, who paid regular visits to Germany to decide which projects they might be interested in supporting. On September 20, 1929, a letter from the NDW, translated by someone either in Germany or the United States into somewhat awkward English, was directed to Dr. Edmund E. Day, the director of Social Science at the Rockefeller Foundation in New York:

Dear Dr. Day:

On the occasion of [your staff member's] last visit to Berlin, I had the opportunity of discussing with him some of the larger common plans to be carried out with the support of the Notgemeinschaft in the field of social sciences. [He] was kind enough to indicate the possibility of soliciting cooperation from the Rockefeller Foundation for researches of that nature. I was pleased to take this suggestion, and in the following wish to draw your attention to one of these general plans taken up by the Notgemeinschaft.

In substance it deals with a comprehensive investigation of the anthropological relations of Germany, with the object of finding a really scientific foundation to judge the anthropological constitution of the population. By this is not meant a one-sided anthropometric survey, but the main idea is the observation of people in their social surroundings, not as isolated zoological objects.[36]

At this point in his letter, Dr. Ott repeated much of what Eugen Fischer had written in a special publication (*Sonderdruck*).[37] Fischer had explained the purpose of the study and the research plan. Without attributing his description to Fisher, Ott covered the same points.

The research was to be a comprehensive study of the anthropological makeup of the German population. It would focus on at least sixty communities, primarily rural, for in-depth analysis. Some industrial towns would also be selected as well as the settled Jewish population of Frankfurt and various towns in which nobility lived. The research anthropologists would examine church records and historical data as well as public health records and would do examinations of individuals. Social and economic conditions would be highlighted, and the scientists would look for evidence of "degeneration" through the distribution of hereditary pathologies. Social pathology would also be studied though a close examination of murderers and "hardened criminals" whose brains would be sent to the Berlin Brain Institute for examination. Birth rates, abortion rates, and possibly blood groups would be added to the record. Even prehistoric skull remains might shed light on the composition of the German people.

The study would be carried out by anthropologists located in the various regions, all of whom would standardize their data collection instruments and agree on research goals in advance of the study. The entire project would be overseen by the NDW through the auspices of the KWIA in Berlin.

During the last year the Notgemeinschaft devoted about $25,000 to the community work mentioned, the results of which lead to hopes of other, more important issues. Each increase of the means available would signify an increased formation of these plans for research and the possibility of an intensification of the work. The Notgemeinschaft would therefore be very pleased if the Rockefeller

Foundation would take into consideration a larger support of these plans. From previous experience, it would be very desirable, if in addition to the means devoted by the Notgemeinschaft, the Rockefeller Foundation would contemplate a yearly contribution of $25,000 for a period of five years.

With kind regards,
Dr. F. Schmidt-Ott
Minister of State[38]

From the beginning of the KWI, the international flair, the modern approach to interdisciplinary science, and the assertive marketing by the KWI scientists had led the Rockefeller Foundation to be positively predisposed to funding its projects. Often the wording in reports by visitors from the foundation was glowing and expressed great sympathy for the scientists working under conditions of hardship because of the effect of World War I reparation payments on the economy. "The project is being conducted with model German thoronous [*sic*] and with the use of many ingenious statistical and mapping devices. The whole thing will cost about 600,000 marks. The director of the project alleges that the Government would have given their mailing matters the franking privilege, had the postal revenues not been pledged to the service of the Young loan. If this is so, it is a striking example of how severely reparations burden certain types of scientific work."[39]

This particular project was one of the first anthropological ventures that the Rockefeller Foundation funded for the KWIA in response to the request from Dr. Schmidt-Ott. It was grandiose in both size and intentions, reminiscent of a research proposal from a naive student who has not yet learned to limit the scope of study. Yet to those following the agendas of German anthropologists through the years, this project would not have been unfamiliar. Indeed, it was virtually the same project that the German government had rejected more than a decade earlier as far too expensive. Fischer described the new project thus: "Today our plans for achieving this increasingly important goal are different. We believe that the earlier plan to investigate as many people in various age groups in all of Germany [students and soldiers] does not take us to our goal. The population mix in the cities that have grown gigantically in the meantime and the population fluctuations in the industrial areas are so overwhelming that in this investigation the results would be skewed by these mixed areas and would distort the results."[40]

Fischer believed that this project should be part of an international effort and mentioned that Polish anthropologists were making great strides in such studies. He was particularly interested in tracing the systemic relationships between prehominids and Germans. "We do not know if our people is a Cro-

Magnon race. We know less about the Prussians than the southern Germans.
. . . Finally, we have to think of the foreign Germans. Here anthropology has
a new problem of great interest. Whether without crossing or mixing, through
their own development, eventual incest, or through some kind of environmental influence (climate, altitude, lifestyles, etc.) the progeny of German
immigrants have changed over the centuries or whether there was crossing
with the former population and what came of that. These are questions of
great importance, for there are areas where large numbers in relatively pure
form are located."[41]

This use of the term "foreign Germans" was a veiled reference to the Jews
in Germany. He was interested in the extent to which their genetic heritage
was present in the German population. In Berlin, where most German Jews
lived, 40 percent of the marriages were mixed. Without conducting a "genetic
investigation," it would be quite clear that the total population had many
genetic influences from its Jewish citizens.

The way the Rockefeller Foundation staff described it, the project would
create a "cultural atlas" of the German people. The Germans described it
differently. They called the project "Racial Knowledge about the German
People" (*Rassenkunde des deutschen Volkes*). It would continue the racial
mapping of the German territory that had been an interest of European
anthropologists for almost one hundred years.

The Museum for Ethnology and Folk Traditions (*Museum für Völkerkunde*)
in Hamburg was one of the institutions that would provide staff to gather the
information for the massive study discussed by Ott and Fischer. Because of
this participation, the Rockefeller staff person visiting the project also arrived
to look over the museum and its staff. In his diary, this person noted his impressions of that visit:

> [The] purpose is to establish a cultural atlas of the German speaking peoples.
> Some 15,000 places being studied by the questionnaire method. Some 150 ques-
> tions covering beliefs, terminology of common objects, etc. etc. When these are
> plotted on maps, unexpected relationships are revealed. Thus the plotting of the
> term haystack appears to show from what districts of old Germany come the set-
> tlers of the Eastern frontier. The concordance of a number of facts will establish,
> it is believed, historical sequences which cannot be established by direct histori-
> cal investigations. These maps when completed should throw considerable light
> on sequences of cultural diffusion and existence of distinct cultural areas within
> the areas populated by Germans.
>
> This is the best museum of cultural anthropology in Germany. Dr. T[hilenius]'s
> creation. Collections beautifully arranged. It makes the Paris Trocadero look very
> sick. Dr. T. is about 70 years of age—gray hair, full beard, erect, vigorous—a re-

markable and winning person. Dr. Scheidt is about 35—a voluminous writer, a dynamo of energy and a fountain of enthusiasm. The fastest talker I have ever heard in my life. His personal traits stand in the way of his promotion.

This is one of the centers handling the big cooperative anthropological research project the R.F. is financing. In a number of villages in this district S[cheidt] has taken physical measurements of every single person, traced back the genealogical line to about 1650. This study has already revealed interesting results of radical changes in economic bases of life upon family survivals. Now they are beginning on the more cultural aspects of the problem the presence of various artifacts and how they come into the community, attitudes toward them. Later they will study attitudes toward concepts. The technical organization of the work is truly remarkable. Very desirable to send over here young American anthropologists and sociologists providing they have a real mastery of German.[42]

Walter Scheidt, the anthropologist who elicited such enthusiasm from the Rockefeller representative, was well known in Germany. The author of *Allgemeine Rassenkunde* (Common Racial Knowledge), published in 1925, he was very much interested in racial studies. "Although many anthropologists continued to define anthropology as the 'natural history of humanity' and 'ethnology' as the 'cultural history of humanity,' . . . by the mid-1920s even this distinction had been called into question." Scheidt now defined ethnology as the study of "the influence of race on culture" and anthropology as the study of "the influence of culture on race."[43]

Scheidt believed that anthropologists and those using their methods could solve the problems of society by using both physical and social anthropology to alter traits within the population. This combination of the two fields was new to anthropological thought and seemed to promise advances not only to the German population but evidently also to the American. For Germany, undergoing the social turmoil caused by the defeat of World War I and the terrible inflation of the 1920s, this was a particularly attractive idea.

In 1930, Scheidt wrote: "Population biology, biological culture, and civilization research create the content of cultural biology from which the knowledge of genetic capabilities must be enhanced if anthropology is to become the field of Race Hygiene. Finally, the restrictive after-effects of an unfortunate [term] 'physical anthropology' will have to be overcome in order . . . that we can look at culture history and social science as an absolute. Thus, anthropology can become THE research into the laws of societal life, and thus the art of racial hygiene."[44]

The Rockefeller Foundation, indeed, was interested in supporting this research and spent little time deciding to allot $125,000 for it.[45] The money would be paid to the NDW, with the understanding that it would be passed on to the KWIA for an anthropological study of the German population. The grant would be paid out "over a period of five years beginning January 1, 1930, with the understanding that not more than $25,000 shall be available during any one year."[46] This study was to be nationwide in scope and would provide "results" that would be shared with "the numerous parties who are having a share in the project."[47] The funding and other involvement of the Rockefeller Foundation with the KWIA was transmitted through the Paris office of the foundation through a cost-reimbursement plan with the understanding that the NDW would continue to pay its share of the project.

The study was carried out in different locations with many of the same scientists in leading roles as had been proposed by the anthropological commission several years earlier and then in the letter from the secretary of the minister of state. For example, Fischer was now not the newcomer to the project but its director. Dr. Thilenius, no longer in Breslau but in Hamburg at the Museum for Ethnology and Folk Traditions,[48] was joined by his co-worker, Dr. Scheidt, while Dr. Eichstedt represented Breslau. Others were Dr. Aichel from Kiel; Dr. Jacobi from Stadtroda; Dr. Vogt in Berlin-Buch; Dr. Martin-Oppenheim, Dr. Reid, Dr. Ruedin, and Dr. Ruedin-Mollison from Munich; Dr. Vierenstein from Straubing; Professor Munter in Heidelberg; and Dr. Saller in Göttingen.[49]

Documents show that many staff members of the Rockefeller Foundation examined the project both before funding and while it was under way. They found Professor Fischer "cooperative" but the KWIA "is very nicely housed and equipped but one did not gain the impression of scientific activity commensurate with the equipment."[50]

The economic crisis of 1929 hit the KWI as it did every other institution in Germany. In spite of that, the Rockefeller Foundation continued its funding of this project and others that it had begun in conjunction with the KWI. The KWIA was without reserve funds, and its appropriations from the NDW and other sources had dropped. Rockefeller staff reported:

> The income of the Institute has been provided from grants of the Kaiser Wilhelm Gesellschaft, the Government, the Notgemeinschaft, and local organizations. Reductions have occurred in subventions from all sources during the past two years, as follows:

	Kaiser Wilhelm Gesellschaft	Total
1930–1931	90,594 R.M.	127,319 R.M.
1931–1932	76,000 R.M.	97,045 R.M.
1932–1933	65,000 R.M.	71,000 R.M.

Since the staff, which is paid largely out of the Kaiser Wilhelm Gesellschaft grant, has been kept intact, reductions in income have affected chiefly expendable supplies including animals, and special technical and clerical assistance.[51]

However, the anthropological teams continued to conduct their studies and by 1933 had completed and published ten of them, with ten more ready for publication. This was a disappointing outcome for such an immense project. The publisher threatened to pull out of the project, as he had lost a great deal of money on it. Fischer then requested that the Rockefeller Foundation pay for publication of the rest of the studies out of foundation funds. The Rockefeller grant money for the project had not been earmarked for publication, but after some discussion, the foundation decided to grant Fischer's request. They informed him that no further money for this project, however, would be forthcoming.[52]

Twin Research at the KWIA

The other research that the KWIA was pursuing at the same time was varied and intriguing to the Rockefeller Foundation. Fischer was conducting studies at Berlin-Buch, a public general hospital in a Berlin suburb. "[Fischer] has available to him and his associates some 4,000 insane patients and the criminals in various institutions in and around Berlin. His own particular problems are studies of twins, both fraternal and identical. He is studying such problems in connection with tuberculosis, criminal tendencies and mental disorders. One of his associates, a doctor totally disabled during the war, is studying some 12,000 X-ray photographs of the torso and is accummulating [sic] a series of data having to do with the inheritance of those who have an abnormal number of ribs."[53]

In addition, Otmar Freiherr von Verschuer, under Fischer's direction, had become director of the Division on Twin Research. Fischer described the importance of the twin studies as follows: "Identical, or monozygotic, twins have always the same heredity. Fraternal, or dizygotic, twins have a different heredity. In principle, they are submitted to the action of the same environment. The most important differences in the characteristics between the monozygotic and dizygotic pairs prove the action of heredity and allow a summing up of the action of environment. Thus, twin research is by far the most important method of study of human heredity."[54]

Twin research had racial implications for the KWIA as well. Fischer believed that research on twins would enlighten scientists about the development and nature of races and address questions of racial mixing, racial capabilities, and racial degeneration. Verschuer had written for Ploetz's journal that twin research would allow a further distinction of good and bad genetic material through which healthy lines could be encouraged and sick ones "turned off."[55]

Fischer and Verschuer selected 4,000 twins from the rosters of Berlin schools. From these twins, they were able to examine the largest number of twins ever entered into a research study, more than 500 pairs. How the selection was made is not known. The researchers most likely made measurements of the twins but, in addition, studied "resistance to infectious disease," namely tuberculosis. Comparing single and double ovum twin pairs, "Diehl and v. Verschuer found the proof of inheritance."[56] They looked at cancer within twin pairs, as well, and the effects of heredity versus environment on its appearance in individuals.

Another major study of the KWIA in 1932 had to do with "the effects on succeeding generations of agents toxic for the germ plasm, for example, X-ray, lead, mercury, and certain gland extracts, with particular reference to malformations and general deterioration in racial stock." These were animal experiments and followed upon investigations by scientists in other institutes. They were expensive undertakings because of the high cost of the chemicals used and the large number of animals required. "As many as 1,200 rats may be employed for a single experiment." This project required 6,120 RM per year to continue.[57] Fischer also reported that he and Verschuer examined twins at their births along with their placentas. Where and how this took place also was not explained. Fischer requested 6,200 RM from the Rockefeller Foundation for this study.

The Rockefeller Foundation supported the grant over a three-year period for these two projects, based on the following considerations:

1. The Kaiser Wilhelm Institute of Anthropology, in its four years of operation, has demonstrated its claim to a position of leadership in the advancement of knowledge in its special fields of operation. The fact that during this period some 166 papers have been published is an indication of the activity of the Institute's staff.

2. As in the case of other KWG institutes of medicine and biology, there is wide and liberal local support, chiefly from government sources. It is probable that but for the severity of the present economic depression, the activities of the Institute could and would be maintained at a normal level without outside aid.

3. The importance of the two research projects for which aid is recommended is beyond question. Furthermore, the kind of aid proposed—assistance for materials and technical help, with no contribution to professional salaries or general maintenance, and with no commitment for future support, is in harmony

with our normal research aid program. In brief, it is not necessary, in this instance, by reason of the emergency character of the appeal, to liberalize the proposed grant by permitting its use for general budget deficit.

4. The scope of the Institute's activities makes its work of interest not only to the MS [Medical Sciences], but to the SS [Social Sciences] and NS [Natural Sciences] as well, and the directors of the latter divisions for Europe support this proposal for aid to the Institute.[58]

The Rockefeller Foundation granted 36,960 RM to the KWIA to be payable over a three-year period for the two studies to be carried out under the direction of Eugen Fischer. For other work of the institute, Fischer had to find additional sources of income. For instance, he was very interested in the work of Franz Boas, the student of Virchow who had emigrated to the United States and conducted studies following the humanistic path of his mentor. Boas claimed that his research showed that among immigrants, the size of the body, the shape of the head, and the age of onset of puberty changed with successive generations after migration. As Fischer stated with such prescience, they too were "conducting thorough-going investigations of East Judah immigrants to Berlin since 1918 (parents and children)."[59] By this reference, he meant, of course, Jews from Eastern Europe.

The KWIA also was studying the causes of birthrate decline under the leadership of Professor Hermann Muckermann. He sent out thousands of questionnaires and needed support for their analysis, although he already had many publications from his work. Other topics that interested Fischer and his colleagues were "Psychological investigations of inheritance of mental predispositions, investigation of embryons with regard to the embryonic origin of racial characteristics of the skull, hair, hand, etc. Further study of bastards among half-breeds here in Berlin. Hereditability research among criminals and prostitutes. Hereditability research of the vertebral column, nerve plexus, cranial structures, etc.—in man and animal. All this work is in full activity and it has to be carried on, with the meager resources of the Institute, by the exercise of extreme economy and by personal sacrifice on the part of collaborators."[60]

Precursors of Nazi Anthropology

In 1933, Eugen Fischer was arguably the most important and respected anthropologist in Germany. Based on his studies of mixed-race people in South Africa, he saw some positive outcomes of different groups coming together and reproducing. He argued that the *mixture* of three racial groups, the Alpine, Dinaric, and the Nordic, strengthened the German Volk, making them healthier and more intelligent. Each race contributed its own special emphasis to the mix, making all a little more complete. Fischer believed that the true anthropologist is one who is interested in the physical development of human beings over time and the morphological distinctions they display. The anthropologist is interested, as well, in the *systematic* comparison of present-day humans with fossils and "recent primates." The ethnologist is concerned with the present day, or the "ethnological present," a synthesis of information about the cultural group that may not all be current or exhibited at the present time.

Fischer had doubts early in his career that a distinct differentiation of races was possible. "There are so many characteristics, so many difficulties, indeed unsolvable! And when we consider all the possible environmental influences that might modify the outward appearance, then the possibility disappears totally that we can divide up the races anatomically and find the genetic key."[61] Furthermore, Fischer viewed the concepts "Volk" and "race" as different but related. He saw Volk as large groups of people with commonalities in their cultural traits, whereas race, according to Fischer, was a systems phenomenon, looking back over time to prehominids. It could be seen as the common genetic inherited form of physical and psychological traits that characterize a population. Every Volk is potentially comprised of many or several races. Only when a Volk was comprised of only one race could one use the term to mean race.

Hans F. K. Günther, who had heard Fischer's lectures while studying at the University of Freiburg, was a popularizer of "scientific" concepts and by far the more widely read of the two. While Fischer's book *Kultur der Gegenwart* (Present-day Culture) received a good response on the market as a basic text, Günther's book *Rassenkunde des deutschen Volkes* (Racial Studies of the German People) was reprinted sixteen times, for a total of more than 50,000 books.[62] While the two books shared many of the same ideas, Günther did not believe that the Nordic race was a result of race mixing and did not advocate racial mixing of any kind. And his "expert" message was the one that most of the German people read.

The large sales of Günther's book indicate that the German people had an interest in race and concerns about their own place in the illustrated racial hierarchy that Günther offered them. Despite the distinguished legacy of Beethoven and Goethe, the German people had just lost World War I and were defeated in body and spirit. Then, too, they were faced with the approach of the modern world, the declining power of the church and community tradition, the growth of big industry, and the appearance of new forms of art and modern ways of life.

Fischer had hoped that the racial studies of the German people would definitively place before science the variability that existed in the present-day Germany of the early 1930s. Under his direction, anthropologists went from community to community measuring their subjects and conducting ethnographic inquiries, but they met with great resistance among the population to this probing and prying. Even with Rockefeller funding, the resistance of the population was so great that progress was difficult. Fischer and his distinguished colleagues had enormous plans, but the results were disappointing and even embarrassing.

Notes

1. Segal, *Die Hohen Priester der Vernichtung,* 11.

2. Lösch, *Rasse als Konstrukt,* 27.

3. See chapter 9 for a discussion of the skull and skeleton collection still found in the Natural History Museum in Vienna, Austria.

4. Segal, *Die Hohen Priester der Vernichtung,* 11.

5. Proctor, "From Anthropologie to Rassenkunde," 143.

6. These ideas are still distributed in the United States by at least one publisher. They form the basis of a neoracist philosophy cloaked in pseudo-intellectualism. See Kühl, *Nazi Connection,* chap. 1.

7. Spencer, *History of Physical Anthropology,* 871.

8. For instance, *Landeskunde* is translated "geography" and would not include, except as an aside, mythological or folk beliefs about land formation and usage.

9. Zimmerman, *Anthropology and Antihumanism in Imperial Germany,* 4–5. See also Massin, "From Virchow to Fischer," 83.

10. Lösch, *Rasse als Konstrukt,* 26–27.

11. See Penny, "Cosmopolitan Visions and Municipal Displays."

12. Kelly, *Descent of Darwinism,* 23.

13. See <http://www.strangescience.net/haeckel.htm>; <http://www.uemp.berkeley.edu/history/haeckel.htm>; and <http://www.nceas.ucsb.edu/-alroy/lefa/Haeckel.htm>.

14. Junker and Hossfeld, *Die Entdeckung der Evolution,* 133.

15. Some of Haeckel's ideas were used in later Nazi theorizing, but there is no evidence that the regime specifically used his ideas to substantiate Nazi philosophy. In fact, a clear distancing from Haeckel is seen in a letter from the main office of the Culture-Political Archives to the German Office of Adult Education. "[One] has to take into account that the racial teaching of the National Socialists holds its distance from the human evolution school, which constantly changes elements of its scientific theories. It is [held hostage] to its basic tenets, which at this time reflect Haeck-

el's thoughts and thereby is thought by the public, not entirely without cause, to serve the materialist-monist ideas" (quoted in Brömer, Hossfeld, and Rupke, *Evolutionsbiologie von Darwin bis heute*, 293).

16. Lösch, *Rasse als Konstrukt*, 31.

17. Segal, *Die Hohen Priester der Vernichtung*, 25.

18. Quoted in Lösch, *Rasse als Konstrukt*, 33.

19. See Zimmerman, *Anthropology and Antihumanism in Imperial Germany*. The description of anthropology in this time period is thoughtfully presented in this book, and the implications of what Zimmerman calls "antihumanism" are fully realized in the next period of German anthropological history.

20. Ploetz, *Archiv für Rassen- und Gesellschaftsbiologie* 24:7. The author has taken a little liberty with the translation in order to make the English more coherent.

21. Ammon, *Gesellschaftsordnung und ihre natürlichen Grundlagen*, 288.

22. Stölting, "Die anthroposoziologische Schule," 149.

23. Lösch, *Rasse als Konstrukt*, 43.

24. E. Fischer, "Anthropologische Erforschung der deutschen Bevölkerung."

25. Ibid.

26. Ibid.

27. Lösch, *Rasse als Konstrukt*, 42–45.

28. Harwood, "Rise of the Party-Political Professor," 23.

29. Szöllösi-Janze, "Der Wissenschaftler als Experte," 48.

30. Ibid., 55.

31. RAC 1.1, A, 717, Box 10, Folder 64, n.d., 2.

32. Proctor, "From Anthropologie to Rassenkunde," 145.

33. RAC 1.1, A, 717, Box 10, Folder 64, 6–7.

34. RAC 6.1, Series 1.1, Box 4, Folder 46, May 22, 1931.

35. RAC 1.1, A, 717, Box 10, Folder 63, June 7, 1932.

36. RAC 1.1, A, 10, Box 20, Folder 187, Sept. 20, 1929, 1.

37. E. Fischer, "Anthropologische Erforschung der deutschen Bevölkerung."

38. RAC 1.1, A, 10, Box 20, Folder 187, Sept. 20, 1929, 4.

39. Ibid., Jan. 3, 1931.

40. E. Fischer, "Anthropologische Erforschung der deutschen Bevölkerung."

41. Ibid.

42. RAC 1.1, A, 10, Box 20, Folder 187, Jan. 3, 1931.

43. Proctor, "From Anthropologie to Rassenkunde," 147.

44. Scheidt, "Rassenbiologie und Kulturpolitik," 58–59.

45. RAC 1.1, A, 10, Box 20, Folder 187. The application was made on September 5, 1929, and granted on November 14 of the same year.

46. Ibid.

47. Ibid.

48. Vossen, "Die Entwicklung der Europa-Abteilung am Hamburgischen Museum für Völkerkunde," 73.

49. Lösch, *Rasse als Konstrukt*, 200.

50. RAC 1.1, A, Box 40, Folder 63, Jan. 13, 1931.

51. RAC 1.1, A, 717, Box 10, Folder 63, n.d.

52. RAC 1.1, A, 10, Box 20, Folder 187, date unclear (probably Aug. 24, 1935).

53. RAC 1.1, A, 717, Box 10, Folder 63, Jan. 21, 1932.

54. Ibid., Feb. 16, 1932, 2.

55. Verschuer, "Vom Umfang der erblichen Belastung am deutschen Volke," 238.

56. RAC 1.1, A, 717, Box 10, Folder 63, Feb. 16, 1932, 2.

57. Ibid., May 13, 1932, 4.

58. Ibid.

59. Ibid., Feb. 16, 1932, 3.

60. Ibid.

61. E. Fischer, "Die Rassenmerkmale des Menschen als Domesticationserscheinungen," 520.

62. Lösch, *Rasse als Konstrukt,* 134–35.

CHAPTER THREE

The Rise of Hitler and His Embrace
of Anthropology

The Book in Hitler's Library

While working in the Library of Congress in the early stages of research for this book, I wrote a request slip for the classic textbook of German anthropology from the 1920s: *Menschliche Erblichkeitslehre und Rassenhygiene* (Human Heredity and Racial Hygiene), by Erwin Baur, Eugen Fischer, and Fritz Lenz. My request form was returned with the information that this book could be found in the rare books division. I left the main reading room and went upstairs, thinking to myself how fortunate I was to do this work in such an extraordinary environment. The Library of Congress, certainly the most beautiful building in Washington, D.C., recently had been refurbished in the original colors of the Jeffersonian era—salmons, turquoises, pale greens and yellows. The main reading room, under its vaulting glass dome, made reading day in and day out seem an experience of great importance and mitigated the sadness, anger, and despair often brought on by the words on the page. It heightened the excitement of piecing together a hidden chapter of history. Now I could see a rare book without special permission or any particular barriers placed in my way. The democratic procedures of the Library of Congress, where anyone who has a legitimate interest can get a user's card in a matter of minutes and have access to such documents, was in stark contrast to some of the libraries and archives I had used in Europe.[1]

I ordered the book, wondering why it would be such a rare item. Other volumes, even those written in the 1800s, had been available in the main reading room. In a few minutes, the book arrived with the information that it had been found among Hitler's personal library. On the first page was a dedication to Hitler by the publisher, J. F. Lehmann. "To Adolf Hitler, the primary fighter for the meaningful recognition of the race question as the most important cornerstone in our deepening knowledge."[2] I was stunned.

This book presented the biological-anthropological view of race and eugenics, the study of the manipulation of propagation to achieve certain ends. For the authors, the ends envisioned were the identification of races of people, each with distinguishable characteristics that separated them from all others. Under the book's assumptions, Germans could build a stronger, more beautiful, and more intelligent Nordic race by carefully choosing mates with outstanding racial features. This book was meant to be used as a textbook but also found its way into homes where well-read people could incorporate these ideas into their own Weltanschauung.

J. F. Lehmann, who so thoughtfully provided the not yet elected Hitler with this anthropology textbook, was a right-wing publisher. Books emanating from his publishing house represented reactionary thinking but were not just racist tracts. They were written by authors with reputations as acknowledged scientists. Lehmann had his own goal in his publishing undertakings. His goal was to revitalize the spirit of the German people, which he felt had been damaged by the First World War, and his mission was to build national self-confidence by promoting the idea of the superiority of the Nordic race. For this purpose, Eugen Fischer was a good author for Lehmann to represent. The first book by Fischer he published was *Kultur der Gegenwart* in 1923, and in the same year he published Günther's *Rassenkunde des deutschen Volkes*. Lehmann paid the costs of publishing both books, and he also paid for several years of Günther's studies in anthropology.[3]

Lehmann had another tie to anthropology: His daughter had married Bruno K. Schultz, an anthropologist of some note who edited the renowned *Anthropologischer Anzeiger* and the more popular racist journal *Volk und Rasse*. He received the Eagle Cross of the German Reich and honorary doctorates from the University of Tübingen and the University of Munich before he died in 1935, and he was proud of his part in bringing the eugenics agenda before the German people and popularizing the ideas on which Hitler built his empire.[4] Lehmann did not live long enough to see exactly how influential he had been and what his publishing had helped to reap. His publishing house and his own personal efforts provided the venue in which a supposedly scientific basis for Hitlerian ideology could be established.

Hitler's Rise to Power

The life story of Adolf Hitler is well known and has been presented in detail and with various interpretations over the years.[5] It is only necessary here to place his life in context so that we can better understand his connection to anthropology and its role in his movement. Hitler was born in 1889 in Austria to a customs official and his third wife. His childhood was unexceptional, and he attended school without showing any signs of being an outstanding student. At age twelve, he asked his father if he could leave school and study art. His father refused that request. Adolf remained in school until he graduated at age sixteen, a favorite of neither students nor teachers.[6]

Failing to be admitted to art school in Vienna, Hitler mourned the death of his beloved mother and the depressing outlook for his future as he sank into poverty. He moved in and out of homeless shelters in Linz and Vienna, Austria, and at a men's residence for poor but employed young men. Hitler spent his time reading racist theory, writing, and doing artwork, which he sold to merchants in the form of postcards. In the dormitory, he found an audience for his increasingly vehement views on politics and practiced his oratory.

In 1913, Hitler, now twenty years old, moved to a dingy rented room in Munich to avoid military conscription in Austria and registered himself with the police as "stateless." The Austrian police tracked him down and forced him to appear for the medical examination required for induction. This exam found him to be in no condition for military service, and he was allowed to return to Munich.[7]

The First World War shook Hitler from his lethargy. This time he was able to enlist in Bavaria and served with aplomb, despite only rising to the rank of corporal.[8] He won several commendations, including the Iron Cross for bravery. He was wounded several times in the four years he served as a soldier, the last time with chlorine gas that blinded him for a time. While he was recuperating, Germany capitulated.

In the revolutionary days that followed, no one knew who would rule the independent state of Bavaria or Germany as a whole. For a brief time, there was a communist-led republic (*Räterepublik*) that took hold in Bavaria, but that was broken and replaced with military rule.[9] Hitler joined others at the University of Munich for training in paramilitary activities. While there, he found an even larger audience for his speeches and developed a following. Asked to write a statement on the appropriate attitude toward Jews, Hitler wrote his first political document on the subject in 1919. Sounding like an anthropologist of his era, he wrote: "In general the Jew has preserved his race and character through thousands of years of inbreeding, often within very close family relationships, and he has been more successful in this than most of the people among whom he lives."[10]

The Weimar Republic was established in 1919 after the disastrous years of the First World War and was intended to bring to Germany a modern, parliamentary system of government. It incorporated elements of the constitutions of Western Europe and the United States, as well as the German Constitution of 1849. Hitler joined the National Socialist German Workers Party (*Nationalsozialistische Deutsche Arbeiter Partei*, or NSDAP) and gave his first major address to a crowd of several thousand on February 20, 1920, in the Munich Hofbräuhaus. On that evening and subsequently, Hitler whipped the crowds into a frenzy with anti-Semitic and anti-Bolshevik rhetoric, often combining his two hatreds into ranting about "Jewish Bolshevism." Hitler also started to develop his own army to increase his protection and to institute fear and terror in others. The number of these troops grew to the thousands in the early 1920s and were paid for by donations and subscriptions of the party faithful, industrialists, and large business owners, who were attracted to Hitler's anti-Semitism and bellicosity.

On September 30, 1923, Hitler, who was becoming well known, was invited to visit Richard Wagner's son Siegfried and his English-born wife in Bayreuth. Also in attendance was Houston Stewart Chamberlain, a man whose philosophy of social Darwinism had so much influenced German anthropologists. The members of the group admired one another immensely. Chamberlain later wrote Hitler: "At one blow you have transformed the state of my soul. That Germany in her hour of need has produced a Hitler testifies to its vitality. . . . Now at last I am able to sleep peacefully and I shall have no need to wake up again. God Protect you!"[11]

In 1923, Hitler and the NSDAP attempted an unsuccessful coup. Hitler was arrested and incarcerated in Landsberg Prison. He used this time to write *Mein Kampf*, which was part autobiography, part political tract. Here he spelled out his philosophy and his plans in enough detail for it to have been a clear warning to those thousands who read it. In 1924, he was released from prison and resumed his political party activity.

As a result of the economic crisis, in 1929 the Weimar Republic crumbled. A plethora of political parties and splinter groups competed for power amid growing social unrest and disintegration. The political coalition of the Social Democratic Party (*Sozialdemokratische Partei Deutschlands*, or SPD) and several others fell apart in 1930, and in that same year, the NSDAP became the second strongest parliamentary party in Germany.[12] Turmoil continued in Germany but became pronounced as the Depression of 1929 deepened.

With bad economic times, Hitler had a stronger drawing card with the German workers and middle class. Many industrialists and bankers felt Hitler offered a buffer against the communists. Their objective was to use the NSDAP as a tool to oppose the leftist parties and labor unions but to keep Hitler in line by surrounding him with conservative cabinet ministers. They were prepared to circumvent the parliamentary party system to carry out this strategy.[13]

The NSDAP, while still the strongest party, had garnered only 33 percent of the votes in the election on November 6, 1932, and had actually lost seats in the *Reichstag* (parliament) since the previous election. The other large German parties received about 37 percent of the vote.[14] No party had a clear majority, and the formation of a new government had to be negotiated.

On January 30, 1933, Hitler took over from the *Reichspräsident,* Field Marshal Paul von Hindenburg, and became chancellor of Germany. Hindenburg had been the Reich president since 1925 and was neither a democrat nor a progressive, but he had been a stable force and a prominent figure since the First World War. By 1933 he was old and weak, completely controlled by those around him.

Many Jews were not immediately worried when Hindenburg named Hitler chancellor. They saw Hindenburg, the president, as the rock in the storm, "the peaceful politician . . . whose sense of justice and loyalty to the constitution we can trust. . . . we are convinced that no one would dare to touch our constitutional rights."[15] Thus declared the Presidium of the Central Organization of German Citizens of the Jewish Faith, the largest Jewish organization in Germany at that time.

Hitler Consolidates His Power

Hitler's first cabinet had only three Nazi Party members, including himself. The vice chancellor was a member of the Catholic Zentrum Party. The other key cabinet posts were filled by men from nationalist and conservative parties who were already in office.

President Hindenburg, sick and ineffectual, ordered the Reichstag to be disbanded on February 1, with the backing of the conservatives.[16] Hermann Göring, president of the Reichstag as well as Reich commissioner for Prussia, used emergency measures to dismiss the Prussian parliament and ordered new elections on March 5, 1933, intending to continue strengthening the police to "clean up" the political scene. Two Nazi organizations, the SA (*Sturmabteilungen*) and the SS (*Schutzstaffeln*), were deputized as auxiliary police. This 50,000-man force patrolled the streets with the regular police. Meetings of the Communist Party (*Kommunistische Partei Deutschlands,* or KPD), the SPD, and the Zentrum Party were now forbidden and their campaign materials confiscated.

Hitler held a meeting with industrialists and the commanders of the army and navy on February 3, 1933, to solidify the power of the NSDAP. There he spoke of the plans for Nazi domestic policy: a complete reversal of the current German situation and no tolerance for any indication of opposition to his goals. "Whoever doesn't let himself be taught must be bent." He declared there must be a total extermination of Marxism, the military must be rearmed, and the draft reinstated. Rearming the military would be the most important task for the success of the reunification of the political power of Germany.[17]

Gustav Krupp von Bohlen und Halbach, a major arms manufacturer usually referred to simply as Krupp, thanked Hitler and assured him of his backers' concurrence with his thoughts. He felt it was "high time for Germany finally to get clarity on domestic policy." The request of Göring at the close of the meeting to support the NSDAP in the next parliamentary election did not fall on deaf ears: An election fund of three million RM flowed from the coffers of industrialists and bankers.[18]

The NSDAP was not so certain the victory was in their grasp for the election of March 5, but on the evening of February 27 the Reichstag burned. A young Dutch communist was the accused perpetrator, but there has always been doubt about his guilt. Many believe that the Nazis planned and instigated the fire themselves.[19] Göring rushed to declare that this was "the beacon for a communist uprising" in conspiracy with the SPD.[20] As commissioner of Prussia, he ordered the immediate arrest of representatives and functionaries of the KPD and the suspension of communist and social democratic newspapers. In addition, throughout the entire nation, the SS and SA auxiliary police prepared to arrest leaders of the leftist parties, Jews who were members of the workers' parties, and middle-class intellectuals who had spoken out against the Nazis before 1933.

The Reich president's Order for the Protection of People and State (*Verordnung zum Schutz von Volk und Staat*) of February 28, 1933, ordered the first dismantling of the German Constitution: "[A]s a defensive measure against communist acts of violence endangering the State . . . [this act imposes] restrictions on personal liberty, the right of free expression of opinion, including freedom of the press, on the right of assembly and association. And violations of privacy of postal, telegraph, and telephone communications, and warrants for house-searches, orders for confiscation as well as restrictions on property rights are permissible beyond the legal limits otherwise prescribed."[21]

At the same time, an unremitting propaganda campaign designed to arouse panic poured over the German people. Left-wing parties were suppressed and blamed for the Reichstag fire. The Communist Party was decimated and existed thereafter only as an underground movement.[22]

The SA set up "wild" (spontaneous) concentration camps in prisons and penitentiaries, barracks, and abandoned buildings, particularly in the middle of Berlin, to further promote their terror. They also used castles, storage buildings, and empty factories.[23] In this atmosphere, the vote of March 5 took place. The NSDAP received 17.3 million votes and, by joining with only one of the small nationalist parties, reached its goal of an absolute majority in the Reichstag.

Now the Nazis directed their terror not only against political parties and activists but toward all organized opponents of the regime. Jews were not yet direct targets but were pressured at every turn to leave the country and were rapidly losing all civil protection. The minister of the interior announced the establishment of concentration camps, while the "Political Police Commander" of Bavaria and head of the SS, Heinrich Himmler, announced on March 20, 1933, the new concentration camp known as Dachau.

The new parliament was sworn in with great pomp on March 21, 1933, in the *Garnisonskirche* (garrison church) in Potsdam in the presence of the president. The sermon was given by the Lutheran bishop, Otto Dibelius. "[I]f it comes to the life or death of the nation, then state power must be established vigorously and powerfully, both externally and internally. We learned from Dr. Martin Luther that the church should not interfere in the legitimate power of the state when it does what it is called to do. However, we also know that Luther with the same seriousness called on Christian leadership not to denigrate their God-given office through revenge and arrogance, that he supported justice and humanity as soon as order was restored. . . . state office must not be mixed with personal caprice."[24]

This tentative protest against Nazi terror, this reference to Luther as an admonition to reestablish justice, resulted in Dibelius's being removed from his position as the general superintendent of Kurmark. There were many ministers and church workers who experienced the brutal actions of the SA and SS as they protested against the state seizure of the Protestant state church. However, the main administrative bodies of the Protestant church accepted the "Law of the State-Church Relations with the Spiritual and Church Employees." Under this law, only those who could support the national state and the Protestant church without reservation could be church employees. All others would be sent into retirement along with "those who could not be trusted." Those who did not have an Aryan pedigree or were married to a non-Aryan would not be allowed to serve as a minister or employee of the church administration. Ministers and employees who could not match these requirements were to be dismissed or forcibly retired.[25]

In the Catholic Church, many priests and bishops stood up and warned of the philosophy of National Socialism and forbade Catholics to join the

NSDAP.[26] In order to counterbalance that message, the German ambassador presented a memorandum to the Vatican on March 16, 1933. "Since the National Socialist Party came to power in Germany, its Führer has shown his strong will not only in his words but also in his actions in terms of his program for fighting communism and atheism to bring about a religious and cultural revival of the people."[27] On March 28, the Catholic bishops gave a statement in which they withdrew their previous warnings and rescinded their resolution against membership in the NSDAP. They trusted the assurance that Hitler had given in his explanation of the German government's position and the negotiations between it and the Vatican, and on July 20, a concordat was signed between them.[28]

The Prussian minister for science, art, and education dismissed almost all of the provincial church administrators. The SA and the police occupied the office of the Protestant press. Positions opened through this seizure were then given to members of the Nazi organization of German Christians (*Deutsche Christen*). The Protestant church's old Prussian Union received a telegram that read like an order: "We have God and Adolf Hitler to thank for turning back the threat of Bolshevistic chaos. Only a nation that is preserved can preserve the church."[29] The head of the Protestant church in Germany stated: "It is in the state's own self-interest that it tolerate no resistance of any kind from the people or the church. Any attempt at such resistance must be viewed as treason against the people and state. My job and that of those around me . . . is [to see] that authority will not be sabotaged . . . is to keep a sharp eye out on the activities of church groups and clubs. . . . It is recommended that the ministers be forewarned to speak to [their parishioners] about this."[30] Catholic and Protestant church authorities were therefore in lockstep with the Nazi regime.

As the churches were lining up behind Hitler, so was industry. In a statement to the Reichstag on March 23, 1933, Hitler quoted the chairman of the Organization of German Industry, who expressed the unanimous opinions of the board. "'The election established a basis for a stable government, and it has put aside the disturbances and the constant political swings of the past that so badly damaged economic initiative. The German industry, which sees itself as an important and vital factor for the national reconstruction, is ready . . . to work energetically, and the Reich's Organization of German Industry, as its economic representative, will do everything to help the government in its difficult work.'"[31]

The Nazi regime was now ready to change the content of the constitution without regard to parliament. The Reichstag, on the same day, by more than a two-thirds majority, endorsed the Enabling Law (*Ermächtigungsgesetz*), which nullified the constitution and the parliament. Political parties and constitutional safeguards were destroyed.

The Order of Defense against Secret Attacks against the Government of the National Revolution established penalties for any verbal criticism of the Nazi revolution. It created special courts that could operate without any prior hearing, without being called into session, and without any defense protection for the accused. By the end of April 1933, in Prussia alone, there were 30,000 arrests, most for only a few days or weeks, but enough to thoroughly frighten opponents of Hitler.

At the same time, the SA instituted an anti-Semitic outcry. Joseph Goebbels, minister for propaganda and communication, and Julius Streicher, publisher of the anti-Semitic paper *Der Stürmer* and administrator (*Gauleiter*) of Nuremberg, organized a widespread boycott against the Jews in Germany beginning April 1, 1933. The SA and the SS troops, who now went into action like clockwork, occupied and blocked every store and business and every office in which a Jewish doctor, lawyer, or judge practiced. They were not yet ready to set fire to the buildings or smash businesses, but on every building, they plastered and painted signs: "Jews out!" and "Germans! Don't buy from Jews!" Many Jews and gentiles did not respond to the boycott but continued their patterns of shopping and seeking professional advice. However, the pressure of the Nazis had its effect on the general population, who were intimidated and feared reprisals. The regime called off the boycott after a day, but there followed a string of anti-Jewish laws and practices.

The weeks of increasing terror and debilitating anxiety went by, and in the German state of Prussia alone, in the first few months of Hitler's rule, 25,000 people were in prisons and concentration camps in "protective custody."[32]

Gleichschaltung

"Bringing into line" can be expressed in German in just one word: *Gleichschaltung*. There was no room for deviation under the Leader Principle (*Führer Princip*). Everything had to line up with the ideas of the leader, and although that authority could be handed down to men in charge of other parts of the Nazi apparatus, the conformity to basic tenets of Nazi ideology and to the ultimate rule of Hitler was inescapable.

The Nazi regime now proceeded more vigorously against the surviving opposition. On the morning of May 2, 1933, the mobile troops of the SA and the German Workers' Front (*Deutsche Arbeitsfront,* or DAF), the new state-initiated organization for workers, swept through the entire country, taking over operations and offices of independent unions and even the Workers'

Bank (*Arbeiterbank*). Many of the leading union officials were taken into "protective custody" and sent to concentration camps, union newspapers were forbidden, and confiscated union funds were made available to the DAF as a part of the NSDAP. The members of the independent unions now were forced to join these new organizations.

The Law for the Restoration of Civil Service (*Gesetz zur Wiederherstellung des Berufsbeamtentums*), established in April 1933, restricted unwanted Jewish and Polish civil servants from working for the government or any agency receiving government support. From then on, there were "Aryan" and "non-Aryan" clauses. Nazi students nailed up "Ten Theses against the Non-German Spirit," which said in part:

> Our dangerous adversary is the Jew and those who belong to him. The Jew can only think Jewish; if he writes in German, he lies. The German who writes in German but does not think like a German is a traitor! The student who does not write or speak like a German is completely thoughtless. We will regard the Jews as foreigners. We take our "Volkstum" seriously.
>
> We demand therefore from the censor: Jewish works only appear in the Hebrew language. If they appear in German, it is made clear that they are translated. Make a regulation against the misuse of the German language. German script is only at the disposal of Germans. The non-German spirit will be wiped out of the public libraries.[33]

In this way, the national mode was prepared for the book burning on May 10, 1933, in which books by those identified as Jews as well as progressive and leftists authors, including internationally acclaimed literary and scientific books, were hurled into huge bonfires. A further order removed Jewish professors from their lecture halls. In all, 1,684 scholars were removed from their positions.[34] On September 22, 1933, the Nazi regime set up the so-called Reich Culture Board, which excluded Jews from all cultural activities. An Editors' Law was created under which it was required that all editors and their spouses be of Aryan descent. No longer were Jewish lawyers, patent attorneys, and tax advisers allowed to practice. Jewish doctors, dentists, and dental technicians were not allowed to see patients insured by state plans—in other words, the vast majority of the non-Jewish population.[35]

Political parties were either banned or dissolved themselves. A law of July 14, 1933, forbade new parties. It consisted of only two paragraphs:

1. In Germany there is only one political party, the Nationalsozialistische Deutsche Arbeiter Partei.
2. Whoever tries to organize support for another political party or to build a new party—to the extent that he is not subject to a higher penalty—will be sentenced to three years in the penitentiary or jail for six months to three years.[36]

In this context, all other areas of life fell into line: business groups, farmer cooperatives, unions, administrative bodies. The key governmental and police functions in the hands of the Nazis further enforced the "Führer" dictatorship. Jews and opponents of the system were locked out of every possibility of participation in their country's civic affairs.

The National Organization of German Industry and the Organization of United German Employers, which already had initiated an advisory group for the "Adolf Hitler Fund for the German Economy," contributed annually 0.5 percent of the annual wages of their workers. By 1945, when it was dissolved, it had brought a total of 700 million RM to support the terror organizations, the Nazi SA and SS.[37]

The Response of the Anthropological Establishment

Both a carrot and a stick were held out to anthropologists in the Third Reich. Hitler was talking their language in many instances, although the establishment anthropologists had been more careful in mincing their words. It was clear from the beginning that they could play a big role in the new government, that money would be available for research, and that they would have power over research subjects. And, not an insignificant consideration, order would be restored. It was also clear that Germany was now a terror state, at least for those who did not agree with the reigning power.

Eugen Fischer was a member of a nationalist, conservative political party at the time Hitler came to power, and to many in the Nazi leadership, he was a suspicious character. As the country's leading anthropologist, he had spoken in ambivalent terms about the Nordic race, racial mixing, and the embodiment of race within national groups.

A campaign of intrigue against Fischer started, based on his pre-1933 research reports supporting the idea that racial mixing might have some positive outcomes.[38] He was called to the SS Office of Population and Genetic Health (*SS-Amt für Bevölkerungspolitik und Erbgesundheitspflege*) for questioning in the first days of the new regime. During the interrogation, officials made it clear that he would have a very restricted position and would be required to retire at age sixty-five, in 1939, if he did not agree to the line set out by the racial policy groups.

It took Fischer no time at all to decide to be a player in the new system. As rector of the University of Berlin as well as director of the KWIA, he did not want to go into retirement and lose his public voice. Besides, there was little in the Nazi regime to which he stood in opposition. He endorsed the concept of "Volk," the idea that national and ethnic groups were homogeneous entities and should be fostered if they were of value and should be suppressed if they were not. Fischer had on many occasions expressed almost the same thing that Hitler published in *Mein Kampf.*

> The *völkisch* [racially and ethnically homogeneous] state must make up for what everyone else today has neglected in this field. It must set race in the center of all life. It must take care to keep it pure. It must declare the child to be the most precious treasure of the people. It must see to it that only the healthy beget children. . . . [C]onversely it must be considered reprehensible to withhold healthy children from the nation. . . . It must put the most modern medical means in the service of this knowledge. It must declare unfit for propagation all who are in anyway visibly sick or who have inherited a disease and can therefore pass it on, and put this into actual practice.[39]

Hitler's words could have been taken from a tract by any one of a number of anthropologists or eugenicists of the time, and not only Germans.

To solidify his position and show his solidarity with the new regime, Fischer gave a speech on July 29, 1933, at the University of Berlin entitled "The Concept of the Volk-State, as Viewed Biologically." In it Fischer warned of the mistaken belief that cultured people could not be subject to degeneration and even extinction. According to Fischer, Gobineau could be criticized for his mistakes, but what a shame that his basic idea of the different valuation of human races was not taken seriously! We know about race, Fischer exclaimed, we know about genetic illnesses, and we know the laws of racial mixing. Now we have to determine what it means for the state: "From the beginning, the NSDAP placed genetic health as first in their program, next to race purity. They stood more than anyone else on the standpoint of a pure race for the Volk. Their great Führer has made his plans not just through thinking and reflecting but through a feeling, a healthy instinct, and a living sense for the racial meaning of the roots of honest German Volk."[40]

Eugen Fischer, who at first was not so sure about the Nazi idea of a pure German race, soon was able to tell a different story to a learned audience.

> We need—I repeat again—an *Erbpflege* [literally, a fostering of heredity], in large part conscious and goal-directed. *Erbpflege* is a better word for genetics than racial hygiene, it promotes those who are healthy in mind and body, those with a Germanic heritage, those who carry our way of life. Only that is a population policy! If finally such is enacted, it is not too late to save our people, our German people . . . to [bring them to] the fortified National Socialist state, a state that we all want, that is supported by our sense of duty, based on an ethical understanding of the future of our people.[41]

The population policy of which Fischer spoke had a positive and negative ideal. On the positive side, the German supremacists, of whom Fischer was definitely one, wanted to see the Aryan population grow. On the negative side, they wanted to see the non-Aryan population disappear. Reports of Aryan population growth were met with great jubilation throughout the years of Hitler's reign, as evidenced in periodic notices in such journals as *Volk und Rasse.*

Long before the Reich Citizenship Law (*Reichsbürgergesetz*) was enacted in September 1935, spelling out the definition of a Jew became critical to the enforcement of the new German government policy. Now, employees throughout Germany had to prove that they had no "Jewish blood" and were "pure Germans" in order to continue in their jobs. For academics, this was the last of any Jewish participation in the universities. Particularly in the field of ethnology, colleagues denounced one another as they rushed to line up with the new regime.[42] Kinship formed the basis of determining who was Jewish and who was not. A Jew was defined under the Nuremberg Laws of November 1935 as a person

—descended from three Jewish grandparents;
—descended from two Jewish grandparents and belonging to a Jewish religious community on September 15, 1935, or on a subsequent date; or
—married to a Jewish person on September 15, 1935, or on a subsequent date.

In addition, the offspring of a marriage contracted with a "three-quarters" or "full Jew" after September 15, 1935, or the offspring of an extramarital relationship with a "three-quarters" or "full Jew" born after July 31, 1936, were also considered Jewish.[43]

Although this law was not drafted by anthropologists, who better understood kinship and were in a position to certify it? Fischer made use of this expertise to further the fortunes of the KWIA. An examination was needed when church records did not establish the ethnicity of a person. The examination, when it was performed, consisted of a blood test, a look at the shape and physiology of the eye and the shape of the head, and the taking of a photograph from the front and in profile. In the end, the decision was based on personal opinion, for there were no criteria to determine from an examination who was Jewish. Throughout the country, people rushed to find *Gutachter* (certifiers). Universities performed the service free of charge. Fischer rebelled against this volunteer service, however. "I would urgently advise against doing these certifications without cost. First, it is really not clear why some who are economically capable of paying for the time, especially the scientific time, furnished by public institutions do not pay for the trouble."[44]

Later, in 1938, Fischer declared that his institute prepared about seventy certificates yearly, bringing in an income of 1,652 RM in 1935–36 and 1,117 RM from April to August 1936.[45] According to the Interior Ministry, each certificate should cost about 90 RM. Most people seeking or requiring a certificate could pay for it themselves, which would leave only a shortfall of 1,350 RM per year to the KWIA as a whole.[46] Although eventually the government allowed the institute to keep the money it collected, it argued that the "research value" alone of doing the racial certifications should be a reward, particularly to the university departments of anthropology.[47]

Certainly, at first, many German anthropologists, although interested in race, were not in agreement with the racial doctrines that the Nazis espoused. The KWG, not a government agency but a recipient of government funding, was obliged to rid itself of Jewish workers and politically left-leaning personnel. The anthropologists at the KWIA immediately set about cleansing their institute of these colleagues.

Max Planck, a physicist, had become director of the entire KWI complex at the beginning of the Nazi era and remained its director until after the war. He had a personal relationship with Albert Einstein and had been instrumental in bringing him to Berlin before the First World War. Einstein was in the United States when Hitler came to power and wrote that he would not return under the current conditions of intolerance, inequality, and obvious discrimination. Planck chastised him for making these views public and privately wrote to Einstein that he would only make matters worse for his "racial and religious brethren" by openly opposing Hitler.[48] Planck did go to see Hitler to tell him that the removal of Jewish scientists from the KWI would mean far fewer Nobel prizes in the future.[49] This did not impress Hitler, who was determined that Germany would thrive without Jews. Nor did Hitler's unwillingness to consider another solution deter Planck from continuing his work at the KWG and complying with every government regulation. He declared in July 1933, "I am honored to inform the Minister of the Interior that the Kaiser-Wilhelm-Gesellschaft for the Advancement of Science is willing to place itself systematically at the service of the Reich in the area of racial hygienic research."[50] For this purpose, he had appointed Erwin Baur, Eugen Fischer, and Ernst Rüdin to serve in such a commission.[51]

More and more, the questions of race had to be resolved in courts of law. And the cases revolved around ever-growing groups of people: homosexuals, Roma, the handicapped, and bastards, among others. Racial courts were established by the Nazis to handle violations of racial codes, to settle racial questions, and to enforce the racial standards. Societal standards, in general, were also to be determined in this way.

Anthropologists at the KWIA, who were the most prestigious of the new breed of "racial scientists," were asked to serve, and they did. In the "Report of Activities" of the institute from July 1933 to April 1935, Fischer reported:

> Dr. Gütt, the ministerial director, met on July, 1933, with the board of directors and stated that it was in the government's best interest and its wish that exactly this institute be ready to advise on the enactment of laws relating to sterilization. This institute should perform research on the genetically ill and provide the clinical training and activities of a medical force trained in genetics and racial biology. The institute has tried to do this without restraint since that time. I have been aware that much of my scientific work has been somewhat reduced or given to others, but that did not stop me. I am of the opinion that at the present time as we build the peoples' State, no other institution can serve this task as well as we, and it must be our priority. We have all done this—division leaders, assistants, and volunteers—to the greatest degree possible.[52]

Fischer then went on to say that Professor Otmar von Verschuer, at that time second-in-command at the KWIA, had been a member of the Genetic Health Court (*Erbgesundheitsgericht*) "for a long time." Fischer himself had been a member of the Appellate Genetic Health Court in Berlin "from the beginning."

The Genetic Health Courts had a rapid influence and a chilling effect on the population. Those ordered to be sterilized because of what was thought to be a genetic flaw in their makeup could appeal their cases. In the first two months after the courts were established, the first court in Berlin heard 348 cases, of which 325 appeals were rejected and the sterilizations ordered.[53]

Making the laws regarding genetic health was a major thrust in the first months of the Nazi administration. Hitler had been interested in eugenics for years and wasted no time translating that interest into the kinds of legislation that many anthropologists had been enthusiastically suggesting. The Nazis were encouraged by international support for their party's eugenic ideology and lost no time in passing their first law, the Law for the Prevention of Congenitally Ill Progeny (*Gesetz zur Verhütung erbkranken Nachwuchses*), on July 14, 1933.[54] This law stated that certain categories of persons could be sterilized, including genetically mentally retarded, schizophrenics, manic depressives, epileptics, those with Huntington's chorea, the genetically blind, the genetically deaf, and those with severe physical deformities. This legislation was followed by another law allowing for the sterilization of criminals. Soon, the law also allowed for the sterilization of "Foreigners who make their home in Germany." This category included Roma and, eventually, after April 1943, Jews who were deprived of their citizenship under a new Nazi law. However, by that time, they had already been slated for deportation and later death.

Many anthropologists greeted the laws with a certain satisfaction. Hans Weinert heartily approved. "It is a biologically based marvel that National Socialist Germany with the only possible lawful help has progressed. One can only conquer genetic illnesses when one precludes the sick strain from the hereditary stream; that means one must prohibit these genetically ill people from reproducing. For the cases where a simple instruction or institutionalization does not suffice, we have produced the Law for the Prevention of Congenitally Ill Progeny in full consciousness of our responsibility."[55]

Hitler had intended to develop measures to eliminate congenital physical and mental illness but felt it necessary to wait until he began a war before instituting the most radical euthanasia practices. There had been so little effective opposition to his policies, however, that he started earlier and on July 3, 1934, announced the Law for the Unification of Health Administration, which allowed for payment to health care personnel for ascertaining racial and hereditary characteristics that under law should be reported. As of August 18, 1939, midwives were instructed to report the birth of any defective child to the Office of Public Health immediately. For their troubles, they would receive a small payment.[56] Health care personnel were obliged to report any cases of mental illness or severe physical disabilities to the authorities. If such cases were not reported, the doctor or nurse could be held responsible and punished.

Professor Muckermann, who was also a Catholic theologian, was still in the employ of the KWIA at the time. Fischer reported in his yearly summary of activities that 1933 had found Muckermann with "an intensive public speaking schedule . . . that served well to spread eugenic thinking throughout Germany."[57] In one such address, Muckermann stated: "It is also most regrettable that German literature and German art and much more that belongs to the German cultural life are unfortunately for our Volk and our youth in the hands of Jews. Some of [the Jews] are of good will, I won't argue that, but they should not be allowed to be middlemen to the pure German ways. . . . I emphasize, therefore, the demand that one immediately shuns, because of the possibility of deforming the native race, each marriage of a native-race German with a foreign-race person."[58]

Certainly, the training of SS doctors was an important part of the service the KWIA was providing for the state. In a textbook for doctors used at that time, Eugen Fischer stated that the cultural life of humankind involves a domestication in which many weak and sick individuals come to be tolerated but that this would not occur in free nature, where variation and mutations would not survive. The textbook went on to explain the implications of "contraselection" and made the beginning arguments for euthanasia.

In the first year and a half of the regime, the KWIA trained 1,100 doctors in the theory and practice of racial hygiene.[59] These doctors were trained by the anthropologists to be ruthless in their approach to their patients. As the years went by, however, the training at the KWIA was totally insufficient. Although racial study was included in medical schools right from the start of the Third Reich, the number of people who could teach this new subject was small. The quality of the courses was often challenged.[60] Despite that, changes were made in the medical curriculum throughout Germany to accommodate the racial hygiene emphasis. "In medical studies, next to other subjects, required courses in Racial Hygiene and Genetics have been added to those in which general exams will be given. The training time for doctors is shortened by two years. This is accomplished by reducing the studies from eleven to ten semesters, reducing the State Examination from one year to a half a year and melding the practice year into one of the academic years."[61]

By the late 1930s, most of the significant university positions in anthropology were being vetted by the KWIA in Berlin, which by now had a sterling record of loyalty to the government and its racial policies. It is safe to assume that few, if any, anthropologists had positions in German universities who were not ideologically committed to racial studies and actions to make Germany and the Reich uniform in its population. Racial certification was done by anthropology departments throughout Germany, and research was parceled out to universities in Marburg, Munich, Jena, Gera, Leipzig, Frankfurt, Vienna, Graz, and numerous other cities.

It is interesting to compare the KWIA director's report from the years 1933, 1935, and 1940. In 1933, Fischer reported that they were involved with the racial studies sponsored by the Rockefeller Foundation.[62] They were also studying, on the basis of families, instances of anomalies and illnesses as well as instances of special cognitive or other talents. They were studying twins to determine the biological influences on the life of the Volk. The staff members were giving lectures on race, genetic pathology, and eugenics as well as on conducting examinations. They were giving continuing education courses to doctors, teachers, and social workers. They were doing genetic counseling and determination of fatherhood. They were watching over the racial and genetic tendencies of the Volk, making the necessary suggestions for racial "measures" to the state and influencing lawmaking.[63]

In 1935, Fischer reported that the KWIA had been devoted to the scientific support and practical application of racial and population policies of the new state.[64] It had carried out the wish of the Prussian health minister, Dr. Gütt, without fail in advising on laws regarding sterilization research on genetic pathology and training of doctors in racial biology. To all the other groups they had continued to teach, they had added parish ministers. They were teaching at the organizations of the state and smaller organizations. Not only were they teaching lawyers and judges but sitting on the courts themselves. Verschuer was directing the Comprehensive Clinic for Genetic and Racial Care. They were providing certificates regarding race, paternity, and genetic problems.[65] In addition, there was a new Division of Genetic Psychology in the KWIA.

In 1940, Eugen Fischer wrote in his report: "The coming victorious end of the war and the powerful growth of the Great German Reich presents us with new duties. Even if all parts of the war-related areas like physics, chemistry, and technology stand in the foreground, everything that belongs to leading the people should in the immediate future be of utmost importance. Questions of genetic health, race, human selection, the environment. Our Institute goes to meet the new challenges."[66]

Since the rise of Hitler to power, the staff had published 190 articles and books. They were still giving continuing education courses in government departments and to the usual array of professions. They were providing the same kinds of certification but had added certificates for those being resettled. They now listed their Genetic-Biological Central Collection as an accomplishment. It included collections, among other things, of organs of children, adult twins, and Jews.[67]

The KWIA was tied to the state in every conceivable way. It worked with all the organs of the new government as they came into existence. In this symbiotic relationship, the KWIA gave its scientific credentials to the new regime and in return became a key player in the policy, legal, and administrative areas of government.[68]

Continuation of Rockefeller Foundation Support

By the time Hitler was named chancellor of Germany in 1933, the KWIA was a major research center in Germany. It had changed its focus and its name to become the Institute for Anthropology, Human Heredity, and Genetics. Due to the world financial crisis, it had a reduced budget of 71,200 RM, of which 12,345.51 RM, over 17 percent of the total, came from the Rockefeller Foundation.[69] By 1935, the budget of the KWIA had risen to 140,000 RM, in large part because of the critical role it was playing in racial policy.[70] Eugen

Fischer had a powerful position as head of the institute and also as rector of the University of Berlin.

Internal documents at the Rockefeller Foundation indicate that its officials watched the development of the Nazi regime but were not particularly concerned with supporting a research entity that became closely aligned, because of funding and policy, with the new government. Correspondence that remains shows that officials were aware of the anti-Semitic policies that came into force, but year by year the grants continued.[71] In June 1933, a foundation official in New York wrote: "It remains to be seen whether any attempt may be made by the authorities to use these studies in any way to support the theories of the National Socialist Party. There seems no reason to believe at the moment that the scientific character of the studies will be influenced by the doctrines of the regime."[72] In response to this optimistic portrayal of where the foundation's money had gone, another official answered: "I wish to thank you and Mr. Kittredge for the progress report on the anthropological studies of the population of Germany. It is gratifying to know that so much work has been done on this study and that its conclusions may have some real influence in the present confused state of the German mind on the race question."[73]

The Rockefeller Foundation shifted its interest from racial studies to twin research in the beginning of the Hitler era. Twins held the key to questions of heredity versus environment. The studies at the KWIA were the domain of Otmar von Verschuer, who had been a professor at Frankfurt and maintained a post there as well as in Berlin. The Rockefeller Foundation made a grant of 12,320 RM in July 1934 "towards the expenses of research on twins and on the effect of poisons on the germ plasm, under the direction of Professor Eugen Fischer."[74]

In August of 1939, an exchange of letters between a Dr. Raschhofer and Tracy Kittredge of the Rockefeller Foundation provided an indication that the foundation staff was concerned about the fate of people in Eastern Europe. Raschhofer wrote Kittredge to thank him for the foundation's support of his work as part of the racial studies group and to ask what would happen to the study of "minority problems" that he had worked to develop. He explained that he had been distracted from completion of the work by illness, unexpected responsibilities in his position in the university, the new political realities, and taking part "in legal actions" (by which he probably meant conducting racial certifications). He wondered if the foundation might publish his findings.

Kittredge's answer is instructive. After explaining that the foundation left it to the researcher to find publication outlets, he gave what might be taken as a mild, ironic rebuke to this active participant in the Nazi effort. "It would perhaps be of interest to give, as you suggest, a rather careful summary and historical description of the position of the Minorities in Central and Eastern Europe and of the efforts which were made to provide them with some form of international guarantee and protections."[75]

The Rockefeller Foundation made no reference to the fate of the Jews in Germany, which was becoming more critical each year that the Hitler reign continued. Beginning with general harassment, the discrimination and terror had grown to encompass the blocking of almost all routes to work, culture, and civic life. Protections given other German citizens were removed, until there was no law that would stand between the Jew and the vicious government. Many fled the country.

The Nuremberg Laws were passed in September 1935. With this step, Jews lost their full rights to German citizenship and became "subjects" of the German state, or second-class citizens. They were not allowed to marry non-Jews nor employ them. On the night of November 8, 1938, with exact forethought and planning, the SA and SS stormed Jewish businesses and places of worship, burning and destroying mainstays of Jewish life in Germany. Massive roundups of Jews for the first time brought them into concentration camps like Buchenwald, Dachau, and Sachsenhausen where, separated from other prisoners, they were in large numbers driven to their deaths or suffered unspeakably. Those lucky enough to obtain an exit visa could leave Germany with little more than the clothes on their backs. The remaining Jews left in their communities were "fined" one billion RM.[76] The Third Reich was using Jewish assets to develop the "new order."

The diabolical system of indirect administration of Nazi laws and orders now came into effect for the Jews as it had for the concentration camp prisoners earlier. Representatives of the tortured groups were set up to create their own enforcement mechanisms under the scrutiny of the Nazi SS. Thus, in 1939, the Reich's Organization of Jews in Germany (*Reichsvereinigung der Juden in Deutschland*) was established to encourage the out-migration of Jews and to take charge of all Jewish affairs under Nazi direction.[77] Systematic robbery of Jewish belongings, money, and real estate was accomplished.

It appears that the Rockefeller Foundation funding of the KWI ended with the invasion of Poland in 1939. In December 1941, after Hitler declared war on the United States, the United States declared unconditional war on Germany and the other Axis Powers. By January 1942, the United States along with Great Britain, the Soviet Union, China, and twenty-two other countries became the Allied Powers. Before the end of the war, ten more countries had joined the fight against Germany and her Axis allies.

Notes

1. Over the decade in which I was using archives in Europe, the rules and regulations became less restrictive, and the archivists became ever more helpful.

2. Baur, Fischer, and Lenz, *Menschliche Erblichkeitslehre und Rassenhygiene,* handwritten inscription on flyleaf.

3. Lösch, *Rasse als Konstrukt,* 137–38.

4. See Lehmann, *J. F. Lehmann, ein Leben im Kampf für Deutschland.* See also Günther, "Berichte."

5. Some of these biographies that the reader may wish to read are Fest, *Hitler;* Kershaw, *Hitler;* and Stone, *Hitler.*

6. Payne, *Life and Death of Adolf Hitler,* 33–41.

7. Fest, *Hitler,* 58–62.

8. According to one account, Hitler's commanding officer reported that he could not promote Hitler further because he lacked leadership qualities. Noakes and Pridham, *Nazism,* 1:10.

9. Stürmer, *German Empire,* 125.

10. Quoted in Payne, *Life and Death of Adolf Hitler,* 130.

11. Quoted in ibid., 171.

12. Grebing, *History of the German Labour Movement,* 131.

13. Kershaw, *Nazi Dictatorship* (2d ed.), 42–43; Kühnl, *Der deutsche Faschismus in Quellen und Dokumenten,* 88–89.

14. Tyrell, "Das Scheitern der Weimarer Republik und der Aufstieg der NSDAP," 196–97.

15. Quoted in Benz, "Realität und Illusion," 119–20.

16. Burleigh, *Third Reich,* 140–56. The political intrigues of the 1932–34 period are too complex to describe here in detail and are somewhat tangential to this book's theme. For a chronicle of these days, see Broszat and Frei, *Das Dritte Reich im Überblick;* and Kühnl, *Der deutsche Faschismus in Quellen und Dokumenten,* 193.

17. Quoted in Kühnl, *Der deutsche Faschismus in Quellen und Dokumenten,* 208–9.

18. Quoted in Kühnrich, *Der KZ-Staat,* 5–7s.

19. Noakes and Pridham, *Nazism,* 1:139.

20. Quoted in Broszat and Frei, *Das Dritte Reich im Überblick,* 203.

21. Noakes and Pridham, *Nazism,* 1:142.

22. Tyrell, "Towards Dictatorship," 35–36.

23. Kühnrich and Kogan, *Der SS Staat,* 59–60.

24. Quoted in Kühnl, *Der deutsche Faschismus in Quellen und Dokumenten,* 223.

25. Ibid., 224.

26. Kretschmar, *Dokumente zur Kirchenpolitik des Dritten Reiches,* 23.

27. Quoted in ibid., 17.
28. Ibid., 20.
29. Quoted in ibid., 70–71.
30. Quoted in ibid., 74.
31. Quoted in Kühnl, *Der deutsche Faschismus in Quellen und Dokumenten*, 204–5.
32. Weinmann, *Das nationalsozialistische Lagersystem*, xc.
33. Quoted in Hirsch and Schuder, *Der Gelbe Fleck*, 539–41.
34. Noakes and Pridham, *Nazism*, 1:443.
35. Hirsch and Schuder, *Der Gelbe Fleck*, 541–50.
36. Quoted in Kühnl, *Der deutsche Faschismus in Quellen und Dokumenten*, 200–201.
37. Kühnrich, *Der KZ-Staat*, 96–98.
38. Lösch, *Rasse als Konstrukt*, 234–53.
39. Hitler, *Mein Kampf*, 403–4.
40. E. Fischer, "Der Begriff des völkischen Staates, biologisch betrachtet," speech delivered July 29, 1933, Berlin; copy in the Library of Congress.
41. RAC 1.1, A, 10, Box 20, Folder 187, E. Fischer, "Die Fortschritte bei der menschlichen Erblehre als Grundlage eugenischer Bevölkerungspolitik," 71 (source unidentified).
42. Mosen, *Der koloniale Traum*, 12.
43. Hilberg, *Destruction of the European Jews*, 31.
44. MPGA, I. Abt., Rep. 1A., Nr. 2399/3, Bl. 89.
45. Ibid., Bl. 90.
46. Ibid., Bl. 80.
47. Ibid.
48. Quoted in Walker, *Nazi Science*, 71.
49. Stern, *Einstein's German World*, 54.
50. Planck to Frick (minister of the interior), quoted in Lösch, *Rasse als Konstrukt*, 312.
51. Pollak, *Rassenwahn und Wissenschaft*, 408.
52. MPGA, I. Abt., Rep. 1A., Nr. 2404/3, Bl. 49.
53. Proctor, *Racial Hygiene*, 106.
54. Klee, *Dokumente zur "Euthanasie,"* 51.
55. Brömer, Hossfeld, and Rupke, *Evolutionsbiologie von Darwin bis heute*, 274.
56. Lifton, *Nazi Doctors*, 52.
57. MPGA, I Abt., Rep 1A, Nr. 2404/2, 14–16.
58. Quoted in Klee, *Dokumente zur "Euthanasie,"* 58
59. Proctor, *Racial Hygiene*, 42.
60. Kater, *Doctors under Hitler*, 116.
61. Schubert, "Mitteilungen zur Rassenpflege- und Bevölkerungspolitik," 226.
62. MPGA, I. Abt., Rep. 1A., Nr. 2404/2, Bl. 15.
63. Ibid., Bl. 18–19.
64. MPGA, I. Abt., Rep. 1A., Nr. 2399/2, Bl. 52.
65. Ibid., Nr. 2404/3, Bl. 49–50.

66. Ibid., Nr. 2400/11, Bl. 159.

67. Ibid., Nr. 2404/4, Bl. 57–59.

68. Pollak, *Rassenwahn und Wissenschaft,* 51–56.

69. RAC 1.1, A, 717, Box 10, Folder 63, May 13, 1932; RAC 1.1, A, Box 4, Folder 46, July 16, 1933.

70. Proctor, *Racial Hygiene,* 42.

71. RAC 1.1, A, 717, Box 4, Folder 46, July 16, 1933.

72. RAC 1.1, A, Box 20, Folder 187, June 27, 1933.

73. RAC 1.1, S, 717, Box 20, Folder 187, June 27, 1933.

74. RAC 1.1, A, 717, Box 10, Folder 63, July 23, 1934.

75. RAC 1.1, A, 717, Box 21, Folder 189, Aug. 5 and 9, 1939.

76. Bauer, *History of the Holocaust,* 102–3, 109.

77. Frei, "Die Juden im NS-Staat," 130–31.

CHAPTER FOUR

The Discovery in the Smithsonian

Serendipity

As the archivist brought the rolling cart to the table where I sat in the Smithsonian Institution's National Anthropological Archives (NAA-SI) that day when I found the anthropological collection of Nazi materials (see introduction), she was as curious as I. The boxes on the top tray of the cart were tied in cord that seemed to be as old as the boxes themselves. Carefully, I untied the first box. It appeared to me that it had never been opened. In a neat row were envelopes, each stamped with a swastika and marked with a number in the top corner. The swatches of hair, the little curls, were hair samples from research subjects.

Hair shaven from heads, hair stuffed into mattresses, hair used to make rugs carries a million stories gathered into vivid, visual Holocaust images. Looking at these hair samples brought forth these nightmares, as well as a hint that each piece had come from an individual with an infinitely sad history. We were chastened.

I had planned to use the NAA-SI to find out what American anthropologists had known about the work of their German colleagues in the Third Reich.[1] When I recognized the name of the Institute for German Work in the East (*Institut für Deutsche Ostarbeit,* or IDO) on the list of materials in the archive from previous reading I had done, I was excited by the thought that here in the nation's capital there might be new data about anthropology in the Third Reich. The archivist in charge of the small visitors' library that day had been surprised by my request to see the IDO collection. She gave me the acquisition information for the collection and told me that the crates in which the collection was to be found were in the same state as they had been delivered at the end of World War II; the materials in them had never been shelved.

The NAA-SI provided me with the memos related to the IDO collection. Accession notes, the statement that an archivist writes to describe something being acquired for a collection, were in the form of internal notes and memos that had been collected and chronologically rearranged by a staff physical anthropologist on April 20, 1989. The content of the memo written to the director of the NAA-SI stated that accession 176,333 "has been divided between the Dept. Anthropology (Ethnology, Physical and the NAA-SI); Div. Cultural History, HMAH; the National Gallery and some to Dumbarton Oaks. Only anthropometric instruments were retained in the physical collections."[2]

The accession notes indicated that the collection had come as a permanent loan from the Intelligence Division of the War Department of the Pentagon to the U.S. National Museum as a joint accession to the Physical Anthropology and Ethnology Divisions on June 11, 1947. The original accession memo written by the associate curator of the Division of Physical Anthropology described the collection and the way it had found its place in the Smithsonian.[3]

> On February 6, 1947, Capt. Joost of the Medical Intelligence Section, Surgeon General's Office, telephoned to inquire if the Division of Physical Anthropology, U.S. National Museum, would be interested in securing original anthropometric data, instruments, photographs and other data on Eastern European peoples. He indicated that his section had received a large shipment of confiscated material collected by the Germans, and since seven large wooden boxes contained anthropological material of no value to Medical Intelligence, he was anxious to place them in a federal institution specializing in such matters. After consultation with Mr. Setzler, I asked Capt. Joost if the cases could be sent to the National Museum for inspection. Capt. Joost informed us that since there was British cooperation in securing these cases, they would have to be accepted as a permanent loan instead of a transfer.
>
> The seven boxes arrived at the Museum on February 7, but lacked the anthropometric instruments which will be forwarded shortly. If in good condition, these instruments would be of considerable value to the Division of Physical Anthropology since they are apparently standard-make (Hermann, Zurich). The anthropological data was [sic] collected by German anthropologists working in the "Sektion Rassen- und Volkstumsforschung of the Institut für Deutsche Ostarbeit," under direction of Dr. E. Riemann. Headquarters for the Institut were at Krakau, Poland, and the work was performed on subject peoples, mostly southern Poles, Huzuls, Ukrainians, in 1942–1944. The anthropometric data, of most interest to us, were apparently secured with traditional German thoroughness, and are tied in with excellent photos and negatives, hair samples, contour tracings of the head and nasal region, personal and medical information for each subject. Many of these data are already seriated and statistically analyzed. Emphasis was placed on place

of birth and family genealogy since the Institut had a side project of unscrambling subject people by means of name analysis.

Racially the Huzuls are the most interesting since they are the mountaineer descendants of Slavic pioneers who moved into the Carpathians as early as the 8th Century A.D., and through isolation have remained distinctive. They were studied by the village, a geographical factor of considerable importance.

The Institut also took many excellent photographs of cultural specimens in Polish museums. There is a large series of well-documented photos of bronze brooches, etc., roughly 8th century on. A number of plates and color slides of tapestries, native houses, family groups and the like, a voluminous bibliographic file of references pertaining to anthropology of the area is included.

Not all the material is of anthropological interest. Two boxes contain personnel files, apparently on people working for the Institut. These data, and possibly others, will be returned to the Surgeon General's [sic] with the suggestion that the Eastern European Bureau, Division of Research for Europe, Department of State, would be interested in examining them.

I respectfully submit that the various anthropometric measuring instruments, anthropometric data, photographs of living peoples, head contour tracings, hair samples, dermatoglyphics, and medical and family records would be a valuable addition to the Division of Physical Anthropology. The photographs are especially valuable for our files, which have poor representation for Eastern Europe. The anthropometric data, with other pertinent records, will be further analyzed, looking toward possible publication by the Division. The hair samples and finger prints can be studied by others and correlated with the anthropometric data. The instruments can be used to great advantage in the Division, and would permit us to render loan service. The cultural specimens may be of interest to the other Divisions in the Department of Anthropology.

The principal purpose of this memorandum is to obtain your opinion as to whether the National Museum should accept this material on the basis of a *permanent loan*. The selection I have made will naturally be subject to Dr. T. Dale Stewart's reactions after his return from Guatemala. If this procedure meets with your approval a letter will be prepared for your signature acknowledging receipt of this material but no formal accession will be made until after Dr. Stewart has had an opportunity to examine the collection.

Respectfully submitted,
(Associate Curator, Division of Physical Anthropology)

The archivist who helped me that day and I were both overwhelmed by the implications of this collection and the lack of context provided for it. It seemed as if the curator who had written the note had no idea of the horrors that stood behind the anthropological data and instruments. As the archivist took the cart with the IDO boxes away, I asked that if the NAA-SI decided to further explore this cache of materials, would they please inform me?

A few weeks later, I received a call from the NAA-SI, asking if I would be interested in cataloging the IDO collection. Of course, I was very interested. This might be a rare opportunity to gain insight into the primary research materials and data of Nazi anthropologists. On the day I began, the director of the NAA-SI took me around the archives and introduced me to the small staff and the volunteers. One of the archivists took me to the second-floor archival space, which was connected to the small rooms on the first floor of the Natural History Museum of the Smithsonian by several back stairways. There, in warehouse-like spaces, were a few desks, a long table, and then rows and rows of shelves filled with neat gray boxes of varying sizes and shapes. I was given an array of empty boxes, pencils, and thin white cotton gloves. Thus equipped, I was ready to begin.

I started unpacking the first crate, noting each item as I removed it. The crate was filled with small boxes and bundles of heavy papers wrapped in brown paper, each labeled with names, dates, and places. It was easy to see that the names were those of the primary researcher, the dates were the time of the particular gathering of the sample or data, and the place was where the materials originated.

My colleague from Germany, Gerhard Zeidler, who had worked as an archivist in a concentration camp memorial and with whom I had recently published a book on concentration camp memorials,[4] was available and came to help. He could read the handwritten notes on the packages better than I, being familiar with the German handwriting of the 1940s. We began in earnest.

When we had unpacked everything, we found that there were not only hair samples but fingerprints, body outlines with pubic hair crudely sketched in, and hundreds of pages of penciled drawings in circular shapes. The note on the package explained that these were head circumferences, but they looked like circles drawn with a geometric tool on large sheets of thin white paper. There were also various kinds of questionnaires, twelve in all, inquiring about health, family history, work history, genealogies, household goods, and schooling. There were snapshots, mostly unlabeled, taken in Poland perhaps, and hundreds of labeled slides of the faces of villagers. There were large file cards with pictures attached and often genealogies of the individual's family. There were also boxes and boxes of bibliographic cards like those used in libraries and what appeared to be inventory lists from ethnographic museums.

Papers in the collection seemed to have been taken from file cabinets. Some explained the administrative functions of the office from which the collection came, others were reprinted articles, reports of travel to sites, and a list of publications. A routing list gave names of people who should see a particular document. It would be hard to make sense of the collection, I thought, but at least there were some progress reports that gave us the most basic information. We were dealing with the part of the IDO called the Section on Race and "Volkstum" Research, the SRV.

My German colleague suggested that we start with the list of publications and go to the Library of Congress to see if any of the journal articles written by the staff of the IDO were there. I thought such a search would be useless, for I had never heard of the journals listed and could not imagine that these articles, published in occupied Poland, could be found in Washington. And it was no surprise that, indeed, they were not on the computer at the library. We asked for help, and the librarian suggested that we try the old card catalog located off of the main reading room. There, in the dusky, deserted rows of the old wooden file cabinets were long and narrow file drawers, which we searched by hand, going through our list of authors, journal titles, and subject areas to see what we could find. Most of the articles in the IDO publication list were there; later, we found the rest in the state libraries in Berlin and the archive of the Jagiellonian University (*Uniwersytet Jagiellonski Archiwum*, or UJA) in Kraków, Poland.

Gerhard Zeidler working on the IDO collection at the Smithsonian's National Anthropological Archives. Author's personal photo collection.

Background to the Collection: The Second World War Begins

Hitler annexed Czechoslovakia in the spring of 1939 and immediately started planning the takeover of Poland. To assure that there would be no interference from the Soviet Union, a nonaggression pact between Germany and the Soviet Union was signed on August 23 in Moscow. Stalin made this pact with Hitler, the outspoken enemy of communism, perhaps in part because he had no faith that France and Britain would defend Poland but would leave Russia to fight the German behemoth. Being in a nonaggressive alliance with Hitler meant that war could be held off for a time, and Russia would gain a part of the Polish spoils. The pact brought the release of communist and leftist political prisoners in German concentration camps, at least for a short time.

On September 1, 1939, the Germans struck. The Polish military was prepared for a World War I combat scenario but unprepared for the lightning speed with which Germany attacked. On September 3, France and Britain declared war on Germany, but by then the frontier between Germany and Poland was breached, and by October 6, the last organized Polish military resistance fell. Everything happened so fast that the West was caught off guard.

The Soviet Union and Germany divided the Polish territory between them. The Soviets got Galicia in eastern Poland, while the western part of Poland was absorbed into Germany and became part of the Reich. The area bordering Germany was renamed the *Warthegau,* a part of Poland that had been in German hands before 1919. It had been given to Poland after World War I as part of the Versailles Treaty. The population was a mix of people, most of whom traced their roots to a German background, to a Polish background, or both.

The central part of Poland, also taken by Germany, was renamed the *Generalgouvernement* (GG) and eventually encompassed the Warsaw, Kraków, Radom, and Lublin districts.[5] The GG was developed with a particular purpose in mind. The territory would not just be plundered but would be developed as a resource for Germany. Its population would serve as a permanent labor pool for German demands. The population itself, "Jews, Polacks, and riff-raff," would be "cleaned up."[6]

Poor in colonies, Germany had suffered in comparison to other European states like France and England, which grew their wealth through colonization of parts of Africa and Asia. The Germans now hoped to colonize the lands to the east. Hans Frank, named *Generalgouverneur* of the GG, described the area as follows: "This area has been German-inspired for centuries, with rich German cultural, economic, and technical work, with German indus-

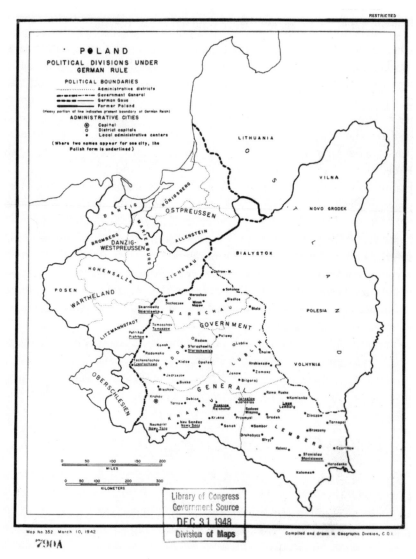

Map drawn by American government staff members of occupied Poland in 1942 showing administrative divisions.

triousness and German know-how. German command of this area is therefore justified historically through the deeds of our forefathers. [We] today have the job of keeping the many millions of Poles and Ukrainians in lawful, war-relevant, stern order, [providing] peace and security so that [we can] place them, for their own good, in the service of the development of Europe."[7]

For Germany, the peace with the Soviet Union was only a temporary measure. It gave Hitler time to move westward into the low countries and France, and then into Norway and Denmark. In 1940, Germans began submarine actions in the Atlantic, Pacific, and Indian Oceans. In spring 1941, they moved through Rumania into southeastern Europe and Greece. In the midst of this expanded war, Germany invaded the Soviet Union on June 22, 1941, retrieving all Polish territory before advancing still further eastward.

Measures against Jews

For the Jews in Germany, repression in 1938 and the following years became almost unbearable. In a policy paper from the state's Foreign Office (*Auswärtiges Amt*), the goal of the 1938 Jewish policy was clearly stated:

> Jewish independent businesses [with the exception of those owned by foreigners] will be totally erased from view on the street. The liquidation of ownership of large concerns, factories, houses, and land will gradually be encouraged, so that in the foreseeable future there will be no more mention of Jewish ownership in Germany.
>
> The ultimate goal of the German Jewish policy is the emigration of all living Jews in the area of the Reich.[8]

Jews had already been forced to take "Sara" or "Israel" as their official first names and carry the letter "J" on their passports. Ghettos had been formed in large cities of Germany to house Jewish work commandos. In October 1938, the first major expulsion of Jews took place when 17,000 Jews of Polish origin were deported and transported over the border into Poland. By the beginning of the war a year later, about half of the Jews in Austria and Germany had left their countries of origin.[9] In February 1939, the order came that all Jews should leave Germany without taking their belongings with them, but by September almost all permission to leave Germany had been rescinded. By October 1, 1941, the exits were totally blocked, and the remaining 163,869 Jews were virtually trapped.[10]

Quickly, the state acted to set aside certain areas where Jews had to live. They could only shop at certain hours, could not travel freely, could not practice their professions, could not be on the streets without their armbands. More and more transports left for the east.[11]

The Nazis established the first ghetto in Poland by October 1939. Piotrków Tribunalski, Łódź, and then Warsaw became centers of Jewish population concentrations. The ghettos experienced various degrees of isolation, the worst being Łódź, where there was absolutely no sanctioned contact with the outside. Housing, food, and sanitation were all lacking, making survival a daily struggle. Tens of thousands died of starvation and untreated illness-es.[12] Non-Jewish citizens were forcibly moved from their living quarters in areas designated as ghettos to make room for the Jews. This also caused hard-ships as reported in England by the Polish government-in-exile. "The for-mation of nationally exclusive residential quarters causes enormous social and economic complications. It is enough to mention the tragedies of mixed marriages, the loss of clientele, the costs of resettlement, and the destruction of property incurred in the course of resettlements, disturbances in supplies of rationed foodstuffs, confusion in the work of the police, church parishes, telephone services, gas and power stations, and so on. Waste, administrative malfunction, and chaos appear everywhere. The populace suffers indescrib-ably, especially since resources and human resilience have already been ex-hausted."[13] The burden on the Jews was traumatic. In occupied Poland, Jews were dispossessed of their property, terrorized, left without legal recourse, and subjected to any humiliation the Germans chose to visit upon them.

The War of Occupation

The military takeover of Poland was not Hitler's only goal. He simultaneously wanted to follow a population plan that would remove all elements in Pol-ish society that were unwanted (*unerwünscht*). At first, he could not target the communists because of the Soviet pact, but he could get rid of the Jews, the nobility, and the intellectuals. To accomplish this, Hitler sent in mobile death squads to move with or ahead of the army as it carried out its inva-sion, but with a different aim. They were to do "special operations," such as kill large numbers of these "enemies" of the Reich as fast as possible. Lists were prepared of government leaders, nobility, clergy, professionals, and in-tellectuals slated for the firing squads.[14] "The goal was to liberate the army's rear areas by killing Jews, Gypsies, and community activists."[15] The *Ein-satzgruppen* (mobile death squads) provided backup for the regular army and got rid of possible resistance through terror. It was murder under the guise of war in a multipronged attack on the people of Poland.

Heinrich Himmler was the person in charge of the Einsatzgruppen. Hit-ler had chosen Himmler to lead his paramilitary forces, the SA and the SS, in the late 1920s. In 1929, Hitler appointed Himmler to be *Reichsführer SS*. Under Himmler's command, the SS became more than a terrorizing mili-tary force; it became a major business center, creating new ventures in all areas of enterprise from bottled water to building supplies. All of these entrepre-neurial parts of the SS used the concentration camps as centers of production, providers of research subjects, and employment opportunities for their own people. It provided funding for its own operations.

Himmler was a well-organized and ruthless commander, grounded in racial ideology. He had also steeped himself in anthropology and had read the anthropologists' books on race, including Hans Günther's.[16] In 1935, alongside his other massive responsibilities for reorganizing German society into a military, fascist state, he founded the *Ahnenerbe,* an organization within the SS representing the German Ancestral Heritage Society and dedicated to proving racial hypotheses.[17] Within this structure, he gave prominence to well-educated SS elite who adhered to the goal of developing a new and supposedly scientific agenda that could be pursued under various auspices.

Himmler was determined to lead the cultural and social assault on Poland as well as the military and police functions. He wanted full control, but Hitler appointed Hans Frank, a man of ambition, immense ego, and limited intellect, to be governor of the GG instead, while Himmler was appointed the Reich Commissar for the Strengthening of the German People (*Reichskommissar für die Festigung deutschen Volkstums,* or RKF). This division of labor meant that Himmler was in charge of reordering the population groups in Poland through murder, deportation to slave labor, and assigning racial identities, while Frank was in charge of administering the GG, exploiting resources, and culturally diverting the country to a German model of racial separation and hierarchies.

The Development of the IDO

For decades before the rise of Hitler, Germany's interest in "the East" was pronounced. Settlers from German-speaking areas had settled there for centuries, some maintaining their linguistic and cultural ties to their original homeland and others fully assimilating. Organizations of nationalists, academics, and politicians had supported these German minorities in Poland and further east by funding schools and supporting enclaves and had agitated for German control of the area. The term "East Research" (*Ostforschung*) was familiar, and the effort was led by prominent scholars.[18]

With the onset of the war, a series of institutes sprang into being in various locations of the occupied territory. They were established not only to satisfy the desire to exploit the resources of the territories but to put a scientific face on events, to justify to Germans the rape of Poland, and to satisfy the ideological fantasies of the German leaders. These groups were formed without any thought as to their importance to the war effort. They included the Reich Foundation for German Research in the East and the Reinhard-Heydrich-Foundation, both in Posen (Poznań), the Reich Foundation for Scientific Research in Prague, and Alfred Rosenberg's Reich Center for Research in the East inside the Ministry for the Occupied East Territories.[19]

The IDO was such an endeavor. This collection of units functioned as a think-tank, with each institute exploring its own scientific, or pseudo-scientific, purpose. It was opened on Hitler's birthday, April 20, 1940, by Hans Frank. Frank intended that each of the institutes would mark his regime with an academic atmosphere and yet produce useful plans and strategies for exploiting the resources of the newly acquired land. The order establishing the IDO made its mission clear. "The mission of the Institut für Deutsche Ostarbeit is to lay out all the fundamental issues of the Eastern [occupied] lands as far as they affect the Generalgouvernement and to provide scientific findings, as well as publicize and disseminate [these findings]. To fulfill this task, the Institut für Deutsche Ostarbeit will work together with other institutions with similar missions."[20] "Institutions with similar missions" not only were the quasi-academic and scientific institutions but the police and security agencies, the racial bureaus, and, finally, the extermination apparatus of the state.

Frank was the president of the IDO, and he appointed Wilhelm Coblitz as its director. Coblitz was responsible for establishing a functioning institute, for selecting the leading positions, and for seeing to it that the IDO was linked sufficiently with other organizations, such as those dealing with population issues and security. The IDO, located in Kraków, had outposts in Lemberg and Warsaw, which were under Coblitz's authority.

There were eleven "sections" of the IDO, including:

—Prehistory
—History
—Art History
—Law
—Economy
—Linguistics
—Agriculture
—Geology
—Landscape and Gardening
—Forestry and Woodworking
—Race and "Volkstum" Research (including a division for research on Jews, the *Judenreferat*)

The IDO, in some respects, took on the character of a university without students and, indeed, was housed in Kraków's Jagiellonian University. Five months before the IDO opened, and just one month after the invasion of Poland, the Germans announced to the university professors that they must attend an important meeting. Such an order could hardly be ignored. In all, 183 professors appeared, but the meeting was promptly dismissed. All present were arrested and packed into buses headed for Sachsenhausen, a concentration camp north of Berlin, where virtually all of the Jewish professors and most of the rest eventually were killed or died under the extreme and torturous conditions.[21] This cleared the way for a new direction in the institute, which was slated to become a university specializing in "racial science," and made space for the offices of the IDO.

The courtyard of the Jagiellonian University Archive Building in Kraków, Poland. Author's personal photo collection.

The beautiful buildings of the Jagiellonian University, which dated back to the age of Copernicus, were more impressive than the new buildings of the KWIA in Berlin. The administrative structure of the two institutes was similar but not identical. Whereas the KWIA was involved in teaching, advising government agencies, conducting racial examinations, and sometimes doing rather sophisticated research under the best-known scientists, the IDO was busy with exploitation, doing racial investigations, and serving the government's population policy with young and relatively inexperienced Nazi academic staff. It set about discovering what human resources and cultural riches were available for exploitation for the Reich.

The IDO had a publishing and propaganda function and produced its own journals. The journals published in the first months of the occupation were glossy, and some were even printed with covers of a simulated gold, making them look like art magazines. The articles were varied. Some explained the nature of the occupation, what was expected, the problems encountered, and the administrative functions. Others set about justifying the conquest of Poland, explaining over and over again how this land could and should be considered German. There was a great deal of attention given in these journals to two major figures: Copernicus, the astronomer, and Veit Stoss, the wood carver who had done magnificent altars in Kraków and elsewhere in Poland. There was an urgency to show these men to be Germans, for the Poles had been declared an inferior race who would now only be educated to the sixth grade at best. Genius among them was inexplicable unless it could be shown to have German roots. Another propaganda function of the IDO was the creation of traveling exhibits to bring back to the Reich. Much like the exhibits already on display in Germany that had displayed the Jew as less than human, these exhibits displayed the Pole as a permanently inferior type, suitable only for labor under supervision. One of the first tasks of the IDO was to produce an exhibit called "German Volkstum in the Area of the Weichsel [Vistula River]." A description of the parts of the exhibit indicates that topics would be displayed, such as the German development of cities, the German farmer settlements of the Middle Ages, and the influence of Germanic law, woodwork, house types, and church architecture. Other exhibits showed the prehistoric finds from Poland or the German heritage that could be traced there.

The *Berliner Morgenpost* reported in February 1942 that one of these exhibits was currently showing in the capital city. The reporter expressed amazement that "amidst the wastelands of Polish mismanagement or Bolshevist lack of culture" remnants of German culture from bygone eras were exposed in the photographs on exhibit. It cheered the reawakening of German influence in the east.[22]

Prehistory had an important role in the ideological underpinnings of the Nazi state. Himmler's *Ahnenerbe,* along with other government agencies, carried on a continual search for prehistoric finds that would confirm the early and important contributions to civilization by the "Aryan race."[23] The symbolic value of these finds played well into the hands of racial mythology and the development of ultranationalism. Some believe that it was also one of the foundations for eventual genocide.[24] Slave laborers under gunpoint were used to excavate the sites.

In order to exploit the country's cultural heritage, the IDO had to discover what resources were available in the former Poland. IDO staff plundered libraries from public and private collections and made decisions about which books would be sent back to Germany. They took bibliographic cards from libraries, assessed them for the usefulness of the material, and then made decisions about what should be done with the books.[25]

At about the same time, the Frankfurt am Main Institute for the Research of the Jewish Question started a collection of Jewish literature. Much of the library assembled in that institute came from Eastern Europe, including 280,000 volumes from the occupied eastern lands.[26] In 1942, the staff reported that it had made 13,258 separate notes in its research into Polish bibliographic sources. Many of these were historical descriptions of settlements in which the anthropologists had an interest in the racial composition of the population. They had assembled these notes and placed them in a card catalog, which was "completed up to the letter 'J.'"[27] Museums were cataloged for the same purpose. This took a great deal of effort and time. The German staff needed the assistance of Polish workers and requisitioned many who were experts in their fields. By providing assistance to the Germans, these Poles unwillingly helped to destroy their own cultural heritage.[28]

It was not the Poles who were blameworthy, however, but the invaders whose personal greed almost exceeded that of their country. They enriched their homes back in Germany with the paintings and artifacts of museums and public buildings. In 1942, the provincial curator of just one of Germany's states had "requisitioned nearly eighty repositories in castles, monasteries, parish houses, and warehouses" for the purpose of storing stolen artworks and cultural goods.[29] The spoils of exploitation of those "eliminated" from consideration did not extend only to the newly conquered territory. The aryanization of businesses brought great prizes to the German people.

> Each week in the Hamburg harbor, beginning in 1941, huge quantities of household goods belonging to Jews of Hamburg, then of all Germany, and ultimately from throughout western Europe, were sold or auctioned; furs, carpets, and period furniture were especially in demand. But linen, lamps, tableware, and children's

An ethnographic museum in Chochołóv, Poland. Author's personal photo collection.

toys were also sold at bargain-basement prices. In Hamburg alone during the war years, linens and furnishings totaling 60,000 metric tons were sold. At least 100,000 residents of Hamburg bought something at the auction of "Jewish goods." That the objects had belonged to Jews was widely known.[30]

The IDO's SRV: An Overview

The NAA-SI collection represents the work of primarily one section of the IDO: the SRV. In the *Cassell's New German Dictionary* of 1936, revised in 1938, the word "Volkstum" does not appear. It was an invention of the Nazi era. Later, in the *Pocket Oxford German Dictionary* (1975), it is defined as "national characteristics." The term encompasses much of what is usually known as "culture" in ethnographic research, including ways of life of the group and its artifacts. However, the researcher who used the term "Volkstum" in the Nazi era was not interested in the perceptions of the people about their own culture but merely interested in the German view of what they observed. Of course, these observations were premised on the Nazi ideology.

The SRV had a relatively small number of permanent staff members augmented by six Polish assistants, who were paid about 25 percent of their German colleagues' wages.[31] The staff consisted at various times of Anton Plügel, who acted as section leader for Erhard Riemann during periods when Riemann was on active duty in the army; Heinrich Gottong, adviser (*Refer-*

ent); Elfriede Fliethmann, adviser; and Elisabeth Nonnenmacher, scientific assistant. Gottong was the first to come to the section in October 1940. Plügel followed in February of 1941 and brought on Fliethmann in July of that year. Riemann did not arrive until April 1941. Ingeborg Sydow worked in the section from September 1941 to March 1943. Sydow did not have the necessary background for work in Europe, according to Riemann, and left the institute in 1943. Dora Kahlich worked periodically, conducting research in the field under the direction of Plügel.

In her letter of application for the position of assistant in the SRV, Fliethmann gave as her references Dr. Plügel, Dr. Tuppa in Vienna, and Dr. Routil. She was twenty-six years old, single, and described herself as "previously" Lutheran and now simply "a believer in God." She had been a member of the Nazi Party since 1937. She had worked in Vienna producing certificates of race, which led her to her dissertation topic, "Racial Investigations in Two Villages," which she completed under the leadership of Eberhard Geyer. Her transcripts show that she had studied geography and history from 1934 to 1936, when she changed to a major in anthropology.

A different kind of anthropologist, Werner Radig, was called to the IDO Section on Prehistory. He held at the same time a position in Alfred Rosenberg's apparatus. Rosenberg placed Radig in the IDO in keeping with the mandate to maintain close cooperation among state agencies.[32]

Rosenberg had been a member of the Nazi Party from its inception. He was the author of a publication in 1930 that was believed to have influenced Hitler's thinking. It blamed modern liberal thinking for allowing Jews to gain power and urged Germany to take the lead once again. Born in Estonia and a veteran of the Russian army in World War I, Rosenberg came to Germany after the Russian Revolution. Despite his very difficult personality and his infighting with Himmler, he grew in power from his position as the editor of the *Völkischer Beobachter* to Reich Minister for the Occupied Eastern Territories (*Reichsminister für die besetzten Ostgebiete*).[33]

Rosenberg was particularly important to the IDO in his role of creating liaisons among this academic-appearing institution, the Nazi Party, and the military. Among other positions, he had held the party post of overseer of the total schooling and mental and philosophical preparation for the party. Even more important to the IDO was Rosenberg's role in leading the Institute for Research on the Jewish Question (*Institut zur Erforschung der Judenfrage*). When he gained governmental rather than party power, he was the point man in the government for planning and executing the robbing of art and literature from the eastern occupied lands, and he retained his interest in producing propaganda and training other people to produce it.[34]

Dr. Gottong was given the particular assignment of dealing with political problems in the Polish population. His job was to discover and win back individuals or small villages where the German blood was "trickling away." Gottong was a student of the racial anthropologist Hans Günther and had been sent to the IDO as a representative of Rosenberg's Institute for Research on the Jewish Question. Dr. Fliethmann was the assistant to Gottong during much of her tenure at the IDO.

Plügel, although a young man of twenty-nine when he came to the IDO, had a history in "East Research" from the "race, state, and cultural-political standpoint." He had studied for six years in the anthropology and ethnology department at the University of Vienna, where he obtained substantial training in both theory and practice. His main field was ethnology, but he paired his interest with a deep commitment to the Nazi Party starting when he was only sixteen years old. A party member at seventeen, Plügel worked in the youth division of the organization in Austria and Germany. He worked closely on race questions with organizations of the state, the party, and the police. In 1940, Plügel was sent to Kraków to work in the Nazi Party education office and in museum work.[35] He soon combined those jobs with the one at the IDO. His job description found in his personnel file was as follows:

The [relevance of] research on Race and Volkstum in the east for many current practical tasks of the administration cannot be delayed because it is linked to racial and Volk-political measures of greatest importance. Plügel's duties will include:

—Racial investigations of certain individual groups of population in the GG;
—Racial-biological investigation of Polish resistance members;
—Racial-biological investigation of groups whose value cannot immediately be determined, such as the Gorale, Ukrainian groups, etc.;
—Identifying groups or clans that are suitable for Germanization [*Eindeutschung*];
—Providing information about German blood that is dissipating in the east;
—Racial-biological investigations of family members of people of the east to determine to what extent their work in the Reich would create a biological contact with our Volk.
—Putting our Volk in contact with those in the east and seeing what the results are.[36]

Many of the "Reich" personnel in the SRV were Austrians, with ties to either the University of Vienna or Vienna's Natural History Museum. Vienna was considered the experimental location for much of the actions against Jews. With a population of 200,000 Jews, most of whom lived in Vienna, Austria had massive numbers of people on whom to try new orders and procedures. Many of these Jews had come from Poland in the last one hundred years and were not as integrated into Viennese life as were the Jews from Berlin.[37] Although the Nazis maintained some secrecy about what was transpiring, public humiliation of Jews in the streets of Vienna and depletion of Jewish assets into government coffers went very smoothly for them in Austria, often with the enthusiastic endorsement of the non-Jewish population.

Two Viennese professors, Robert Routil and Eberhard Geyer, were important sources for the recommendation of people to the SRV. Routil was an avid racial researcher who had made plaster casts of the heads and bodies of prisoners of war in World War I (see chapter 1). Both he and Geyer devoted themselves to racial science.

Clearly, Routil, Geyer, and other anthropologists had some indication of the mass annihilation that was to be ordered four years later, for there was an impetus to these anthropologists to collect and save reminders of the disappearing Jews. Following the pogrom on November 8 and 9, 1938, university and museum anthropologists had rushed to a stadium where Jews had been rounded up and interned to make plaster-cast masks of hundreds of prisoners. Haste was necessary, for these prisoners were being deported to Buchenwald, and many would not return.[38]

The Ideology and Mission of the SRV

The staff members felt they had a mission. They were in the forefront of applying racial theory in the field. They often sounded almost intoxicated with the power they had to make a "new world" based on their long-held beliefs.

> The Volkstum Division is making efforts to carry the concept of ethnic research far beyond what has hitherto been understood by the term as it is used in academic circles. This ethnic research requires the total encompassing of the life history of peoples, what they carry with them from all sides, such as their racial history, their biology, their demographics, sociology, ethno-politics, and Volk psychology. Ethnic investigation includes the health of a people, including their limitations due to inherited illnesses and conditions. It includes the [cultural] movements of the people, their customs and expressions of them in form and content, the feeling for nationhood and mythmaking, the problems and conflicts on the speech and ethnic boundaries, and much more. In short, all that contributes to a group's active or passive expression of race and identity.[39]

The anthropologists believed that Middle and Eastern Europe were comprised of various "racial strains." Under the prevailing philosophy, each group should be assessed according to how the capabilities of its people could best assist in the development of the "New Order" of Nazi Germany.[40] In practice, this meant that the anthropologists of the IDO and their staffs intended to cast a thick net of investigations over the GG to aid in this sorting of population groups.

Their ideas had mirrored Himmler's, which he expressed in a speech on May 15, 1940. "[We] have no interest to lump together all the peoples of the east. . . . to the contrary, we want to divide them into many parts and splinters . . . so that we have not only the Poles and the Jews [but also] the Ukrainians, the White Russians, the Gorale, the Lemken, and the Kaschuben. . . . But even within the [German] Volk we have splinters and particles to sort out."[41]

The German anthropologists, who earlier felt that the Poles had made important contributions to the mapping of groups within their country, were now unsatisfied with the descriptions of populations they could obtain from Polish scientists. "There is little worth in the materials presented to us by Polish anthropologists due to their peculiar point of view and the methods used. There is virtually no material on the races and their distribution; everything remains for the German scientists to do."[42]

The major ideological concern of the German Reich was that of "blood and land" (*Blut und Boden*). They wanted to bring Germans back into the Reich and move less worthy people away from the original German territory. To do this, it was necessary to know the composition of various groups within Poland, particularly in the Warthegau and the GG. The anthropological investigations would "splinter" the groups, as Himmler had wanted, and each would carry with it a fate determined by the Nazi regime.

One of the major missions of the SRV was to work cooperatively with other administrative agencies of the Reich. In a document found in the NAA-SI collection, this cooperation was described as follows:

—Appointment of the Section Leader [Plügel] as scientific colleague in the *Volksdeutsche Mittelstelle* [Ethnic German Liaison Office, an organization for the support of population groups being moved from one location to another];
—Involvement in the field trip on February 12–14, 1943, under the theme "German Research in the Area near the Carpathians and Weichsel in Service of Practical Volkstum Work";
—Alignment of the Section's work to the necessities of practical Volkstum policies and Volkstum work;
—Examinations for certification of race for isolated settlements in the GG and to ascertain the degree to which German blood has infiltrated Poland;
—Card file creation;
—Teacher training for instructors coming into the eastern lands from the Reich;
—Preparation of the "Village Book" given out by the GG, particularly Paragraph V;
—Cooperative work on the journal "Colonial Letters" and on the "German Calendar" in GG;

—Advice regarding compiling school materials, fairy tales, and song books for children of German heritage; and

—Oversight of the compilation of information for the service of other agencies of the government.

In addition to this work for the Mittelstelle, the SRV also provided certificates of race to the Population and Social Work Department of the Kinship Office (*Sippenstelle*) and took part in investigations in Haczow for the college of ethnic studies of the NSDAP. They worked on the German-language atlas being produced in Marburg by taking recordings of speech while doing their other work. Intermittently, they worked with the following institutions:

—Museum of German Folk Knowledge (*Volkskunde*) in Berlin
—Museum of Folk Knowledge in Vienna
—Kaiser-Friedrich-Museum in Posen (Poznań)
—Collections from the City of Breslau
—Organization (*Volksbund*) for the Germans in Foreign Lands
—German Foreign Institute in Stuttgart
—Institute for Folk Knowledge of the University of Breslau
—Hofkammer-Archive in Vienna[43]

The staff of the SRV also worked with the Institute for Anthropology of the University of Vienna to conduct joint anthropological research and with the Institute for Psychological Anthropology of the University of Marburg to carry out anthropological investigations.[44]

By 1943, the SRV was more focused on practical matters. "Seldom has a region within Europe been so racially mixed and presented with the resulting ethnic problems as the Generalgouvernement. To investigate the full range of ethnic expression and to make the results useful to the state officials is the job of the Section."[45] In this report, it is clear that another concern bothered the Germans. Many Poles were being sent to the Reich to work as slave laborers. Would they "mix" with the people there, infecting the "pure" German population with inferior genes? Only Poles with predominantly "Aryan" features could be risked. The anthropologists had to find these people and identify them.

The Work of the SRV

When the SRV was established, it was divided into three divisions: Ethnology, Anthropology, and Volkstum Research. (There is only information on the Ethnology and Volkstum Research Divisions in the NAA-SI collection.) In reality, the divisions are hard to distinguish. The staff did some racial certifying, but it does not appear from the materials available that it was a major

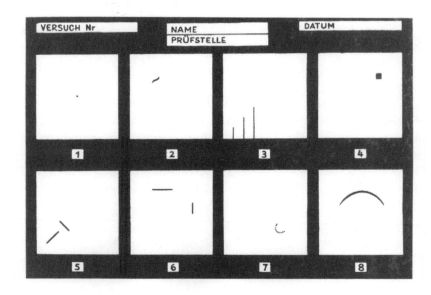

A template for a psychological test given to children in occupied Poland. The purpose of these projective tests is unknown. NAA-SI, IDO Collection.

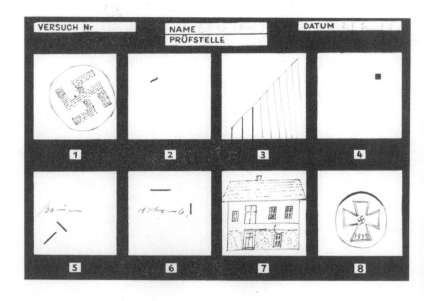

A completed psychological projective test given to children in occupied Poland. NAA-SI, IDO Collection.

focus of their work. Trained SS personnel probably did most of this certifying in the GG, with the IDO staff called in for difficult cases. More important was the work of advising and working closely with the larger Nazi bureaucracies dealing with racial matters.

And, just as the anthropologists in Berlin had discovered, the anthropologists at the IDO now found that they could have input into the creation of new laws and regulations regarding Jews and other minorities. This must have been exhilarating for academics, who previously had had little influence over more than their own research. Thus, in January 1940, Riemann wrote to the SRV on "justice": "The higher SS and Police Führer have given notice that because of the numerous sentences of Jews and Poles to long terms of confinement, the prisons are overfilled, and a large number of sentences cannot be carried out. It has been suggested that these sentences be served in enforced labor. This suggestion is approved of here. I propose that this suggestion . . . a judicially recognized sentence of enforced labor [be carried out] according to the decision of the courts."[46]

Nor did the staff members of the IDO live in isolation in Kraków. They traveled back to the Reich to meet with family, with members of their professions, and with party and state officials. For instance, on March 26, 1941, Dr. Peter-Heinz Seraphim, a member of the IDO, gave a lecture entitled "Population and Political-Economic Problems of a European Solution to the Jewish Question" at the celebration of the opening of Rosenberg's Foreign Office of Higher Education in Frankfurt am Main. The invited guests included several hundred of the SS and party leadership, as well as university professors such as honored guest Eugen Fischer of the KWIA. Also on the speakers' list was Rosenberg himself, who spoke on the topic "The Jewish Question as World Problem."[47]

The SRV grouped its work into three spheres of interest: Jews; those thought to have some German heredity; and those who were "Slavic" or "Mongoloid" in character. These investigative efforts were carried out without any apparent plan to prioritize research subjects or venues. Perhaps, some of the choices were made with regard to available SS protection or the need for information about groups about to be moved. Of course, the work in which the division was engaged was not the usual academic research. It had a practical application in solving "real problems" of the Reich in its handling of population groups. The SS and the security police assisted in all of the research and, in return, had full access to the results.[48]

Aside from gathering data on the Jews living in the ghetto in Tarnów (see chapter 1), it is not known if the SRV conducted other research among Jews. Dora Kahlich, who had worked with Fliethmann in Tarnów, had previously studied Jews in a retirement home in Vienna and perhaps in another institution as well. She and Fliethmann would have liked to continue work in Jewish settlements in the GG, but there is no evidence that other ghettos were studied in connection with the IDO work. An effort to find Jews living in their original settlements in rural areas was unsuccessful. Even with the help of Dr. Salomon Czortkower, "a well-known anthropologist-archaeologist, whose great-grandfather is said to be of Aryan descent," none were intact in the Galician District.[49] The commander of the Security Police in Galicia could only recommend the confiscated literature on the subject.

The Gorale, or mountain people of southwestern Poland, were another group of great interest to the anthropologists of the IDO. There may have been several reasons for this interest. One was that the area is among the most beautiful in Poland. Located in the Tatra Mountains, it is set among dramatic peaks, clear streams, and long meadows. The people were picturesque, wearing a particularly colorful costume with metal spangles that could be traced over time and from village to village. Ethnographers had done a great deal of work in the area, and there were ethnographic museums in several towns, including the ski resort of Zakopane.[50]

A Gorale wedding. Anthropologists collected pictures out of the photo albums and off the walls of homes in the towns that interested them. This wedding party might have been photographed by the anthropologists themselves, but more likely the photograph was confiscated from the family, because investigators usually maintained a distinct distance between themselves and their subjects. NAA-SI, IDO Collection.

A group of ethnographic interest to Nazi anthropologists were the Gorale of southwestern Poland. Shown is a Goral man in traditional costume. NAA-SI, IDO Collection.

As their colleagues were called into active military service, the women in the SRV gained greater recognition and responsibility. They went into the field without male coworkers but with strong support from the SS. Elfriede Fliethmann was the primary researcher for racial research in the village of Hanczowa. In a letter to Dora Kahlich, she described her work as follows:

The investigations in Hanczowa were again a handicap-race, as one can only wish, with train delays, wagon rides in the night in typical Polish farm carts, unexpected overnights, luckily in orderly *Meierhof* [farms of people of German heritage]. After two full days, we had succeeded in traversing the 180 kilometers from Kraków to Hanczowa. The rebellion on the part of the population was again very strong, so that we could only [do our] work with the [help of the] border patrol and police. I, naturally, was once again half dead from anger, but in spite of that, grateful for the good food and lodging of the local minister (Greek Orthodox ministers are allowed to marry) and the teacher who served well. The people themselves were interesting, one could see such a strong Eastern component that they were quite different from the Poles. One sees the really crude Eastern and East Baltic types among them. The Slavic influence wins out over the Dinaric. Pure Dinaric does not come to the foreground: most of the people are an unhappy mix of East European and Dinaric elements, medium height and slim, with little hands and feet and large noses and strong jaws. I am analyzing this material and am anxious to compare it with the Gorale.

. . . I am making myself completely independent. If they [IDO colleagues] want something from me, fine, but I do not go to them.[51]

Fliethmann's trip back to Kraków was also difficult. "As I drove back from Hanczowa, I was almost hit by an avalanche. Workers there loaded a car with stones and as I drove past, they threw a whole load at me. Luckily nothing happened to me, but you can imagine my fury."[52]

The SRV's importance is described in a 1943 report by an unknown author as follows: "Seldom has another area presented the possibility of looking at the settlement of two tragically dovetailed people as exactly this German-Slavic border area." It was decided that the main thrust of the research would be on German Volk in the area, in order to find out how much German influence remained in their way of life. "[The anthropologists] will look at the ways of country life, above all, the way farm houses are built, for the indications of various Volk cultures and especially the German contribution. They will look at names of places, flowers, and personal names for their ability to show the origins of the people. They will gather songs, sayings, fairy tales, and scientifically review them. The villages of Szaflary and other places where Gorale live will be the focus of the investigations."[53]

The SRV had originally been under the direction of Plügel, but according to Riemann, who took over the leadership of the section in November 1942, Plügel was not focused, and the SRV had not accomplished what it should have. There was no clear line drawn between the divisions within the organization. Plügel had spent most of his time building up the race research activities at the cost of Volkstum research. Heinrich Gottong, who should have been in charge, worked exclusively on questions of German settlements.[54]

Fliethmann tried to get extra help in the summer of 1942. She contacted a Fräulein Block at the KWIA in Berlin to say that she hoped Dr. Gottong could arrange her move to the IDO at the completion of her studies. Although Gottong had probably already told Block of the duties, Fliethmann reiterated them:

1. Systematic racial studies of the people of the GG,
2. Racial and genetic studies of Jews,
3. Special studies of those with a German heritage,
4. Racial studies of prisoners of war in concentration camps and prisoner of war camps.[55]

She said that there was a lot of work to do, but it lent itself to independence. This was obviously very appealing to Fliethmann.

Changes in the Organization of the SRV

Thus, by 1943, there were changes in the organization of the SRV. The three divisions, Ethnology, Anthropology, and Volkstum Research, had changed to a different set of titles: Volkstum Research, Race Research, and Jewish Research.[56] The staff was reduced in size. It now had a section leader, two major staff people in military service and another on leave, two German assistants, and six Polish workers.

In 1944, the report on the accomplishments of the SRV repeated many of the mission statements given before, but it added a particularly important note. "Thus the Section fulfills in a special way its political assignment in that it places itself in service to the security and development of German national characteristics in the east."[57]

Riemann did not clear up the administrative problems, although that might have been considered his job. Interested in philology and racial mapping, he tried to create in occupied Poland racial mapping studies similar to those done by the KWIA but without much success. For that purpose, he developed numerous questionnaires, often changing the content so that the data could never be analyzed across sites. Riemann hoped to make teams composed of one IDO researcher, one Polish anthropologist, and one photographer. Altogether, the teams would cover 1,250 villages. The NAA-SI collection represents most of what he was able to accomplish, only a small fraction of his ambitious plan. Riemann's work in philology was published after the war as scientific linguistics studies. Most of his proposed picture archive now resides at the NAA-SI.

The Race Research Division was led by Elfriede Fliethmann during the absence of Plügel and Gottong, when they were called to active duty. However, Dr. Fliethmann married in October 1943 and worked only half-time from October 1943 to January 1944, when she moved back to the Reich. Dr. Josef Sommerfeldt then took over the position. Fliethmann remained on call from Berlin, where she lived with her husband. The division found that it was absolutely imperative to carry out the mapping of "living races" in the GG so that "living Volk groups could be compared and ordered according to a racial standpoint with the German *Völkskörper* [gene pool of the German people]. The basic demand is made to investigate the people as extensively as possible . . . so that the changing relationships between racial composition and cultural expression, between environmentally impacting appearances and underlying conditions, and finally the reasons for destruction or encouragement [of the original German culture] are observed."[58]

The villages used in this study included those for whom materials are found in the NAA-SI collection. They included those that the Germans believed were settled in the sixteenth century, such as Golkowitz, Neu-Sandez, Borowa, Wawzenczce, Witow, Szaflary, Hanczowa, Jaslo, and others. Dr. Fliethmann would analyze the morphological values with help from the Anthropological Institute of the University of Vienna.

Another task of the SRV was to investigate the Poles and Ukrainians selected for slave labor in the Reich. They were examined in delousing centers in Kraków and in transit camps. Also, members of the German Special Service (*Sonderdienst*), the Polish Building Service (*Baudienst*), and the Jewish families in Tarnów were examined.[59]

The Division on Jewish Research was developed under the direction of Dr. Sommerfeldt. According to Riemann in a report of 1943, Sommerfeldt was more knowledgeable and more competent than others in the division and thus was given more independence. He had published a wide array of racist articles and made a name for himself in the Reich.[60] Sommerfeldt had also worked in close association with Alfred Rosenberg and his Reich Institute for the History of New Germany (*Reichsinstitut für Geschichte des neuen Deutschlands*) and particularly the Division for Research on the Jewish Question. In a publication, Sommerfeldt explained how research on Jews had changed since Hitler came to power.

[F]rom the beginning the German research on Jews and the [previous] Jewish-run research work had a hostile relationship, for they were working towards contradictory goals. The German research tried to prove the necessity for the destruction of Jews, plus the exclusion of the Jewish race from the Aryan Volk. But the Jewish research group attempted to find a justification of Jewish history and of Jewish existence today. In the spirit of the National Socialist war, [German research on Jews] will seamlessly and exhaustively [provide] the basis of the global extermination of Jews and his exclusion from the Aryan Volk.[61]

Coblitz expressed the same thought in his statement, "Jewish research in the institute will be carried out in the closest coordination with the party and the state," when he was called to be a member of Rosenberg's Frankfurt Institute for Research on the Jewish Question.[62]

The mission of this division could be described in a forthright way. The staff collected written material about Jews and hoped to publish materials showing the negative results of the racial mixing of societies in the occupied lands. "The final goal of all the individual research projects is the production of a history and course of study of the Jewish question in order to immunize the coming generations against renewed domination tendencies of Jews."[63] Sommerfeldt wanted to do this by a careful review of the literature that would show the ways in which Eastern European Jews had reached the highest governmental and cultural positions in Germany in earlier times and how closely the "unhealthy" fate of those times was linked to the Jews.[64] This division would also provide information about the "traditional hatred" of Poles toward Jews. It would cull out the sayings, expressions, books, and common materials that showed this antipathy. And Sommerfeldt was as good as his promise; a raft of such publications appeared during the war years.[65]

Riemann stated in the beginning of 1943 that the "solution to the Jewish question is the job of the political leadership. The necessary reasons for this action stem from history, and the sound justification for these reasons in the future is the task of science."[66]

The End of the IDO in Kraków

When it became apparent that the war was going badly for Germany, the IDO in Kraków began to pack up and move back to the Reich. However, it still carried out its propaganda function by producing exhibits to remind Germans of their right to be in the occupied territory.

> As a special work plan in the year 1944, the Section is preparing a large exhibit on the Volk history in the Generalgouvernement that comes from a German heritage. In this exhibit a major theme will be the in-migration of Germans to the GG, creating an overlayment of German culture. This was already a major theme of earlier exhibits, only now it will be [only a part]. Instead, the agricultural-farm culture of the German isolated settlements will come to the fore. I must say that the creation of this exhibit is extraordinarily difficult, for the archival and museum artifacts are packed and not available.[67]

And soon everything was packed up and sent back to the Reich. Only a few papers remained that told of the workings of the SRV. Some remained in Kraków, some ended up in the German archives, and others, surprisingly, showed up in an archive in a museum in Washington, D.C. Without the self-serving publication of details of the work of the SRV, there would be no way to interpret accurately the artifacts of research housed in the Natural History Museum of the Smithsonian Institution. The Library of Congress provided the vital link to understanding the collection of perhaps the last indication of racial "science" as it was practiced on a captive people slated for slavery and death.

Notes

1. At that time, the NAA-SI occupied a small set of library-like offices on the first floor of the Smithsonian's Natural History Museum, although it has since moved to the Smithsonian's Museum Support Center in Suitland, Maryland.

2. NAA-SI memo from D. Schmidt to Jim Glenn, Apr. 20, 1989, concerning 1947 accession from the War Dept. of anthropological materials from the Institut fur [sic] Deutsche Ostarbeit.

3. NAA-SI memo from Marshall T. Newman to Dr. Witmore, Feb. 14, 1947, concerning accession #176333.

4. See Schafft and Zeidler, Die KZ-Mahn- und Gedenkstätten in Deutschland.

5. The area known as "East Galicia" was added to the GG in July 1941 on Hitler's orders.

6. Broszat, Nationalsozialistische Polenpolitik, 22.

7. H. Frank, "Das Führerprinzip in der Verwaltung," 213.

8. Quoted in Poliakov and Wulf, Das Dritte Reich und die Juden, 177.

9. Bauer, History of the Holocaust, 109.

10. Weinmann, Das nationalsozialistische Lagersystem, cxiv.

11. Victor Klemperer describes in diary form the increasing oppression of Jews throughout the war in his two-volume work, I Will Bear Witness.

12. Bauer, History of the Holocaust, 153–55.

13. "Activities of occupation authorities on the territory of the Republic between September 1 and November 1, 1940," Report of the Research Bureau of the Polish Government-in-Exile, quoted in Gutman and Krakowski, Unequal Victims, 45.

14. Nicholas, Rape of Europa, 61.

15. Testimony of Otto Ohlendorf, head of Einsatzgruppe D, at International Military Tribunal for Major War Criminals, Apr. 24, 1947, quoted in Arad, Krakowski, and Spector, Einsatzgruppen Reports, ix.

16. Breitman, Architect of Genocide, 34.

17. Taylor and Shaw, Third Reich Almanac, 27.

18. Klessmann, Die Selbstbehauptung einer Nation, 26.

19. Ibid., 61.

20. BAL, R52 IV.

21. Burleigh, *Germany Turns Eastward,* 253.

22. Quoted in Nicholas, *Rape of Europa,* 71.

23. Arnold, "Past as Propaganda," 464–78.

24. Arnold, "Justifing Genocide," 95.

25. Adam Cieslak, note in Schafft and Zeidler, "'Antropologia' Trzeciej Rzeszy," 13.

26. Poliakov and Wulf, *Das Dritte Reich und die Juden,* 28–30.

27. NAA-SI, IDO Collection, 1.20, Bericht, Oct. 23, 1942. (All NAA-SI citations are to the IDO Collection.)

28. There is a great deal of debate about issues of collaboration between Poles and Germans within the IDO. This research could identify no willing or enthusiastic assistance provided by Poles to their German occupiers.

29. Nicholas, *Rape of Europa,* 78.

30. Herbert, "Extermination Policy," 29.

31. NAA-SI, 1.16, SRV.

32. BAL, R52 IV, 138:88.

33. Taylor and Shaw, *Third Reich Almanac,* 282. See also Breitman, *Architect of Genocide,* 183–84.

34. Jacobsen, "Structure of Nazi Foreign Policy," 72–74; Weiss, *Biographisches Lexikon zum Dritten Reich,* 385–86.

35. Linimayr, *Wiener Völkerkunde im Nationalsozialismus,* 64–65. Plügel's museum work seems to have been in inventorying ethnographic museums and helping to mount propaganda exhibits.

36. BAL, R52 IV, 85:35.

37. Bauer, *History of the Holocaust,* 105.

38. See Knigge, *Vom Antlitz zur Maske.*

39. Gottong, "Bedeutung und Aufgaben der Sektion Rassen- und Volkstumsforschung," 35–36.

40. Ibid., 30.

41. Quoted in Gumkowski, *Poland under Occupation,* 38.

42. Ernst R. Fugmann, "Das wirtschaftsgeographische Gefüge des Generalgouvernements," unidentified article in a collection at the Bundesarchiv Berlin-Lichterfelde.

43. NAA-SI, 1.16, SRV, n.d.

44. Ibid.

45. Ibid., 1.7, Bericht, Dec. 31, 1942, 1.

46. BAL, R52 II, 251, fol. 1–15.

47. Proctor, *Racial Hygiene,* 211.

48. NAA-SI, 1.15, Gliederung der Sektion.

49. UJA, IDO Collection, Folder 70, Letter from Kommandeur of the Sicherheitspolizei and the SD in District Galicia to SRV. (All UJA citations are to the IDO Collection.)

50. Fliethmann, "Bericht über anthropologisch-ethnologische Untersuchungen in Szaflary und Witow, zwei Goralenorte im Kreise Neumarkt," 272–76.

51. UJA, Folder 70, Letter from Dr. Fliethmann to Dr. Kahlich, n.d.

52. Ibid., Letter from Dr. Fliethmann to Frau Furtek, Oct. 29, 1942.

53. NAA-SI, 1.15, 1944, 2.

54. Ibid., 1.10, Arbeitsbericht der SRV, July 7, 1943.

55. UJA, Folder 70, Letter from Dr. Fliethmann to Frl. Block, June 16, 1942.

56. NAA-SI, 1.15, Arbeitsbericht der SRV, July 7, 1943.

57. Ibid., 1.14, SRV, June 21, 1944.

58. Ibid., 1.15.

59. Ibid., 1.7, Bericht, Dec. 31, 1943.

60. Goguel, "Über die Mitwirkung deutscher Wissenschaftler am Okkupationsregime in Polen im Zweiten Weltkrieg," 159–60.

61. Sommerfeldt, "Die Aufgaben des Referats Judenforschung," 29.

62. Quoted in ibid., 35.

63. Ibid., 31.

64. Ibid.

65. Ibid., 64–79. See also Sommerfeldt, "Die Juden in den polnischen Sprichwörtern und sprichwörtlichen Redensarten," 313–29; "Das Schicksal der jüdischen Bauernkolonisation Josefs II in Galizien," 29–41; "Galizien und die ersten russisch-jüdischen Auswanderungswellen nach Amerika," 187–96; and "Judenstaatsprojekte in der polnischen Publizistik des 19. Jahrhunderts," 14–26.

66. NAA-SI, 1.7, Bericht, Dec. 31, 1943, 17. What Riemann meant by this was that in the future people might not understand why the Jews had to be eliminated. Anthropologists would leave a written record explaining the necessity for the exterminations.

67. Ibid., 1.15, Gliederung der Sektion.

CHAPTER FIVE

Population Selection and Relocation in the Midst of War

The IDO and the Establishment of Auschwitz

The IDO can be better understood if we return to the beginning of the invasion of Poland and look more closely at Germany's ambitions for this "colonized" area.[1] Hitler and his Nazi leadership had complicated goals that included the relocation of population groups and ways of life of the people in occupied countries in order to achieve an ordered, hierarchical world society led by Germans and the "Aryan race." This involved assigning roles to each group according to their perceived degree of closeness to or separation from a racial ideal. At the losing end of this continuum, people would be isolated and finally exterminated, while at the winning end, they would be considered "real Germans." This continuum had a geographic component, with some exceptions: the farther west and north, the closer to being "German," and the farther east and south, the more removed from the Aryan people.[2]

The war had gone smoothly for the Germans in the first years, and almost all who worked enthusiastically for the Reich were confident in its outcome. On April 27, 1940, the first transport of 2,500 Roma were sent to the GG from Germany's *Altreich,* that geographic area defined by the boundaries in place prior to 1939.[3] In 1941, an additional 5,000 were sent to Łódź.[4] They, too, were slated eventually to suffer extermination. By 1943, the Germans had expelled virtually all Jews from the Altreich. They had been "resettled" in ghettos throughout the former Poland, while some were sent to Auschwitz and to Theresienstadt. Their extermination was under way. In a similar manner, the Roma populations had been identified and, to the extent possible, all were sent to ghettos.

Germany broke its pact with the Soviet Union, invading on June 22, 1941, and taking the Ukraine, Belorussia, the Baltic state, and much of European Russia. The military operation went under the name "Barbarossa." At the same time, the reordering of population groups in the newly conquered territories was being planned under the name "General Plan East" (*Generalplan Ost*). Under this plan, "thirty-one million Slavs would be deported over the next thirty years to Siberia, where they would be allowed to die. Sixty-five percent of the west Ukrainian people would have the same fate. The Jews were not a consideration, as the plan for their disappearance had already been made."[5]

The Einsatzgruppen moved with the German Army through eastern Poland, and as they marched eastward they massacred Jews, educated people, communist leaders, and resisters. Captured Soviet soldiers were left to die in makeshift camps until the beginning of 1942. After that, they were sent to Germany as slave laborers. Anthropologists continued the work of Routil and Luschan in the First World War, who had used these population holding areas to do "ethnographic studies" and to measure prisoners with their anthropometric tools and construct masks of the people held under very dire circumstances.[6]

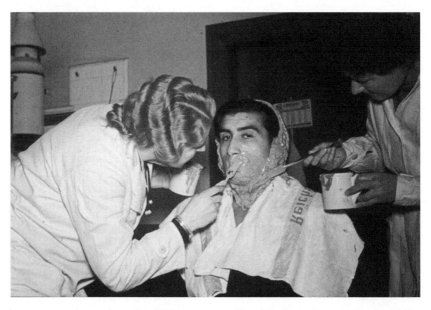

A Roma man being encased in a plaster material by an anthropologist making a mold of his head. Bundesarchiv Lichterfelde.

The absurdity of doing ethnographic studies of Soviets in prisoner-of-war camps can hardly be overemphasized, yet under SS supervision, anthropologists such as Wolfgang Abel of the KWIA did just that.[7] The conditions under which the prisoners were held reflected the Nazi belief that their lives had no value.

> Up to 55 million Soviet citizens were in German hands [at one time or another] during the war; Soviet land was laid waste; in the occupied areas, women, children, and the elderly were harassed; and the Soviet citizens capable of work were treated barbarically. Almost 3 million "Eastern" workers were in commandos in Germany [and] 1.5 million Soviet citizens were exploited as work slaves for German purposes. This is to say nothing of the prisoners of war, who were left to starve in cold blood or murdered—more than 3 million in fact. In the winter of 1942–43, 6,000 soldiers of the Red Army died daily in the custody of the German Army.[8]

The idea of Auschwitz as a major camp that would enslave and finally exterminate millions of prisoners began a year and a half after the invasion of Poland. A member of the IDO, Fritz Arlt, a well-known, twenty-nine-year-old intellectual with a doctorate in anthropology, had a major role to play in the exploration and assessment of the site at the beginning of 1941.[9] Arlt, who was Himmler's representative responsible for the expulsion of Poles and the new settlement of Germans, felt the site was ideal for a major death camp and a slave labor camp.[10] The Jewish and Polish homes in the area would make excellent living quarters for the camp's Nazi staff. He suggested that a transport could bring 1,000 prisoners and could arrive at any time. This transport should be comprised of 800 Poles and 200 Jews, of whom 50 might be capable of work. The following transports would come from Brzeszcze. This would allow the relocation administration to take the homes of those "evacuated" Jews and use them for new "settlers." In that same transport would be Jews from Pulawy and Harmence. In Pulawy, it was not only the houses that were the booty but also the land.

Arlt's plan was that the first slave labor effort in Auschwitz would involve the shoe factory Bata, and the stock in that company had to be either bought up or taken over. Arlt planned to put a notice in a finance journal informing stockholders that they would have a chance to sell their stock at the price they would have gotten on the day Germany marched into Poland. If they did not register to sell within a certain time from the date of the notice, the stock would be confiscated, and no further action would be needed. Himmler had other ideas for the industrial uses of Auschwitz that he developed with the IG-Farben industries.[11] With this banal beginning, and with the cooperative help of Arlt, the most significant death camp of World War II was established in the GG. Its purpose was to get rid of unwanted people, use people and body parts for medical and sadistic experimentation, free up their property and goods for the German state, and provide the state with slave labor. This describes Auschwitz for its entire period of operation as a death camp from the fall of 1941 until the arrival of Soviet troops brought it to an end on January 27, 1945.[12]

The War in the East

In 1942, the Nazi army moved toward the Caucasus region and into the southern Volga River area in order to secure the oil reserves. In this way, they could control a strategic transport system. Their march to the east reached as far as it ever would in that year, and the logistics to supply troops with food, clothing, and weapons became critical. Natural forces or saboteurs could disrupt thousands of miles of supply lines between the homeland and the front. The ability of the Germans to fight the war was seriously impaired by the distance they had successfully covered in the U.S.S.R.[13]

The Germans encircled Leningrad (St. Petersburg) in the summer of 1942. The army intended to starve civilians and the Soviet Army into submission, but a year later, with terrible losses on both sides, the Germans were forced to retreat. By the end of 1942, the German Army was in Stalingrad. The fight for the city was a standoff, again with a huge loss of life. Here, the Red army was successful in encircling the Nazi army. In February 1943, the Germans capitulated in Stalingrad and later that year withdrew from Leningrad. From July 1943, the German Army was in retreat from the east back toward their homeland.[14]

It cannot be forgotten, however, that this was a world war and was fought in many other arenas and on several continents. The United States, Britain, and the Allies had also entered the war at the end of 1941 and fought not only in Asia and Africa but in the Western European sphere, trying to gain ground so that they could meet their Soviet allies moving in from the east. This would signal the complete defeat of the Germans, but the victory was still years down the road.

As Himmler looked back on the war against the Soviet Union in October 1943, he regretted that the Germans had so badly underestimated the Soviets, both in their communist convictions, which made them tough fighters, and in their usefulness as prisoners. "We did not value then the great mass of men as we do today, as raw material, as a workforce. In the final analysis, when I think of the generations [to come] it is not a big issue, but it is a pity today because of the lack of workers [for Germany]; the [Soviet] prisoners died by the tens and hundreds of thousands from exhaustion and hunger."[15]

The German alliance was also falling apart in late 1942 and 1943. Italy left the fold, and Rumania and Hungary were ineffectual partners in the German cause. For most Germans, winning the war was no longer a certainty. Realization of the coming defeat only grew in 1944. The German people themselves were feeling the effects of the war, living with less food, increasing bombing attacks, and their men at the front.

Jews in Occupied Poland

Himmler understood that every party functionary would speak of the murder of the Jews. Even those who agreed with the Nazi belief that these measures had to be taken would know a single Jew who was "different from the rest" and would want to save that one person. This had to be stopped. Himmler urged people to think of how much more difficult it would have been if, in the midst of clearing bombed cities and while experiencing the terrible difficulties of war, there were still Jews acting as "secret saboteurs, agents, and agitators. . . . Collectively, we can say that we have fulfilled the most difficult job [extermination of Jews] because we love our folk. And we have not injured our inner selves, our souls, or our characters [in the process]."[16]

Extermination through unlivable circumstances was the first strategy used by the Nazis, and thus they defined the killing fields. The Warsaw Ghetto was the largest, established in October 1940. It held in all about 350,000 Jews, or about 30 percent of the city's population, crowded into less than 3 percent of its territory.[17]

The ghetto of Łódź, one of the most significant in Poland, was more directly related to the work of anthropologists. Created in a poor and neglected part of the city, but previously a very successful textile center, it grew to house hundreds of thousands, of whom few survived. Many of the Jews brought to Łódź were from the Altreich or former Austria. They were allowed to bring only a few of their belongings with them. When they were sent out to work camps, their belongings were even more restricted.

> For summer, the Jews can bring a shirt, one pair of pants, one pair of underpants, one skirt, one pair of socks, one pair of shoes, and one cap. Any other clothing will be taken and kept with careful attention to registering it. In the sleeping room there will be one straw sack, one blanket, one towel. For everyone there will be a table and chairs if they are available. There should be a firm nail in the bed rail for each person to hang clothes for the night. Hair should be kept short and

body hair too. After work, each prisoner should inspect his clothes for lice and carefully inspect his body. In the interest of public health, every prisoner should be in the camp by 7 p.m. One day a week, the Jews should not work but clean their clothes and their camp.

County Commissioner [*Kreiskommissar*] of Posen[18]

The administrative costs of the population policy were extremely high. Yet, sources of income were available, at least at first. For example, in Łódź, a Jew's property belonged to the state after his or her death. Thus, after paying fines and fees until there was no more money in the community, the Germans were still able to find a source of income from the Jews well into the 1940s.[19] For example, the estimated income (in reichsmarks) for the ghetto of Łódź in 1943 was as follows:[20]

Support from the Altreich		4,614,411.93
Support from outside the Altreich		93,014.32
Support from the GG		304,685.37
Reichsmark collections from the Jewish elders		1,803,570.76
Confiscation of former Jewish requisitions		57,257.11
Profits from the sale of confiscated goods		585,604.53
From furs	1,302,344.51	
From goods [from factories]	62,069.79	
From valuables	55,909.62	

However, the ghetto could not any longer pay for itself. The poverty of the Jews after years of robbery by the Reich was apparent.

It is in the nature of things, that little by little, the available income will be used up. For example, the sum of 1,081,900.47 RM, which was promised in January, had sunk to 160,764 RM. In other words, it had declined about 85 percent. In the coming year, we cannot depend on anything. Therefore, the leadership of the ghetto administration has a hard job that has to be solved through the liquidation of the belongings of the newcomers [Jews]. In 1942 the income covered the expenses, although even then a little had to be brought in from the sale of the belongings left behind [in the Altreich].

So in 1943, we have to reckon with about 30 percent of what we need and the rest . . . must be obtained through the rational increase in the rate of work by about 30 percent in order to come out without a contribution from the Reich. The increased number of newcomers cannot be seen to result in a signification capital surplus that will absolutely cover the 3,000,000 RM [that are needed].[21]

The Łódź Ghetto eventually housed at one time or another 200,000 people during its existence. Of these, 45,000 died of hunger and disease. Yet, the deaths never kept up with the transports, so that until the end, more and more people entered the ghetto in utter despair. "Because there is no room to expand, there has reached an almost unbearable density. The Jews are more hopeless, for they fear they will be evacuated out of Poland."[22]

The Selection Principle

The ideology of blood and land (*Blut und Boden*), previously an ideology without particular referent, now became concrete. The biological and cultural heritage of the people, their "blood," should be homogeneous within the land or area in which they lived. This required the state to check all persons' history to determine their proper place of residence and to make every attempt to move them there. More than a duty, it was carried out with enormous optimism and enthusiasm. Even Fischer at the KWIA was an enthusiastic supporter of the policy. "The new German state will be the first in history, as our genial Führer recently said, that will build its people out of blood and race. So must each political regulation regarding the population be so scientifically supported that it will be untouchable and will work far into the future."[23]

The sorting process was handled primarily through the Reich Security Main Office (*Reichssicherheitshauptamt*, or RSHA) by Himmler, who was also the Reich Commissar for the Strengthening of the German People (RKF). Many different offices and institutes contributed to determining what groups belonged in which geographic areas, however.[24] Intellectuals and scientists, often anthropologists, provided the support for this decision-making process. As a result of this activity, for several years there was an almost unimaginable movement of people in Eastern Europe from place to place.

The problems of selection of "acceptable people" had been encountered within the Altreich in regard to Jews and those of some Jewish ancestry. Racial certifications provided the information needed by the state to know who was to be considered a Jew and who was not. The real problems of selection, however, were found to exist in the GG. Here, the political boundaries that separated Poland and Germany had been variable throughout the centuries, and the people often traced their heritage to both Germany and Poland.

For the anthropologists, the thought of moving people around central Europe to match a highly questionable, if not fictitious, scheme of genetic and cultural heritage was not new. Fischer had promoted the idea for years. In one of his early studies, he discussed the issue of "foreign Germans."[25]

[A]nthropology has a new problem of great interest. Have the offspring of German emigrants changed over the centuries without crossing or mixing [with people in countries into which they moved but rather] through their own development, such as possible incest, or through some kind of environmental influence such as climate, altitude, lifestyles, etc.? Or was there crossing with the foregoing population, and [if so] what came of that? These are questions of great importance for there are areas where large numbers [of people of German heritage] live in relatively pure form.[26]

Nazi anthropologists believed that the movements of Indo-Germanic peoples from the east to the west had begun a few centuries before Christ. This rich Bronze Age culture was characterized by a strong Nordic influence that continued into the late Stone Age in the eastern part of Poland (the *Weichselland*). There had been a great deal of race mixing during this time, which was increased by the Turkish invasions. Then the Nordic peoples came down from Scandinavia and the Baltic Sea into the Weichselland and either pushed the other races out or, in some cases, mixed with them. They were farmers and shepherds. Thus, according to this mythology, the land could be considered a "German homeland."[27]

According to Anton Plügel of the SRV division of the IDO, the Slavic people moved into this region in the seventh century. He speculated that they did not conquer the land but only settled where land was already devoid of Nordic people, who had left to explore further. The Slavs procreated so fast, according to Plügel, that soon they were in the majority. The Germans claimed that even in this prehistoric time, the leadership was "Nordic," as witnessed through archaeological finds. The problem the Nazi regime faced was to reestablish this dominance, and the anthropologists of the Third Reich were eager to do their part.

Complicating the picture for Plügel was his vision of the migrating shepherds that came from the north Balkans, the so-called Walachen people, who were descendants of a Rumanian people. They spread over the Carpathians. Among these groups were also "Indo-Asian Gypsies" who spread into the population as well. "And finally we are not able to forget the large number of Jews, who joined the population of this area, and who have left in many ways their visible traces in the racial substance. Strange but true, it is a historical picture of a gruesome tearing, a disintegration of strength and folk and races in this area. We could only expect a terrible racial picture as we marched into the Generalgouvernement into this colorful, almost lawless place and, in the beginning, confused [*verwirrende*] in its disparity and contradictions."[28]

While the anthropologists believed that there were "Nordic elements" in Poland, they could not determine the percentage of each of the races, however, or their exact location. Plügel guessed that perhaps one-sixth of the population had "Nordic or related blood."[29] The Polish upper class was believed to be "very Nordic," but they were also usually not salvageable because of their political opposition to Hitler and his regime.

All of these speculations were important, for the rules of the game made their practical application deadly for great numbers of people. Himmler's words display the great ruthlessness with which the conquered people were treated:

> The basic rule of the SS man is absolute: honest, respectful, true, and comradely to all who share our blood, and otherwise to no one. How it is with the Russians, as well as the Czechs, is totally unimportant to us. We will take back the good blood of our kind that is in these people by robbing them of their children and raising them with us, if necessary. If the others live well or starve to death interests me only as far as we need them as slaves for our culture; otherwise I am not interested at all. Whether 10,000 Russian women fall from exhaustion in building fortifications for tanks or not interests me only as far as the fortifications for Germany get finished. We will never be raw and heartless where we do not need to be; that is clear. We Germans are the only ones in the world who behave well toward animals, and we will also behave well to these human animals. But it is a crime against our blood to worry about them and to bring our ideals to bear upon them, so that our sons and grandchildren will have a harder time with them.[30]

Auslese, Ausmerzen, and Anthropological Theory

Establishing dominance would require the Germans to pursue an extreme form of social Darwinism. In doing so, they adopted not only the vocabulary of Darwin but the vocabulary of the vineyard. *Auslese,* or selection, is a common German word used regularly in reference to the production of good wine, and it sometimes appears on bottles, indicating that inferior grapes had been sorted out before processing. Likewise, the word *Ausmerzen,* a term used in the breeding of sheep, is the process by which a negative selection is made between the animals acceptable for breeding and inferior animals—those destined for slaughter.[31] These words became the standard parlance of the Nazis as they spoke of human beings who were identified for continued use for the Reich or for destruction.[32]

On what basis were people selected? The racial investigators would say, "on the basis of German blood." Yet, no blood tests were done, and no basis in fact existed for determining who was a "real" German. And because the blood of human beings does not reveal racial differences, such tests would have been fruitless anyway. In practice, the people living in Germany who were neither Jews, Roma, nor any other darker-skinned minority and who were neither physically nor mentally disabled were part of the Auslese, the positive selection of the folk. The others would be *ausgemerzt,* or selected out for "resettlement" in the east.

The anthropologist Otto Reche of Leipzig University's Institute for Race and Ethnology (*Institut für Rassen- und Völkerkunde*) and an adviser to the Race and Settlement Main Office of the SS (*SS-Rasse- und Siedlungshauptamt,* or RuSHA) was one of those concerned with the possible "bastardization" of the German Volk who were slated to "resettle" in the Polish territory. To diminish this possibility, Reche suggested that all Jews and Poles be placed in their own geographic territories. He further urged that each new settler in the region who claimed a German heritage be racially investigated. With the backing of Fischer and Fritz Lenz of the KWIA, he determined that standardized "racial tests" should be conducted, rather than simply using criteria such as blue eyes and blond hair.[33]

Reche was not a newcomer to the anthropological scene. Born in 1879, he had held many important positions as an anthropologist and ethnographer. Among his other accomplishments, he had developed the method of determining paternity used in the Viennese racial courts. In 1943 Reche stated: "All the precursors that are mentioned in connection with the development of humans and the propagation of races can be explained through genetics. Without the appearance of inherited differences, without Auslese and Ausmerze, we would never have developed a higher ability [*Bildung*], the highest capacity among the most competent races and groups; it would have never come to a higher human culture."[34]

Anthropologists and the Implementation of the Selection Principles

As we have seen in chapter 3, anthropologists had influenced Hitler's policies from the beginning. Now he could use their ideas to further his program in its actual implementation. The anthropologists' statements and Hitler's program fit hand in glove. In a speech in October 1939, Hitler declared, "The new order and the new construction of economic life, the transportation and, therefore, also the development of culture and civilization . . . and a new order of ethnographic relationships will create better lines of separation [among people] in the end."[35]

With these marching orders, the anthropologists and other producers of racial certifications began to examine the people of Poland for the express purpose of determining how the separation should proceed. First, Jews had to be identified and initially placed in a ghetto, "for the Jew is not only a danger for the German people but for all the people of Europe and, as this

war has made clear, for the whole world."[36] Jews were not difficult to identify. Census lists provided the necessary information. The real difficulties appeared among the broader population groups.

The Deutsche Volksliste

A peculiar artifact of the racial selection practice was the *Deutsche Volksliste*
(DVL), a list of ethnic Germans created by order of Hans Frank on January
26, 1940. This census of all people who could claim some degree of German
heritage required a complicated system of examinations and investigations
of individuals in Poland. The product of these evaluations was a passport-
like document indicating the level of "Germanness" an inhabitant of occupied Poland could claim.[37]

Special offices were set up throughout the Warthegau, the new district
adjoining the Altreich set aside in occupied Poland for population groups
designated as German, and throughout the GG in county seats to issue these
passes and to keep track of the hundreds of thousands of people who were
being according to their degree of German biological and ethnic heritage.
Each office had a leader, an office manager, a member of the security forces,
two advisers from the category of Poles considered to be ethnically German,
and secretarial help as needed.[38]

For Polish women, being placed in category 1 or 2 on the DVL meant that
there were privileges that could be claimed. Deportation to the east was less
likely; it was possible to have better housing and ration cards for food. Polish men, however, while being able to claim improved rations, might also be
called into the military or paramilitary to subdue their own people or those
of countries to the east. They might also be "privileged" enough to be sent
to the Altreich to work on farms or in munitions factories. The Germans
looked forward to increasing the number of members of the German Volk
(*Volksdeutsche*) through this kind of instant population growth, and there
would be more possibilities of "strengthening the nation." However, the ideology was strict; German "blood" had to be reclaimed, but it could not be
contaminated by "foreign blood." According to Himmler, "It would be irre-
sponsible to take the Water Poles, the Kaschuben, and the German-Polish
mixtures of Slavic blood into the German gene pool [*Völkskörper*] without
a racial examination. In order to prohibit the most severe damage, the most
troublesome elements should be wiped out [*ausgemerzt*] before they are
[mistakenly] taken into the Deutsche Volksliste."[39]

Everyone who wanted to claim a Volksdeutsche status had to file an application with certain information: family name, all first names of family
members, dates and places of birth, residence, nationality, and ethnicity. The

card was stamped "German," "Polish," or "Stateless" (in the case of Jews or Roma). The levels of "Germanness" that would be indicated on the card were:

I. Both parents German
II. Husband German, wife Polish
    A. Children brought up to be German
    B. Children brought up to be Polish
III. Husband Polish, wife German
    A. Children brought up to be German
    B. Children brought up to be Polish
IV. (Unmarried) German living in the GG
V. Husband German, wife "foreign blood" (Jewish or Roma)
VI. Husband "foreign blood," wife German[40]

There were many problems with implementing the DVL. Most significantly, the Germans doing the certifying soon found that the genetic heritage itself was not very meaningful. Far more important was the relationship of the individual to the cultural heritage. One official stated frankly: "German Volk are those who feel they belong to the German Volk and acknowledge that through their actions, such as their language, how they bring up their children, their culture, etc. A more specific definition of the concept 'Member of the German Volk' is simply not possible."[41]

Because of the benefits that could accrue to those who could claim Germanness, there were those living in Poland who would do so despite having fought against the Germans, having assimilated into Polish communities completely, or having forgotten the German language over generations. Those in charge tried to eliminate these people, and one inspector wrote, "The question of who can be allowed to be German will be decided not only through blood and his relationship before the war [to all things German] but through his present acknowledgment [of his Germanness]."[42]

Printing and distributing the questionnaires that formed the basis of decision making was expensive and time-consuming. In the city of Łódź, for example, it took ten minutes for each applicant working with a staff person at the branch office to complete the paperwork. Therefore, if the office could do only 48 per day, and there were 30,000 applicants, it would take nearly two years to complete the list.[43] Nor did this account for all the complicated cases.

For the bureaucrats, it seemed that all of the possibilities for categorizing those people with some German heritage had been covered, yet even with their forethought, there were many cases that did not fit neatly into the scheme. For example, a member of the Security Service (*Sicherheitsdienst*, or SD) of the SS in Poznań wrote to his supervisor in 1943 that he was having trouble with the many "wild marriages" that had occurred between Poles and Germans through the years. The married partners were easy to classify, but their children were more complicated. Should they be registered with the RuSHA and thereafter placed in category 3 of the DVL? The operating theory was that families should be examined together and treated as a group, for the genetic characteristics relevant to the placement on the list would be more likely to show up within the total group.[44] In addition, there was consideration that there would be less disruption and complaint if families shared the same fate.

Each case was handled individually. Sometimes, the children were seen as "competent to be Germans," sometimes even the Polish member of the family might be viewed as "a welcome addition to the German Volkstum." However, there were many cases where the German partner was placed on the DVL, but the children and husband were not. In those cases, the Polish partner was placed in category 4, a dangerous position to hold.[45]

The decision made concerning these mixed marriages was supposed to be based on the person's profession and work record, his or her social standing, whether or not the person had a criminal record, and the cleanliness of the household. If there was a positive outcome, family members should all be considered German, and if negative, they should all be removed from the DVL. It was decided that in order to keep rebellion to a minimum, the pass should not be rescinded until the person was assigned a place on a transport either to a death camp or into slave labor in a munitions factory or concentration camp.[46] The only people who were exempt from this fate were those in categories 1 and 2. All in groups 3 or 4 had to have a further racial examination and would be treated as "unworthy" (*unwertig*).[47]

It happened often that the family was evaluated in such a way that different members were assigned to different categories. The children's ration cards then had to be decided upon on a case-by-case basis. Would they get the rations of the German part or the Polish part of the family? In one case, the wife of a Pole was placed on the DVL; her Polish husband had died fighting on the side of the Germans when Poland tried to defend itself against the Nazi invasion (September 1939). Could she get special ration cards for her children who were half Polish? The decisions made in many of these individual cases made people so angry that they chose not to cooperate with the Germans, and they were "lost to the German Volkstum."[48]

Another issue concerned the common-law marriages between Poles and Germans in cases where financial difficulties might have precluded a formal wedding and a signed certificate. A solution was found, and the rules were stated thus:

1. The partnership has to be ended if there are no children. If the pair is racially "highly valued" [*hochwertig*] or in Category I or II, there is a possibility of their remaining together, but only if they move to the Altreich, where they would then be Germanized [*eingedeutscht*].
2. If there are children, they will not be entered on the Volksliste, or if they are already on it, they will be removed.
3. If there was a marriage before September 1, 1939, and there were children, the family needs a racial certificate.

It is forbidden to have a marriage between a German and a Pole. If the couple and children are not judged suitable for a move to the Altreich, the SS must be informed, and they will be treated as criminals.[49]

This classification meant they most likely would be placed in a labor camp in Germany or Poland.

Increasingly, as the Poles realized what lay in store for them, they were anxious to do what they could to save themselves. Many paid local officials to vouch for their relationship to German blood and culture. Graft and corruption at the local DVL offices grew.[50] Categories 3 and 4 required special examinations. Those who were unworthy had to be removed immediately and sent to a concentration camp. For those who were considered worthy to be sent to the Altreich, there could be no more contact with Poland or anything Polish. Their children would be sent to boarding schools and separated from their parents. The parents would be given an adviser who would check on the progress of their Germanization. Those in category 3 would get no support for their new existence, but damages would be paid for what they left behind.[51]

As Himmler had promised, some children in the occupied lands were singled out to be "saved" for the German Reich. One reason behind this move was to increase the population, which was suffering from a shortage of men in the homeland and a falling birthrate. Other reasons were to provide a growing workforce for the Reich and to mitigate the feelings of loss among women who were of childbearing age but who, due to the war, would not have the opportunity to have a family. Children under the age of ten or twelve were considered for foster care in German homes if the Public Health Office (*Städtische Gesundheitsamt*) certified their "racial value."[52]

The other side of the coin was the situation of the children of possible German heritage who were living in Polish foster homes and institutions. They were to be removed and placed with Germans. Ultimately, these decisions were made in the most ruthless manner.

There is always the danger that when a country goes beyond its borders, it will bring its people in contact with others of lesser worth. Evacuation of the foreign elements is then the responsible result of racial-political thinking. One can see the German influence in the middle class and in the farmer class of west Poland. The cultural achievements of Poles are due to the German part of their heritage. Many are German without knowing it. . . . We have no interest in preserving a Polish race, even if it has character in a class. Therefore, the welfare of Polish children should be determined only by their racial value.[53]

The number of children who were considered for assimilation into the German Volk was not small. Indeed, in Łódź 1,400 foster children were in question.[54] The Public Health Office under the direction of Herbert Grohmann was very interested in this problem, and although he wanted to bring as many children as possible into the Reich, he found that many of them were "suspiciously Jewish." A true racial examination could not be conducted until they were two or three years of age.[55] This created its own problems. Many Germans in Litzmannstadt (Łódź) had taken Polish foster children under the age of three and wanted to get clothing for them through the welfare offices. The Public Health Office refused their requests because "it [only] concerns children here who have a certificate from the Public Health Office [indicating] that they can be Germanized and that they are in every way racially valuable children."[56]

Grohmann was an anthropologist and a staff member of the KWIA and

Polish children were the subject of investigation in several towns and villages of Poland. Often their teachers, if they did not have a German heritage, were murdered by the Nazis as part of an effort to rid Poland of its educated class. NAA-SI, IDO Collection.

was also a key person in the development and practice of racial segregation under the Nazis. A member of the Nazi Party and the SS before 1933, in 1936 he joined the Office of Population and Genetic Health. He took the KWIA genetic biology course from November 1936 to July 1937. Fischer was so pleased with this student that, in 1938, he took Grohmann on as his assistant. As soon as Germany marched into Poland, Grohmann took over the job as medical director (*Obermedizinalrat*) of the Public Health Office of Łódź. He retained his post at the KWIA until 1943, however, an example of the scientific institute's interest in racial sorting in the east.[57]

In at least one instance, Grohmann asked that Eugen Fischer verify his suspicions that a child was actually half Jewish although the mother claimed otherwise. The case involved a woman in Kraków who was accused of having a child by her Jewish husband from whom she was divorced. Although she was remarried, the woman's claim that the child was not from the first marriage was not believed by others, and she was brought to Grohmann, who examined her, her child, her first and second husbands, and two men with whom she claimed to have had sexual intercourse. Grohmann was not completely certain and wrote to the National Kinship Office (*Reichssippenamt*) to ask if the case could not be referred to his former employer, Eugen Fischer. Over a period of months, various offices examined the voluminous documentation, but no decision is recorded in the archival record.[58]

Grohmann was very worried about the speed with which the unwanted people could be removed and their belongings, land, and housing made available to the "Germans" who were to be resettled in the Warthegau. He believed that disastrous epidemics threatened not only civilians but soldiers. He urged a quick answer to race and ethnic-political questions, suggesting that the danger of potential epidemics

is made worse by the increasing need for Polish workers in the Altreich. Racial hygiene and ethnic-biological questions are not meaningful and, for the moment, play only a secondary role. It is important to find a quick answer to race and ethnic-political questions. Therefore, for the work of the Section on Genetic and Race Hygiene of the Public Health Service, the following procedures must be followed:

1. German Volk must be supported in their resettlement [in the GG] through the development of generous policies. It is terribly important to support the growth of this group. Racially and ethnically worthwhile classes of people must reproduce in large numbers.
2. The foreign people, especially the Polish Volk, cannot be moved out soon and, therefore, measures must be taken that lessen their possibility of reproduction. All must fall either into the group of Ausmerze or into the group of Auslese, with the purpose being to either hinder reproduction or encourage it in those

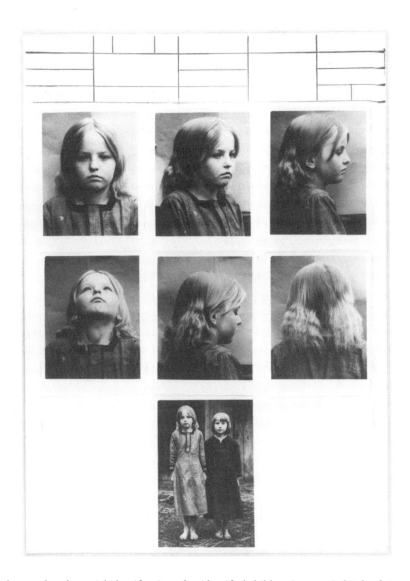

Photos taken for racial identification of unidentified children in occupied Poland. Because they were blond, they were in danger of being taken from their home and sent to Germany for "Germanization" and possible adoption by a German family. NAA-SI, IDO Collection.

who are worthy. Foreign bloodlines must be eliminated from the German Volk to further the cleansing of the Warthegau. The enactment of these measures is in line with the Volk's policy goal: Warthegau = German Volk.

Later, Grohmann made this point even more clearly: "It was always the purpose of the state to get rid of the minorities within its boundaries through special measures that would destroy strange ethnic groups. How this would be done would be determined by the ruling Zeitgeist. Either they would be assimilated or they would be eliminated down to the last person. The aborigines are going to get the second version. It is hard and brutal."[59]

Grohmann's initial suggestions were the following:

1. Keep young Polish men away from women until they reach an older age through the use of work camps. Men should be kept until twenty-five and women until twenty-one.
2. Tax illegitimate fathers for child support.
3. Give privileges to unmarried and fatherless men.
4. Bring married men into forced labor in the Altreich.
5. Sterilize the primitive Polish class.
6. Make laws for the foreigners (Poles) that would accomplish the goal.

In addition, all children between the ages of six and twelve would be placed in boarding schools, and all those under two, if they passed the racial certification, would be Germanized.[60]

From 1940 to 1942, 70,929 racial examinations were conducted on people in Łódź, all under the direction of Grohmann. Over time, as the work became more time consuming, the interest in conducting the exams waned. As of January 1942, no more exams were given for categories 4 and 5. They were considered expendable and were disposed of as the regime saw fit. (Sometimes transports were sent to death camps and sometimes to slave labor camps. The decision probably hinged on the current requests for slave labor.) Those in category 3 also had little chance to escape slave labor or death.[61]

Less than half of 1 percent of those examined were considered totally German (category 1). The vast majority were placed in categories 2 (35 percent) or 3 (52.75 percent). Categories 4 and 5 together made up fewer than 10 percent. Twenty percent of the people did not appear for the exam when it was scheduled. (If found, they would be sent immediately to a concentration or death camp, thus their failure to appear indicated how much the Poles feared the outcome of the exam.)[62]

The people examined who "failed the test" by falling into categories 4 or 5 were placed on a special list, and these lists were secretly given to many different officials and offices. To the extent possible, these people were to be used as "cannon fodder" and were sent to the local military headquarters. But even here, some standard of Germanness had to be met. In the Warthegau, there were 1,186 families that fell into this category.[63] A letter from the administrator to the RuSHA in Poznań indicated that 957 people were racially excluded from moving to the Altreich but could be sent to the military. This would allow draft numbers for the Warthegau contingent to be fulfilled. The disposal of the women and children is not known specifically, but most likely they were executed. The following statement hints at this solution: "It's going to cause trouble to take away the identification card, so just get it over with. Under no circumstances should these people be sent to the Altreich. Those in Group IV should be sent to the SS and put into a concentration camp. If the children are given to relatives to raise, they will become the most fantastic opponents of the Germans. Therefore, their passes should be taken away, and they should be put into protective custody [*Schutzhaft*]."[64]

When a genetic defect or a long-term illness was suspected among those who were examined, regardless of the group into which they fell, they were sent to a doctor who, through sterilization, guaranteed that no harm would come to future generations. Marriages were no longer allowed for people in categories 3 and 4, and those in category 2 could not marry out of their group.[65]

The Immigrants

As the anthropologists conducted racial examinations to sort the people in the GG, the German Army was advancing through the Soviet Union. Administrators of the Resettlement Program (*Umsiedlungsprogramm*) worked the area as soon as the armed forces had cleared it, in order to move large numbers of people with German heritage into the Warthegau. The Germans promised land and a better way of life within the German territory to thousands of farmers and their families if they would move to the west from Galicia and the Ukraine. Some were enthusiastic about the promises, while others were skeptical. In the midst of a war of gigantic proportions, Hitler and his ideologues were so driven by this philosophy that they found it necessary to continue to reorder the population groups to accomplish their Blut und Boden program, regardless of the resources it demanded.

Observers from various offices related to the population movements kept accounts of the transfers of people. A secret report dated April 19, 1940, stated: "The occupied farms are guarded by the Volksdeutsche Police Auxiliary. . . . the wooden floors are freshly scrubbed, the clay floors are swept. In the pantry are several sacks of flour and a barrel of preserved meat. We found large pieces of smoked meat hanging under the roof. In the stalls the cattle waited: horses, cows, pigs, also chickens are there. As one young Volksdeutscher with a four-child family took possession of such a farm, he said: 'In Wolhynien I never had it so good.'"[66] The reporter also looked into the house of a Polish family who had not been moved out. "A single room with eight people that I counted. The women have their Sunday dresses on . . . the men stay in the background. Their thoughts are not hard to decipher."[67]

But not all of the immigrants, or *Umsiedler* (resettlers), as they were called, found such a welcoming environment. In a secret report from 1940, it is revealed that the Poles burned two large barns of the settlers. The settlers became very frightened of being left in areas where Poles were living. They did not want to get out of their wagons when they were brought into the villages. An SS officer complained that the person from the police academy "has a big mouth but is too sentimental to simply put a few of these rebellious Poles up against the wall."[68]

The immigrants were usually moved in large caravans with their belongings on farm wagons and carts, driving their cattle with them. Along the way, they were given the bare basic care in transit camps (*Zwischenlager*). Usually nothing went smoothly. The Umsiedler came as families, and some were old or sick. The administration had to deal with a raft of complaints and provide answers to hundreds of individual situations.[69] A description of the situation as early as 1940 depicts the trauma that awaited even those belonging to the more favored groups of resettlers:

> The situation in Krakau is quite terrible. There is no food to be had. The Germans [*Reichsdeutsche*] who work there have to eat in restaurants. Apples cost three RM a pound and butter is almost impossible to get. Fourteen wagons are sent from Krakau each day with food for soldiers on the front. The political situation is also not good. The Poles are at least rebellious inside themselves. For instance, they did not come out to see the magnificent fireworks for the Führer's birthday. The return of Poles from the Warthegau was halted and they were sent off to Germany in forced labor before they ever got to Krakau. They never got out of the trains.
>
> Twelve thousand people from the Ukraine, Russians and Jews have been sent from Russia to the GG. In Bialystok 1,000 Volksdeutsche are sitting waiting for placement. It is said that thousands of children have died due to the resettlement efforts. The [German] settlers are better workers and have more skill than the Volksdeutsche. There is resentment.[70]

After the attack on the Soviet Union at the end of 1941, racial examiners were overwhelmed with the numbers of people they should have been assessing for racial classifications. There was no time for any serious effort to be made. One of the examiners reported that the efforts in eastern Poland and the Ukraine were very superficial.

The Pole who is being examined walks by an SS man who has been trained in racial questions. If the person is capable of being German [*eindeutschungsfähig*] then this person will be sent to an intermediary camp in Litzmannstadt [Łódź] with a German ration card, etc. There are two ways of practicing the racial separation. The one decides about German capacity by the nature of the applicant: his looks, his character, his manner. The other identification is only by his appearance. Which way is the right way, history will tell.

In the recent past, the new immigrants have gotten along quite well. Among the Volksdeutsche, however, there is the feeling that the new immigrants will take their jobs. Some want to go back to the Baltic and Bessarabia after the Soviets are driven out.

The attitudes of the Poles have not changed in the last three months. There are many complaints about the work habits of the Poles. Whenever punishable offenses were seen they were quickly handled. When the Pole, Max Magdanski, was being moved out of his farm, he attacked the local administrator with an iron bar. He was sentenced to death. Poles are complaining that they are placed on the same level as the Jews.[71]

In the report of the same time period from the town of Hohensalza, the administrator said that the Poles had strengthened their resistance since the United States entered the war. And there was another problem that was not anticipated: the Volksdeutsche found it difficult to recognize their German heritage and get over their friendliness to the Poles. They spoke Polish more fluently than German, although it was now against the law to speak Polish in public. He reported that the Poles were working badly, which may have been caused by the minimal rations they received and the propaganda spread by means of flyers that called for slowdowns. Their butter ration had been taken away, because butter had to be reserved for the soldiers. Because the men were not allowed to marry until they reached the age of twenty-five, many Poles were living together illegally.[72]

The extent of the movement of people can hardly be imagined. For example, in one forty-seven-day period in the relatively small area of Galicia, 3,885 families comprising 35,448 people were moved into an area from which 31,276 families with 193,539 individuals were removed.[73] The entire situation was made worse by the fact that the Nazis appointed county administrators who knew nothing of public administration. People who were expelled from their homes often complained to a higher official, and the county-level administrator would have to allow them to return. In the time that had elapsed, often the home had been completely ransacked and new people had moved in and were reluctant to leave. Violence often ensued. One estimate was that four to five thousand Volksdeutsche died violently in the years of occupation.[74]

The social scientists of the IDO began to speak of "overpopulation," and one of them, Dr. Helmut Meinhold, suggested taking people from "overpopulated regions" and sending them to other places where they would receive the simplest accommodations.[75] By November 1942, 835,000 people in the GG were working under slavery conditions in the Altreich, and the majority of Polish Jews had been murdered. Meinhold was still concerned about continuing "overpopulation" and sought "rational" ways to have these "unnecessary eaters" (*nutzlose Esser*) serve the Reich or be removed from it.[76]

Slave Labor

Shortly before the Second World War began, labor shortages in Germany became serious. Mandatory labor laws brought more people into the workforce, but there was still not enough labor. The ideology of the Nazi Party had emphasized the role of the wife and mother in the home and initially discouraged women in the workforce. As of the end of 1936, however, working-class German women were not only allowed to work but were required to do so. When the war began on September 1, 1939, women and girls were required to join mandatory labor crews at first for six months and later for a year.

German slave labor policy shifted from year to year as the regime moved toward war and then into combat. Even today, it is hard to comprehend the contradictory and counterproductive purposes and practices the Germans made of slave labor, although recently an excellent account of the rationale of these policies and practices has appeared.[77] The Third Reich depended on slave labor from all of the occupied lands in Europe, using prisoners in its factories and concentration camps as "horsepower" to save machinery and raw materials. Men, women, and children were exploited as workhorses and slave laborers under terrorizing conditions. Slaves laborers were also used as technicians and skilled workers in the production of "wonder weapons" never before known in warfare. These weapons terrorized England and the Low Countries, and prisoners feared that they could be directed at their own compatriots.

The German racial planners were always concerned with the possibility that Poles would have sexual relations with Germans, resulting in offspring of "impure blood." The selection of able-bodied Polish men who could serve the Reich had to be based, therefore, on the degree of danger they posed to the German gene pool. Only those who would not create such problems could be sent into slave labor in the Altreich. (Late in the war, the Germans did not make these distinctions, for the demand for munitions workers was simply too great. The Poles and other "Slavic" people were kept tightly isolated from the German population, however.)

Women were also brought into the Altreich to work under varying conditions of virtual imprisonment. At the end of the war, there were almost two million foreign women in some form of enforced labor in Germany.[78] These measures served two purposes: there would be fewer pregnancies and births in occupied Poland and more laborers for the Reich. Sometimes, however, women were already pregnant when they arrived at their destination or became pregnant despite the restrictions of their new life. At first, pregnant women workers were sent back to Poland, but this entailed costs that the German Reich did not want to pay. They also did not want to give the women an easy way out of the forced labor pool. Some women also tried to get pregnant so they would not be sent to bordellos.[79]

After much discussion, it was decided that those capable of work would not be sent back if they became pregnant. Instead, so-called foreign children care centers (*Ausländerkinderpflegestätten*) would be developed at their place of work. Costs would be borne by the German Workers' Front (DAF). This would also take care of another problem; some women were taken from their villages with their small children in tow. Unwilling to leave their babies and small children behind, the women being abducted into slave labor had simply grabbed them and taken them along on the trucks carrying them into the Altreich.

While the "foreign children care centers" sound like a humane solution to the child care problems, in fact these children and infants were subject to conditions that could not sustain life, and most died.[80] Those of "racially worthy stock" were not cared for in these places but were handled as if they were German children. They were adopted into German families or cared for in German foster homes. If a woman in slave labor refused to name the father and give his racial history, she would be sent to the police and treated as a criminal.[81]

Slave labor began to take many forms. As the labor shortage became acute and Germany had access to occupied lands, foreign workers were brought into the country as forced labor (*Zwangsarbeiter*) to work in agriculture and war-related industry.[82] This released Germans to serve in the army. The conditions they experienced were not usually as terrible as those of the concentration camp inmates, and they had some rights. However, these rights could be taken away at any time, and the Zwangsarbeiter could be thrown into a concentration camp. This might occur if there was an infraction of rules, if the concentration camps needed more workers, or if a particular skill was needed. At the same time that Zwangsarbeiter were being "recruited," those who were caught in any act of resistance were immediately sent to the concentration camps. By the end of the war, the differences in the treatment

A graveyard without identifying information where slave laborers and their children are buried in Rudolstadt, Germany. The graves are marked with stones placed there during the Soviet occupation. Author's personal photo collection.

among the categories of prisoners diminished, and almost all were treated brutally.[83]

Slave Labor on Farms and in Towns

The impressed laborers from Eastern Europe (with their clothing marked *Ost* for the Soviet region and *P* for Poland) were mostly used in agriculture or in unskilled jobs in the armaments industry. In the early years of the war, the impressed labor from the Western European countries were placed more often in semiskilled or technical jobs and usually wore no particular mark on their clothing. If they were placed in towns, they had to be in their barracks in the evening. Those from the western countries received a small wage and were able to return home for periodic respites. Some used this opportunity to go underground and join the resistance, but most lived in fear of the monolithic power of the occupying forces and returned to Germany when they were recalled.

The occupation of Austria and the larger part of Czechoslovakia in 1938 and 1939 secured material and labor resources for the Reich. The Reich Defense Advisory, under Göring's direction, reported in June 1939 about the work potential of the prisoners and that of future prisoners of war. In the lands plundered by the German armed forces, there would be an almost endless supply of male and female labor. All those who in any way showed opposition to the occupation regime would be sent immediately to the concentration camps. Those who were identified as subhuman, because they did not fit the requirements of the "Aryan race," would also be incarcerated in camps but under conditions that would lead to their death.[84]

To explore ways of handling labor problems, Nazi officials at Peenemünde inspected the Heinkel Works in Oranienburg, which used prisoners from the Sachsenhausen Concentration Camp. A memorandum written on April 16,

Prisoners or slave laborers were used to excavate Polish ground for prehistoric remains that were often sent back to Germany to build museum and university collections. NAA-SI, IDO Collection.

1943, summarizing findings, describes the reasons why the war industry should use concentration camp prisoners:

> [P]risoner deployment in general has yielded considerable advantages compared to the previous deployment of foreigners, in particular since all tasks not directly involving labor deployment have been taken over by the SS and since [the use of] prisoners offers greater assurance of secrecy. The entire area in which the prisoners are deployed is fenced in, specifically first with a barbed wire trip entanglement one meter wide, next a barbed wire fence carrying an electrical charge, and at a distance of three to four meters another barbed wire fence. In the space between the two barbed wire fences, there are five-meter-high wooden towers at certain intervals, which are manned by sentries and equipped with floodlights and machine guns. At this time, about 130 SS men are being deployed to guard the 4,000 prisoners for whom special quarters either exist or are being provided.[85]

Slave Labor in Concentration Camps

Several authors have pointed out that the concept of slave labor does not describe what was found in the concentration camp system of the Third Reich.[86] Usually, a slave has enough value to the owner to provide an incentive for keeping that slave alive and able to produce a lifetime of free labor. Many concentration camp prisoners, on the other hand, particularly at the end of the war, were subjected to a policy of "death through work" (*Vernichtung durch Arbeit*), a system of annihilation of all workers, regardless of their contributions. In the camp, the slave had no individual worth, and there was no need to keep him or her alive for more than a few months. There was an unending supply of this labor to be "used up," as Nazi documents expressed it.[87]

The prisoners of the concentration camps were, at first, virtually all Germans, political opponents of or resisters to the state on the basis of philosophy and belief. Their task was to build the concentration camps and the infrastructure for them and also to work in SS enterprises that helped to support the new police state. Hard labor was part of the terror apparatus designed to drive prisoners to despair and to keep them from revolt. Under the slogan "Work makes one free," the Nazis cynically spoke of "reeducation through work," with the promise of release for "successful" prisoners. In fact, there were some releases of prisoners from concentration camps in the years 1935–37 under the hidden agenda that the potential for incarceration in concentration camps would inhibit criticism and rebellion among German citizens. When the German troops invaded the Soviet Union, the number of prisoners in the vast variety of camps grew exponentially to literally millions.[88] Most of the concentration camp prisoners died in custody or experienced freedom again only when the Allies liberated the camps.

Tens of thousands of German Jews were imprisoned in concentration camps following the November pogrom in 1938, and many were given work details and subjected to conditions far harsher than those of the non-Jewish prisoners. This often was done for no purpose beyond the torture such orders entailed. Policy held that Jews were to be excluded from any work that was vital to the war effort, for the long-range plan was their elimination, and no part of production should become dependent on them.[89] However, like other policies, this one was adhered to only when it was convenient for the SS. As a matter of fact, a small percentage of the Jewish prisoners were used consistently for war-related production in concentration camps in Germany and in many of the death camps in the east. Recently, it has been discovered that as many as 300 slave labor camps existed for Jews in the GG.[90]

Sadistic practices were employed under the rubric of "reeducation," and the work itself was of less importance than it would become later, when the war demanded a total commitment. In 1942, Himmler, as head of the SS, wrote: "It is still very important to state that the question of investigating the prisoners and the purpose of reeducating those in the concentration camps who are trainable remains unchanged. If not, the idea could emerge that we arrest people in order to use them as a labor force. Or that we use those who are arrested [that way]. . . . Even though we must extract a 100 percent level of effort [from the prisoners], I am still of the opinion that the camp commander must try to reeducate those who can be rehabilitated."[91] This was a total sham, however. Virtually no effort was given to Nazi indoctrination or education. Almost no inmates were released after the war began, and few survived the entire Nazi era.

Financing and Complicity in the Use of Slave Labor

Hitler encountered no organized opposition to his slave labor policy from the German people. Their own unions had been destroyed, and their leaders were in concentration camps or in exile. Many had been murdered.

Many industrialists had not supported Hitler initially, but their enthusiasm grew with changes in the German economy and the reindustrialization of the state. Göring enlisted them in the militarization effort. The boundaries separating the private and public sectors were blurred, and many industrial leaders served in semiofficial capacities in the government.[92] They gained many advantages in the process, such as the destruction of the unions, stabilization of the reichsmark without its devaluation, and wage controls.[93] Eventually, however, as the state became central to all phases of the economy, finance, and labor markets, competition with private industry became more pronounced.

Firms and factories confiscated through the Nazi aryanization policy often were perpetuated by the SS as their own industries. The first SS industries included a publishing house for propaganda, a construction firm, and a factory for making dishes. All of these endeavors lost money until the SS began to use the labor available to them in the concentration camps. Starting with only a few enterprises, the SS had dominion over more than 150 industries by the end of the war.[94] Most of these were directly related to weapons production and the support of the people in uniform, but their harmless names hid the nature of their activities, which were in direct contradiction to the Geneva Accords established before and after World War I. For example, the notorious practice in which prisoners were forced, at a very heavy toll, to break rocks and cart them by hand and with wagons from deep in stone quarries to collection points on the ground above the pits served a "national interest." These very rocks would build the autobahns and the massive structures that would last 1,000 years, according to the fantasies of the architects of the Third Reich.[95]

Throughout Hitler's reign, government, banks, and industrial monopolies were in symbiotic relationships with one another, each profiting from the other, each manipulating the situation for an advantage. The government allowed huge profits and lavish life styles, and it encouraged the growth of industry through research and development.[96] It also created bureaucratic nightmares and encouraged industrialists to become partners in the murder of millions of their compatriots and neighbors to the east and west, north and south. While industry did not make policy, many industrial leaders, middle managers, and common workers were engaged as willing and knowing participants in all aspects of slave labor in the concentration camps, outer camps, and commandos. A group of business leaders and corporate executives, "Himmler's Circle of Friends," met once a month to discuss labor issues with the SS leader and contributed millions of reichsmarks for his personal discretionary use.[97] Their thoughts and concerns, their greedy desire for more human production energy, were certainly expressed and became part of the modus operandi of the Third Reich.

In March 1942, Hitler named Fritz Sauckel, the district leader (*Gauleiter*) of the Nazi Party of Thüringen, to the post of general administrator of the labor force. In making the appointment, Hitler stated: "To guarantee the necessary labor force for the entire war economy, especially for armaments, [we are] required [to have] uniform direction for the utilization of all available labor corresponding to the needs of the war economy. [This means] workers recruited abroad, prisoners of war, as well as the mobilization of all, as yet, unused labor in the Greater German Reich, including the Protectorate, the GG, and the occupied territories."[98]

Sauckel could call up thousands of slave laborers from occupied lands any time he was informed of a need. He introduced a plan in Western Europe of giving out ration cards only when able-bodied men and women registered with the labor office, making it easier to round them up unobtrusively when the time came. He was not always as subtle when dealing in the east, and often towns would be emptied of all their young men and many of the women, who would then be sent to camps in the west. His operating principle was "All the men must be fed, sheltered, and treated in such a way as to exploit them to the highest possible extent at the lowest conceivable degree of expenditure."[99]

By September 30, 1944, there were thirteen million men in the German armed forces, and four million more had died or were badly wounded.[100] Bombing raids had taken their toll on the workforce within Germany, and the citizens were discouraged. They were ready for all the slave labor they could obtain, no questions asked. They had to repair the buildings, homes, and factories as fast as they could, with little help. Concentration camp labor was needed throughout Germany. Small camps or commandos sprang up around the countryside to fill particular needs. These were filled with slave laborers from the east, predominantly Soviets sent back from towns and villages annihilated by the German Army.[101]

The SS had run a very large rental agency, meting out prisoner labor at a few reichsmarks per day since the beginning of the war. The SS made the prisoners available, at a price, to the private industries in Germany and, eventually, to virtually any enterprise, and often even to households, that needed labor. Because selection of prisoners suited for particular work was rare, and because prisoners did not intend to help the German war effort against their own compatriots, the factory owners did not get consistent help from the slave labor. They also had to deal with the SS on many issues they felt they should handle themselves. Despite these annoyances, the industries used more and more impressed laborers. The price they paid was calculated to take into account the reduced level of work that could be expected from the underfed, overworked men and women of the concentration camps. In general, the individuals, firms, and factories that used slave labor paid 6 RM for skilled labor and 4 RM for unskilled labor per prisoner, per day, to the SS, creating large coffers. Costs of maintaining the prisoners were kept as contained as possible, running 1.22 RM per day for females and 1.34 RM for males.[102]

The SS had transportation difficulties and, therefore, built camps or outer camps near the industries that "rented" slave laborers. Also, the industries

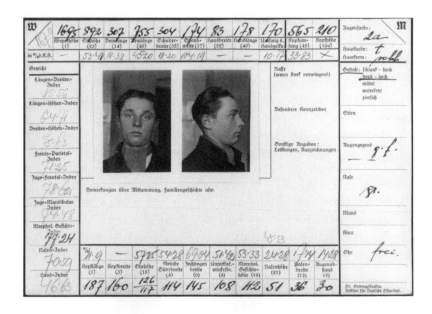

Front and back of an index card with picture identification of a young man in the *Baudienst*, a category of slave laborers in occupied Poland. NAA-SI, IDO Collection.

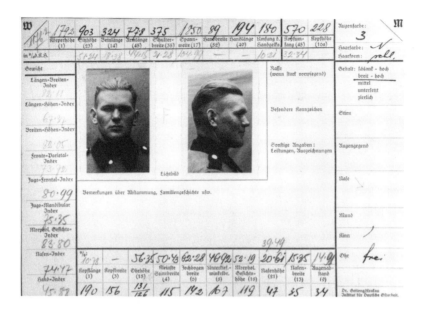

Front and back of an index card with picture identification of a member of the *Sonderdienst,* a group of men believed to have a German heritage who served in paramilitary and policing positions. NAA-SI, IDO Collection.

themselves built factories very near the main concentration camps. A model for slave labor in concentration camps, and the largest example, was the IG-Farben Buna Works in Auschwitz-Monowitz. In order to have a continual supply of slave laborers, IG-Farben used its own funds to build a special concentration camp especially for "Poles and Jews." Director Ambros stated on April 12, 1941, "our friendship with the SS is turning out to be very prosperous."[103]

On February 1, 1942, the Main Office for Economy and Administration of the SS (*SS-Wirtschafts-Verwaltungshauptamt*, or WVHA) was established under the direction of Oswald Pohl, a longtime member of the NSDAP. The WVHA was responsible for the aryanization program (taking Jewish property and putting it into the hands of the state) for the SS enterprises and the organization of slave labor. Among its duties, the WVHA was responsible for the administration of concentration camps under its Office Group D. Pohl explained before the Nuremberg tribunal after the war how slave labor was allocated to industry.

> The enterprises would apply either to the camp commandant directly or to the Office D II—it depended on their connections and on their situation. The camp commandant then had to visit the enterprise and discuss with the manager questions of billeting, feeding, and medical welfare of the laborers. In this respect, he had to report to the Office D II; Office D II then would discuss these applications with the armament ministry and would receive a certificate confirming the necessity of the particular allocation. The applications having thus been prepared, Gluecks, usually accompanied by Maurer, would see me about once a week, submit the applications to me, and I approved them. Only then, would the camp commandant, through Office D II, receive the order to furnish the inmates.[104]

The "total war" engendered a further intensification of the armed forces mobilization and an increase in war production. The decreasing potential labor force within Germany meant that the shortfall would be made up for by impressed labor from the occupied countries. In 1941, there were three and one-half million foreign workers and POWs working in the Reich, but in 1944 this had risen to almost seven million, or 20 percent of the total labor force, a quarter of whom were women.[105]

With the defeats in battle, Germany began to look for the answer to its wartime problems in technology and "wonder weapons."[106] From 1943 onward, the race was on to develop rockets and firepower. The tide turned from impressed farm labor as a model to slavery in factories and underground tunnels where rockets could be built. All available resources were directed toward this end under the leadership of Albert Speer. Conditions in concentration camps were brutal under all circumstances, but the murderous pace of production, and particularly the building of underground weapons and rocket plants, demonstrated a new kind of inhumanity.

At the end of February 1944, a new organization, the *Jägerstab*, was formed between industry and the national air ministry. Airplanes and rockets were produced in a variety of sites, with more caves and tunnels being carved out of stone and rock throughout central Germany. Outer camps sprang up by the hundreds. The conditions under which the concentration camp prisoners had to work were the worst that had been known to that time. A prisoner was expected to live about nine months and then die from the work itself. Few prisoners digging and blasting rock in the outer camps and commandos lasted even that long; three months was the average for them. Ellrich, Langenstein-Zwieberge, Heimkehle: the names of these "construction brigades" were remembered by the very few survivors with absolute horror.[107]

As Germany clearly began to lose the war, a decision was made to bring the Jewish prisoners who were still alive and could still work back into central Germany and work them to death in weapons production. Ignoring once again the ideology of Blut und Boden in order to solve economic and war-related labor problems, Nazis transported Jews from eastern camps like Auschwitz, Gross Rosen, and Stutthof back to Germany. At first, selections were made based on perceived strength and ability, but a short time later, the prisoners were sent west to avoid their discovery at the death camps and to erase evidence of the mass murders that had occurred there. Most of these prisoners, numbering in the tens of thousands, died of hunger and exposure on the transports.

Few Nazi anthropologists ever saw the fate to which they sentenced their subjects when they made their racial selections. Yet, they were well aware of the camps and were the recipients of what they had to offer: free labor, subjects for further research and experimentation, and body parts from those already deceased. The anthropologists' initial enthusiastic planning and participation in population segregation and differentiation contributed to the human travesties that followed.

Notes

1. The use of the word "colony" in regard to lands overtaken by Germany was common. It is clear that part of the self-deception of the Nazis, as they committed atrocities and crimes against other lands and people, was that they were doing what other countries had also done: developing their colonies. In some regards, colonial development in the African subcontinent had also been as brutal as the pregenocidal occupation of Germany's conquered territory.

2. The Germans became allied with the Japanese as part of the Axis Powers but did not carry their phobia about "Mongoloid races" into this pact. Typically, the Nazi ideology could be shelved when a greater need arose.

3. Rose, *"Den Rauch hatten wir täglich vor Augen,"* 148–49.

4. Ibid., 166.

5. Pohl, *Nationalsozialistische Judenverfolgung in Ostgalizien 1941–1944*, 97.

6. Routil, "Das Erscheinungsbild gefangener Polen aus dem Weltkrieg," 129–43.

7. Lösch, *Rasse als Konstruct*, 402–3.

8. Benz, *Feindbild und Vorurteil*, 23.

9. NA, T-76, Roll 9, 380623–626, Aktenvermerk über die Dienstreise vom 10.2.41 nach Auschwitz und Chielmek zusammen mit Dr. Arlt und Pg. Korn. Kattowitz, Feb. 11, 1941.

10. Steinbacher, "In the Shadow of Auschwitz," 284.

11. See Borkin, *Crime and Punishment of I. G. Farben.*

12. Strzelecka and Setkiewicz, "Construction, Expansion and Development of the Camp and Its Branches," 69.

13. Burleigh, *Third Reich*, 492.

14. Stokesbury, *Short History of World War II*, 232–44.

15. International Military Tribunal, *Trial of the Major War Criminals*, 29:112.

16. Ibid., 145–46.

17. United States Holocaust Memorial Museum, *Historical Atlas of the Holocaust*, 36.

18. PA, Katalog 1/"O" 299 Reichsstatthalter, Signatur. 1214, Unterbringung der Juden in Gettos, Anordnung für Judenlager, n.d. (All PA citations are to Katalog 1/"O" 299 Reichsstatthalter.)

19. Ibid., Auszug aus dem Reichsgesetzblatt Teil I, Nr. 64, July 2, 1943.

20. Ibid., Voraussichtliche finanzielle Entwicklung der Gettoverwaltung im Wirtschafts- und Kalenderjahr 1943 (Litzmannstadt).

21. Ibid.

22. PA, Signatur. 1131, Reichstatthalter Rassiche Musterung von Angehörigen der Abteilung III und IV, Oct. 1–Dec. 31, 1941.

23. MPGA, I Abt, Rep 0001 A, Nr. 2404/2, Seiten 22–26, Eugen Fischer, Speech given at the opening of the Forschungsinstitut zur wissenschaftlichen Unterbauung deutschvölkischer, rassenhygienischer Bevölkerungspolitik, n.d.

24. One of these departments or institutes was the Volksdeutsche Mittelstelle.

25. See E. Fischer, "Anthropologische Erforschung der deutschen Bevölkerung."

26. Ibid., 4.

27. Plügel, "Das Rassenbild des Vorfeldes im deutschen Osten," 8.

28. Ibid., 9.

29. Ibid., 12.

30. International Military Tribunal, *Trial of the Major War Criminals*, 29:123.

31. Klee, *Deutsche Medizin im Dritten Reich*, 37, note 23.

32. See Klemperer, *Language of the Third Reich.*

33. Haar, "'Ostforschung' und 'Lebensraum'-Politik," 457–58.

34. Quoted in Broemer, Hossfeld, and Rupke, *Evolutionsbiologie von Darwin bis heute,* 266.

35. Quoted in Kundt, "Entstehung, Probleme, Grundsätze und Form der Verwaltung des Generalgouvernements," 53.

36. Ibid.

37. Waltemath, "Deutsches Blut im polnischen Volke," 91–92.

38. PA, Signatur. 1106, Richtlinien für die Erfassung der deutschen Volkszugehörigkeit, n.d.

39. PA, Signatur. 1114, Rassische Überprüfung der Angehörigen der Abteilung 3, Mar. 26, 1943.

40. PA, Signatur. 1106.

41. PA, Signatur. 1108, Abschrift! Der Reichsminister des Innern Berlin, Mar. 29, 1939.

42. Hans Kopf, "Zur Entscheidung über die deutsche Volkszugehörigkeit," 16–18 (mimeograph), n.d., copy in LA.

43. PA, Signatur. 1108.

44. PA, Signatur. 1101, Verkehr Deutscher mit Polen, Entwurf eines Runderlasses, n.d.

45. Ibid.

46. PA, Signatur. 1114.

47. Ibid.

48. PA, Signatur. 1124, Behandlung der Mischehen der deutschen VL, n.d.

49. PA, Signatur. 1101, Verkehr Deutscher mit Polen, Aktenvermerk, Jan. 6, 1943.

50. PA, Signatur. 1113, Geheim! Posen 20. Jun. 40. An die Zentralstelle der DVL Posen. Abschrift, June 20, 1940.

51. PA, Signatur. 1130, Verkehr Deutscher mit Polen, n.d.

52. PA, Signatur. 1137, Eindeutschung polnischer Waisenkinder, n.d.

53. Ibid.

54. Ibid.

55. Ibid.

56. PA, Signatur. 2134, Erziehung von polnischen Kindern in deutschen Haushaltungen von Litzmannstadt. Spinnstoffausweise für Polen, n.d.

57. Lösch, *Rasse als Konstruct,* 357–58.

58. LA, Signatur. 31867, Gesundheitsamt, Letter from Grohmann to the director of the Reichssippenamt, Sept. 10, 1941.

59. PA, Signatur. 1137, Abschrift Erb- und Rassenpflege als Grundlagen biologischer Volkstumspolitik. Dr. Grohmann, Oct. 7, 1941.

60. Ibid.

61. PA, Signatur. 1131, Rassische Musterung von Angehörigen der Abteilungen III und IV, n.d.

62. Ibid., Vertraulich. Bericht über die Eignungsuntersuchungen in der DVL. SS-RuSHA Aussenstelle Litzmannstadt, May 29, 1942.

63. Ibid., Bericht über die Eignungsuntersuchungen in der DVL im Reichsgau Wartheland, n.d.

64. Ibid., Vermerk, June 19, 1942. Behandlung der rassisch abgelehnten Personen der Abt. 3 und 4 der DVL, soweit ihnen bereits Ausweise ausgehändigt worden sind.

65. Ibid., Vertraulicher Bericht, May 29, 1942.

66. BAK, R57 (neu), Band 15. Geheim! Bericht Dr. Quiring Nr. 9, Apr. 19, 1940, 4–5.

67. Ibid., 6.

68. Ibid., 2.

69. PA, Signatur. 2202, Umsiedlerkreisfürsorge, n.d.

70. BAK, R57 (neu 25) Standort 10, Magazin 1 1A Akten K.2.03, Reihe 117, Dienstreise nach Kraków und Warthegau, Apr. 10, 1940.

71. Ibid., Vertraulich. Lagebericht für die Zeit, Oct. 1– Dec. 31, 1941.

72. PA, Signatur. 1131, Reichstatthalter Rassische Musterung von Angehörigen der Abteilung III und IV. Lagebericht Hohensalsa, Oct. 1–Dec. 31, 1941.

73. NA, T-74, Roll 3, 373225–228.

74. Broszat, *Nationalsozialistische Polenpolitik*, 47.

75. See Meinhold, "Die Arbeitsreserven des Generalgouvernements," 273–91.

76. Aly and Heim, *Vordenker der Vernichtung*, 477; Klee, *Dokumente zur "Euthanasie*," 85–86.

77. See Allen, *Business of Genocide*.

78. See Gisela Schwarz, *Kinder, die nicht zählten*.

79. Ibid., 142–43.

80. Schafft, "Civic Denial and the Memory of War," 266.

81. PA, Signatur. 2199, Polnische Rückkehrer aus dem Altreich (Arbeiterinnen), Aug. 13, 1941.

82. The logistics required to transport thousands of workers at one time placed a large burden on German resources. For a document describing the process, see BAL, R-52, Folder 252, 1–125.

83. Vetulani-Belfoure, *In einem deutschen Städtchen*, 169–90.

84. See Drobisch and Wieland, *System der NS-Konzentrationslager, 1933–1939*.

85. Freiburg Stadtarchiv RH8/v 1210, 105–6.

86. Ferenz, *Less than Slaves*, frontispiece, xvii.

87. See Kaienburg, *Vernichtung durch Arbeit*; and Wysocki, *Arbeit für den Krieg*.

88. Allen, *Business of Genocide*, 132.

89. Ferenz, *Less than Slaves*, 13.

90. Pohl, "Murder of Jews in the General Government," 98.

91. Quoted in Kühnrich, *Der KZ-Staat*, 77.

92. See, among others, Rasch, "Forschung zwischen Staat und Industrie," 373–97; Allen, *Business of Genocide*, 165–71; and Simpson, *Splendid Blond Beast*, 59–74.

93. Homze, *Foreign Labor in Nazi Germany*, 7.

94. Weinmann, *Das nationalsozialistische Lagersystem*, lxxiii.

95. Ibid., lxxiv.

96. See Kaufmann, *Geschichte der Kaiser-Wilhelm-Gesellschaft im Nationalsozialismus*.

97. Ferenz, *Less than Slaves*, 26.

98. Quoted in Rich, *Hitler's War Aims*, 71.

99. International Military Tribunal, *Trial of the Major War Criminals*, 29:57.

100. Blaich, *Wirtschaft und Rüstung im Dritten Reich*, 36.

101. Lord Russell of Liverpool, *Scourge of the Swastika*, 147.

102. Distel and Jakusch, *Concentration Camp Dachau, 1933–1945*, 139.

103. Quoted in Kühnrich, *Der KZ-Staat*, 102.

104. Quoted in Ferenz, *Less than Slaves*, 109.

105. Homze, *Foreign Labor in Nazi Germany*, 65, 195; Blaich, *Wirtschaft und Rüstung im Dritten Reich*, 41.

106. See Neufeld, "Introduction: Mittelbau-Dora-Secret Weapons and Slave Labor" and *Rocket and the Reich.*

107. Fröbe, *Deutsche Wirtschaft*, 40.

Anthropology and Medicine in the Third Reich

The goal of the anthropologists who were active under the Nazi regime was to create a state in which the German gene pool became homogeneous and the racial and genetic qualities of the citizens matched their national identity as Germans. All of these people would live in or adjacent to the geographical area referred to as the Altreich, or the original Reich. These would be the most valuable of all possible people, the perfect race, the "master race." Others would be ranked according to their near or distant relationship to the ideal and would be assigned their life chances and living space based on these calculations. All anthropological investigations and activities in Germany and occupied lands led to this goal.

This Blut und Boden policy could be achieved either by moving massive numbers of people in order to realign them or by getting rid of the people who did not fit the picture of this rarefied German state. Eliminating the unwanted from the German gene pool could be done slowly through sterilization or, as the policy makers later decided, more quickly through murder.

As part of the Gleichschaltung process, which brought all endeavors in line with the Nazi agenda and ideology, the KWIA willingly committed itself in writing to "the service of the Volk, the war, and the policies" of the government.[1] As we have already seen, the KWIA had begun this cooperation with curricula development and training courses for SS doctors and other health professionals in the concepts and praxis of "racial hygiene." It had provided the techniques and training to produce racial certificates and had even done the examinations. It had laid the groundwork for the development of law and policy to begin "racial cleansing." Now, it would enter into the most dangerous, gruesome, and deadly period of Nazi anthropological endeavor.

Sterilization

Anthropology had been linked to medicine from the very beginning of the discipline through a common interest in anatomy and morphology. Many anthropologists believed that these fields moved their scientific efforts forward. Medicine had not advanced to the point in the 1930s whereby most chronic and genetic illnesses, much less mental illnesses, could be treated effectively. Therefore, it was not surprising that those within the eugenics movement, in which both anthropologists and medical doctors were very active, began to discuss sterilization as a way of improving human genetic "stock," not only in Germany but elsewhere. In this, as in other efforts, anthropologists and medical doctors worked together closely throughout the years of the Third Reich.

At the beginning of the Third Reich, before Germany invaded other countries, the major effort was to rid the Fatherland of what the Nazi anthropologists and other policy makers considered inferior genes.[2] This was often spoken of as "race and population policies." These policies had many facets. "We know what race is, and [we know about] the genetic illnesses, and we know absolutely how they are inherited. What is missing is the understanding of the number and the distribution of the individual racial and healthy and sick *genetic lines* among our Volk" (emphasis added).[3]

This "distribution" was the picture of genetic abilities and disabilities among various parts of the population. While it was not stated as such, "genetic lines" referred to groups of people who should be encouraged to reproduce and those who should not. These groups were often coterminous with social class, ethnic, and religious groupings within German society. Eugen Fischer and his colleagues believed that genetic illness was not randomly distributed but rather much more prevalent in certain "genetic lines." These lines, they believed, should be identified and eliminated.

A resolution of the 1934 meeting of the International Federation of Eugenic Organizations, meeting in Switzerland, stated that all governments should adopt eugenic principles for their own good.[4] This argument followed the same line espoused by the German anthropologists. Such measures already in place in the United States, which had the earliest eugenic laws, included sterilization of the mentally handicapped, the mentally ill, and certain criminals and even restricted immigration according to race and nationality. Mercy killing was not widespread nor approved. Although the laws permitting sterilization existed in many countries, only in the Third Reich did these laws provide the groundwork for mass murder. The number of those sterilized in other countries was not in any way as large nor as great a percentage of the population as it was in Germany, nor did it ultimately have the same meaning.[5]

Most cities in Germany developed plans to carry out the new sterilization law. In Frankfurt am Main, the city and the university worked together to set up the university's Institute for Hereditary Biology and Racial Hygiene (*Universitäts-Institut für Erbbiologie und Rassenhygiene*) and called Otmar von Verschuer, medical doctor and anthropologist, to be the director in 1935.[6] Verschuer came from Berlin's KWIA to do this but retained his ties there as well. He was enthusiastic about the new law and its results.

> We know today that the life of a Volk is only guaranteed when the racial unique-ness and hereditary health of the gene pool [*Völkskörper*] is maintained. The nub of the population policy in the Third Reich is therefore: hereditary and racial care or hygiene. . . .
> The National Socialistic State with exceptional energy has assumed [the respon-sibility] for the practical administration of hereditary and racial care. The first goal was the fight against racial alienation through the Jews. The second deed is the damming up [i.e., sterilization] of those with hereditary illnesses through the Law for Prevention of Congenitally Ill Progeny. In the two years since [this law] has been in place, approximately 100,000 sterilizations have been carried out.[7]

Verschuer, being an enthusiastic Nazi and well positioned in the appara-tus, consolidated all the tasks of the new law under his control. The institute took over all the jobs in the area of racial hygiene that had previously be-longed to the Public Health Department of the city. The institute would pro-vide racial certificates in the Frankfurt/Main area, investigate all marriages, sterilization, and immigration questions, and take over *all* certifications and questions concerning heredity. The Public Health Office would be given a "guest room" in the institute, but would not be independent of Verschuer's operation.[8] Undoubtedly, this was to prevent any nonconformity with the new law by liberal bureaucrats in the left-leaning city of Frankfurt.

In 1935, discussions among anthropologists and medical doctors began about the fate of children born in the Rhineland of French colonial fathers and German mothers during the French occupation of that area following the First World War. These "colored" children, referred to in the literature as the "Rhineland bastards" (*Rheinlandbastarde*) did not seem to fall within the established law. It was decided that they should be sterilized after being examined by Dr. Karl Abel and Eugen Fischer from Berlin's KWIA and two assistants of Verschuer in Frankfurt. At first, there was a plan to discuss the sterilization with the children's mothers, but in 1937 they were simply taken from their homes and transported to centers where Fischer, Abel, or Herbert Gölner certified that each was of African ancestry, whereby the deed was done.[9] By 1937, approximately 500 children were unlawfully sterilized in university clinics under secret orders from Hitler.[10]

Several years later, Fischer spoke of this action against the children as one of the foundations on which theory and practice were built in the Third Reich. Perhaps his complicated expression reveals his own ambivalence about the illegal act he had perpetrated:

> Further, the Institute (KWIA) devoted itself to the development of hereditary studies in their unique, apparent, and single underpinning of racial studies—all racial studies—and further, naturally, all racial policies stem from the information about the heredity of racial characteristics. The method here is the research of racial mixing. Partly here in the homeland [Rhineland] bastards (Abel), other bastards (Fischer, Tao), partly through the research trips supported by the Institute (Chile, Schäuble; Trinidad, Hauschild; Southwest-Africa, Lichtenecker). New outcomes of racial hereditary investigations are achieved that serve racial policy directly.[11]

In the years that Verschuer held the position in Frankfurt as a virtual racial hygiene czar, he used a variety of anthropological methods to increase his scientific claims for the rectitude of his decisions. He developed kinship charts and took various photographs to include with his racial certificates. And perhaps it was this anthropological work that attracted Josef Mengele to the KWIA, where he was made assistant to Verschuer in 1937. He remained there until he entered the SS in 1940, where he became the battalion doctor of the SS-Division Wiking (one of the early Einsatzgruppen) and, in 1943, the head doctor of Auschwitz. Verschuer left two years later to assume Fischer's position as director of the KWIA in Berlin. Verschuer and Mengele worked together continually until the end of the war, although from different locations.

Early Medical Experimentation and Twins Research

As was noted in chapter 3, twin research was a major research interest of the KWIA in the prewar years. One of the earliest expressions of interest in twin research came in a letter from the NDW to the Rockefeller Foundation. In a 1929 request for funding for ethnographic-racial studies, the NDW also requested funding for twin research.[12]

Almost a decade later, the KWIA sent a report to the European office of the Rockefeller Foundation about the state of their twin research. In the first year of Hitler's rule, 1933–34, fifty pairs of single-egg twins and fifty pairs of double-egg twins had been X-rayed. The results would not only be published but presented at an anatomy congress in Würzburg. "The work goes on . . . for twin research can give us here the basic important hints of the genetic character of certain illnesses."[13]

The first evidence of mistreatment of twins during research is found in the following year's report from the KWIA to the Rockefeller Foundation. After describing all the advances that had been made in the year and the various directions the research was taking, Fischer noted that he and his colleagues had tested the reactions of twins to substances such as atropine, pilocarpine, denonoline, and histomine.[14] They determined that following the ingestion of the chemicals, the pulse, blood pressure, and saliva were more similar among identical twins than fraternal twins. He felt that this was evidence that the chemically induced reactions were hereditary.[15]

In a report about the clinical genetic research in the Rudolf Virchow Hospital, Fischer stated, "The professional colleagues, even the X-ray Institute of the hospital, have given their support for medical specialists' examinations. Furthermore, we have the possibility to admit sick or well persons for research purposes to the hospital, even when [we do not intend] to effect a cure for the patient. From this go-ahead, we could use up to 365 hospital days a year. It is, for example, therefore possible to bring in the healthy partner of a sick twin for clinical observation."[16]

Research and experimentation were widespread and supported by the central funding organs for science in Germany. Patients subject to research were referred to as *Krankengut,* literally "sick goods." At other times, research subjects were referred to as simply "material." Thus, insulin shock therapy, cardiazol, and other chemical substances were given to "clinically sick goods" to test their effects on the brain.[17]

The value of pursuing twin research was assessed differently in internal memos versus the reports that the KWIA sent to the Rockefeller Foundation. Internally, Fischer said that the reasons he saw for conducting research on twins were to promote "positive racial hygiene" and to be able to "influence the biological basis of culture."[18] This certainly could be interpreted to mean that, if one determined the biological basis for disabilities, there would be more justification for performing interventions to prevent such hereditary strains in the population. Fischer reported to the Rockefeller Foundation that he personally oversaw all research and could vouch for its value. He mentioned neither racial hygiene nor the biological basis of culture. "Twin re-

The anthropological interest in twin research began prior to World War II and continued through the Auschwitz experiments. This picture of Polish twins was found in the
Institut für Deutsche Ostarbeit files at the NAA-SI. It was taken as part of anthropological fieldwork in the period 1940–44. NAA-SI, IDO Collection.

search is the best instrument for studies of heredity. Also this research is ex-
traordinarily important for the recognition of the hereditary underlying
causes of illnesses. We know today that many illnesses have an underlying
hereditary cause, but we do not know the course these illnesses will take in
the individual family or person. This will be the next large assignment of twin
research."[19]

In another document, Fischer explained the interest in twin research a
third way: "With regard to many characteristics of mankind, corporal as well
as mental, twin-research of itself makes it possible to fix the limits of the parts
played by inheritance and by outside action."[20] This "nurture/nature" dichot-
omy suited the verbiage of the Rockefeller Foundation but did not necessarily represent its true interests. Certainly the foundation's interest in eugenics did not exclude a belief in the efficacy of sterilization.[21]

Research centers in Germany, other than the KWIA, also were interested
in twin research. The so-called Hamburg Division for Twin Research applied
for funds,[22] pointing out that they would choose non-Aryan children and the
politically unwanted for their investigations, "especially children descended

from Jewish parents or grandparents. It is sufficient if one parent or a part of the grandparents is not Aryan. This is particularly worthy of selection if one of the parents or grandparents belonged to the Jewish religion . . . [or if they] were politically active in the Communist or Social Democratic welfare or equivalent organizations, or if they worked in the spirit of these organizations."[23]

The psychological development of twins became a great interest of the KWIA. It was not based on a need to know more about human development but was primarily reflective of a long-term interest in the criminal personality. Dr. Kurt Gottschaldt led this effort. He had a remarkable idea: to start camps for children in Berlin and bring twins in for study in a "natural environment." "Since the establishment of the Division for Hereditary Psychology [Abteilung für Erbpsychologie] in 1935 the [field of] hereditary psychology has also become a task-centered focus of the institute. Through the idea of twin camps (Gottschaldt), psychological hereditary investigations were able to be freed of the mistakes of the laboratory research. The first steps in this new and difficult field are finished; they build the basis of a yet to be developed racial psychology."[24]

In 1936, Gottschaldt examined 26 twin pairs for several weeks. In the next year, with support of government funding, he held a camp in northern Germany for 180 twins. Gottschaldt had the help of 14 counselor-researchers. "In addition to the genetic-psychological questions, the assignment was also to increase the understanding of the racial-psychological differences among the children."[25] These so-called races consisted of children from northern Germany, central Germany, and southern Germany.[26] About five years later, such camps were instituted in Auschwitz for more nefarious purposes.

The Euthanasia Programs

The Law for the Protection of Hereditary Health of the German Volk (Gesetz zum Schutze der Erbgesundheit des deutschen Volkes) was passed in October 1935 but not put into effect on a large scale until 1939. This law allowed for the elimination of the mentally ill or other "unnecessary eaters." This was the first time that the economic value of persons was to be used as a cause for putting them to death, and it spelled a major step in a continuing deterioration of Nazi moral valuation of human life. When the war began, the law became an economic policy. It was hoped that this action would also free beds in asylums and hospitals for the anticipated war casualties.[27]

Fischer expressed his personal satisfaction that anthropologists had such an influence on the genetic laws that developed over these years. "No one could have guessed that the studies of Gregor Mendel on peas could develop into the basis of hereditary health laws or that my bastard studies of 1908 would one day be able to provide the support of the racial laws."[28]

Actions against Children

The first actions initiated by the Nazi regime in its administration of euthanasia were directed at children. When health care personnel identified children falling into the categories listed under the law as eligible for euthanasia, these children were generally sent to an institution at least for an evaluation. Shortly thereafter, the parents of these children were notified that they had died of natural causes.[29]

The children were often killed with overdoses of Luminal or injections of gasoline.[30] Some children were not ill at all but merely had been identified as Jewish or Gypsy and, if caught in the net, exterminated. Children were also subject to sterilization, and many Gypsy children were treated with radiation as a form of castration. Children whose parents were mentally ill were in danger of being arrested for sabotage or resistance. Children were also subject to medical experimentation.[31]

Churches or the state administered most of the institutions to which sick and disabled children were sent or were cared for on a long-term basis, and the personnel trained to care for children often did so with a religious commitment. The effectiveness of the propaganda that surrounded the euthanasia program, as well as techniques developed to hide the truth of the children's fate, must be credited to a large extent for the acceptance of euthanasia against children. On the other hand, the penalties for speaking of the fate of the children were severe, and many found what they saw and experienced frightening. Many dared to speak of it only to their priests and clergy.

The T4 Program

The adult euthanasia program began in 1939 with the purpose of killing all patients in mental hospitals and asylums. It was organized differently from the children's program and began with adult patients in psychiatric hospitals suffering chronic illnesses. It was thought to be controversial enough that the program would need secrecy. Thus, it was given a code name, T4, after the address of the Work Group of Sanatoriums and Nursing Homes (*Reichsarbeitsgemeinshaft Heil- und Pflegeanstalten*), located at 4 Tiergarten Street. The administrators for the program included Dr. Karl Brandt and Dr. Leonardo Conti, who, while not anthropologists, were serving during this time on the KWIA's governing bodies (*Kuratorium*).[32]

Conti, serving as *Reichsärzteführer,* or a kind of surgeon general of the country, had a talk with Hitler in 1939. Conti had already begun killing mental pa-tients in and outside of Germany, and Hitler was quick to give permission for this action. Philipp Bouhler and Karl Brandt had the primary responsibility for carrying out the euthanasia laws. Hitler wrote to Brandt and Bouhler, or-dering "the authority to be extended namely to certain doctors to provide a mercy killing to incurable patients on the basis of their own judgment in light of a critical assessment of the illness."[33]

Under T4, all mental hospitals and asylums were coordinated. A question-naire was sent to all directors, who were asked to assess their inmates. The completed questionnaires were sent to Tiergarten Street, and a group from the Reich Ministry of the Interior decided who would be killed.[34] Those who could not work, had been in an asylum for five years or more, had a criminal history, or did not possess German nationality were the most likely victims. So many forms had to be completed that many assistants to the program were necessary. Many doctors who were requested to take part in the euthanasia program refused. This was allowed so long as they kept the request secret.[35]

As the program went on, it became more sophisticated. It was apparent that some parents or family members would complain and cause trouble, even though this could be dangerous for them. Therefore, new procedures were instituted to allow time for these complaints to subside. Patients were taken from the asylum and moved once or twice before being sent to a eu-thanasia center. If family members inquired and seemed anxious, the patient might be released to their care. Time was also allowed for the bureaucratic paperwork to be completed. Eventually, the directors were given an exemp-tion for up to 25 percent of the cases, and they could keep these patients from the transport. They often chose those with whom they had special relation-ships or those whose families might raise questions.[36]

The need for secrecy regarding euthanasia and sterilization, while at the same time propaganda programs were carried on to encourage acceptance of the concepts, was exhibited most directly by the placement of the T4 pro-gram inside the Reich chancellery, of which both Bouhler and Brandt were members. Here, policy could be made and carried out without danger that exact information would filter out through the bureaucracy to the public. This served two purposes: It forestalled active resistance, and it gave cover to those who were willing to go along with the policy but did not want to commit themselves in public.[37]

Bouhler and Brandt were charged with assigning responsibility to physi-cians to make careful diagnoses and to provide a merciful death to their se-lected victims. This was only a pretense, however, and never was a major concern. As the questionnaires were returned from all of the mental institutions in the Reich, they were sent to a committee of three certifiers, who marked a plus or a minus next to all items on the list and initialed the questionnaire. The final step was the signature of an academic professor in psychiatry. This was pro forma, requiring no examination or knowledge of the patient or person in question. Thus, thousands of cases could be handled in a matter of weeks.

Many criteria were used to select the victims for this program, but the most important was the economic consideration: Could the patient work, or would he or she be a burden on the state? Patients with mental and physical illnesses and conditions that were terminal in nature or did not lend themselves to cures were the first to be at risk for euthanasia.

Action T4 signaled the beginning of euthanasia in earnest. After receiving the certificate from three doctors, the patient would be transported by buses provided by the euthanasia administration to one of the several killing centers.[38] In order to keep the victims quiet once they arrived in these centers, a false sense of security was established through a doctor's supposed examination of the naked patient. The doctor at this time established a false reason for the death that was about to occur. Pushed into the gas chamber, the victims suffered a slow and excruciating death from carbon monoxide that lasted as long as twenty minutes. A death certificate was prepared with the previously established fictitious cause of death and also a fictitious place and date. The goal was to have nothing that could be traced. These notices of death were sent to the homes of the deceased, often accompanied by an urn of ashes. The euthanasia centers included Hadamar, Grafeneck, Bernburg, Hartheim, Brandenburg, and Sonnenstein. A description of the gassing was provided at a trial after the war:

> In the asylum Sonnenstein the gassing went as follows: The sick were transported to Sonnenstein in the buses with green painted windows and were taken to a reception room where their identities were certified. Dr. Schumann and Dr. Schmalengbach assessed them in the next room. About 60 patients were examined in about two hours. If the doctor decided on gas, the patient would be taken by the health care workers, among whom were the defendants Felfe, Gäbler and Räpke, to the separate disrobing room where they had to take their clothing off. Very weak patients were disrobed by the personnel. The patients were told that they had to be bathed. From the disrobing room, there were stairs that went to a room in the basement that was next to the gas chamber. The health care workers brought them that far, and then very reliable SS personnel took over. After the health care workers left, the patients were brought into the gas chamber. The gas itself was turned on by a doctor. It lasted a few minutes. . . . the defendants Felfe, Gäbler and Räpke, as helpers in the gassing, served as regular "hangmen."[39]

People with disabilities were murdered not only in the institutions devoted to euthanasia. With the blanket approval of the state, doctors and other personnel were encouraged to examine patients in every hospital and nursing home to determine if a given patient was a burden on society or might pass on defective genes to a new generation. If the individual was capable of working for the state, sterilization was the preferred method of "racial safeguarding." Those living in institutions and financially supported by the state were in the most danger of being eliminated or sterilized. Even with home care, however, the person not fitting the image of the inherently healthy (*erbgesund*) individual was in danger of being sent to such a center to be killed.

The T4 program extended to all Jews after April 1940. All Jewish patients were to be inventoried, and as the troops moved eastward, sanatoriums and asylums were emptied. The patients were summarily killed, sent to killing centers, or taken to extermination camps in the east. Einsatzgruppen killed thousands of mental patients as they marched through occupied lands. Many were shot in their beds. Patients without family connections or who had incurable conditions were simply killed. Others were transported elsewhere before being disposed of in any way possible. Many from the Danzig and Pomeranian regions were transported to the town of Neustadt in west Prussia and killed in a forest nearby. Prisoners from the Stutthof Concentration Camp dug large pits to serve as mass graves. About 3,500 were killed there, including the prisoners who had been unwilling witnesses.[40] The Czechoslovakia War Crimes Commission estimated the number of murdered mental patients and aged in that country alone to be about 275,000.[41] Even more were killed in the Soviet Union. There is no way of ascertaining the actual number of those murdered, for there were no complete records kept of exterminations of the handicapped.[42]

T4 personnel, including Viktor Brack and Bouhler, spent much of the winter of 1941–42 consulting about the construction of death camps in the eastern occupied territories. The following year saw them again in the east, where they remained until June 1942. "Eventually, T4 men comprised almost the entire personnel of the extermination camps. . . . Altogether, at least ninety T4 men were assigned to Belzec, Sobibór, and Treblinka."[43]

The euthanasia laws brought about a reaction from German church leaders and the German population. Although code names were used and the causes of death were hidden, many families realized what had happened to their loved ones. Families received multiple urns of the remains of their loved one, a death notice gave a cause that could not have been true for a particular patient, or a death notice was received before the actual date of the death.[44]

Parents and relatives of children who were killed often complained to authorities and the church. Some doctors refused to participate in these practices. Rumors circulated among the population about the people who were being killed and the circumstances under which they died. The medical profession was implicated in every step from decision making to actual murder. Nurses and midwives were sometimes very damaged psychologically by their participation in the euthanasia program and complained to their ministers and priests. Individual church leaders voiced opposition, but the official organs of the Protestant church were silent. The Catholic Church asked that its people be excused from the program, but this was not allowed. On December 2, 1940, the Vatican issued a statement saying that the direct killing of an innocent person because of mental or physical defects was not allowed under Church doctrine. The Church did not try to stop the program, however. An individual cleric, the bishop of Münster, Cardinal August Count von Galen, on August 3, 1941, spoke from the pulpit against the euthanasia program. He explained the Nazi laws regarding the taking of human life and condemned them and gave examples of people who had been put to death for their physical or mental characteristics.[45]

Hitler could not withstand the growing criticism, and at the end of August 1941, he gave the order to stop the official euthanasia program. The institutions were closed, and the use of gas chambers was discontinued for the time being at the euthanasia centers. Dr. Brandt figured there was a savings of exactly 141,775,573 RM through the euthanasia program, a calculation based upon the amount of food that would have been consumed had the victims remained alive.[46] Many professionals were implicated in the euthanasia program. Most of them cooperated and endorsed the program, and many had to face their responsibility in war crime trials after the war.[47]

The number of people exterminated in the T4 program is not certain, for as the process continued, less care was given to registering victims. In addition, many of the records were destroyed before the end of the war. Brack and Brandt estimated that between 50,000 and 60,000 persons were murdered through euthanasia institutions, but later accounting indicates that the goal of 70,000 was exceeded by a few hundred.[48] And this was only up to the date when the T4 program was officially ended. Thereafter, euthanasia, whose very concept stemmed from anthropological theory and whose practice was organized by those intimately connected to the KWIA, continued in other ways.

Wild Euthanasia

After the order was given to discontinue the killing centers, one might have assumed that the euthanasia had ended, but this was not the case.[49] A period of "wild euthanasia" ensued. Children, who had been the first victims, were also the last. They were killed, as before, through shots of petrol, overdoses of medicine, and other means, but increasingly many were simply left to starve.

The chancellery made its plans and prescribed actions known to the medical community. On August 17, 1943, asylum directors came to a meeting of the medical chief of the T4. They were told at this meeting that they could kill patients at their own discretion.[50] No longer did they need to bother with the certifiers or any other formality.

Thus, doctors continued, with encouragement from the state, to kill patients, no longer bothered by a bureaucratic structure to supervise their actions. In some ways, this made it easier for them to do away with patients on their own initiative. They were assured that they would in no way endanger their practice by conducting euthanasia or sterilization. Killing by gas within the geographical boundary of the Reich was no longer an approved method, but killing through starvation, drugs, and shootings occurred inside and outside concentration camps. Children continued to be killed in institutions throughout the Reich. Young adults were reclassified as children for the purposes of killing them.

Action 14f13

Shortly before Hitler called a stop to official euthanasia, another action was begun within the concentration camp system. Until the very end of 1938, the concentration camp system had as its primary objective the incarceration and punishment of political opponents to Hitler.[51] The camps were filled with communists, Social Democrats, and prisoners of conscience. This changed with the major Jewish pogrom, Crystal Night (*Reichskristallnacht*) in November 1938 and the onset of war in September 1939. Suddenly, the camps filled with Jews and people who had formed the resistance to Hitler in many other countries. Germans represented only 5 to 10 percent of the population of the camps.[52]

It is not a coincidence that euthanasia began in earnest at this time as well. The Germans were at war and were prepared to cast a blind eye on horrors close to home. Propaganda under the Nazis was highly developed and effectively painted euthanasia as mercy killing. Films were shown widely to audiences throughout the country about the despair caused by incurable genetic defects. And all people knew that asking too many questions could land one before the Gestapo.

The concentration camps spread in Germany, and the number of inmates rose with each year of the war. These inmates were totally without rights of any kind and could be used for the sadistic pleasure of guards, for hard labor, or for medical experimentation.[53] It became clear in the postwar years that the number of concentration camps or holding areas similar to concentration camps was enormous. These included work training camps, camps for those moved out of their homelands, "Germanizing" camps for children in Poland, ghettos, prisoner-of-war camps, youth camps, camps for foreign workers, police camps, infant and small children camps, SS special camps, Gestapo camps, Department of Justice camps, forced labor camps for Jewish men and women, forced labor camps for Roma, concentration camps, wild concentration camps, outer camps of major concentration camps, building brigades from major concentration camps, and death camps.[54] Today, one cannot travel more than several miles in Germany without coming to a site of a former camp (*Lager*) of one kind or another.

Doctors examining prisoners were again able to designate prisoners for extermination primarily on the basis of inability to work because of illnesses like tuberculosis or chronic diarrhea or because of injuries. Others could be singled out for experimentation. Many of the experiments were developed to provide information to the military for treatment of armed services personnel. Many more were carried out on the whim of SS doctors who had been trained in anthropological institutes and university departments to view "hereditary" illnesses and "racial" differences as inherently dangerous to the German Volk. Why should they not feel free to do what they liked, to play with these "lives unworthy of life" in any way their scientism indicated would be interesting? It was sanctioned by the government, by their peers, by their professional organizations, and, ultimately, their own consciences.

In one experiment, the German Institute for Aviation in Berlin provided a mobile low-pressure chamber to the Dachau Concentration Camp to conduct high-altitude experiments on prisoners. The altitudinal pressure could be simulated within the chamber to produce the effects of pressure on a pilot bailing out at twelve to forty kilometers above sea level. The request for prisoners to be used in this series of experiments went through Brandt to Himmler and resulted in several hundred prisoners, primarily Jews, Poles, and Russian prisoners of war, being subjected to the most terrible torture. "Through the window of the van, I have seen the people lying on the floor of the van. Most of the prisoners died from these experiments, from internal hemorrhages of the lungs or brain. The survivors coughed blood when taken out. It was my job to take the bodies out and as soon as they were found to be dead to send the internal organs to Munich for study."[55]

Freezing experiments were also undertaken at Dachau for the German Air Force. They were planned and carried out by university professors from Kiel. In this series of experiments, as many as 300 prisoners were submerged in freezing water and kept there until their rectal temperatures had dropped to

86 degrees Fahrenheit. All were unconscious. In one version of the experiment, each of the prisoners was placed in bed with one or two naked women, prisoners of Ravensbrück who had been transported to Dachau for this purpose. A letter from Himmler to *SS Obergruppenführer* (SS Lieutenant General) Pohl spelled out the care that must be taken in selecting the women to take part in this experiment. In this case, a girl with "Aryan" appearance appealed to him, and he wanted to be sure that in the future all such girls would not be put in harm's way.

> During my visit in Dachau on November 13, 1942, I had the following thoughts about the experiments there regarding the saving of men who through "undercooling" in ice and snow or in water, hovered in danger of their lives and [who] should be saved by all means.
>
> I ordered that for experiments in warming these under-cooled [subjects], particular women should be brought in from the concentration camp. Four girls were brought in who were in the concentration camp because of their loose lifestyles; actually they were in danger of venereal disease because they were whores. Among the four was a 21 year old girl, Ursula Krause, who certainly should not have been brought in. This K. was a foster child and already had had venereal disease twice. In spite of that, she is the type of girl who should be the last to be taken on in such an experiment, but should be saved for the German Volk and her later life.[56]

One of the experimenters concluded in a report that "only those experimental subjects whose physical condition permitted sexual intercourse rewarmed themselves remarkably quickly and showed an equally strikingly rapid return to complete physical well-being." One in three of the subjects of the experiment died.[57]

Women were used for experimentation, particularly in Ravensbrück, a large concentration camp for women. Among other uses to which these "test rabbits," as they were called, were put was to test the sulfa drugs being developed in wartime. These experiments were supervised by the chief surgeon of the SS and the police, who was also Himmler's personal physician and later became the president of the German Red Cross.[58] The subjects were surgically infected with bacilli, using slivers of wood and glass. Those who did not die were permanently maimed by the experiment. At the same time, the women of Ravensbrück were selected for experimentation in bone, nerve, and muscle transplantation, again with disastrous results.[59]

These few examples do not describe the extent or the variety of experimentation within camps. The prisoners could be used for any reason at all for random or very carefully planned experimentation. As we have seen, this experimentation was an escalation of what had taken place in Germany since prewar times, but now it could be done with no regard for the victims what-soever.

As the war progressed, the major consideration of the worth of a human being was economically based. When a prisoner could not work productively, he or she could be taken to the nearest euthanasia center to be gassed. In addition, political and racially based decisions played a major role in life-and-death decisions. This meant that any kind of murderous act could be carried out without repercussions from the SS until 1942, when the order was passed that prisoners were not to be killed if they were capable of working. In the end phase of the war, no body, no matter how damaged, could be spared. Death through work was the preferred solution.[60]

Concentration camp authorities had the option of using the facilities at the five euthanasia centers whenever they wanted to do so. Under the category "14f13" as cause of death, all mentally or physically defective inmates could be killed. According to testimony of a former camp physician at Buchenwald, W. Hoven, "all the Jewish inmates of the Buchenwald concentration camp were to be included in this extermination programme. In accordance with these orders, 300 to 400 Jewish prisoners of different nationalities were sent to the euthanasia station at Bernburg for extermination."[61]

In cases of overcrowding, insufficient work for the prisoners, or for other reasons, prisoners could be eliminated by transporting them out of the camp. A commission of physicians visited a number of concentration camps in the winter of 1941 and chose prisoners who would be "assigned special treatment" under 14f13. In this way, 5,000 Jewish prisoners from Buchenwald, Gross Ros-en, Neuengamme, Ravensbrück, and Sachsenhausen were murdered in Bern-burg. In other places, such as Mittelbau-Dora in Nordhausen, prisoners could be sent to a holding area and left without food or water until they died.[62]

It was not only Jews who fell under the 14f13 regulation. Prisoners with tuberculosis who had lost the will to live and work, those with serious inju-ries, and others who somehow came under the negative scrutiny of camp personnel were all subject to selection. Finally, even the slave laborers from the occupied countries were included in 14f13. Those who were too ill to send back to their countries and could no longer work could be disposed of on the spot.[63]

The Wannsee Conference

On January 20, 1942, a conference was held in a villa on the beautiful lake in the outskirts of Berlin called Wannsee. The purpose of the conference was to determine what would now happen to the Jews, for it seemed as if all the money that could be gotten from them had been extracted through fines, fees, and the confiscation of goods. Jews, Roma, the handicapped, communists, and other opponents of Hitler were being murdered on a large scale by Einsatzgruppen and the German Army (*Wehrmacht*). Those living in ghettos in Eastern Europe were not able to produce enough to pay for themselves anymore. It was time for a "final solution" to the Jewish problem, one that would, through technological means, bring an end to all Jews and other unwanted elements in society.

The conference was called by Reinhard Heydrich, chief of the RSHA, protector of Bohemia and Moravia (Czechoslovakia), and head of the SD, the secret police branch of the SS. He had been meeting with Hitler, Himmler, and a few others to discuss the next step in the "biological solution" to the "Jewish problem."[64] Using a directive from Göring to come up with a "final solution" as the point of departure, Heydrich sent out the invitations.[65] Of the fourteen participants, each with a particular responsibility for a region or an administrative function in the occupied territory, seven had doctorates.[66] They represented the highest ranks of the civil service: the undersecretaries in government offices. Heydrich was not convinced that they would all endorse the final elimination of the Jews and their necessary involvement in it. To his surprise, there was not only acceptance but an enthusiastic endorsement of the idea. The participants each offered suggestions of how they could help.[67]

The conference dealt with practical matters. The conferees addressed issues of how to make the victims stateless so that no one could inquire about their fates, how to extract the last of their economic value from them right down to their gold teeth, how the trains could handle their ordinary schedules while transporting hundreds of thousands of victims to the east, and how the police could round up stragglers.[68] No minutes of the meeting have been found, only a protocol that speaks in the obscure language that made the deeds more palatable and more deniable to the bureaucracy, both then and later. Two issues were clear, however. Not only were the ghettos not paying for themselves anymore but there was a public health threat of large-scale infections and epidemics to the occupying forces and others of "worthy blood." And certainly, they felt, the houses belonging to Jews, their businesses, and any other property should be disposed of once and for all.[69]

The Wannsee Conference brought Adolf Eichmann to the foreground as the logistics expert who could move the Jews eastward. He had control of parts of thirty different administrative entities to make this happen. Eichmann was a midlevel functionary under Heydrich, but the "Final Solution" made him into a key player in the genocide. His testimony after the war provided information about events and the psychological context of the Holocaust.[70]

In November 1941, the death camp Belzec was established in the GG.[71] Brack sent technical personnel from the euthanasia center called Sonnenstein to help begin the mass executions by gas. Auschwitz was opened that fall, and Chelmno was opened in December. Other death camps sometimes cited are Jungfernhof near Riga and Maly-Trostinec near Minsk.[72] All of them were characterized by the factorylike nature of the killing machine, through which as many as three million people—men, women, and children—were murdered in three years. In May 1942, an attempt on Heydrich's life led to his death a week later. The next two extermination camps, Sobibór and Treblinka, became monuments to the anger his assassination caused. This culminated in *Aktion Reinhard,* which marked the beginning of massive extermination of the Jews in the eastern occupied lands.[73]

Medical Experimentation in Auschwitz

Eugen Fischer announced in a report dated December 4, 1940, that the next year at the KWIA would see a research emphasis on phenogenesis, or the appearance of abnormalities. This was not only of theoretical interest but was supposed to have practical applications for "racial hygiene," as well. As an example of this practical use, he put forth several questions:

> [T]he inherited polydactyl condition appears sometimes as six fingers on both hands and feet, sometimes only on hands or on one extremity, sometimes as normal six fingers, sometimes as a stump next to the little finger or only as a bone on the knuckle of the little finger. Why? When does it appear in the embryo and why does the deformity occur in so many different ways? What determines the various degrees? Or in the normal area, when is a Negro embryo distinguishable from a European embryo? Could one make a contribution in this way to the question of when the first [sign] of racial difference appears and how these differences develop over time and to what degree?[74]

These thoughts were not new to Fischer. In 1936, he had written the German Research Society that "racial differences between Negroes and Europeans can be identified in the embryo. This evidence is the single weapon [against] the outlandish Jewish propaganda, which wants to ascribe differences in grown men to environmental influences."[75] Fischer combined in this statement his interest in abnormalities with questions of race. His reliance on Verschuer for expertise in this field is seen in Fischer's assigning the chap-

The doorway of the Auschwitz Archives inside the Auschwitz Memorial
Museum. Author's personal photo collection.

ter "Anomalies of the Body Form" to him in the edited book *Erbpathologie*
(Hereditary Pathology) published in 1940.[76]

Fischer stated in this 1940 report that Professor Hans Nachtsheim, who
worked in the KWIA as the head of experimental hereditary pathology,
would be studying genetically "ill" rabbits to see if malformations could
be bred and would then kill them to "capture" the embryos. "And then, as
something new, I will string this phenogenetic investigation out in normal,

Medical record from Auschwitz taken on August 21, 1944, showing a drawing of a pair of lungs. The clinical diagnosis: "twin." The X-ray result: "No apparent sign of infection." This prisoner would be used for experimentation, and this may have been the initial diagnosis. Auschwitz-Birkenau Museum Archives.

that is, racial and individual characteristics, in animals, but then also in human embryos. . . . The phenogenetic research, especially in humans, needs . . . a large amount of embryonic material. It takes a great deal of time to collect that. And so it must be collected over years in order to prepare for future research."[77]

When Verschuer took over the directorship of the KWIA in 1942 as Fischer retired, he wrote to a colleague expressing the exact wish that Fischer had uttered.[78] He wanted to concentrate on phenogenetics and had a plan to collect embryos from women's clinics and hospitals throughout Germany. However, fulfilling the wish of Fischer and Verschuer for embryos did not depend upon the patient gathering of human material from public sources. A surfeit of skeletons, eyes, embryos, and disembodied heads of children were sent from Auschwitz to the KWIA in the coming years.[79]

Dr. Josef Mengele, who had joined Verschuer in Frankfurt as his assistant, joined him again at the KWIA in 1942. He divided his time between his responsibilities to the SS and the KWIA, perhaps planning the research with Verschuer that the latter would conduct with the Berlin institute when he became the head doctor at Auschwitz in 1943.[80]

Mengele was a person of particular habits. Some said that he looked like a movie star. He moved in an elegant fashion, always carefully dressed in uniform. The camp for twins, which had already been established at Auschwitz prior to his arrival, was improved through his intervention. A kindergarten was set up, and the children received special rations. They routinely called him "Uncle" or even "Papa." This behavior stood in stark contrast to his absolutely emotionless approach to experiments. He would treat children with sulfa drugs and vitamins then send them "for further treatment to the gas chamber."[81]

Mengele also had a genetic malady of his own: He had no incisors. This strange formation of his teeth, in some way, may have contributed to his obsession with genetic flaws, but it was an obsession that he shared with many colleagues.[82]

Mengele was not a trained surgeon but had no qualms about performing surgery on his subjects. He was known to operate on Roma for the purpose of sterilization and on children for other purposes. One prisoner, a doctor who assisted Mengele, reported after the war on what happened to a "twin pair named Guido and Nina not much older than four years." "Mengele picked them up and brought them back in a perverse, stumplike way. They were—like Siamese twins—sewed together at the back. At the same time, Mengele had joined their arteries. Their wounds festered, they screamed day and night. Somehow their mother, I remember her name was Stella, got morphine for them and thus could end their suffering."[83]

As Mengele was called to Auschwitz to become the head of the medical department there, he did not break his ties to the KWIA. On the contrary, an arrangement was made for him to send research samples on a regular basis back to Berlin where other anthropologists could work on them.

At the KWIA in Berlin, Verschuer had another assistant, Dr. Karin Magnussen. Magnussen, whose value to the Nazi Party was proven early in her career, was a member of the Racial Policy Office of the party and had important credentials as a biologist. She warned of the many dangers that confronted Germany—from Negroes, "Gypsies," but especially Jews, whom she viewed as a treacherous 1 percent of the German population. She wrote textbooks for biology teachers. She was not modest in her proposals for policy in many different areas, including settlement, eastern land development, slave labor, and citizenship.[84]

Magnussen had practical interests in addition to her more theoretical policy interests. She was particularly interested in the inheritance of eye color and worked with Verschuer from 1940 until 1945 on that topic, often using twins. Mengele provided her with eyes removed from prisoners, often children, in Auschwitz. His assistants packed them in glass bottles and sent them to Berlin.[85] It is unknown how many twin pairs Mengele had under his control in Auschwitz, nor from whom such body parts were taken, nor how many of them were exploited unto death for other experiments. At the time of the liberation of the camp by Soviet troops, there were 200 children still alive in the twin barracks.[86]

Notes

1. MPGA, I Abt., Rep. 1A, Nr. 2400/1, Bl. 159–67. Eugen Fischer's report to Board of Trustees of the KWIA, 1.

2. See Aly, Chroust, and Pross, *Cleansing the Fatherland.*

3. MPGA, I Abt, Rep 0001 A, Nr. 2404/2, Eugen Fischer, Speech given at the opening of the Forschungsinstitute zur wissenschaftlichen Unterbauung deutschvölkischer, rassenhygienischer Bevölkerungspolitik, n.d., 1.

4. Kühl, *Nazi Connection,* 27–29.

5. Ibid.; Friedlander, *Origins of Nazi Genocide,* 3–9.

6. Daum and Deppe, *Zwangssterilisation in Frankfurt am Main, 1933–1945,* 64.

7. Verschuer, "Rassenhygiene als Wissenschaft und Staatsaufgabe," 17.

8. Daum and Deppe, *Zwangssterilisation in Frankfurt am Main, 1933–1945,* 63–83.

9. Proctor, *Racial Hygiene,* 113.

10. Ibid., 112.

11. MPGA, I Abt., Rep. 1A, Nr. 2400/1, Bl. 159–67, 3.

12. RAC 1.1, A, 10, Box 20, Folder 187, Sept. 5, 1929.

13. RAC 1.1, A, Box 4, Folder 46, Aug. 23, 1934 (Letter from Fischer to Lambert).

14. The author could find no listing for a substance called "denonoline" in either German or English sources.

15. RAC 1.1, A, 717, Box 10, Folder 63, Aug. 23, 1935 (Letter from Fischer to Rockefeller Foundation).

16. MPGA, I Abt., Rep. 1A, Nr. 2399/1, Nov. 23, 1933, 17.

17. BAK, R73, Archiv Signatur. 14717, Standort 10, Magazin 1, Akten K. 2.03, Reihe 126, Letter from Oberarzt Dr. Selback to NDW, Dec. 12, 1942.

18. MPGA, I Abt., Rep. 1A, Nr. 2404/2, Tätigkeitsbericht KWIA 1933, 14–17.

19. RAC 1.1, A, 717, Box 10, Folder 63, Aug. 23, 1935.

20. Ibid., Feb. 16, 1932, 2.

21. Friedlander, *Origins of Nazi Genocide,* 13.

22. This was most likely the Institut für Zwillings- und Erbforschung der II. Medizinischen Klinik und Poliklinik des Universtätskrankenhauses in Hamburg-Eppendorf. See BAK, R73, Archiv Signatur. 11956.

23. BAK, R73, Archiv Signatur. 15170, Anweisung für die Abt. Zwillinge.

24. MPGA, I Abt., Rep. 1A, Nr. 2400/1, Bl. 159–67, 3.

25. Quoted in Suttinger, "Zwillingslager Norderney," 23–25.

26. This interest in the "races" of southern Germany was exhibited in the Anthropological Institute of the University of Munich. Its director, Professor Th. Mollison, requested skeletons from southern German common graves in September 1939: "It concerns the technical preparation of material, in order to make a scientific work available. . . . It is addressing the . . . solution to the question of racial dispersion in southern Germany that is continuing to be important" (BAK, R73, Archiv Signatur. 13217, Letter from Anthropologisches Institut Universität München to Deutsche Forschungsgemeinschaft, Nov. 21, 1939).

27. Friedlander, *Origins of Nazi Genocide,* 64.

28. MPGA, I Abt., Rep. 1A, Nr. 2400/1, Bl. 159–67.

29. Lifton, *Nazi Doctors,* 54–55.

30. Kogon, Longbein, and Rückerl, *Die nationalsozialistischen Massentötungen durch Giftgas,* 29.

31. Rose, *"Den Rauch hatten wir täglich vor Augen,"* 280–307.

32. MPGA, I Abt., Rep. 1A, Nr. 2400/1, Bl. 159–67.

33. Quoted in Baader, Cramer, and Winter, *Verlegt nach Hadamar,* 20.

34. Aly, "Medicine against the Useless," 22.

35. Lifton, *Nazi Doctors,* 51–57. See also Proctor, *Racial Hygiene,* 251–81.

36. Aly, "Medicine against the Useless," 40–42.

37. Ibid., 31.

38. It is reasonable to believe that almost all of these doctors had been trained in anthropology and racial hygiene at the KWIA.

39. Quoted in Jensch, *Euthanasie—Aktion "T4,"* 6–7.

40. Friedlander, *Origins of Nazi Genocide,* 136–37.

41. Cohen, *Human Behavior in Concentration Camps,* 108.

42. Friedlander's account is one of the most complete to date. See *Origins of Nazi Genocide,* 136–86.

43. Ibid., 297.

44. Lifton, *Nazi Doctors,* 75.

45. Ibid., 80–95. See also Noakes and Pridham, *Nazism,* 2:1034–35.

46. Noakes and Pridham, *Nazism,* 2:1042.

47. See Annas and Grodin, *Nazi Doctors and the Nuremberg Code.*

48. Aly, "Medicine against the Useless," 39.

49. Weinmann, *Das nationalsozialistische Lagersystem,* xv–xvi.

50. Noakes and Pridham, *Nazism,* 2:1047.

51. Sofsky, *Order of Terror,* 37.

52. Ibid., 34.

53. Publications, including prisoner narratives, are available at concentration camp memorial sites and show the effect of a political system that had abolished virtually all civil rights.

54. Weinmann, *Das nationalsozialistische Lagersystem,* cxl–cxlii.

55. Cohen, *Human Behavior in Concentration Camps,* 84.

56. International Military Tribunal, *Trial of the Major War Criminals,* 27:349.

57. Cohen, *Human Behavior in Concentration Camps,* 86–87.

58. Ibid., 89.

59. Ibid., 91–92.

60. Müller-Hill, *Murderous Science,* 63–65.

61. Quoted in Cohen, *Human Behavior in Concentration Camps,* 110.

62. Schafft and Zeidler, *Die KZ-Mahn -und Gedenkstätten in Deutschland,* 172.

63. Friedlander, *Origins of Nazi Genocide,* 161.

64. Aly, *Endlösung,* 357–58. Heydrich's given name may have been Süss, and his parents are believed by many to have been Jewish.

65. Arendt, *Eichmann in Jerusalem,* 78.

66. Müller-Hill, *Murderous Science,* 49.

67. Arendt, *Eichmann in Jerusalem,* 100.

68. Ibid., 102.

69. Aly, *Endlösung,* 364–66.

70. See Arendt, *Eichmann in Jerusalem.*

71. Aly, *Endlösung,* 359.

72. Gudrun Schwarz, *Die nationalsozialistischen Lager,* 211.

73. Ibid., 248, 252–54.

74. MPGA, I Abt., Rep. 1A, Nr. 2400/1, Bl. 159–67, 5–6. The author has taken a certain liberty in translating the last sentence to make it more understandable in English.

75. BAK, R73, Archiv Signatur. 15966.

76. See Verschuer, "Anomalien der Körperform."

77. MPGA, I Abt., Rep. 1A, Nr. 2400/1, Bl. 159–67, 7–8.

78. MPGA, V a, Abt., Rep. 0016, Nr. 1, 2, or 11, Oct. 16, 1942. Fischer lost his only son in the war at this time and suffered from knee problems. He wanted to retire to the small town where he had maintained a home. He may also have seen the direction the institute was taking and the coming defeat of Germany and decided to protect himself from liability.

79. Klee, *Auschwitz, die NS Medizin und ihre Opfer,* 450–56.

80. Ibid., 457.

81. Ibid., 464–67.

82. Kater, *Doctors under Hitler,* 234.

83. Quoted in Rose, *"Den Rauch hatten wir täglich vor Augen,"* 243.

84. See Magnussen, *Rassen- und bevölkerungspolitisches Rüstzeug.*

85. Klee, *Auschwitz, die NS Medizin und ihre Opfer,* 486.

86. "Erinnerung an den Teufel," *Der Spiegel,* June 11, 2001, 224–25.

CHAPTER SEVEN

The End of the War and the Aftermath

The End of the War in Germany and Poland

The concentration camps in Europe were filled to overflowing. Death camps were established in former Poland. From 1942 until the last months of the war, millions were annihilated. Unlike concentration camps that were located in the Altreich as well as in occupied lands, where prisoners' labor was valued for at least several months before their death, the main purpose of the death camps was to kill people sent there as soon as possible. Exceptions were made for prisoners who had a skill that was especially needed, strength to do the work in the crematoria or elsewhere, or those who were being used for experimentation. Most, numbering eventually in the millions, were eliminated quickly.

Some of these death camps were liberated by the Soviet forces in the summer of 1944, but others, like Auschwitz, were left intact for another half year. The first death camp to be liberated was Majdanek, where about 400,000 prisoners had died, most of them Jews.[1] This was followed by Belzec, Sobibór, and Treblinka. The news of Majdanek was widely circulated by the Soviets, but they did not publicize the other liberations. Many in the western nations were still questioning the truthfulness of the reports they did receive until almost the end of the war.[2]

The Soviet Union had suffered tremendous losses in its homeland, and soldiers had battled through their own devastated country before arriving in Poland. By one estimate, the Soviets suffered seven and a half million military war dead between 1939 and 1945.[3] By the end of summer 1944, the troops were exhausted and having difficulty with their supply lines. The distance that supplies had to travel from inside the Soviet Union to the Vistula in occupied Poland presented them with the same kind of dilemma the Germans had faced going in the other direction. In addition, the German troops had destroyed the railroad tracks as they retreated, leaving only roads over which to transport supplies. Whether for logistic reasons or those of strategy, the Soviet troops stopped their offensive in the middle of Poland until January 1945. For those still in captivity, the halt in the Soviet offensive was disastrous. Thousands more were annihilated before the Red army resumed its push westward and liberated Auschwitz on January 27.

Those few who survived the Polish camps and experienced liberation were faced with a desperate search for a safe place to go. It was not always possible to return home, for many villages, towns, and cities had been decimated, and often all of a survivor's relatives had been killed. Jewish survivors in particular faced absolute devastation of family and community. Even if other family members had survived, individuals usually could not find each other immediately. Anti-Semitism, simple hatred of the returnees, and fear that they might once again claim what was theirs made parts of the Polish population vicious enemies of Jewish survivors and turned some places into death traps. Many survivors sought safe havens where they could and had little means of communicating with others who might have survived.

Like the Jews, the Roma had been targeted throughout Europe by the Nazis as a "biological group" for whom annihilation did not need to be justified on any other grounds.[4] They had been targets of despicable anthropological investigations, partly for their physical characteristics, which were considered exotic, and partly for their cultural patterns, which were viewed as asocial. Central to the persecution of the Roma was Robert Ritter, an educational psychologist and medical doctor with a specialty in child psychiatry. He hired many anthropologists for his Research Institute for Racial Hygiene and Population Biology. He wanted them to study the "Gypsies" because they presented such a particular case; coming from India, they should have been considered Indo-European, one of the Aryan peoples. Among the anthropologists hired by Ritter were Adolf Würth, Gerhard Stein, Sophie Ehrhardt, and Eva Justin, several of whom had earned doctorates in anthropology by writing dissertations on "Gypsies."[5] Their research on genealogies had facilitated the roundups of Roma throughout Germany, and their anthropological interests in the exotic ways of the Gypsies paved the way for special attention to be given to this victim group. In Auschwitz and Ravensbrück, Roma were incarcerated in special barracks, "observed" in "family camps," subjected to medical experimentation, and finally murdered en masse within a few days in the gas chambers.

At the end of the war in Germany, corpses, not only in death camps but also in concentration camps, could no longer be disposed of quickly enough, and they piled up inside and outside barracks and sheds, or were stacked like cordwood, or were thrown into pits. The number of deaths from starvation, epidemics, and exposure within the camps was only exceeded by the loss of life on death marches, in which hundreds of thousands of human wrecks were driven across Germany by their captors in the face of advancing Allied troops. In the last months of the war, there was no German policy for handling the concentration camp prisoners; there was only the order to evacuate the camps and get rid of the evidence. Driving the prisoners in their rags with no proper footwear on forced marches through the late winter and early spring weather, with no plan for obtaining food and water, was a strategy meant to kill as many of them as possible. The remnants of human beings from the camps died or were shot by the side of the road or in woods and fields where they stopped for the night. Death was everywhere.

The German population had a long history of witnessing. They had seen people simply disappear from their neighborhoods. They had seen the trains loaded with their Jewish neighbors on their way to "resettlement" in the east. They had worked beside slave laborers in factories and on their farms. Many had taken the opportunity to hire such laborers from nearby concentration camps to help with their gardening or manual labor around their homes. Germans were exposed to a large number of concentration camps and a huge number of outer camps and commandos spread throughout the countryside and in towns and cities. Most Germans could not claim total ignorance of the camps' existence or some knowledge of their true nature. They had witnessed brutality before and had suffered themselves under bombing raids, food shortages, and work quotas. Finally, many also witnessed the forced marches of the concentration camp survivors, and most Germans were terrified of the prisoners' illness, anger, and thirst for justified revenge.[6]

Fifty years later, on a day of commemoration at the former site of the concentration camp Langenstein Zwieberge, a bus tour took a group of survivors and their supporters along the route of the forced 1945 death march. Throughout Germany in the last days of the war, concentration camps were abandoned and the prisoners were literally marched to death on Germany's roads.

As we passed through one village, an Italian survivor insisted that the bus stop and we get out. He recognized a particular street and house. He said, "Here is where we stumbled through the streets, and the people threw water at us and yelled at us to hurry on and get out of their town. They wouldn't let us stop. But I saw a place where I could hide and got over the fence into the garden." As he showed us the exact house, an elderly woman came to the gate to ask what we wanted. We explained that this gentleman was a former prisoner in a Nazi camp and was retracing his route on the death march. She told us to go away. As we talked to her a little longer, she said that she remembered that event and did not want to see any survivor. He had put her family in danger, even though he had only hid for a few minutes. A German in the tour group suggested to me that the townspeople might have thrown water on the prisoners on a warm day to cool them. I asked the Italian survivor what he thought of this idea, and he screamed in a fury, "Idiocy! They wanted to get rid of us!"[7]

Very few prisoners escaped from death marches. They were often hunted down by young Nazis, their parents, or their grandparents. Some 1,016 prisoners, for example, were killed on April 13, 1945, in Gardelegen. The events of this particular massacre involved prisoners from many different concentration camps who were gathered together and marched until their SS guards had to stop to rest. Not knowing what to do with these human remnants, the guards consulted with the town leaders, who led them to a huge barn. When all the prisoners were inside, the captors threw gasoline on the hay and onto the prisoners themselves and then set fire to the barn. With all the exits blocked and men with rifles guarding on all sides to shoot anyone who might try to escape, the prisoners were burned alive.[8] Those few prisoners who had managed to escape before the others were herded into the barn met with various fates. Some were hunted like animals, while others were taken in by German townspeople, who through pity or in the hope of getting a reprieve from the approaching Allied forces, hid them until they could be liberated.[9]

Liberation, when it came in the spring of 1945, arrived on different days in different places for the slave laborers of the Third Reich. As Allied forces pushed through Germany, they found and liberated survivors in camps, the horror of which they could scarcely fathom. Often, they could smell the decomposing bodies before the camp came into view. Some of the prisoners appeared scarcely human in their catatonic state of near death. Others rushed the liberators with a frenzy that almost caused the soldiers to panic.[10] In Germany, 750,000 prisoners survived the concentration camps, only a fraction of whom were Jewish.[11] Few of the Jews deported to the east by 1942 had survived. Germany was almost *Judenrein,* free of Jews, just as the Nazis had wished.

There were nearly eight million slave laborers in the Third Reich in August 1944, and at the end of the war, they began to escape their bonds and hide out in cities and in the countryside.[12] Many lived by plundering what they could. If caught, they were immediately executed. As the Allies came into areas, the slave laborers were set free and could try to return home, although all transportation systems were in ruins. Many did not want to go home to the east and found themselves labeled "displaced persons," awaiting a plan for resettlement. Soviet citizens, both slave laborers in farms and factories and prisoners of war in concentration camps, were ordered by their government to return immediately.[13] The Soviet Union placed them under suspicion of having collaborated with the enemy. Many were imprisoned again in the Soviet Union for this imagined crime.

The End of the IDO

In the beginning of June 1944, plans were under way to move the IDO out of Kraków, which was in the hands of the German War Advisory Office under the direction of Dr. Erich Pietsch.[14] Not everyone connected with the IDO was evacuated from Kraków at this time. As all the other Germans were packing and leaving, Dr. Erhard Riemann was still attempting to show the German presence! Riemann, the director of the SRV, was authorized to mount an exhibition in Kraków's art museum on the topic of German Volkstum in the GG. It was to be a traveling exhibit, shown first in Kraków and then moved to the Altreich. The exhibit was closed two days after it opened in Kraków.[15]

The SRV was declared to have a "decisive meaning for the war"; its staff and documents needed to be protected along with those sections having to do with the technical sciences.[16] In order to be outside the range of the battles raging on the eastern front, materials would be stored in a safe place in two "castles," which were actually large villas, in the County (*Gau*) Bayreuth, in the district of Cham. One villa, Schloss Zandt, was privately owned by Ernst Mik, who voluntarily or involuntarily relinquished it to the county. Mik was paid 600 RM a month for the property, concluding the deal on July 21, 1944, and had six weeks to remove his belongings.[17] A week later, there was more urgency, and the fine points of land transfer were forgotten, as the following memo from the director of the IDO shows:

> To the Leadership of the Gau, Bayreuth: . . . Because of the military situation the storage must be carried out immediately. Please allow the takeover of Schloss Miltach for the storage of the library and private quarters in Miltach and Zandt. Also it is requested in case Mik hesitates, [that you] threaten police eviction of Zandt, for trucks with important war-related materials are arriving now.
>   Dr. Coblitz[18]

Schloss Miltach was more difficult to obtain. It was in the hands of an elderly woman whose arrogant son, who referred to himself as "Dr. Dr. Edwin Oertel,"[19] had fled from Berlin to Starnberg am See, a village near Munich. He came to Cham to handle the matters involving the requisition of the property. He informed Dr. Coblitz that the castle had been used to house the art collection of his father, which was one of the most extensive private collections in Germany. Furthermore, he maintained, with the destruction of so many treasures in national galleries, such a collection demanded even more protection.[20]

The IDO wanted to take eight rooms, which, according to Dr. Oertel, would need repair, including the cleaning of the fireplaces, installation of lights, telephone, and new windows. Certainly, while this was going on, the rooms would be of little use, and the paintings had to be protected. He complained that the IDO staff had thrown his belongings, which he had removed from Berlin and had stored in the castle, unceremoniously into one room. There they were "piled as high as mountains" and had been damaged in the process. Cabinets and cupboards, as well as silverware and dishes, had been put to use by the new inhabitants of the castle without his permission. He was very angry and worried about his treasures.

By this time, there was a general order in effect that no building, including renovations, could be started by any government agency. The scientists at Schloss Zandt, however, wrote to the Organization Todt, the logistics agency of the Nazi government, to express their dire need for building onto the villa. "The chemical-physical part of the Institute that is stored at Zandt is one of the few such research institutes that is not out of commission due to bombs."[21] Arrangements were made to bring chemicals, equipment, books, and documents through the customs at the border of what is now the Czech Republic without paying any costs. By the end of the month, materials were being stored also in the dance hall of the Old Post Tavern in Zandt.[22]

The situation with Dr. Oertel did not resolve itself easily. He vowed to tell of the IDO's scandalous misappropriation of his property to authorities in both Berlin and Munich. These threats were taken seriously and were the subject of a report within the IDO, which said that this defamation would be "embarrassing to the staff and damaging to the Institute."[23] With great care, the staff tried to placate Dr. Oertel but finally used the castle as they intended.

There was no heat in most of the rooms of the villa, so the staff of the IDO, twelve men and fifteen women, had to find quarters in the town. During the day, they worked in unheated rooms.[24] Dr. Oertel continued to plague the staff. One day in October 1944, he barged into the room of one of the staff and shouted at Dr. Hildebrandt, "This isn't even a Polish mess here anymore; it is a Jewish mess!" The staff assured him that some of the materials had been sorted and boxed for storage and placed in the front hall, such as those from the SRV, at which point he screamed incessantly about the "Jewish mess."[25]

In November 1944, prisoners from the Flossenbürg Concentration Camp were ordered to go to Kraków to finish packing the IDO for their storage in

Schloss Miltach in southern Germany, where IDO materials were stored at the end of the war. Author's personal photo collection.

the west.[26] As the goods and even more evacuees arrived in Cham, rooms were in short supply. Dr. Josef Sommerfeldt and his wife, who had joined him, were relegated to two beds in a bakery, while others stayed with the blacksmith, the midwife, or the school teacher.[27] Most of the men were called into some kind of military service. Sommerfeldt was exempted because of his highly valued anti-Semitic writing, which was still considered vital to the war effort, even with publication possibilities extremely limited.[28] Dr. Oertel temporarily forgot his worries about the state of the villa and worried instead about the safety of the structure from air attacks. Under the American occupation, IDO director Coblitz made payments to his staff until June 1945, and back rent on the villa was turned over to Dr. Oertel at that time as well.

The End of the KWIA

Otmar von Verschuer replaced Eugen Fischer as director at the KWIA on October 1, 1942, with the greatest respect and affection for the "Father of Hereditary Studies," but from that time onward, Verschuer put his own stamp on the institute. His relationship with the younger members of his staff grew, and the importance of the concentration camp connection as an unlimited resource of human "material" became pivotal. Money appeared to be no

problem. Josef Mengele, one of those assistants, had a close personal relationship with Verschuer. He ate dinner at the Verschuer home and considered the
older man almost a father figure.[29] When Mengele was in Berlin, he spent
almost every day at the KWIA. The relationship between the two men remained close while Mengele was at Auschwitz, but evidence of any communication between them disappeared when each man sought to save himself
at the end of the war.

Mengele was one of the many anthropologists or SS doctors trained in
anthropology who made their way to Auschwitz. Professor Abel had made
the case to the SS in 1943 that these anthropologists could look at prisoners
of war in the concentration camps and find some, particularly among the
Russians, who would be quite acceptable for *Eindeutschung,* or "Germanization."[30] This would solve a big problem for the military authorities, because
all soldiers in the German Army had to be "Aryan." Given the great need for
frontline combatants, this idea was seized upon, and soon anthropologists
were asked to assess the "human material" found in the camps.

Anthropologists had another job at Auschwitz. Among the first anthropologists the SS intended to send there were Heinrich Rübel, Hans Endres,
and Hans Fleischhacker. The purpose of the assignment was to examine 150
persons that Adolf Eichmann had identified as being "of interest," perhaps
for their so-called Jewish characteristics. With this anthropological certification, they could be sent to the gas chambers and their body parts and skeletons sent to Professor Hirt in Strasburg for his anthropological collection.[31]

Karin Magnussen, although a zoologist by training, worked for the KWIA
as one of Verschuer's assistants. She took pictures of the eyes of twins at the
KWIA before they were sent to Auschwitz. Later, she obtained specimens
from Mengele in Auschwitz to help pursue her research on heterochromia
of the iris, a condition in which an individual has eyes of different colors. One
report by an inmate physician indicates that six twins and a family with eight
members were selected from the Gypsy Camp and killed so that their eyes
could be "harvested" for Magnussen's and Verschuer's research.[32] Sufficient
numbers of eyes for her research were sent to Berlin to assure that the research
agenda of the KWIA would be supported.[33]

Meanwhile, in Berlin, Verschuer understood the danger that the KWIA
faced from bombings in and around the city. As early as July 1943, he began
to search for places to store research data and specimens.[34] On November 23,
1943, the bombing in Berlin was so intense that the main part of the city center, a major church, the Philharmonic, and other historic sites were lost. All
of the men in the institute were called to protect the city. This left Magnussen, as a single woman, alone to lead what research could be conducted. More

materials of the KWIA were stored to the north at the estate of one of Kurt Gottschaldt friends in Mecklenberg. Still, the institute remained open, and staff members pitched in to secure the roof, the windows, and the other vulnerable parts of the edifice.

Fischer, living in active retirement in Freiburg, finally had to evacuate his home and newly designed and constructed work space shortly before Christmas 1944. Bombing had finally destroyed much of Freiburg, and Fischer feared he would be first in line to be taken as a hostage or called as a witness. He found shelter with his unmarried daughter in a village in southern Germany. Shortly thereafter, Verschuer sought refuge in the large farm his family owned, only a few kilometers away from Fischer's retreat. Both men continued their work, Fischer writing his memoirs, and Verschuer writing the year-end report for the KWIA and making inventories of the institute, which was now widely scattered.[35]

At the same time, Mengele rushed to leave Auschwitz as the Russians approached. After all, his records showed that the survival rate of his twins was less than 10 percent.[36] He was certainly going to have to pay a price for his research. On January 17, 1945, Mengele destroyed records, said good-bye to his assistant, Dr. Puzyna, the Polish anthropologist who was also a prisoner, and left Auschwitz.[37] Starting his long journey, Mengele went first to the concentration camp Gross Rosen, where he stayed until February 18. During this period, Verschuer left Berlin with documents and destroyed his correspondence with Mengele.[38] Mengele then joined a field hospital, where he stayed until May 1945.

One cannot avoid speaking of Max Planck, the director of the entire KWI for the entire period of the Second World War. A renowned physicist, he was no more involved with the KWIA than one would expect of a general director, or what today would be known as a CEO. Planck was not an early Nazi enthusiast but managed to speak in ways that were acceptable to many. For instance, he was most unhappy when, in 1920, anti-Semitic attacks prevented Albert Einstein from speaking at the hundredth anniversary meeting of the German Natural Scientists and Physicians, and he objected publicly. In finding someone to take Einstein's place, he wrote that the change in speakers had its advantages. "Namely, it serves to demonstrate that the theory of relativity is not exclusively Jewish, and it takes the wind out of the sails of anyone still wont to think that the entire principle of relativity is nothing but an artful personal advertisement for Mr. Einstein."[39]

Planck is known to have gone to Hitler after he took power to tell him that the Nobel Prizes so often bestowed upon KWI scientists would be fewer if Jewish scientists were excluded from their professional pursuits. Hitler was not willing to accept this argument and, indeed, felt challenged then and in the future to assert Germany's ability to prosper without Jews. This private meeting, from which no minutes were taken, has been taken as an icon of Planck's "resistance" and undoubtedly has been promoted by those who had something to gain from the retention of the reputation of a major German scientist. In fact, Planck refused to protest the dismissal of German Jewish scientists and other employees from the KWI, stating, "If today 30 professors stand up and protest . . . then tomorrow 150 will come to declare their solidarity with Hitler because they want the [vacated] positions."[40]

Planck's son, Erwin, was involved with people who were active Nazi resisters. After the attempt on Hitler's life in the summer of 1944, Erwin was arrested and sentenced to death. The elder Planck had ties to Himmler, perhaps through Himmler's interests in the KWIA-Auschwitz human experiments but more likely through the entire war effort, of which the KWI was a vital part. The KWI, a cooperating institute within the Third Reich, could be called upon to conduct a variety of research and scientific or quasi-scientific tasks as the need arose. Certainly, the KWI had also cooperated with Himmler in propagating botanical plants in Auschwitz, which would seem innocuous except for the fact that, in concentration camps, human ashes were often used as fertilizer.[41]

Planck believed that these ties to Himmler could save his son. This was not the case, however, and Erwin Planck was executed on January 23, 1945.[42]

War Trials

The Nuremberg Trials

Beginning in 1942, there was talk of a military tribunal that would be set up when the war came to an end.[43] This idea gained momentum as the end came into sight, and it was decided by the Allied Powers that the trials would take place in Germany despite the many problems this decision presented. Germans, particularly those of the right wing, referred to it as the "Tribunal of the Victors."[44] In general, questions of justice and questions of the rationality of conducting such a series of trials in a war-torn country were raised on many sides. There were also questions of the Allied bombing of civilian population centers without clear military targets. Would the Allies set themselves up for scrutiny?

For many of the crimes of the Third Reich, no single geographical jurisdiction was relevant; they simply occurred across prior or current national boundaries. An agreement was reached in August 1945 to hold trials for crimes with no specific geographic jurisdiction at the International Military Court in Nuremberg. Those suspected war criminals whose crimes were committed in a particular location would be sent back to those countries for trial. Four Nazi organizations were also charged: the political leadership of the Nazi Party, the Security Service, the Gestapo, and the SS. The Nuremberg Trials would concentrate on war crimes, crimes against peace, and crimes against humanity.

The trials began on November 20, 1945, and lasted for ten months. Twenty-one of the high-ranking Nazi Party officials were tried. Judges were chosen from the four Allied countries, the United States, France, Great Britain, and the Soviet Union, each of which had different legal codes. A meeting prior to the trials set the rules for the International Military Tribunal.

The prosecutors were selected by the Allies, and the defenders were German. The defense attorneys did not have the resources of the prosecutors and thus prepared their defenses based on precedents in international law.[45] Death sentences were given to eleven of the defendants, including Hans Frank, who had been governor of the GG. He was the only one of the twenty-one defendants who expressed guilt and shame. He said, "A thousand years will pass and still this guilt of Germany will not have been erased."[46]

The Doctor Trials

The series of trials legally referred to as the *United States of America v. Karl Brandt et al.* brought twenty-three defendants, mostly physicians, to the court in Nuremberg in December 1946. Dr. Leonardo Conti, the head of public health, took his own life in 1945 and so could not be tried. The trials concluded eight months later, with death sentences given to seven defendants, including Karl Brandt and Rudolf Brandt, who had conducted concentration camp experiments, and Viktor Brack, who had run the far-reaching euthanasia action, the T4 program.

Accounts of the concentration camp experiments in high-altitude and low-pressure effects on human subjects were brought before the court. Freezing experiments, malaria experiments, and mustard gas experiments were also described in detail as the defendants who had conducted them stood before the judges. Victims and witnesses testified about the pain experienced by female victims in Ravensbrück and the victims of the sea-water experiments, the typhus experiments, and the sterilization experiments.[47]

The Soviets, in their part of the now-divided Germany, wanted to have their own trials for doctors, assistants, and nurses. Some of these people were already in custody, particularly those from the Sonnenstein institution outside of Dresden. People who suspected that family members had been murdered through euthanasia actions came forward to make serious charges.

These questions needed to be resolved. Some of them were resolved through trials, but many suspected perpetrators were summarily imprisoned in "special camps" on the sites of the old concentration camps.

The anthropological profession in Germany, which had done so much to prepare the way for the experiments and had trained the doctors in the theory and practice of "life unworthy of life," was not specifically cited in the courts during any of the trials. How many of the doctors had been trained by anthropologists in racial hygiene? How many anthropologists advised on the experiments or used the information from them? It would have been appropriate to ask these questions and to bring those responsible before the judges. In the end, among those who received sentences, four were later brought to the United States by the U.S. military under "Operation Paperclip" to enhance the U.S. biological warfare capability. Others went on to employment in various capacities or continued to practice medicine in Germany or work in the German pharmaceutical industry.[48]

The trials of those responsible for slave labor ended in convictions for many of the SS but for only a few industrialists. Fritz Sauckel and Oswald Pohl, who organized the slave labor forces in Germany during the war, were sentenced to death and executed. Albert Speer received a sentence of twenty years. Himmler committed suicide in the face of certain hanging. The anthropologists who had sorted the people according to their "racial" profiles were very seldom identified as perpetrators in regard to slave labor. It was their decisions, however, and their development of policies and procedures that had decided the fate of millions.

Of the industrialists who had used slave labor by the hundreds of thousands, few suffered for long. In 1951, John J. McCloy, the U.S. high commissioner in Germany, announced an amnesty and set them free.[49] It took almost sixty years after the war ended for slave laborers to begin to receive pitiful amounts of compensation for their suffering in the war years. Few alive were in any position to go through the complicated process to claim the funds. It was, and remains, a travesty.

Anthropologists after the War

Hiding and working on a farm in southern Germany for a few years, Josef Mengele eventually escaped to South America, where he continued to live out of sight for the rest of his life. Any communication he might have had with his former colleagues is not known. He died by drowning in 1979.[50]

Planck, who had suffered tremendous personal losses as a result of the war, stood by his old colleagues after the war, despite the fact that he knew the nature of the research and applied work they had done. In at least two cases, Planck intervened for particularly odious colleagues. Ernst Rüdin was a psychiatrist who had sought to prove that mental illness was hereditary and advocated the elimination of people with such illnesses as a necessity for a healthy nation. He had been one of the intellectual supporters of the euthanasia program. As director of the Kaiser Wilhelm Institute of Genealogy in Munich, he directed the construction of "genetic registries" that played a major role in determining who would live and who would die.[51] Planck urged that Rüdin be freed because he knew "that [Rüdin] never allowed political motives to influence his scientific work." Planck also protected Ernst Telschow, who had been a member of the Nazi Party since 1933, had held important positions in the Third Reich, and had a leading role in the KWI.[52] Planck's usefulness to his old Nazi colleagues came to an end in 1947 when he died at nearly ninety.

Perhaps because of Planck's legendary meeting with Hitler, or because his son had died as an opponent of Hitler, or because Planck was such an outstanding physicist, his reputation survived after the war. Yet, it was Planck who, as early as 1936, signed his name on the annual report of the KWI in which this statement about the accomplishments of the KWIA appeared:

> The inner design of the Institute shows the single leadership of a director under whom it is divided in three departments that appear in the name of the Institute. However, the development of the science of man, not to mention the work of the Institute itself, has simply made itself into Human Heredity. The old empirical anthropology is dead. Descriptive racial studies alone are worthless. Human heredity studies [*Menschliche Erblehre*] encompasses the entire field. Anthropology, which includes race studies, is biological, not descriptive science. Without heredity studies there are no racial studies, but simply pure measuring technology or history. And racial hygiene and eugenics are applied human heredity studies. So, dividing this institute into three divisions is only an administrative technicality; under their leader, the work field and the work procedures are not different from one another, rather they complement and crosscut each other constantly.[53]

Today, the KWG is known as the Max Planck Society (*Max Planck Gesellschaft*), and numerous schools and other institutions throughout Germany are named for him as well. Yet, this man signed the yearly reports of the KWIA when he was the director, with information in his possession about the activities that were undertaken. He knew.

In 1946, efforts began to rebuild the KWIA. Fischer and Verschuer corresponded about the possibilities of moving it out of the city of Berlin and perhaps to Verschuer's familiar university in Frankfurt am Main, where Fischer felt more certain that the Americans would protect the institute.[54] This was not so easy, however, because in Berlin, opposition to the further involvement of Fischer and Verschuer was growing. Denunciations of their roles in the Nazi era came from the colleagues who had been dismissed in 1933, as well as from a few remaining colleagues in the KWIA who had reservations. Kurt Gottschaldt and Hans Nachtsheim were most likely to benefit from the dismissal of Verschuer's claim to a continuing interest in the directorship.

In order to proceed further with their influence as anthropologists, Fischer and Verschuer had to present themselves to the occupying forces for denazification. Fischer informed Verschuer in a letter that he wanted to go through with this intimidating procedure and submit an affidavit of his noncomplicity. "I am of the opinion that the time has come that I do that. Don't you think so? But I don't want to send it in without going over a few points with you first."[55]

Interestingly enough, the correspondence between Verschuer and Fischer is missing from the archives for the period in which they continued to correspond about their presentation of "facts" to the denazification offices. At this time, however, Gottschaldt and Nachtsheim were joined by Robert Havemann, who instituted a public denunciation of the KWIA's Auschwitz connection and Verschuer's part in it. Gottschaldt and Havemann had become communists, and Havemann became both a citizen and a critic of the GDR (East Germany).

Verschuer attempted to make his case to the new director of the KWG, Otto Hahn. "You see the justification of my point of view. . . . it deals with not only my person but also my Institute and my science and how it was and will continue to be."[56] However, Hahn decided to suspend Verschuer and suggested that he rehabilitate himself.

Verschuer may have prepared himself for denazification interviews, but in any case, he was sought out by the American Counter Intelligence Corps in his retreat at the family estate for questioning. As a result of the interrogations, Verschuer was restricted to the village, and to prevent him from moving around Germany or out of the country, his passport was taken. However, in a month, the passport was returned, and all restrictions were lifted.

Verschuer's troubles were not over, however. Otto Hahn set up a commission at the KWG to investigate charges against him. Under the leadership of a judge, Kurt von Lewinski of the KWG's Institute of Law, four members of the KWG, Otto Warburg, Havemann, Gottschaldt, and Nachtsheim, contemplated not only questions of specific guilt but the scientific value of Verschuer's body of work. Their decision was severe: Not only was Verschuer's link to Auschwitz established but he was judged to be a "racial fanatic." Thus ended Verschuer's career at the KWIA.[57] Hermann Muckermann, who had been a racist even in the 1920s, became the new director of the KWG for

Applied Anthropology, which was still heavily influenced by his interest in eugenics.

Verschuer successfully completed the denazification process in November 1946, was declared a "fellow traveler," and fined 600 RM.[58] He was free to continue his career, even if it would not be in Berlin. Fischer completed his denazification a little later and was fined 300 RM for being a fellow traveler.[59]

Muckermann's first report as director of the reinstituted Institute of Anthropology in the Sciences and Humanities (*Institut für angewandte Anthropologie*) summarized the outcomes of denazification:

> Today Eugen Fischer is back in his hometown of Freiburg im Breisgau, where he is continuing his life's work as one of our foremost anthropologists. Otmar von Verschuer, to whom twin research is indebted for many great advances, left Berlin-Dahlem in 1945. Today, as Professor of Human Genetics, he directs a newly founded institute dedicated to its study at the University of Münster. Fritz Lenz, whose contributions to shaping the study of human heredity, and its applications, are very highly valued, also left Berlin-Dahlem in 1945. Today, he directs an institute for the study of human heredity in conjunction with his teaching at the University of Göttingen. Hans Nachtsheim stayed at our institute right up to the end. Today he directs the Institute for Comparative Biology and Pathology of Heredity within the German Research University and in conjunction with a chair of General Biology and Genetics at the Free University in Berlin-Dahlem.[60]

Of those Muckermann did not mention, Karin Magnussen was certainly of note. She went on to become a teacher in Bremen and engaged in a lively correspondence with Fischer. She wanted to continue to study the eyes of Roma, but Fischer advised strictly against that. "If the clan were not such a criminal society," wrote Magnussen, "I would try to work further on them, for there are Auschwitz Gypsies still walking around here whom one could ask, but I do not want to make contact with them." Fischer replied, "I want to advise you in general—and you allow me to give advice, for you see that I help you where I can—that you still refrain from every attempt to publish Gypsy material, whether about living or dead for a time."[61]

Efforts to explore Magnussen's culpability continued throughout her life, but with the help of institutional interests, she was able to live to be almost ninety without any public acknowledgment of her involvement with Auschwitz. In 1952, she was able to report to Fischer:

> I attended a conference [Congress for Research of the Constitution] again for the first time [since the war]. It was extremely pleasant how our Dahlem School [KWIA], that people had [tried to discredit], again stands in first place. No Frenchman made sarcastic remarks about us anthropologists as they had before;

there were none there. I was heartily greeted by the chair, Kretschmer, as the most senior of the anthropologists; Verschuer held the first session, and his two assistants, Duis and Gerhardt, both of whom were my students in Dahlem, gave the first lectures. I was named "Honorable Member" of the Society. So, Dahlem blooms further![62]

The IDO

After the war, the staff of the SRV went their separate ways. Eberhard Geyer, who had provided the IDO with his students, Elfriede Fliethmann and Dora Kahlich, had died on the Russian front in 1940. Fliethmann, who had left Kraków in 1943 with her husband, relocated in Berlin. She received more education in history and then became the director of a girls' school. One of her grandchildren was adopted from an Asian country, which apparently never elicited any racial commentary from her. She supported a more liberal and tolerant position as she grew older and apparently never told her family any details of her earlier work.[63]

To the best of my knowledge, none of the anthropologists in the IDO were brought to court after the war for their work in Poland. Most went back to their previous jobs or developed a new line of work. Dora Kahlich's husband was killed in March 1944 in Poland on a tour of duty, and she never remarried. She became an independent consultant to the Viennese Paternity Court (*Österreichische Gerichte im Vaterschaftsachen*) until this system came to an end in the mid-1950s. She then became a private assistant to an anthropology professor. When she died, an obituary written by her colleague K. Tuppa, who had also been a convinced Nazi, described her career in sparkling terms, never mentioning the work she had done for the IDO. Tuppa euphemistically described Kahlich's work as follows: "One of her large series of research in a German village in Poland in the year 1942 delivered an extensive amount of material that however through the unfavorable times could not be analyzed."[64]

Most of the men in the SRV, such as Plügel and Sommerfeldt, disappeared. Erhard Riemann continued to write about the loss of "East Germany," which he defined as (postwar Polish) Prussia and Silesia.[65] In other words, in print, he continued to deny the validity of the postwar boundaries. However, his published documentation on German-Polish names, which he had gathered to support the work of racial judgments and used to place individuals on the DVL, appeared to offend no one.[66] He became a professor of German ethnology (*Volkskunde*) and linguistic research at the University of Kiel in 1964 and led the Commission for East German Ethnology.[67]

Peter-Heinz Seraphim, the vicious anti-Semite, went on to teach economics of Eastern Europe at the University of Munich in 1948. A prolific writer, Seraphim's dozen books are still on the Library of Congress shelves, written during and after the war. They bear such titles (translated into English) as "Economic Cooperatives in East Europe" (1950), "The Economy of East Germany before and after the Second World War" (1950), "East Germany and Today's Poland" (1954), and "The Expelled from Their Homeland [*Heimatvertriebene*] in the Soviet Zone of Germany" (1954). Like Riemann, Seraphim found an audience for his view that "East Germany" (Poland) had been "lost." By continuing to assert the name of Germany for Polish land, they made it clear that no matter what the boundaries were after the war, Germany legitimately laid claim to land east of the Oder-Neisse line. This point of view had a great deal of support in German academic circles, as it had before and during the war.[68]

Losses

It is a hopeless task to try to enumerate the millions of people lost either as combatants or civilians in Europe between 1933 and 1945. The attempted annihilation of the Jews and "Gypsies," while not totally succeeding according to Nazi plans, eliminated close to *seven million* people. It is truly impossible to say with certainty how many victims fell to the Nazis in any group. The best figures for the losses of life among Jews in Europe during the Third Reich are arrived at by comparing census figures before and after the war. The terrible disruption of family and community life can never be estimated. Into the generations following World War II, children of survivors have suffered the effects of their parents' terrible experiences. There is no way to conceptualize these losses, much less count them.

The losses among the Roma were unacknowledged following the war and have remained unfairly challenged by some Holocaust scholars on several grounds. Because many Roma were taken into custody initially for being "asocial," the misapprehension remains among some that they were not racially persecuted. Another misapprehension is that the Roma were not persecuted if they were "settled," not "wandering Gypsies." Of course, these are both totally false assumptions, and we now know that probably half a million Roma were lost in the Holocaust.[69] Many actions against human beings perpetrated by the Nazis were called "Jewish actions," but they swept up or targeted Roma as well. Therefore, in many ways, the tragedy of these people is both underestimated and misunderstood. For these reasons, it took four decades following the war before the Roma were legitimately considered a "victim group" and eligible for German government compensation.[70]

The murder of Polish intellectuals, teachers, and people with a higher education left that country after the war with a grim shortage of physicians and dentists, attorneys, teachers, professors, technicians, and clergy.[71] Other people who might have gone on to live out their life spans instead were murdered through euthanasia actions.

There are still other losses that are often overlooked that are worth discussing in the context of anthropological responsibility. They are the losses from the sterilization, *Lebensborn,* and forced evacuation programs in which anthropologists had a part.

Those Who Were Sterilized

Sterilization was the first of many actions that the anthropologists had supported in Nazi Germany. By the end of the war, an estimated 350,000 people had been sterilized.[72] For many years, the extent of this tragedy was not known. Victims who had survived the war did not always know what had happened to them. Often, they had been operated upon as children. Others were ashamed. Only when Klara Novak, a victim of sterilization herself, began to speak out and organize others to seek compensation did a general awareness of these crimes against both men and women become widespread.[73]

Novak's publication of oral histories, such as those that follow, was an important turning point.

> I was born in Hamburg in 1921. My older brother was a member of the Communist Party and was taken to the concentration camp Fuhlsbüttel and later to Auschwitz. For that reason it was claimed that my mother could not raise her children correctly, and she lost her right to keep her children. My sister and I were also blamed. My two sisters and I were sent to a home, and I, at age 10, to an orphanage. At age 15, I was sterilized. At that time my sisters were too.
>   . . . In the work camp Tiefstack we had to lay railroad tracks. I became the ward of Dr. Käthe Petersen when I was 21 years old. She brought me when I was 22 to the SS-bordello in the concentration camp Buchenwald. There I was very badly mishandled and beaten by SS people. One bit me so in the breast that I developed an infection that caused me to lose the breast. The other breast has been operated on twice. I still have scars on my head from the beatings that I received, and my hearing also suffered. I am 90 percent disabled.[74]

*   *   *

> I was born in January 1902 in Frankfurt am Main. After I left school, I got an apprenticeship in the fashion industry. At 17, I recognized with horror that I loved peo-

ple of my own sex. I couldn't believe it. Why me? But I couldn't get over it. The neighbors told my mother that it would have been better if I had been born a girl.

At 18, I left my parents' house. They couldn't take my ways and we had arguments. I couldn't take it. In 1930 I found a man with whom I lived for seven years. He was a Jew, and I also became acquainted with his parents at that time. They had a big textile company in Frankfurt. It was a quiet, beautiful friendship. Through betrayal, we were taken in 1937 and brought to a prison near Lüneburg. How my friend died, I can imagine. To this day, I never found out.

After serving my one-and-a-half-year sentence, I was not free, but with 20 other men was sent to the death camp Flossenbürg. There we were beaten, the hair shaved off, and then had to walk past an SS man who looked each of us over.

He said to me, "The Führer has reserved a *zentner* [50 kilograms] of coals for you too." They broke out my two gold teeth. . . . Now and then I was taken to the infirmary and treated by doctors. . . . I got a lot of injections. Once I woke up from the narcotics and felt a small sack on my stomach. I noticed that I had been operated on. It was done under narcotics, I never saw an operation room.[75]

Lebensborn

It is easy to overlook the *Lebensborn* program that the Nazis had initiated, for the human tragedy caused by the confiscation of children in occupied lands is less obvious than the actual deaths engendered by other Nazi acts. Yet, for many parents, their children were as lost to them as if they had died. Anthropologists, such as Grohmann from the KWIA, helped in the identification of these children.

Believing that "Aryan" children were needed for the Reich, Lebensborn had a two-pronged approach. On the one hand, women with such characteristics were encouraged to have sex with selected "Nordic" men and produce children for the state. These children would usually be adopted by families wanting and needing children in the Altreich. The second prong was the taking of children who appeared to be "Aryan" from their families or out of institutions and sending them to "home schools," meaning boarding schools in the Altreich, where they could be encultured and then adopted into German families. By some estimates, 10,000 to 15,000 children were "bred" in this way, and in Poland alone, 15,000 to 20,000 children were taken from their families.[76] The end of the war brought great pain to the families who searched for their lost children and pain also to those children conceived not within families but within little more than brothels. Those adopted by German families often were unloved when the adoptive parents did not find the state support they had been promised to help raise these children.

Forced Evacuations

Although it is confusing to compare the perpetrator population with the victim population, sometimes it is relevant. In the years following the war, thirteen million Germans were expelled from Eastern Europe. These people were referred to as the *Vertriebene,* the expelled. Tens of thousands died as they fled to Germany and Austria.[77] This has been the cause of tension for decades between Germany and her neighbors to the east. In discussions among the powerful Vertriebene lobby in Germany, the contribution of Third Reich policies, often developed and set in practice by Nazi anthropologists, is virtually never mentioned. Certainly, the hatred of Germans following the war would not have been engendered to the same extent had not the DVL, the "resettlement" of German Volk, and the forced enslavement of people from occupied lands been enforced during the years 1939–45. And with people like the postwar Riemann and Seraphim publicizing the tragic fate of expelled Germans, while at the same time asserting the legitimacy of German domination of land deemed by law to be Poland, these tensions and mistrust in the former German occupied lands is quite understandable.

Confrontation of the German Public

The German public was the recipient of the rage that filled the Allied soldiers as they marched into Germany, liberated the camps, and set up occupation administrations. People in towns throughout the country were given orders to bury or rebury the dead found in camps and sites where atrocities had taken place. In places like Nordhausen and Gardelegen, the American command told male citizens to come with shovels, wear their best clothes, and bring their best household linens. They then were marched to the mass graves, where they had to climb into them to dig out the half-decayed corpses, wrap them in linen, and carry them in slings made of tablecloths and sheets to new burial grounds. When this was completed, the women in the town had to come to view the bodies and lay flowers on the graves. Until they had done this, no food ration cards would be distributed.[78]

How were the Germans to attribute guilt and blame? They had all read for thirteen years, and even more, the propaganda about "life unworthy of life," of "lesser humans," of scientists who developed this "knowledge" and supported it through research carried on in universities and institutions of great intellectual reputation. Yet, the people who had occupied seats in those universities did not acknowledge their participation and leadership in the horrors of the Third Reich. With very few exceptions, these respected academics and intellectuals walked away and began new lives on the ashes and rubble of that which they had destroyed. The ashes from the crematoria throughout Germany and Poland literally are part of the soil. They were dumped in pits and spilled into lakes and rivers in more towns and villages than one can imagine. The rubble left of lives and lifeways, of families, neighborhoods, shtetls, and rural communities is the social context, the "ground," on which Europe now builds its future.

The memorial stone in front of Schloss Miltach, dedicated to the German soldiers who died in World War II. The victims of the Third Reich and the Jewish Holocaust are not mentioned. Author's personal photo collection.

Notes

1. Bridgman, *End of the Holocaust*, 18.

2. Ibid., 18–21.

3. Taylor and Shaw, *Third Reich Almanac*, 345.

4. Friedlander, *Origins of Nazi Genocide*, xii–xiii.

5. Lewy, *Nazi Persecution of the Gypsies*, 43–49.

6. These assertions come from the author's interviews with hundreds of Germans over a thirteen-year period.

7. These are the author's recollections, not verbatim quotations. This event took place in 1995.

8. Schafft and Zeidler, *Die KZ-Mahn- und Gedenkstätten in Deutschland*, 144–45. See also Stadtmuseum Gardelegen/Abteilung Gedenkstätte, *Tage im April*.

9. Personal survivor testimony in an interview with the author, Gedenkstätte Gardelegen, Apr. 1995.

10. See Bridgman, *End of the Holocaust*.

11. Weinmann, *Das nationalsozialistische Lagersystem*, 133.

12. Burleigh, *Third Reich*, 776.

13. Herbert, *History of Foreign Labor, 1880–1980*, 185.

14. UJA, IDO Collection, Folder 36, Letter from Oberkommando der Wehrmacht to IDO, June 1, 1944. (All UJA citations are to the IDO Collection.)

15. BAL, R52 IV, 142, Nr. 0220896/97.

16. BAL, R52 IV, 13C, 1. See also UJA, Folder 36, Auszug aus dem Schreiben, June 1, 1944.

17. UJA, Folder 2, Vertrag für das IDO.

18. Ibid., Fernschreiben vom July 29, 1944.

19. The double "Dr." title is used in Germany in instances where an individual obtains two doctorates.

20. UJA, Folder 2, Letter from Dr. Oertel to Dr. Coblitz, Aug. 28, 1944, 1–3.

21. UJA, Folder 36, Letter from Dr. Coblitz to Organization Todt Bayreuth, Aug. 17, 1944.

22. UJA, Folder 2, Letter from Dr. Coblitz to Transport Unternehmen Scherbauer (Cham), July 29, 1944.

23. Ibid., Bericht, Aug. 30, 1944, 1–2.

24. Ibid. See also UJA, Folder 2, Landeskunde to Bürgermeister, Oct. 28, 1944.

25. UJA, Folder 2, Abschrift Riemann to Coblitz, Oct. 23, 1944, 2.

26. Goguel, "Über die Mitwirkung deutscher Wissenschaftler am Okkupationsregime in Polen im Zweiten Weltkrieg," 170, and Anhang 3, doc. 11b, 132.

27. UJA, Folder 2, Letter from Dr. Riemann to Forstverwaltung, Kötzting, Oct. 9, 1944.

28. Goguel, "Über die Mitwirkung deutscher Wissenschaftler am Okkupationsregime in Polen im Zweiten Weltkrieg," 162.

29. Matalon Lagnado, *Children of the Flames*, 48.

30. Lösch, *Rasse als Konstrukt*, 402.

31. Ibid., 403.

32. Lewy, *Nazi Persecution of the Gypsies*, 160.

33. Lösch, *Rasse als Konstrukt*, 410–15.

34. Ibid., 423.

35. Ibid., 427.

36. Matalon Lagnado, *Children of the Flames*, 257.

37. Posner and Ware, *Mengele*, 57–58. Dr. Martyna Puzyna, born in 1913, had also been employed by the IDO starting in January 1942, according to documents gathered by the Polish underground and available at the UJA. She and two other Polish assistants in the IDO were caught smuggling documents out of the institute and were sent to Auschwitz. Only Puzyna survived. This information was translated by a colleague in Poland from the Polish journal *Cracovia*.

38. Ibid., 59.

39. Quoted in Stern, *Einstein's German World*, 49.

40. Quoted in ibid., 53.

41. Klee, *Deutsche Medizin im Dritten Reich*, 378–79. Information was gathered at memorial site seminars, particularly Neuengamme.

42. Stern, *Einstein's German World*, 57–58.

43. Kettenacker, "Die Behandlung der Kriegsverbrecher als anglo-amerikanisches Rechtsproblem," 20.

44. Steinbach, "Der Nürnberger Prozess gegen die Hauptkriegsverbrecher," 33.

45. Taylor and Shaw, *Third Reich Almanac*, 243.

46. Quoted in Botting et al., *Aftermath*, 66.

47. Annas and Grodin, *Nazi Doctors and the Nuremberg Code*, 71–84.

48. Ibid., 106–7.

49. Rosenbaum, *Prosecuting Nazi War Criminals*, 86.

50. Weiss, *Biographisches Lexikon zum Dritten Reich*, 316.

51. Annas and Grodin, *Nazi Doctors and the Nuremberg Code*, 20.

52. Klee, *Deutsche Medizin im Dritten Reich*, 368.

53. Planck, *25 Jahre Kaiser-Wilhelm-Gesellschaft*, 118.

54. Lösch, *Rasse als Konstrukt*, 447.

55. Quoted in ibid., 448.

56. Quoted in ibid., 449–50.

57. Ibid., 451–53.

58. Ibid., 455.

59. Ibid., 458; Weindling, "Tales from Nuremberg," 635–52.

60. Quoted in Müller-Hill, *Murderous Science*, 84.

61. Quoted in Klee, *Deutsche Medizin im Dritten Reich*, 365–66.

62. Quoted in ibid., 366.

63. Personal communication with Fliethmann's son, May 7, 2001.

64. Tuppa, "Dora Maria Kahlich-Koenner," 291–92.

65. Riemann, *Preussisches Wörterbuch*, 11.

66. Hebel, *Wer ist Wer?*, 1048.

67. This refers not really to East Germany but to the "lost lands" to the east, exactly where Riemann had served in the IDO.

68. The notion that the legitimate boundaries of Germany extend far to the east of today's recognized boundaries is a popular belief among many Germans. Tour guides of large busloads of Germans are found at sites throughout western Poland proclaiming the "travesty" of the reduced size of the current German state.

69. Rose, *"Den Rauch hatten wir täglich vor Augen,"* 16.

70. Ibid., 344–49.

71. Lukas, *Forgotten Holocaust,* 9. According to Lukas, "Poland lost 45 percent of her physicians and dentists, 57 percent of her attorneys, more than 15 percent of her teachers, 40 percent of her professors, 30 percent of her technicians, and more than 18 percent of her clergy" (ibid.).

72. Hohmann, *Der "Euthanasie" Prozess Dresden 1947,* 18.

73. Klara Novak founded the Bund der "Euthanasie"- Geschädigten und Zwangssterilisierten e.V. in the 1980s and has been a unique force in gaining funding and recognition for victims of sterilization in the Third Reich.

74. Dr. Käthe Petersen was very active as the guardian for a group of "unwanted" people during the Third Reich. She became the regional director of the Social Work Department of Hamburg after 1966. She received many awards, including the national meritorious cross (*Bundesverdienstkreuz*). She was a respected resident of Hamburg and worked until 1978.

75. Quoted in "Bund der 'Euthanasie,'" 22–25 and 31–32.

76. Segal, *Die Hohen Priester der Vernichtung,* 162 and 164.

77. Peter Finn, "Debate Is Rekindled over WWII Expellees—Germans' Plight Evokes New Sympathy," *Washington Post,* Feb. 11, 2002, A18–20.

78. Schafft and Zeidler, *KZ-Mahn- und Gedenkstätten in Deutschland,* 146–47 and 173–74.

CHAPTER EIGHT

Race and Racism

What Is Race?

Discussing the early beliefs about race without first clarifying the latest thinking about this concept could lead to misconceptions. Most people still mistakenly *believe*, for instance, that each of us belongs to a definable race. Skin color, hair type, shape of facial features, and physique are associated with the idea of race in the minds of many people. A writer recently declared that, "With few exceptions, psychologists believe that there are two sexes—male and female—and three (principal) races—Caucasoid, Mongoloid, and Negroid."[1] His point was *not* that this is correct; rather, it is that not only psychologists but most people believe this abbreviated version of human diversity to be true.

The concept of race, according to one prominent physical anthropologist, did not occur to the earliest recorded travelers to distant places, for they were moving slowly on foot or on horseback and saw only a gradual change in the appearance of the people they met.[2] The gradations of appearance seemed natural enough, as indeed they are. It was during the Renaissance, when ocean travel brought travelers to faraway lands, that the sudden differences among population groups startled them. Here were people of size, physique, and skin color very different from what these Europeans had ever seen, and the languages and customs were not at all what they could have imagined. Perhaps they thought these were not really *people* at all. And if they were not human, their riches could be taken from them, they could be put into bondage, they could be subjected and subjugated to the will and whims of their "superiors," since they were outside the moral constraints that applied to fellow human beings.

Seeing other people as fundamentally different from themselves allowed travelers to exploit these strange beings without remorse.[3] Colonial power over the natives could be viewed paternalistically: The exploitation of the natives was for their own good. In this way, the concept of race was associated with power relationships and economic gain. As the colonial era was ushered in at the beginning of the 1600s, the concept of race offered a way to distinguish "us" and "them," a welcome rationalization. "Science" could be used to justify abject racism and proved an instrumental tool for hundreds of years, over oceans and continents.

Armchair anthropologists, using the travel reports of explorers, developed ideas about race through extensive theorizing. They observed the differences among the few prehominid and early hominid skulls and skeletons and then constructed a system of beliefs that would explain diversity over time and over geographic areas. The observable differences among *Homo sapiens,* both living and prehistoric, were then described as races.

For most of the twentieth century, race was defined as the open parts of a closed system, meaning that there are systematic variations of individuals within the human species, but that all of those individuals theoretically are capable of procreating with one another and with no individuals of another species. Attention was given to the number of races and their distinguishing characteristics. Some polygenecists speculated that different races came from different prehominid lines, while others, the monogenecists, proposed only one prehominid line of descent.

Indeed, "race" is a word and a concept that is embedded in our culture. Race is a social fact that determines to some extent life chances and options. Throughout U.S. history, race, along with sex and age, has been a major identifier. However, unlike sex or age, race is a social construct and not a biological fact.[4] While variations among individuals and population groups exist, as everyone can see, it is not possible to divide that variation into biologically meaningful subgroups, or races. What we do observe among human beings are so-called clines, or gradations of difference in specific traits. Gradations of change in any single attribute blend from one individual or group to another. Clines of individual traits are randomly distributed throughout contiguous population groups. As C. Loring Brace pointed out: "[These] traits are under separate genetic control within each species . . . completely unrelated to each other. Early in the 1950s, this [discovery] led to the demonstration that the category of *subspecies* simply could not be used for forms that were reproductively continuous over large areas."[5] This gradation of difference was first proven for animal species and then accepted as true also for humans.

Today, among those in the scientific community in the United States, it is a generally accepted fact that there is as much genetic differentiation within a race, however that is defined, as there is between races. If one used a single trait, such as eye color, one could place all humans in a select number of groups, each based on similarities. The line drawn between groups would be arbitrary, however. Adding a second trait, such as hair type, and trying to make the first set of groupings coterminous with the second would not be possible. The more traits one uses, the more hopeless the task becomes because of the randomness of trait distribution. Not even the Martin-Schultz color chart, used by Nazi anthropologists to distinguish gradients of eye color, could place unwanted population groups in race-specific groups. Only decisions based on social values and preconceived expectations could do that.

The desire to define "us" and "them" appears to be universal, and race is a convenient divider. The characteristic features that most people associate with race are social in nature. These features have no intrinsic value but are used as markers to set apart those who some will define as different. It was not only in Nazi Germany that negative Jewish stereotypes were used; they have been noted as early as the second half of the seventeenth century.[6] At the time of the Second World War in the United States, a widely used negative image of an African American showed a minstrel with thick lips and protruding eyes staring out of a black face. People did not see this image reflected in real people on the street, but many believed the stereotype to be true nonetheless. They were *socially* prepared to do so. The negative image only gave reinforcement to preconceived ideas of difference.

Diversity and Human Variation

In the 1890s, Aurol von Török, a German-speaking Hungarian who held the first anthropological chair at the University of Budapest, made 5,371 measurements on a single skull.[7] He felt the whole morphology movement was fatally flawed and could prove nothing about race. Although many anthropologists were trying to standardize morphological measurements, they were unsuccessful. "Measurements meant to convey 'hard' objective data became so subjective that no two anthropologists could compare their work unless trained in the same school."[8] Thus, all the time-consuming labor that went into measuring thousands of people was based on faulty assumptions.

Johannes Ranke, a noted German anthropologist at the beginning of the twentieth century, came to the conclusion that all of humankind could be placed on a continuum of traits connected by "gradual and uninterrupted transitions."[9] He reached the conclusion that intraethnic variation was greater than the variation between "racial types." Skepticism about the concept of race was widespread in Germany by 1900.[10]

Ashley Montagu, an evolutionary anthropologist whose career spanned most of the twentieth century, was one of the first American anthropologists who disavowed the idea of human races. In 1942, Montagu's book *Man's Most Dangerous Myth: The Fallacy of Race* challenged the idea of biologically determined races.[11] Twenty years later, in 1962, Frank Livingstone, in an article written for *Current Anthropology,* suggested it was time to abandon "the concept of race with reference to the living populations of *Homo sapiens.*"[12] Livingstone's argument was that there are differences among populations of organisms, but "this variability does not conform to discrete packages labeled races. The position can be stated in other words as: There are no races, there are only clines" (defined in the Oxford American Dictionary as "a graded sequence of differences within a species").

Thedosius Dobzhansky, commenting upon Livingstone's ideas, wrote:

I agree with Dr. Livingston that if races have to be "discrete units," then there are no races, and if "race" is used as an "explanation" of the human variability, rather than vice versa then that explanation is invalid. Races are genetically open systems while species are closed ones; therefore races can be discrete only under some exceptional circumstances. Races arise chiefly as a result of the ordering of the genetic variability by natural selection in conformity with the environmental conditions in different territories; therefore the variability precedes race and serves as a raw material for its formation.[13]

Characteristics that are identified with people that come from a certain region of the world were set in place many millennia ago. Many believe that there was some adaptive value to various characteristics that led to their differential selection, but this is not always the case. "We can recognize particular nuances of cheek bone and eye opening formation as recalling the inhabitants of the far East, or the ear shape in Africa, or aspects in the shape of the nose as being peculiarly characteristic of Europe. . . . [T]here is no adaptive value in these nuances of eye, ear, and nose morphology. The only thing we can say about them is that they tend to resemble what can be seen in the region from which the ancestors of those people came."[14]

The British tried to define the concept of race in the mid-1930s as a response to the rise of Hitler. The Race and Culture Committee of the Royal Anthropological Institute was given the task, but after two years of work, it could only arrive at logical definitions. In commenting upon the faulty work of the committee, the editors of the journal *Nature* remarked, "race is pure abstraction."[15] There was no consensus about the definition of race, much less how to measure and assess its possible influence on native abilities.

The American Anthropological Association (AAA) has issued its own position on race, which it maintains on the Internet.[16] This statement is viewed as a working document. It asserts that about 94 percent of DNA is shared within our species and only 6 percent varies among "conventional geographic 'racial' groupings." The statement gives a small history of how the concept of race has been used to distort ideas about human diversity.

> Racial beliefs constitute myths about the diversity in the human species and about the abilities and behavior of people homogenized into "racial" categories. The myths fused behavior and physical features together in the public mind, impeding our comprehension of both biological variations and cultural behavior, implying that both are genetically determined. Racial myths bear no relationship to the reality of human capabilities or behavior. Scientists today find that reliance on such folk beliefs about human differences in research has led to countless errors.[17]

This statement and the remaining discussion not quoted here leave the reader without clear information about whether there is such a thing as race or not. Obviously, to assert that there is no such thing as race is still controversial and is a statement that the AAA is not ready to endorse. Certainly, no one could say that there are a specific number of *definable* races, only populations who share parts of a genetic history.

The major issue is whether we are going to choose to continue to think in typological terms or in terms of process. Typological thinking emphasizes the differences among groups of people and ignores or minimizes the differences within groups.[18] The enormous variation that exists within any group that is artificially seen as belonging together remains the major reason why typological thinking is not adequate.

Perhaps, because it is hard to accept the randomness of human diversity, people seek a rationale to explain diverse characteristics. One wants to know the origin of his or her own "type," and the relatedness one shares with other population groups. An article on DNA mapping was illustrated on the cover of a popular news magazine. Here, it was claimed with some certainty that men and women could find out through mitochondrial DNA their own relationship to original Adams and Eves of hundreds of thousands of years ago. Cutting short the internal discussion and the difficulties still presented to geneticists in making such attempts, the magazine writers promised that within ten years the entire picture of human evolution and its relationship to those on earth today would be revolutionized.[19] This may be true, but the fact today is that human variation is infinite, and yet each one of us shares with each other person a genetic and human history. We humans are all kin.

Beliefs about Race in Germany

A major theme of German anthropologists from the 1800s onward was race. Beginning as a *concept,* a general notion about human evolution and biodiversity, race became a *construct* of interrelated ideas, research agendas, legal prescriptions and prohibitions, and a defining Zeitgeist for the field of German anthropology. Now that the preceding chapters have established the context of the Third Reich and its genocide, it is important to examine how race became such a critical part of the study of German anthropology and how that part of anthropology became a major part of the Nazi ideology. At the same time, in order to place this discussion in a cross-national perspective, it will be useful to see how American anthropologists talked of race in the United States and the kinds of actions that racial and racist thinking led them to take during the war years.

For some time, ideas of race were pursued with no thought given to translating them into a program of action. For most German anthropologists, race was determined at an earlier stage of evolution and was a permanent marker within a group of people. These differences certainly were of interest but not particularly relevant to public policy. "Exotic" people of different skin color were curiosities.[20]

Then why did the Nazis use race to describe differences among people with basically the same identifying characteristics as their German neighbors? They did so because the social categories of Jew, Pole, Serb, Mongol, or Gypsy were of significance to them and could be used to justify policies that furthered their economic and political goals.[21]

When the Nazis began to use ideas about race to plan a new form of society, the theorizing and hypothesizing suddenly became an active pursuit. Individuals and groups were placed on hierarchical scales of fictitious schema of racial classification; and, as we have seen, their options for occupations, living space, and family structure and finally their chance of living or experiencing a quick or slow dispatch to death hinged on the classification into which they fell, according to "scientific" perceptions.

In fact, prior to the Hitler-era, Jews born and living in Germany were Germans in every legal and moral sense.[22] Before the Nazis, Jews and non-Jews had intermarried for generations, and in urban centers, gentiles were often indistinguishable by customs or religion, or lack of religion, from their Jewish neighbors. In Berlin in the 1920s, about one-third of all Jewish married men were married to non-Jewish women, and approximately one-sixth of all Jewish married women were married to non-Jewish men.[23] Likewise, those who survived and returned to their country after the war were again, and in the same way, German, whether or not their non-Jewish neighbors treated them as such.

Anti-Semitism was heightened, though not invented, by the Nazis. The moves that the Nazis wanted to make, however, depended upon the latent anti-Semitism being stirred into a much more virulent emotional response among the Germans. It was necessary for the Nazis to stereotype the Jew in negative ways in order to compel ordinary people to view their friends and neighbors as dangerous enemies. Negative cartoons portraying stereotypes in the Nazi era might show a man with a large, hooked nose and leering eyes or a fat, unattractive woman, images based on perceptions of class, style, and ethnicity. They had nothing to do with observed reality. Later, the same problem presented itself to the Germans when they wanted to separate the Germans and the Poles in occupied Poland. Many Germans who had lived among the Poles, often for generations, intermarried with them. The resulting families were, indeed, "part Polish" and therefore not ready or willing to make these distinctions. The Nazi government provided "assistance," however, through public displays, exhibits, and other incentives to renounce all things Polish and finally by encouraging people to publicly claim their German heritage through the DVL.

Do most people today think of Jews as a race? Members of the Jewish religion, or individuals whose families were, or are, part of the Jewish tradition, come from many parts of the world. They may trace their religious origins to one geographic area but through centuries their ancestors have traveled and lived in different countries and on different continents. For generations, they have intermarried and procreated with people of similar and dissimilar genetic backgrounds. Those from dissimilar backgrounds often have become Jews through religious conversion. Thus, no single physical type, much less a single gene pool, defines Jews, and a so-called Jewish race may have a social meaning in certain contexts but is of no biological significance.

It was quite predictable that Elfriede Fliethmann was taken aback when she measured the Jews in the Tarnów Ghetto (see chapter 1) and found that they had a much more diverse appearance than she had expected. She had expected them to conform to the social definition that was widely promulgated, as if it were physical fact. Fliethmann and Kahlich had been educated in the teachings of the traditional anthropological texts of the German-speaking world of their time. They might have been reassured, when their measurements showed so much variability, if they had remembered the authoritative but patently untrue passage from the Baur, Fischer, and Lenz text that discussed the possibility that Jews were a race. "Those who deny that the Jews are a race are using primarily morphological standards. . . . It depends more on the way of life [*Lebensleistungen*] than on other characteristics: and exactly the Jews are quite uniform in the kind of lifestyle they propagate."[24]

The Jews in the ghettos, however, were very much aware of how many very different lifestyles there were among them. People of various geographic areas and different socioeconomic classes, speaking various languages, were thrown together under circumstances none could have imagined only a few years earlier. These differences caused conflicts within the confined spaces among people who were supposed to be homogeneous. And while Elfriede Fliethmann and Dora Kahlich may have concluded that "you can always tell a Jew when you see one," they certainly knew better than that. Indeed, because that was *not* the truth, many Jews, although a tragically small percentage of the total population, were able to survive the Holocaust.

Beliefs about Race in the United States

Franz Boas, born in Germany and working in the United States as an anthropologist and geographer, studied immigrants in America and discussed the malleability of race, showing that their bodies changed in a relatively rapid period of time due to changes in environment and nutrition. Sophisticated for its time, this study showed statistically that given differing circumstances, people defined as being part of the same group could be expected to physically change over time.[25]

Born to a Jewish family in Minden, Germany, in 1858, Boas was trained in physics and geography and later in anthropology by Rudolf Virchow in a liberal tradition, and throughout his life he was loyal to his own values. In 1887, he emigrated to the United States because he felt there would be greater opportunity in America. Yet, he encountered anti-Semitism as he tried to find employment, and not until 1896 did he receive a position at Columbia University and, a year later, tenure.

Boas engaged in studies of the American Negro almost immediately after assuming the position at Columbia. He believed that all races had the same innate abilities to learn and thrive but that opportunities for schooling and a decent life had to be afforded in order for these to be realized. He belonged to a large number of organizations that promoted equal opportunities and stood against racism.[26]

As Germany turned to fascism, Boas became actively engaged in bringing human rights issues to the attention of both anthropologists and the general public in America and abroad. He influenced a large number of students, who followed his lead in bringing to American anthropology a concern for issues of human rights and racial justice.[27]

As a whole, American anthropologists were neither brave enough nor certain enough of their own positions to support antiracist public positions before 1938. For all of his efforts to enlist other anthropologists in recognizing the dangers of racism, Boas stood quite alone among prominent anthropologists in campaigning against the developing terror in Germany. "Aside from general political anti-fascist activity, there was very little organized response to Nazism among scientists and almost none from official scientific institutions. Scientists reserved their comments, and except for excluding a small number of investigations financed at Columbia, no organized initiative was taken to undermine the scientific claims of Nazi racism. Little immediate response to the Nazi threat emerged among scientists."[28]

Finally in 1939, Boas was successful in making a unified statement on the position of anthropologists toward race when a resolution was presented to the AAA's Committee on Resolutions and passed unanimously. It read:

> Whereas the prime requisites of science are the honest and unbiased search for truth and the freedom to proclaim such truth when discovered and known, and
>
> Whereas anthropology in many countries is being conscripted and its data distorted and misinterpreted to serve the cause of an unscientific racialism rather than the cause of truth:
>
> *Be it resolved,* that the American Anthropological Association repudiates such racialism and adheres to the following statement of facts:
>
> (1) Race involves the inheritance of similar physical variations by large groups of mankind, but its psychological and cultural connotations, if they exist, have not been ascertained by science.
>
> (2) The terms "Aryan" and "Semitic" have no racial significance whatsoever. They simply denote linguistic families.
>
> (3) Anthropology provides no scientific basis for discrimination against any people on the ground of racial inferiority, religious affiliation, or linguistic heritage.[29]

Hrdlička and American Refugee Policy

In 1942, the end of the war was still millions of lost lives away, but it was the beginning of the end. Some of those in power in the United States were already thinking of the stresses victory would place on this nation. Unfortunately, these considerations were not free of racism. This excursion away from our theme of Nazi anthropologists and their activities in the Third Reich is necessary in order to achieve a perspective on the acceptance at that time of a kind of scientism that affected public policy formation even in the United

States. In other words, assertions by scientists had an aura of authority, despite the presence or absence of any supporting evidence.

The anthropological activities in Europe were not well understood in the United States during the war years. While some U.S. anthropologists, such as Boas, were outspoken in their repudiation of using the discipline to support racist ideologies, others raised almost the same racial concerns as did their German and Austrian colleagues.

Aleš Hrdlička was considered by some to be the "father of physical anthropology" in the United States. His career spanned the period from the mid-1890s to his death in 1943. During that time, he studied the fossil record of early humans, human variation, and evolution, conducted research in many areas of the world, and became an expert on Alaskan natives. He collected human materials and added skeletal and soft tissue samples of over 10,000 individuals to the Smithsonian's anthropological collection.[30]

Hrdlička immigrated to the United States from Czechoslovakia in 1882 at the age of thirteen. He studied homeopathic medicine in New York and anthropology in Paris under Leon Manouvrier. In his midthirties, Hrdlička joined the U.S. National Museum's Department of Anthropology, a part of the Smithsonian Institution. In 1928, he helped to found the American Association of Physical Anthropologists and became its first president. Soon after the war began, he spoke and wrote to President Franklin Delano Roosevelt about American foreign policy, including the "Japanese threat" and how to handle it.[31] His papers, left to the NAA-SI, include letters written in 1942, the same year in which the Jewish genocide in Europe became known to the Allies. The letters outlined his advice to President Roosevelt about resettlement of Jewish refugees when the war ended.[32]

A meeting between Hrdlička and President Roosevelt occurred on May 23, 1942. What was discussed is not known, but following the meeting Hrdlička wrote the president and sent him papers pertaining to their conversation. The subtext of his correspondence, both directly and indirectly addressed to Roosevelt, was a concern that the United States might be pushed into increased population diversity through an influx of refugees after the war. Hrdlička made it clear that diversity was to him, and possibly to the president as well, "a large and difficult problem."

> Dear Mr. President:
> The subject you broached in our little conference is one of great importance, and one that, if much future trouble is to be prevented, will have to be given a serious and permanent attention; and it will be most fitting that this country, with you at its head, assume the initiative in the matter.

The problem is not new to me. Already at the time of the World War, I gave a small course of lectures on it before the local YMCA with a number of Congressmen of that time in attendance; and it has been with me in all my travels.

It is a large and difficult problem, and if it is to be satisfactorily solved it will demand the earnest concerted effort of many countries; but solved it must be, and it would be greatly to our and this Country's credit if we could show the ways.

The *least* of these ways would be to make clear the scientific principles of demographic movements and race mixtures. It would be possible today to give categorical answers to these basic questions. This alone, however, while necessary, would remain but an academic expression which, of itself, would probably lead to no activation.

The *medium* way would involve an organization of a small body of our own men qualified on all the main sides of the subject. This body should chart the problem from the anthropological, medical and economic points of view. It would determine the countries that will have to discharge their surplus peoples, and those that might receive them; learn by direct observation, through brief direct field trips, the conditions of the prospective receiving regions; and lay foundations for rational selection and direction of the migrants. Such a body would need some means, which however might be provided, at your invitation, by one or more of our Foundations. It would need cooperation of the Departments of Agriculture and Public Health, to the extent of each contributing one or two experts to its staff. It would have to have a little center of its own, perhaps under the Smithsonian; and would need modest but able clerical help. Such a body could begin to function without delay, and begin to furnish or publish its reports within a few months. But such a body could be only informative and at most advisory. It could not act. There would still be needed another body to institute, direct and supervise the procedures.

The *optimum* way would be to organize and hold, under our American direction, first of all a small Pan-American Congress on Post-War Immigration, inviting each of the Republics to send two or three experts on the matter, with official information as to facilities and desires of their respective countries, and direct knowledge of involved conditions. This should result in the formation and appointment by you of a central "Immigration" nucleus here in Washington, with a small official working subsidiary body in each of the cooperating Republics. This would be first of all a pan-American movement, from which however should eventually develop a World Organization for Emigration, connected as a permanent influential Bureau with the new "League of Nations," or whatever may be formed in place of this.

I stand ready, Mr. President, to do my humble part in anything that you may decide upon, in any position, and without compensation. I will expect your directions.

Sincerely yours,
Aleš Hrdlička[33]

Along with this offer, Hrdlička sent several papers, one entitled "Emigration," another "Racial Mixture," and a third "Race Degeneration." In the first, he warned of the danger of localized overpopulation at the end of the war that could be the cause of more conflict. However, what truly disturbed him was the redistribution of races: "[F]or the next 10–20 years no radical change, unless it be Germany, can be anticipated. The result will be that in 20 years the White populations, except in France and perhaps Germany, will rise by from 5 to 30 percent of their post-war numbers." He predicted that Germany would be "impoverished as well as sobered, and many will want to leave for happier climates. These moreover may be expected to be from among the most sane and industrious, and for them room elsewhere will need to be provided." Here, Hrdlička is most likely referring to the Jewish population of Europe as a group *not* included among the "White populations" that would need resettlement. He again asked for an institute to be set up that would be "one of the permanent and essential parts of the necessary future World organization." Such an institute was created by President Roosevelt and called the "Institute of Population," although no further information about it exists in the NAA-SI.[34]

The next paper, "Racial Mixtures," is a moderate statement on the human inevitability of procreating across borders without negative consequences. "Race Degeneration," however, is more ambivalent. He is concerned, as were Fischer and the Nazi-associated anthropologists, that racial degeneration could be a result of population movements. According to the fears of many of that generation of anthropologists, it would not be the strongest race that survived but the one that produced the most children.

> Races do not live forever. Just as the whole so the parts of humankind change. They differentiate into newer, or daughter-races; they end through exhaustion by wars, famine, disease, the remnant merging with some stronger group; or they degenerate mentally and sink into long dormant states in which they may perish, or from which they may revive for a further course of active existence.
>
> In human history, "race" after "race" has risen to power and cultural prominence, only sooner or later to go down before some stronger group. This up-linger-and-down phenomenon has in fact up to the recent time been the invariable rule. Its principal cause has often been believed to be "race degeneracy."
>
> . . . A temporary deterioration of human groups as that of individuals, is moreover, mostly "curable," and is often cured, on the one hand, through natural elimination of those affected most seriously, and, on the other, through restitution and new adaptations of the remainder . . . and where deterioration does not surpass the limit of the curable it slowly restores and strengthens, until a "normal" status is reached once more, adapted to and mastering the particular place and conditions.

> One of the people in whom such restitution under more favorable conditions may best be studied, and that in various parts of the world, are the Jews.[35]

What is Hrdlička trying to say here? Did he mean that the Jews have been "naturally" reduced in number, and one might find it interesting to see how the regeneration occurs? Did he believe that this reduction in population might even "restore and strengthen" the race? How did Roosevelt understand this poorly delineated argument? How could it have influenced his comprehension of the "natural phenomenon" of mass murder about which he was just becoming aware?

In another document called "Equality of Races," also found in the NAA-SI, Hrdlička delves into the difficulties and potentials of weighing the qualities of races and placing them within a hierarchy of value. He is enamored of the work that has been done on racial morphology. He asks if racial differences might be totally attributable to environment, a position supported by Boas, but finds ultimately that there is no basis for thinking that the "negro" is capable of developing to the position of the American and European races, although there is no way of disproving it either.

> Comparative racial physiology, chemistry and psychology are only in their beginnings. Of the physical studies the most relevant in this connection are those of the brain and the skull, or the head in the living. These researches, too, are far from finished; but enough has already been done for some valid conclusions. These are, in broad lines once more, that within the same stem what differences there are are essentially individual; but that between the moderate zone peoples and those of the tropics, or more particularly, between the whites and the blacks, there are differences that sustain the conclusions arrived at through other considerations.
>
> The point is raised, now and then, that what differences there are between for instance, the white and the negro, are differences in accomplishments, and education, rather than those of potentialities. Should this mean that the brain of the belated group is capable of development, the proposition could readily be assented for there is no evidence or probability to the contrary. But there appears to be no possibility of establishing this thesis that the brains of the belated human groups, such as the negro/negrito, the Bushman-Hottentot, the Melanesians, the Australo-Tanzanines . . . is of equal potentiality with those of the Old American, the English, Scotch, Irish, French, Germans, etc., and that the only differences are in training, enlightenment and opportunity.[36]

President Roosevelt was sufficiently interested in the ideas of Hrdlička to direct his unofficial aide, John Franklin Carter, to be a go-between in developing these ideas into actual plans and policies. Carter was a person Roosevelt used in many politically sensitive areas to gather intelligence. Carter followed up on Hrdlička's idea of an Institute of Population. Carter wrote Hrdlička saying that the president would like to "select a small, informal committee of leading anthropologists in the United States, Mexico and Canada, to come to Washington to conduct exploratory discussions of the ethnological problems anticipated in post-war population movements." Furthermore, the president would "request this committee to formulate agreed opinions as to problems arising out of racial admixtures and to consider the scientific principles involved in the process of miscengenation [sic], as contrasted with the opposing policies of so-called 'racialism.'" The anthropologists should handle these deliberations confidentially with the president, submitting a report to him in writing. Travel expenses would be "defrayed out of funds to be allocated for that purpose by the Office of the President . . . actual practical administration of the project to be conducted by me, unless otherwise instructed, with the help of Dr. Henry Field."[37]

Carter changed the proposed list of participants that Hrdlička had sent him. He took government employees off the list to avoid the committee's having "a government character" and added professors of anthropology "from Harvard, Columbia, Chicago, and California." "For that reason I am taking the responsibility of inviting Professor E. A. Hooton of Harvard University and Professor Ralph Linton of Columbia University also to attend the first meetings."[38] This move may have represented Roosevelt's often-used strategy of pitting various ideas against one another before reaching decisions. Both Linton and Hooton were well-respected anthropologists whom no one could accuse of being racist.

These changes infuriated Hrdlička, who answered, "I could not, if I am to retain my self-respect, accept the present hazy and prospectively subordinate status; nor was this, from what he told me, the intention of the President."[39] With that volley, he threatened to write to the president personally about his decision to remove himself from this activity.

Answering on the same day in a letter marked "Personal and Confidential," Carter urged Hrdlička neither to withdraw from the committee nor to write to the president. Carter answered, "While I am not an anthropologist, I am quite well aware of the political problems entailed in any approach to population problems, and I have undertaken what may well be a thankless task only because the President asked me to do so."[40] A few days later, Carter again wrote to Hrdlička to say that he had spoken to the president and that "he decided to alter his directive after consideration of all the factors involved. . . . I had a fairly full conversation with him—naturally, I showed him all the correspondence between us—and he gave me fresh and explicit instructions. For your convenience, I have summarized his directive in the form of the attached memorandum."[41] Dated August 7, 1942, it read:

Memorandum for Dr. Aleš Hrdlička: Presidential directive,

The President said that he had decided to start this anthropological committee on a much smaller and less formal basis than originally contemplated. He wants
you, Dr. Isaiah Bowman and Dr. Henry Field to be the sole members of the committee for the present. Naturally, he wishes the committee to be free to call in other
consultants not only from this country but from Canada, Mexico and other Lat-
in American countries, as the need arises.

The President wishes this committee of three to attempt to answer the following questions:

1.) Where are the vacant places of the earth suitable for post-war settlement?

2.) What type of people could live in those places?

With regard to 1, the President wants the committee, for the present, to limit
its studies to the following regions:

a.) South America—the plateau land on both sides of the Orinoco River; the
plateau land on the eastern slopes of the Andes down to the Amazon basin.

b.) Central Africa—the plateau land of the eastern Congo basin, Tanganyi-
ka, Uganda, Kenya and southwestern Ethiopia.

In consideration of this problem the President wishes the committee to keep
especially in mind the political fact that the South American nations still insist on
a base stock of their own in regions opened to settlement, that may want a "planned"
melting pot, with a basic "flux" of 30–40% of their own people. This base stock will
naturally include a considerable admixture of Indian blood. The President wishes
to be advised what will happen when various kinds of Europeans—Scandinavian,
Germanic, French, Belgian, North Italian, etc.—are mixed with this South American base stock.

The President specifically asked the committee also to consider such questions
as the following: Is the South Italian stock—say, Sicilian—as good as the North
Italian stock—say, Milanese—if given equal economic and social opportunity?
Thus, in a given case, where 10,000 Italians were to be offer [sic] settlement possibilities, what proportion of the 10,000 should be Northern Italians and what Southern Italians? He also pointed out that most South American countries would be glad
to admit Jewish immigration, it was on the condition that the Jewish group were
not localized in the cities, they they [sic] want no "Jewish colonies," "Italian colonies," etc. How can you resettle the Jews on the land and keep them there? Historically, he pointed out, the Jews were originally an agricultural and pastoral people
and the ghetto system, which had made them predominantly city-dwellers today,
is of comparatively recent origin. He added that modest and reasonable expenses
in connection with the work of this committee would be paid.[42]

The committee did come into existence on October 26, 1942, through a
memo of understanding. In Carter's diary, it became known simply as "Committee M," for "migration." It was not modestly funded but rather lavishly
funded, through a White House slush fund.[43]

What the president and Carter had in mind was larger than what Hrdlička knew. They intended to use Committee M for intelligence-gathering purposes that went beyond questions of immigration and population dynamics.[44] Henry Field became the main player of the three anthropologists on the committee. His contacts in Moscow and the Middle East provided information that the president wanted to have without working through the State Department.[45] So Carter reported to the president:

> The attached "Secret Memorandum on U.S.S.R." was obtained by Henry Field under conditions of extraordinary secrecy from a man who is believed to have accurate and swift means of communication with Moscow. The information is naturally not guaranteed, but the request is specifically made by Field's informant that the State Department be not informed of this channel of communication, especially since the Department recently shot from under us another reliable channel of communication with Moscow and the Middle East. If you wish further substantiating information, I suggest that Dr. Field himself explain verbally the circumstances under which this data was conveyed to him.
>
> J.F.C.[46]

This correspondence raises two questions. To what extent did the three anthropologists and others whom they identified and brought into action create the beginnings of a spy network? And what role did U.S. anthropologists have in developing postwar immigration policies? It is a glimpse into a leading U.S. anthropologist's racial concerns that were shared with the pinnacle of leadership. It sheds light on the limitations placed on Jewish immigration to this country during the prewar and war years when Jews were still able to leave European shores. The most striking conclusion one must reach is that the actual events in Europe were based not solely on humane conclusions about the need to save people's lives but also on consideration of such poorly defined concepts as racial degeneration and the composition of a country's "racial structure."

The Nazi Construction of Race

Nazi anthropologists believed that a race represents a group of people who through their genetic physique, mind, and soul have characteristics that distinguish them from other groups of people. They did not believe that races were synonymous with boundaries of countries, although this was something fervently wished and something toward which they strived. Blut und Boden would be achieved when the homogeneous match between a land and the people that belonged on it, and to it, was achieved. Race was also not coterminous with religion or language. "A Jew who changes his [Jewish] religion for the Christian religion cannot by that act change his racial heredity. He remains as before still a Jew."[47]

Boas's research that showed the malleability of race was very threatening to the racists of Europe and to those in other countries as well. If race was defined on the basis of inherited physical characteristics, what could it mean if these changed due to nutrition and environmental factors? While Boas's ideas were discussed at conferences in Europe throughout the prewar years, German anthropologists remained hostile to them; the malleability of race was anathema to them.

Nor was there agreement about the nature of racial groups found in Germany. Before Hitler came to power, there was discussion about racial groups, their migration, and the numbers one could assign to the German domain. After the assumption of power by Hitler, this discussion changed radically. The phrases "Nordic race" and "Aryan race" became common parlance and replaced to a large extent anthropological discussions of "Dinaric" or "Indo-Germanic." There was no call for investigations that even had the appearance of being unbiased. Such would not have been allowed under the Nazi regime.

This situation must have been difficult for anthropologists who were still attending international meetings as late as 1939. In an article on the international conference of Anthropological and Ethnological Science in Copenhagen, the journal *Rasse* reported that the northern countries pursued a discussion of the race concept that disavowed ancient races.

> The core of the conference was the lectures on the concept of race. Nordenstreng of Sweden painted mankind as a "mixed race from the oldest times." The presence of changing characteristics, for example, within the blond hair color, among other things, Nordenstreng represented as a proof against the existence of pure races. [Nordenstreng believes that] the characteristics that most see absolutely as racial (skin and hair color, stature, head form, etc.) are determined in the largest part through climate and nutrition. As proof, it was enough [for him] to depend on the long since disavowed research of the Jew, Boas. . . . Professor E. Fischer, the leader of the German delegation from Berlin, gave a speech that was the high point of the conference. In an overfilled auditorium, [Fischer] spoke on "Race and Inheritance of Mental Characteristics," and in a clear way, stated that on the basis of today's research results, there is no scientific justification to doubt the heredity also of mental capacity. Jewish and Czech representatives tried to speak out against German science with inconsequential remarks. However, we were able to win out, and as Dr. Gross, the leader of the Reich Office [*Reichsamtsleiter*] declared—"with joy it will be entered in the books that the attitude exactly toward the Jews' dis-

honest services to modern science gradually brought even the most convinced democracies to a very subdued demeanor in regard to their Jewish friends."[48]

A disavowal of the concept of race was not going to occur at this meeting or for many years to come. Instead, the sociolinguistics of race gained dominance. That is, the *talk* of race superseded the *investigation* of race, except where such investigation had political importance.

Speaking of Race

German "blood" became what social scientists call a "trope," a figurative way of speaking, in this case, about exclusion and, finally, in the Third Reich, about elimination. If the Nazis had been interested in exploring the reality of human variation, they might have investigated actual blood groups of different populations. There is no evidence that this occurred on any regular basis. If it had, they would have found no differences among the groups they were studying. Instead, "German blood" became a poetic reference to the essence of "Germanness," which was also referred to as the German *Kulturseele,* or "cultural soul."[49]

"When the question first arose about German Volkstum in conjunction with the goal of stopping a further loss of German [*germanisch-deutschen*] blood in foreign territory, it was concluded that there must be a boundary drawn around our own Volkstum. Seen from the task of reclaiming our own German blood . . ."[50] Thus ran an article in the magazine *Volk und Rasse* in 1942 that went on to engage in a most complicated discussion of how German "blood" had dissipated in foreign lands through centuries and now needed to be "reclaimed" as the land itself was being reclaimed, a rather guileless way of saying it was being occupied.

One might assume that the "loss of German blood" had to do with bleeding on the battle ground, but that was not the meaning. German blood was lost by procreation between Germans and non-Germans. The offspring had, thus, lost their German blood, something that would not have happened had the union been between two Germans. To stop this "blood-letting," race laws forbade sexual contact between Germans and those not considered worthy. No contact between Germans and non-Germans that could result in "inferior" children was allowed. All people who could possibly have sexual contact with Germans were screened for potential "accidents" that might occur. That was the basis of the DVL and the careful selection of even frontline soldiers. (If the soldiers survived the war, they would have the right to emigrate to the Altreich, where they might procreate with German women.)

Germans and Austrians began to speak of their fellow citizens as "foreign people" at the same time citizen rights were removed from the Jews. Thus, the Viennese anthropologist Geyer, who had trained students for the work of the IDO in Poland, wrote to the authorities of the University of Vienna to request ten days of leave. "In order to carry out the racial surveys [*Aufnahmen*] in the Jewish camp of the Gestapo, Vienna II Stadium, I am asking for permission for a leave of absence from September 25 to October 10, 1939. These examinations will be carried out by the Anthropological Department of the Natural History Museum together with the Public Health Office of the city of Vienna, Division of Heredity and Racial Hygiene of Foreign People."[51]

Racial Fears and Racial Hygiene

All of these efforts were part of an overriding fear and insecurity, both about diversity and its potential threat, and insecurity regarding Germany's ability to maintain the boastful promises it had made of a "Thousand-year Reich." Eugen Fischer explained it as follows in 1933:

> We must not make recriminations on our ancestors that they did not try to care for heredity and race, and we should not wonder that the past high cultures, the Greeks, the Romans and others had the same signs of a falling birthrate, misguided selection and nurture [as the Germans]. Regulation of birth, despite the warnings of enlightened people, declined, and we see the results in our own Volk and all European cultures. They did not know better. They did not have any available evidence at hand. Today we have that. The Nazi state is the first that knowingly and generously draws from its resources to eliminate, on the basis of knowledge and with a responsible conscience, damaging coincidences of certain appearances that influence the entire culture.[52]

The "appearances" and "signs" that so concerned Fischer were most likely class-related rather than racial. His fear was that racial degeneration was caused by the "wrong" people having too many children and the "right" people having too few.

The Nazi Party's functionaries spelled out the fears even more clearly. "A particular danger lies also here, that the sinking birthrate does not affect all classes equally, but primarily the hereditarily biologically most valuable part, while the less worthy—the drinkers, psychopaths, criminals, etc.—not hampered by any sense of responsibility, bring an abundant progeny into the world, that populates again a large part of our insane asylums, hospitals for crippled, and prisons."[53]

Not unlike the fears that Hrdlička discussed with Roosevelt, Fischer suspected that an influx of "foreign blood" somehow would damage the culture and civilization of his country. The "wrong" people to the Nazis included those who were not "pure" Aryan or Nordic or Germanic. The fear for Hrdlička and Roosevelt may have been a fear of diversity, a diluting of, in Hrdlička's words, the "base stock."

Care of the body of the German Volk and the present valuable genetic material was covered by a German term, *Volkspflege*. This required good public health leading to the development of a natural biological and racial hygiene in thought and behavior.[54] Smoking and excessive drinking were discouraged through public campaigns. The family was held in sacred honor, and the place of the woman and mother as important, but subservient, was assured. The fact that aside from the propaganda these values were not followed did not occur to many Germans. While mothers and children were given vacations and extra food, women were also required to work, and their men were taken off to war. Male children were indoctrinated in cruel and harsh camps and were required to enter the labor force from age thirteen onward unless they were associated with an elite political or social class.

The belief that the souls of different races were significantly different from one another was another myth of the Nazi anthropologists. "Soul," as used by the Nazis, referred to the aspects of humans that were outside the physical gestalt. A corollary was a belief in the "racial character." Although certifiers were busy throughout the German Reich and occupied lands determining who was Jewish or Slavic simply by appearance or with the help of pseudoscientific tests, at least some members of the party attempted to distinguish character from physical features. "It would be a big mistake if one would place a person in a certain race only on the basis of his outer appearance. The inner character is as, or even more, important in determining membership in a race. A tall man, who outwardly looks like he belongs to the Nordic race disappoints us often through a totally non-Nordic character, while on the other hand, people with dark hair and dark eyes may have 'blond souls.'"[55]

Indeed, such rationales had to be invented. Hitler himself fit no stereotype of the Nordic racial man, nor did many Nazis who were in the most visible positions. Not willing to admit to variation within the body of the German Volk, the theorists of the Nazi state, nevertheless, had to build into their schema explanations for what all Germans saw with their own two eyes.

Notes

1. Fish, "What Anthropologists Can Do in Psychology," 558.
2. Brace, "Concept of Race in Physical Anthropology," 240.

3. See Goldberg, *Racial Subjects.*

4. The author recognizes the pioneering work done by Niels C. Lösch in his ground-breaking book *Rasse als Konstrukt* (Race as Construct). Lösch uses the idea of construct differently than it is being used here. He felt that Eugen Fischer had moved away from the standard concept of race as an observable phenomenon and made it instead an abstraction or a construct (124–25). In this book, the author is presenting the idea of race *as an abstraction* that became *constructed* into a panoply of interrelated laws, regulations, prohibitions, exclusions, inclusions, and consequential actions.

5. Brace, "Concept of Race in Physical Anthropology," 242.

6. Hilberg, *Destruction of the European Jews,* 19.

7. Massin, "From Virchow to Fischer," 107.

8. Barkan, *Retreat from Scientific Racism,* 315–16.

9. Massin, "From Virchow to Fischer," 110–11.

10. Massin's discussion of this critical phase of German anthropology in "From Virchow to Fischer" is an important contribution to understanding the strands of various thought prior to the Nazi regimentation into racist constructions.

11. See Montagu, *Man's Most Dangerous Myth.*

12. Livingstone, "On the Nonexistence of Human Races," 180.

13. Dobzhansky, "Dobzhansky Comments," 182.

14. Brace, "Concept of Race in Physical Anthropology," 251.

15. *Nature,* Apr. 18, 1936, cited in Barkan, *Retreat from Scientific Racism,* 287.

16. See <http://www.aaanet.org/stmts/racepp.htm>.

17. Ibid.

18. Marks, *Evolutionary Anthropology,* 322.

19. *U.S. News and World Report,* Jan. 29, 2001, 34–41.

20. See Zimmerman, *Anthropology and Antihumanism in Imperial Germany.*

21. It is beyond the scope of this book to analyze the Third Reich as a systematic political entity.

22. See Elon, *Pity of It All;* Klemperer, *I Will Bear Witness;* and Jochheim, *Frauenprotest in der Rosenstrasse.*

23. Jochheim, *Frauenprotest in der Rosenstrasse,* 24.

24. Baur, Fischer, and Lenz, *Menschliche Erblichkeitslehre,* 747, quoted in Seidler and Soritsch, *Rassen und Minderheiten,* 26.

25. See Sparks and Jantz, "Reassessment of Human Cranial Plasticity"; and Gravlee, Bernard, and Leonard, "Heredity, Environment, and Cranial Form," 125–38.

26. Barkan, *Retreat from Scientific Racism,* 281–85.

27. Ibid.

28. Barkan, *Retreat from Scientific Racism,* 285.

29. "Report of the Annual Meeting," *American Anthropologist* 41 (Dec. 29, 1939): 303.

30. Montgomery, *Register to the Papers of Aleš Hrdlička,* 1.

31. Ibid., 2.

32. Ibid., 66.

33. NAA-SI, Papers of Aleš Hrdlička, Box 176, Letter from Hrdlička to Franklin Roosevelt, May 27, 1942.

34. Ibid., "Emigration."

35. Ibid., "Race Degeneration."

36. Ibid., "Equality of Races."

37. Ibid., Memorandum for Dr. Hrdlička from John Carter, July 30, 1942.

38. Ibid., Letter from Carter to Hrdlička, July 31, 1942.

39. Ibid., Letter from Hrdlička to Carter, Aug. 3, 1942.

40. Ibid., Letter from Carter to Hrdlička, Aug. 3, 1942.

41. Ibid., Letter from Carter to Hrdlička, Aug. 7, 1942.

42. Ibid., Presidential directive to Dr. Aleš Hrdlička, attached to letter from Carter to Hrdlička, Aug. 7, 1942.

43. FDRL, President's Secretary's File, John F. Carter; M Project File 100, Jan. 1944. Officially, the total amount received by the M Project was $39,052.32 between November 1, 1942, and December 31, 1943. Staff included seven members with three secretaries. Nine specialists were employed on specific assignments. The finances of the M Project were murky, at best. The project had been reapproved on June 28, 1944, by the president. A memorandum dated June 22, 1944, from Miss Tully, the president's personal assistant and confidential secretary, stated that questions had been raised at the State Department about financing the M Project: "Ed Stettinius said, very confidentially, that the State Department really did not know what they were doing and that Mr. Carter receives $10,000 a month and the State Department does not feel that this work is of enough value to warrant spending that amount of money."

44. Persico, *Roosevelt's Secret War,* 118.

45. FDRL, M Project File 100.

46. FDRL, President's Secretary's File, Carter, John F., File 98, Jan.–Feb. 1942, Report on Stalin's "Secret" Board of Strategy, etc., Jan. 7, 1942.

47. NA, T-74, document pages 389101–24, "Erb- und Rassenpflege," A short course about race, heredity, and hereditary health from Dr. W. Stemmler, Wiesbaden Freischulungs-Amt NSDAP, Wiesbaden.

48. "Bericht über die 2. Internationale Tagung für anthropologische und ethnologische Wissenschaften in Kopenhagen," 471–72.

49. See Linke, *German Bodies.*

50. Schubert, "Zur Praxis der Volkstumspolitik," 103.

51. Seidler and Rett, *Rassenhygiene,* 253.

52. E. Fischer, "Die Bedeutung der menschlichen Erblehre."

53. "Erb- und Rassenpflege" (see note 47).

54. Seidler and Rett, *Rassenhygiene,* 250.

55. "Erb- und Rassenpflege."

Professional Denial, Civic Denial, and a Responsible Anthropology

Crime and Punishment

There can be no question that anthropologists in Germany contributed to every phase of the Third Reich as a racist state. They provided theory, policy formation, enforcement, and proactive engagement, and some also participated in, or their careers benefited from, the torture, maiming, and murder of victims. The murders most likely were not committed by the anthropologists' own hands but through prisoner emissaries within the ranks of concentration camps and death camps.[1] The evidence is clear that these anthropologists committed human rights abuses, up to and including participation in the Holocaust (see appendix 1). As Hitler was fighting for power, he found the ideas that he needed already in place. He lent his authority to the racist ideology, and the anthropologists gave him their prestige and their allegiance.

Why is it that only one of the Nazi anthropologists was prosecuted before an international court? Mengele, whose crimes were so obvious and who was not hiding in a laboratory or a university office, was an easy target. He was sentenced in absentia, for he had escaped to South America. Verschuer and Magnussen were under grave suspicion by the prosecutors of the Nuremberg Medical Trials of 1946.[2] Leo Alexander, a neurologist who gathered evidence for the courts, felt they should come before the court as a separate case in a new trial. He was aware of the experimentation on eyes of inmates of Auschwitz and felt there was enough evidence for prosecution. Pressure from Britain and Czechoslovakia was brought to bear, but it was not sufficient. Several reasons for this decision have been proposed. One reason is that the Allies set the standards for prosecution within a very narrow range. They were anxious to have Germany begin its program of medical science again, and they did not want to alert the public to the misuse of science.[3]

Another brush with the courts came from the U.N. War Crimes Commission in May 1945.[4] This also did not result in prosecution, but Verschuer remained suspect. In September 1946, the Berlin office of the U.S. Counsel for War Crimes and its chief research analyst, Manfred Wolfson, recommended that both Verschuer and Magnussen be arrested.

In the final analysis, the decision was made by the British and Americans to resume German medical science and forgo the prosecution of other crimes. In July 1946, Max Planck was invited to come to the Royal Society to be honored on the occasion of its hundredth anniversary. Here, it was decided that the old KWI would now be known as the Max Planck Institute. "Planck became an icon for a new form of scientific organization: the name change symbolized a shift away from imperialist militarism to the idea of a free association of scientists, running their own affairs."[5]

Verschuer had the luck to be saved, in part, because of the very people who condemned him: Robert Havemann and Kurt Gottschaldt. Their ties to the newly created German Democratic Republic (GDR) made it easy for Verschuer to claim that their denunciation was no more than a "communist plot." The beginning of the cold war made Verschuer's attack on his accusers hard for the prosecutors to ignore.

The other Nazi anthropologists' activities during the Third Reich were less easy to discern; their crimes fell within the range of what appeared to be more general scientific work, an area in which great leeway was always granted. Also, weighed against the advances about to be made in science, the rights of the subjects of social and medical research were not generally a matter of concern. This was true not only in Germany but elsewhere. Testing substances on uninformed human subjects was common in most of the technologically advanced countries at that time, and sterilization was not uncommon among asylum inmates and others. Furthermore, the use of human subjects in Germany during the Third Reich was both more random and less attached to specific goals. It was absolutely hostile to human values and sometimes life itself. The exposure of this criminal inhumanity after the war resulted in postwar restrictions on the use of human subjects for scientific experimentation.[6]

Prosecutors focused on finding the Germans who had committed the murders or provided the technology for them. They gave much less thought to those who had provided the rationale for eliminationist anti-Semitism, to those who had designed the methodologies by which one would make judgments of "Jewishness," or to those who used the human "products" of the victims. Prosecutors forgot about those who robbed graves or, through the use of intermediaries, sent people to their graves so that their body parts could be harvested.

Nazi anthropologists committed crimes against Jews by cooperating in firing them from their positions, certifying them as Jewish, deciding court cases about their paternity and social relationships, and training other people in a variety of professions to do the same. Performing medical experimentation and sending individuals to the gas chambers in camps also was done with the assistance of at least some anthropologists.

However, many of the crimes committed by Nazi anthropologists were not against the Jews, per se. Mengele and others harvested the products of the inmates of Auschwitz without regard to race. Roma, homosexuals, those with physical anomalies, twins, prisoners of war, and resistance fighters of many nations did not have a significant voice, nor were they organized to any extent, after the war. Without significant lobbies, they had no effective recourse for recognition or recompense. When some groups were able to organize many years after the war, their demands were rarely met.

Professional Denial

Societies have value systems that are internalized by their members in such a way that not only individual but also civic acts are evaluated and judged to be appropriate or inappropriate.[7] This ethos is embedded in the culture and shared through conversation, body language, and benefits the society offers, such as public esteem, recognition, and advancement in one's profession. The members of a society or group find themselves either congruent with this unstated, but understood, identity or at odds with it. Erich Fromm described this as the production of the "social unconscious."[8]

In the Nazi era, the social unconscious underwent a change. Instead of *sensing* what constituted people like themselves, the Germans were *explicitly told* what it meant to be part of the German "Volk," and the construct was raised to a cult. The rewards and punishments in society became much more explicit than implicit. The sanctions for deviating from the ideal could be deadly. Gleichschaltung, that uniform meshing of all parts of the political and social system to a single organizing *Führer Princip,* or leadership principle, meant that homogeneity was the most valued goal of society.

Fromm postulated that the organizational principles in any society are as unconscious to its citizens as the structure of the unconscious is to any individual. When the Nazi era ended, many of those principles were made explicit and thrown into question, if not disrepute. "Psychoanalyzing the Germans" was fair play for anyone. It seemed to many that the Germans had asked for this scrutiny by claiming during the Third Reich that they were the "master race" and that their destiny was tied to a ruthless elimination of "foreign elements."

The Nazi misconception of German superiority ended in one stroke. At the end of the war, the notion was exposed to the world as a murderous hoax, much to the shame of ordinary Germans. The most that dedicated Nazi anthropologists could hope for was to protect one another from disgrace or, even worse, prison. Due to the political realities of the time, they avoided court trials, but also the German public aided them to sidestep sanctions by their unwillingness to have one more defeat: the loss of respect for their intelligentsia. Few Germans wanted to be too direct or ask too many questions. After all, the Allied Powers were conducting the trials. All the big Nazis would be taken care of soon enough, and who could be sure that he or she did not share a little of the guilt?

For twelve years, the anthropologists of Nazi Germany had been *players.* They had not questioned the system but had been experts in it and had even helped invent it. They knew the language, which they also had helped to establish. They had been more than applied practitioners of their craft; they had been in some of the most respected positions, interacting with government and corporate giants. Anthropology had graduated from a descriptive science to an applied science, as important to the creation of a new state as the products of the most learned physicist or chemist.[9]

Recovering from the Nazi era and building a new and responsible anthropology has not been easy for the Germans. To express the idea that the past plagues the present, they often use the expression "He can't jump over his own shadow," meaning that what happened in the past still affects the present and, perhaps, will even affect the future. The word commonly used in a variety of contexts is *Vergangenheitsbewältigung,* meaning mastery of the past or getting control of the past. Another phrase that comes from an important book title is *die Unfähigkeit zu Trauern,* or "the incapacity to grieve."[10] As anthropologists have often said, when a concept is particularly important to a culture, there will be many ways of expressing it, and there are other expressions that have come into being to describe the Germans' attempt to master specifically the Nazi past as well.

A prominent German anthropologist expressed the difficulty of coming to grips with the past by explaining the dilemma of studying the Nazi anthropological establishment: "The anthropological study of Germany is a matter that inevitably puts cultural anthropologists into a quandary: On the one hand, they are caught between taking a professional approach that entails a receptive, sympathetic attitude toward the object of their study, and on the other, they are reluctant to occupy themselves intensively with the political ideology of the mass murderers and their successors."[11]

This is only one aspect of the reluctance of German anthropologists to attack the issue of their professional past. Young German historians often argue for a "cool" approach to the era of the Third Reich, one that removes the emotion and takes a nuanced look at specific aspects of the time period.[12] Coping with the trauma created by the topic cannot be denied, but this has not kept people in other professions from looking at the anthropological history. Journalists such as Ernst Klee and Götz Aly and geneticist Benno Müller-Hill first documented these actions. Robert Proctor in the United States has written unceasingly about the involvement of social and medical science in the Third Reich. Bettina Arnold has written of the Nazis' use of the archaeological record as justification for racism. And Michael Burleigh has written of the involvement of anthropologists in the occupied east during World War II. These are only a few of a growing number of authors from many disciplines who have begun to explore the anthropological history of Nazi Germany.

There have been serious but sporadic and limited attempts among German anthropologists to discern what responsibilities the discipline actually had for the disaster that was the Third Reich.[13] Several universities have published books exposing the Nazi history of certain departments. Recently, the Max Planck Society has published a two-volume work on the KWI. German anthropologists have written articles about the Third Reich and in the last few years have produced books that deal with the involvement of anthropology specifically in this period.

There is still a professional denial that comes into play that keeps anthropologists from looking closely at the ways in which their discipline was misused in the Third Reich. Denial is a basic working concept in psychology and psychoanalysis but has rarely been used in speaking of professions.[14] Individuals deny some realities that are too painful or traumatic or that invoke uncomfortable emotions. They repress information that they find painful or that causes them stress by repressing or avoiding it. They may also project guilt and responsibility onto others, inaccurately leaving themselves out of the picture.[15] Such denial may work as a short-term coping strategy, but over time, it may prove to be a dysfunctional adaptation that inhibits reality-based thought processes and sets up an unrealistic and unhealthy response to conflict situations.

When a profession denies what its practitioners have done in the past, it leaves the way clear for a lamentable lack of information, a revisionist historical view, a continuation of misconduct, and a repression of those who would attempt to learn from the past. *Professional denial* is similar to *civic denial,* which has been defined previously by this author as "a faulty re-creation of discrediting events by those with direct or indirect governmental authority, in order to make these events appear less damning, more harmless, or to displace blame for their occurrence."[16] Professional denial is created by a silent consensus, and its only authority is the willingness to avoid discussing discrediting events and conform to a version of the past that is nonthreatening to the profession and the individuals within it.

There are several ways in which professional denial comes about and even is enforced. These include sanctions on those who would speak out, limitations and blocks placed on informational sources, and a use of language that limits discourse on the topic.

Sanctions on Those Who Speak Out

Nestbeschmutzer is a German term for one who "dirties the nest." The sanctions that can be placed on someone of this ilk are familiar to us through the phenomenon of the whistle-blower. Like a whistle-blower, the person who informs others or the public of the misdeeds of his or her colleagues, even those separated by time and sometimes space, can become isolated. There may be long years with job loss or without career advancement, without publication possibilities, without friendly interactions at conferences and meetings, without invitations to take serious roles in professional associations. This isolation can rob the lifeblood from a professional.

In any society, there are only a few whistle-blowers. The anticipated and possibly unanticipated consequences of action deter many; the inadvertent discrediting of one's own profession, even in the short run, is not taken lightly. The way some whistle-blowers are handled inhibits others from taking such public stands. This is why legislation was passed in the United States attempting to protect those that would expose dangerous or illegal practices.

An example of the consequences of speaking out about the misdeeds of the profession is the case of Karl Felix Saller.[17] Saller was a student of Rudolf Martin, the director of the Anthropological Institute at the University of Munich. (Martin had a Jewish wife who, long after his death in 1925, was persecuted by the Nazis. She survived Theresienstadt, the "model" concentration camp near Prague.)[18] Martin and Saller followed in the intellectual line of Rudolph Virchow and Johannes Ranke, believing in the malleability of "races" and the inevitability of procreation among groups, making any certain number of definable races difficult, if not impossible, to identify. Like Boas, Virchow's student, they also believed that races were affected by nutrition, climate, physical conditions, and cultural history; races could be viewed as arising from a mixture of inherited and environmental forces.[19]

Martin used his energy to promote social welfare projects alongside his anthropological interests. He arranged with American Quakers to help feed the hungry children of Munich after the First World War, and he wrote, "Tolerance is the first step to inner freedom."[20] In a more critical vein, he wrote in a review of the Baur, Fischer, and Lenz anthropology text, "One always forgets that our European race is no different from a reconstruction of all the more complicated bastard hodgepodge [Bastardgemenge] of people now living on the earth . . . often arranged [in racial groupings] only through conceptualization and common impressions."[21]

The liberal establishment among anthropologists lost its leaders in the 1920s through death and retirement (see chapter 2). Saller came into his own in a different atmosphere from that which Martin had known; it was one influenced most significantly by the racial hygienists and eugenicists. Not surprisingly, having been Martin's student, Saller wrote a dissertation in which he also criticized Lenz's ideas of race, in particular the "Nordic race," using the same idea of race as a "construction" without basis in reality that Martin had.[22]

Saller was not completely in opposition to the mainstream paradigm of the racial hygienists, however. He had been one of the Rockefeller Foundation-sponsored racial researchers in the national study of race in the 1920s and 1930s. He supported sterilization before 1933, even suggesting that more than 10 percent of the population should be sterilized in any generation. According to Saller, reasonable grounds for this action could be bodily weakness, illness, insufficient intelligence, or extraordinary ugliness.[23]

What got Saller into trouble was not his stand on eugenics, which was not significantly different from that of the Nazis, but his belief that races could be defined as geographic, social, or religious groupings.[24] He did not believe that races degenerated through intermingling but quite the opposite: He thought that races reconstituted themselves endlessly, usually to their genetic advantage. Furthermore, the boundaries between races were unclear, and Jews were probably a branch of the "European" race. Saller thought in hierarchical terms when he described "the lower races," such as the Pygmies, Bushmen, Hottentots, Negroes, and Eskimos. He held the common belief of the time that the Jews were part of a "world conspiracy," although he left that undefined.

Undoubtedly, Saller brought this rather mixed message to his students in Munich. After the advent of Hitler, he became accustomed to looking at his students carefully and observing what statements in his lectures they were recording in their notes. Despite his care not to be apprehended for what he said, Saller was caught. One of his students developed a close relationship to the Saller family and, while in their home, gained access to a letter Saller had written in 1932. In it, Saller had said that Hitler and Rosenberg, the head of the Nazi Party's Racial Bureau, talked nonsense (*Blödsinn*) when they spoke of race. The student brought this letter to the authorities, and within a very short time, Saller was relieved of his position at the university. The reason given for the dismissal was that he presented theories of race that did not depend on "blood," but on social conditions and social class, or even religious belief or culture.[25]

There was another reason for the authorities to be anxious to get rid of Saller. He and Friedrich Merkenschlager had written a book about the prehistory of a particular region on the border of Switzerland and Germany, which had been published shortly before this trouble. In it, they had written, "Races are never something that are absolute, but always a balance between heredity and environment. . . . good races have a home, they have a balance with other creatures, with the entire environment and have the strength after a disturbance to find that balance again."[26] These words were intolerable to the Nazi powers. The book was confiscated, Saller was removed from the university, and Merkenschlager, who had either other strikes against him or was without support in high places, was taken to a concentration camp.[27]

Saller had been trained as a medical doctor as well as an anthropologist. Barred from teaching or working any longer in a university, he attempted to practice medicine. As part of his punishment, however, Saller was not allowed to receive insurance payments from his patients; thus, he also could not support himself in this way. Saller retrained in homeopathic medicine and started his own clinic on the Swiss border, with the thought that he might have to flee. As soon as Germany entered the war, he was called to military service, not as a doctor but as a medic with the rank of private. He was not allowed to practice medicine but was kept throughout the war in the service of the German Reich.

Upon the war's end, Saller attempted to recoup his place in the university. The university "rehabilitated" him immediately, but that did not guarantee him a paid position. The position he applied for in the anatomy department was given to Fritz Lenz, Saller's nemesis, who had played such an important role in the Third Reich. Saller complained to the head of the university and finally, six months later, received an explanation. The rector of the university wrote that the cause of Saller's failure to be given an appointment at the university was not based on political grounds but was due to the fact that he had lost his medical knowledge when he took up homeopathy during the years of the Third Reich.

This was not the only, or even the major, reason, however. Three Nazi anthropologists were more directly involved in derailing Saller's career. At the time of Saller's dismissal from the university in 1935, Eugen Fischer had certified to the Nazi Party that Saller was a psychopath. This was to cover the party from any possible criticism, for Saller had a following and was not completely out of line with Nazi ideology. The party's decision could have been unpopular. This certification remained in Saller's file at the university. After the war, Saller was reinstated at the University of Göttingen but had to find a position in the teaching faculty. Lenz then wrote to the head of the medical school, implying once again that Saller was mentally unstable and paranoid.[28] The third denouncer was the racist anthropologist Freiherr Egon von Eichstedt. He wrote to the medical school as well, saying that Saller presented himself as an anti-Nazi but had been positive about the system and even had tried to get a job in its Racial Office. Eichstedt hinted that there was another reason for the dismissal, affirming, but leaving unsaid, the rumor of Saller's "mental illness."

Saller finally obtained a position in Munich in the university's Department of Anthropology and Human Genetics in 1948. He became director of the Anthropological Institute in 1951. He wrote several books, including one of the only books that up to the time of its publication had exposed the anthropologists of the Third Reich by name for what they had said and proposed.[29] He also revised Rudolf Martin's *Lehrbuch der Anthropologie* (Textbook of Anthropology) and *Rassengeschichte der Menschheit* (Racial History of Mankind). In his efforts, Saller often worked together with Ilse Schwidetzky, an old Nazi and student of Eichstedt, in a relationship that remains as puzzling as much of the other aspects of Saller's life and beliefs.

Limitations and Blocks Placed on Informational Sources

When the war came to an end, information about what had actually transpired in the camps and occupied territories became public knowledge only over a period of years, and much remains undiscovered and not discussed. The role of anthropologists in the Third Reich was perhaps better known among the populace than reported in the literature, as the following anecdotes illustrate.

In the 1980s, Benno Müller-Hill tried to gain access to the German Research Society (*Deutsche Forschungsgemeinschaft,* or DFG) records, a primary source of funding of anthropological and other scientific projects in the Third Reich. "As I tried to get the DFG records in 1981, I was told by the staff that the DFG in the Third Reich was not called the DFG and that access to the files was not granted: the files on the DFG were not available on principle."[30] He was told that he would be sued if he persisted.

Robert Proctor, an American expert on German racial policies of the Third

Reich, related to a conference meeting of American anthropologists his experience with his Berlin landlady when he was a student in Germany. He asked her, as he had other Germans, "Why did the Germans kill the Jews?" She answered, "Ach! How would I know? I'm not an anthropologist."

My own experience with the public's awareness of anthropologists came at a meeting of Buchenwald concentration camp survivors in Weimar, Germany. An editor of a small magazine for which I had done some writing asked if I would like to meet some Roma survivors. He brought me to the group and introduced me as a journalist. They were friendly and shook hands. I was not trying to pass as a journalist and said, "Actually, I am an anthropologist." They looked stunned, turned on their heels, and disappeared into the crowd.

The information needed by anthropologists or historians to adequately deal with the Nazi past was not available for many years for a number of reasons. The cold war resulted in a division of archives between the East and the West, and equal access to both sides was virtually impossible to obtain. Thus, the archives in Kraków, Łódź, or Poznań, which I found so helpful, would not have been easily accessible to me before 1990. Second, a variety of German laws prohibited access to certain files and documents for fifty years following the war, thus they became available only in 1995. These were primarily files dealing with individuals. Third, many of the documents and much of the information needed to create a history of the era were destroyed, often intentionally.[31]

Even today, most archives are not as open in Europe as they are in the United States. Many documents that were placed in archives are now missing or have never been collected. In a personal conversation in the early 1990s, the American director of the Berlin Document Center (BDC) told me that he felt certain that some Germans had made connections with BDC staff for the purpose of destroying damaging documentation.[32] In addition, many of those active in the Nazi era seemed to intuit that there would be an early end to the "Thousand-year Reich" and maintained a cover story for how they had spent their time, usually through the use of a university affiliation.

The Max Planck Society Archives (MPGA) that house the KWIA documents are open to the serious researcher without difficulty of access, but they are certainly not complete. There was time enough in the years after the war to cleanse the records of the interchanges with Auschwitz, for example; smoking guns are hard to find. Because so many scientists had protected one another, even those without an explosive past were anxious that others not be discovered.

Even today, those who use the MPGA must have all copies of materials inspected personally by the director, as I learned. When I used the archives for the first time, I was pleased to find that I could copy documents myself at a copy machine in the hallway. Having the documents in hand would be helpful, as I was preparing to leave Berlin. Much to my surprise, the reading room supervisor told me that I could not take the copies with me at that time, that first they would have to be inspected by the director. It was the rule.

I managed to rearrange my schedule to come back to Berlin so that I could pick up the document copies after they had been approved. When I arrived, the friendly reading room supervisor greeted me warmly. "Oh, Frau Schafft! You must live under a lucky star! The Herr Director has finished inspecting your copies and they are ready for you." With a broad smile, he handed them to me, and I was free to leave. The problem was, I had no idea whether some of my copies had been removed or not. I had not kept a separate record of the copies that I made. Was the director acting as a censor?[33]

The double-pronged home of the IDO was the University of Vienna and the National History Museum in Vienna, specifically the university's Institute for Anthropology, now the Department of Biological Archaeology and Anthropology. This institution has worked on its Nazi history during the past years in the midst of people whose loyalty could be expected to be mixed. Some were taught or were directed by people like Geyer and Routil and find it hard to criticize people they may remember fondly. The very directorship of the institution under Routil left the possibility of working through its history virtually impossible for decades.

One senses the conflict still. On a visit to the archives of the museum's anthropology department in 2001, I was met by a staff member of the Department of Biological Anthropology with both interest and reserve. She knew of my work with the NAA-SI and the documents I had archived there. After a brief meeting with the staff, I was told I could look at the literature housed in the archive only if I could name what I wanted to see; I was told that I would not be given access to the card file and could see no records of the IDO because the staff themselves were working on them and hoped to publish from them. I could not have access to information about the postwar careers of the IDO members. I busied myself with reading the articles they had filed of the historical accounts of anthropologists and a few current textbooks. They provided me with information about one recent exhibit.

Perhaps noting my dissatisfaction with this restricted use of what I had assumed was a public resource, one professional staff person asked if I and my husband, who happened to be with me, would like to have a tour of the work space. We assured her we would. She showed us the large laboratory where anthropologists had been working on skulls. On the sides of the cavernous museum room, hundreds of skulls on numerous shelves covered the wall space. Both my husband and I understood our guide to say that there were thousands of skulls, at least half of which had been taken from concentration camps and graves in the Nazi period.[34] I was stunned and asked why the skulls were here and how the anthropologists could bear to work under them. She said that probably no one knew what to do with them. A closer look showed that some were labeled with such banal signs as "Pole" or "Slav." What possible use could they be? I asked if the department would use the skulls for research at a future time and was assured by our guide that they would never do that. Next, we came to a cabinet that our guide opened and showed us the modeled figures of World War I prisoners of war and the life masks described by Routil in his article that is in the Smithsonian IDO collection.[35] To what uses would these prizes from a lost war be put? Why are they kept?

A report on a project of the University of Vienna's Senate throws further light on this dilemma. It attempts to account for the numerous collections made during the Third Reich and quotes a previous university report from 1966 in praising Josef Wastl, the director of the museum's anthropology department from 1941 to 1945: "The great enrichment of anthropological material brought an extensive and scientifically valuable [fund of] research of European and outer European prisoners of war from the Second World War that he carried out under contract with the Academy of Science."[36]

By the latest estimate, the collection residing in the Natural History Museum of Vienna's anthropological division includes or has included the following artifacts:

—28 skulls and death masks of concentration camp victims that were finally buried in 1991;

—29 skulls and plaster casts of Jews that were purchased from the University of Posen (Poznań), plus further collections that included 40,000 individuals from the Stone Age to the nineteenth century, casts and reconstructions from skeletons, plaster masks and busts of living persons and "ideal type" molds, and an X-ray collection;

—15 skulls from Poland as "exhibit objects" and further skulls and plaster casts of Jews from concentration camp victims and Polish resistance fighters;

—350 plaster masks done in the Vienna Stadium, Kaiersteinbruch, and Wolfsberg in 1939; and

—70 face masks done in Hintersdorf.

In addition, 252 graves were excavated in the Döblinger Cemetery, and 182 more graves were identified as having potential for further excavation. Artifacts and human remains collected from these graves are not inventoried.[37]

In World War II, masks were made by the museum anthropologists at the

Masks and miniaturized figures of prisoners of war, probably completed in camps during World War I, stored in cupboards of the Natural History Museum of Vienna in 2001. Author's personal photo collection.

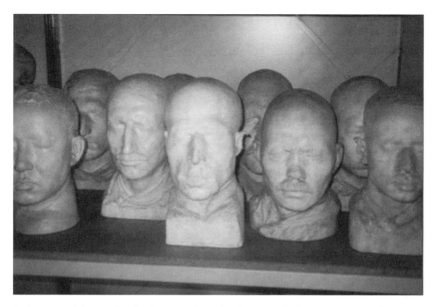

A close-up of the masks of prisoners of war in the Natural History Museum of Vienna in 2001. Author's personal photo collection.

Vienna stadium (see chapter 4). Of the 440 Jewish subjects between the ages of sixteen and eighty-three who were measured using Martin's standardized measurement tools, enough information was collected and masks were made to mount an exhibition under the direction of Josef Wastl for five days in May 1939 at the museum. "They [items in the exhibit] complement the official Nazi race teaching to legitimize scientifically the realization of the obscure, purely ideological differentiation between Jew and non-Jew."[38]

Some of the masks were again displayed in 1999 in an exhibit sponsored by the Foundation of Weimar Classics and the Culture Cities of Europe-Weimar that was mounted by the Buchenwald Memorial Museum and the Natural History Museum of Vienna. The director of the Buchenwald memorial site had written a book about the masks, their history, and the connection of the place, at least through the geographic space it occupied, to Germany's Goethe tradition. The exhibit was developed for a yearlong celebration of Weimar as a "Culture City of Europe," during which many events were planned. The masks and the book written for the exhibition combined the historical record of the 440 Jews who had been handled in this way (343 were killed in Buchenwald) and forty-six drawings by Goethe, Germany's Shakespeare. They were artistically combined so that, if one read the coffee-table book from front to back, one had the history of the 440 Jews from Vienna, but by turning the book

A small example of the skulls in the workrooms of the Natural History Museum of Vienna, summer 2001, labeled "scientifically" as "Pole," "Serb," "Tschechin" (Czech), and "Slovak." Number 320 appears to have had the skull opened for removal of the brain. Author's personal photo collection.

over, one had the story of Goethe in Weimar. The authors believed this showed "the ambivalence of the connection between Buchenwald and Weimar."[39]

A Holocaust survivor who had been imprisoned in Buchenwald, Paul Grünberg, reported in an interview in 1999 that the experience of being modeled for a cast of his head was not the worst of his experiences as a prisoner. "We weren't at all surprised. They [prisoners] didn't have any chance. They were not allowed to ask why one was doing that. They were just an object. They weren't men anymore. One couldn't ask questions or wonder. But that was one of the things that didn't hurt."[40]

The staff member who gave us the tour of the Natural History Museum in Vienna wrote to me to explain that the former Department of Anthropology of the museum has an "osteological collection of about 40,000 skeletons," about 400 of which had been collected between 1938 and 1945. These, she explained, had been reburied.[41] However, 400 is the number of the Buchenwald contingent described in the exhibit book. Certainly, after 1938, many other skeletons and skulls were added to the collection. It seems unrealistic to believe that this was the only time during the Third Reich that the anthropology department had collected human remains for its Viennese museum.

In fact, the diary of Hermann Voss, an anatomist and one of the founders of the Reich University in Poznań during the Third Reich, relates the following: "On Sunday, Herr von H[irschheydt] told me that he had gotten lice on Saturday from a louse-ridden Jewish corpse. He has been making plaster casts of Jewish heads for the Vienna anthropological museum." Hirschheydt died from either that louse or one like it. A footnote adds, "Voss developed a booming trade in skeletons and skulls that he sold to Breslau, Leipzig, Vienna, Königsberg, and Hamburg; he received 15–30 RM per skull, or 150 RM per skeleton."[42]*

Despite these discouraging examples, there is ample evidence that professional denial of the anthropological Nazi past is not the total picture. The neighborhood in which the MPGA is located is the same in which the original institutes were housed. Now integrated into the buildings of Berlin's Free University (*Freien Universität*), the archive building could pass for another villa in this very sedate area of tree-lined streets.

Around the corner from the MPGA is the original building of the KWIA on 22 Ihne Strasse, and on it is a plaque that explains what had happened

---

*I cut the flesh from the bodies of healthy girls for Dr. Mengele's bacteria cultures. I bathed the corpses of cripples and dwarfs in calcium cloride and cooked them in vats, so that the relevant prepared skeletons could be put in the museums of the Third Reich in order that there future generations would have proof of the necessity for the extermination of "inferior races."
—Miklós Nyiszli, prisoner and pathologist under Mengele, 1992

The anthropological collection advanced into one of the largest in Germany. [Speaking of the collection of body parts at the University of Jena]

Pieces Taken Over by Günther in 1936	The Collection in 1953
110 skulls	1,100 skulls
3 skeletons	60 skeletons
76 single bones	10 parts of skeletons
26 casts of prehistoric human remains	11,000 single bones
49 hair samples	175 casts
	39 wet preparations

—Uwe Hossfeld, 2000

within this building. It is one of the most explicit statements of responsibility found anywhere on the history of the Nazi anthropologists:

> The Kaiser Wilhelm Institute for Anthropology, Human Genetics and Eugenics was located in this building between 1929 and 1945.
>
> The Directors, Eugen Fischer (1927–1942) and Otmar von Verschuer (1942–1945) along with their colleagues gave out scientific reasons for the inhuman race and population policies of the Nazi state. As trainers of the SS doctors and eugenicists, through certifications of heredity and compulsory sterilization their work was an active contribution to selection and murder.
>
> Research on twins carried out by the student and personal colleague of Verschuer, Josef Mengele, in concentration camp Auschwitz was planned in this building and supported through the examination of organs of selected and murdered prisoners.
>
> There has been no atonement for these crimes. Von Verschuer was Professor for Genetics until 1965 in Münster.
>
> Scientists must be responsible for the content and impact of their scientific work.[43]

Another encouraging sign was the response of Alfred Kühn, a journal editor, to the submission of a manuscript in 1949 by Karin Magnussen. He refused to provide Magnussen a venue for her work on the eyes that she had collected. Kühn not only rejected her work but was explicit in stating the reasons for his decision.

> Very honorable Fräulein Dr. Magnussen!
>
> Here I am sending back to you the galleys of your work: "The Influence of the Color Gene on the Development of Pigment in the Eyes of the Rabbit." The composition was destroyed at the publishing house [during the war]. The publisher of the journal will not print a new copy of your publication. I will tell you frankly why.
>
> Your National Socialist and anti-Semitic convictions were known to me. Many young people were taken in by these frauds and have in the meantime recognized their mistakes. Whether this is the case with you, I do not know. However, we have discovered that you also worked with human material on Gypsy eyes from the Auschwitz camp in the KWI for Anthropology. It is inconceivable to me how it is possible to have a relationship of any kind with a person connected to this institution. In order not to follow a rumor, we have registered with the Acting Director of the KWI for Anthropology in Dahlem and stated the facts to Professor Nachtsheim.
>
> From here on, we will not take any publication from you. [Making a formal complaint] will not change the outcome.[44]

Magnussen carried on a correspondence with Fischer about this interchange. She was incensed by it but not embarrassed. Fischer offered her solace and some time later referred to Alfred Kühn's letter to Magnussen as "an effrontery and boorish behavior."[45] The editor's rejection was effective, how-

In many European countries, groups of Gypsies wander around. Through their heredity and racial characteristics as well as through their way of life, they are seen as foreign bodies to all people [Volk], less through their numbers and influence than through their strangeness and their remarkable activities.
—Karin Magnussen, 1943

If the [Roma] clan were not so criminal and had not been interned [in Auschwitz] then I would have been able to work on a different analysis for pathological heredity and physiology. . . . If the clan had not been such a criminal society, I now would still try to work on them. . . . there are a lot of Auschwitz Gypsies running around here that one could ask, but I don't want to make contact with them.
—Karin Magnussen, 1950

ever, for later, when Magnussen tried to have the work published through the intervention of an old friend at the KWI, he told her that she should give up the attempt; it was simply tainted.[46]

While the picture was not completely bleak in regard to information about the role of anthropologists in the Third Reich until the 1990s, limitations on the access to information about their crimes allowed the Nazi anthropologists to regain their stature. It is a long and difficult road to making documentation available and accepting responsibility.

The Use of Language and Context

Some aspects of the German language lend themselves to obfuscation. It is acceptable and even preferred in many cases to write in indirect discourse and use a sentence structure that makes determining the agent of action difficult. Sometimes this leads to an inadvertent confusion, and sometimes it leads to a use of language in the service of denial.

There must have been a sense among the anthropologists, even as they were active in the Third Reich, that the new German state would not reshape the world for all time. They were careful. Rarely does one see the word "Jew" in the papers of the university anthropologists or those at the KWIA. (The anthropologists of the IDO used a different, more indirect discourse.) They did not speak of sterilization or euthanasia. They kept the language of their publications free of Nazi jargon. While firing their colleagues for their Jewish backgrounds, sitting on commissions that designed new laws and regulations, and training doctors to dismiss their reservations about "cleansing the society," they were careful to speak in euphemistic terms. So Verschuer could say: "The coming victorious end of the war and the powerful construction of the Greater German Reich also place before our research stations a new task . . . so in the near future everything will be of extraordinary meaning, so to speak, for the importance of developing mankind: questions of heredity, of race, of human selection."[47]

An exception to not directly talking about Jews is found in a textbook written by Karin Magnussen in 1944. After discussing the "Gypsy problem," she turned her attention to the Jews: "For Germany and for many other countries in Europe, the most important racial question is the Jewish question. In the Jewish Volk there are two opposing foreign races: the Preasiatic and the Oriental. The fiction of this race is facilitated through the Moses religion that the larger part of the Jewish Volk belong to, even if by far not all. . . . Through the current war, which is a war of Jews against the Reich, a series of laws is necessary."[48]

As discussed in the previous chapter, many German anthropologists were preoccupied after the war with hiding their Third Reich activities. Within a short time, many were not only back in prestigious positions in universities and institutes but enjoying the respect of their peers and acknowledgment of their earlier work. Magnussen was right when she reported to Fischer that the old gang from the KWIA was back in the midst of the leading anthropological establishment.

As the names of the anthropological perpetrators appeared as respected names in print again, it became harder to make a case against them. Suspicions were not even raised for many years, for their denazification records were held private. This does not mean that they were unaware of the rumors that floated around them or the potential danger that they were encountering. Fischer maintained a correspondence with both Verschuer and Magnussen that survives in his papers and in the MPGA.

Two related problems arose in the use of the names of Nazi anthropologists. The first was the reinstatement of formerly Nazi professors in new positions where they could continue to publish and clear their names through a revised bibliography. In this way, Riemann republished his material from the IDO, housing it in an innocuous shell, as described earlier (see chapter 7). Verschuer, Schwidetzky, Eichstedt, Fischer, and many other Nazi anthropologists found publishers ready to receive their work. The most egregious example is a 1964 article by Verschuer extolling the history of the KWIA without making any mention of the controversy or of crimes against humanity that the institute staff committed.[49]

The second problem was the continued recognition of anthropologists who had been active in the Nazi era without an appreciation of what their past had actually meant. For example, ethnologist Adolf Spamer at the end of the war did not advertise that he had been a Nazi Party member since 1934 and the director of the *Volkskunde* division in the Reich Society for German Volk Research (*Reichsgemeinschaft für Deutsche Volksforschung*).[50] He was successfully appointed to the Technical College (*Technische Hochschule*) of Dresden with the help of a letter written to the university rector by Victor Klemperer, the now-famous diarist, who said, "To be able to count Professor Spamer, such an internationally known man, as a part of the teaching staff would be a great win for the cultural science department."[51]

Spamer responded to the university appointment in a peculiar way. He thanked the school for the appointment but also said that he was particularly pleased that he could step aside from the need to restrict anthropology in a political-propagandistic way and would make up for lost time in earnest work for "a larger organization" (the academy). What he did not recognize was any large break in the discipline between the Nazi era and its aftermath. To him, it was all the same, just a different sponsor.

Dresden was, however, in the GDR (East Germany) at that time, and Spamer's Nazi past did become a point of discussion. As he tried to establish himself within a communist society, he was reminded that there had to be a break with the past. The new anthropology would be general ethnology (*Volkskunde*), in which there were no higher- or lower-valued classes, castes, or peoples, only those that could be described as more- or less-developed.

Ilse Schwidetzky not only managed to hide her past but to become a commentator in her postwar textbooks on Third Reich anthropology. Her opinions went unchallenged, and she was published widely. Thus, as late as 1982, she wrote in *Maus und Schlange* (Mouse and Snake), "What did German anthropology win and lose in the National Socialist time? In the following, I will put together the institutional growth gathered through information from the *Anthropologischer Anzeiger*. It will distinguish between what was profitable to anthropology and what was profitable to nonanthropology."[52] Schwidetzky listed then all of the university positions and those who filled them with no mention of any broader implications. She gave two examples of anthropologists who suffered under the Nazis: a Jewish anthropologist who immigrated and "died in New York"; and Karl Saller, who was removed from his university position.

In another publication, Schwidetzky states chillingly: "A row of new modern statistical investigations has confirmed in meaningful ways the old typological system that was based on observation. And also today, even the anthropologists go back to the basic experience of observations about the geographic differentiation of humans that also gives new impulse to abstract and common, evolutionary-genetic questions, for example."[53]

Relativizing the Past

The request among German historians for a more nuanced picture of the Nazi past too often led to rationalizations, a kind of mild rebuke to those who were active Nazis, and an attempt to relativize the past. For instance, even prolific and thoughtful anthropological historians have stated, "It is necessary to pay attention not only to the politicizing tendencies and discipline's deeds but the total scientific and societal fabric [*Gesamtverflechtungen*] of the academy in the Nazi system and its war."[54] The attempt to place the Nazi past in a context of other eras is also seen in this classic example: "Also in other German universities until now there have only been partially deep or serious discussions of the history of individual disciplines in the various eras— as for example anthropology or genetics in the Weimar Republic, in National Socialism, in the German Democratic Republic, and the Federal Republic of Germany."[55]

However, the Weimar Republic and the cold war were not eras in which anthropology was used as an adjunct to the Holocaust. Thus, these attempts to place this horrific time, which most Americans certainly consider to be unique, within a context of other time periods, as if they were equal, appears disingenuous. This attempt to deal with the past in Germany by making dissimilar events appear equal was made clear to me one day when I visited a museum in Munich, where a Christian church and a Jewish synagogue had been placed together in a context that did not seem quite honest. A particular scene of the city carried the following statement: "Two sacred buildings were destroyed even before the war: the main synagogue near Lenbachplatz and the Protestant Matthäus Church on Sonnenstrasse."[56] The implication was that the two buildings had a similar fate. However, the Matthäus Church was torn down to make way for street construction, and the synagogue was destroyed because it was an unacceptable reminder of Jewish life in the city that was the capital of the Hitler movement.

Another way to relativize the Nazi era was to claim that the academic work was acceptable even when the political slant on things was not. A bifurcation of the academy and the politics is made to appear when, in reality, it did not exist. Verschuer, who remained a member of the Confessing Church, an anti-Nazi institution, throughout the war years, was reported by his son as having said, "Render unto Caesar the things which are Caesar's, and unto God the things which are God's."[57] Having remained a church member did not

We are facing today a serious threat to the survival of the entire European population from the onslaught of Bolshevist Russia. After the victorious conclusion of this war and the guarantee of the racial survival of Europe that will accompany this victory, the future story of race and heredity will depend on two factors: 1. the reproduction of a few nations and the migratory movements to which this will give rise, and 2. the selective processes within individual nations.
—Otmar von Verschuer, 1944

My father favored a strict separation between "pure" science and politics. That was also one of his precepts.
—Helmut von Verschuer, son of Otmar von Verschuer, 1988

preclude him from guilt, nor could one dismiss his murderous activities because he kept them isolated from his "moral life."

The Effects of Nazi Anthropology on the Discipline

In both the United States and the countries that had made up the Third Reich, the postwar era brought about an attempt to look at contemporary problems directly, particularly racism. Anthropologists such as Melville Herskovits, Margaret Mead, and Otto Klineberg, who were Boas's students, made significant differences in the way Americans thought of race.[58] Unfortunately, the change that occurred in Germany and Austria was far less substantial. A change in vocabulary was substituted for substantial redirection of the discipline.

The journal founded by Rudolf Martin reminds its readers of that fact with every issue; under the title of the *Anthropologischer Anzeiger* is the statement "Founded by Rudolf Martin." Perhaps few people know of Martin's position on race or the tragic fate of his wife, but they may remember him as the person who created the eye chart used to determine race and thus the fate of victims. No longer do articles in the journal refer to "race," but occasionally one reads between the lines and finds the content is still there. For instance, in an article comparing body shapes in native British and migrant Pakistani men, the author reverts to the racial term "Whites" in describing his data. "These results indicate that significant ethnic differences exist in trunk and extremity subcutaneous adiposity between Whites and migrant Pakistanis, which cannot be explained by variables like age, and levels of generalized (BMI) and abdominal adiposity (WHR and CI)."[59] The author goes on to say that there was no "ethnic heterogeneity" within each group of subjects when age was controlled. This is not explained, but it shows again the journal's willingness to implicitly refer to the supposed homogeneity of poorly defined groups, using at least one racial term, "white," that has no meaning outside of a racial context.

Notes

1. See the following books for explanations of indirect rule within the Nazi concentration camp system: Sofsky, *Order of Terror;* Drobisch and Wieland, *System der NS-Konzentrationslager, 1933–1939;* and Gudrun Schwarz, *Die nationalsozialistischen Lager.*

2. Weindling, "Tales from Nuremberg," 635–52.

3. Ibid., 637–38.

4. Ibid., 642.

5. Ibid., 648.

6. See Annas and Grodin, *Nazi Doctors and the Nuremberg Code.*

7. See Gillis, *Commemorations;* and Linenthal, *Preserving Memory.*

8. See Fromm, *Beyond the Chains of Illusion.*

9. See Kaufmann, *Geschichte der Kaiser-Wilhelm-Gesellschaft im Nationalsozialismus.* The importance that anthropology was accorded is also seen in the retention of that division of the IDO to the very end, even when other divisions had been dismantled. Anthropology was considered critical to the welfare of the Nazi state.

10. Mitscherlich and Mitscherlich, *Die Unfähigkeit zu Trauern.*

11. Hauschild, Review of *L'quete de la race,* 894–95.

12. Schafft, "Civic Denial and the Memory of War," 261.

13. Many German and Austrian anthropologists have studied their own institutions or other limited aspects of anthropological work in the Third Reich. Marcus Mosen, Niels Lösch, Peter Linemayr, Thomas Hauschild, and a few others have addressed broader aspects of anthropology in the Third Reich.

14. See Freud, *Civilization and Its Discontents.*

15. Schafft, "Civic Denial and the Memory of War," 255–56.

16. Ibid.

17. The following pages on Saller are based on the biography by Lüddecke, *Der "Fall Saller" und die Rassenhygiene.*

18. Ironically, the Martin eye chart, which showed the vast variety of eye colors, was used by Nazi anthropologists to document "race."

19. Lüddecke, *Der "Fall Saller" und die Rassenhygiene,* 57.

20. Quoted in Ziegelmayer, *100 Jahre Anthropologie in München,* 256.

21. Lüddecke, *Der "Fall Saller" und die Rassenhygiene,* 58.

22. Ibid.

23. See Saller, "Eugenische Rundschau."

24. Eugen Fischer had also indicated as much (see chapter 7) when he wrote that the Jews were distinguishable by their religion and cultural characteristics, but he wrote that in a more racist context that was more consistent with the parole of the political powers than Saller's statements. See Baur, Fischer, and Lenz, *Menschliche Erblichkeitslehre*, 747; and Seidler and Soritsch, *Rassen und Minderheiten*, 26.

25. Lüddecke, *Der "Fall Saller" und die Rassenhygiene*, 93.

26. Saller, *Die Rassenlehre des Nationalsozialismus in Wissenschaft und Propaganda*, 38.

27. Lüddecke, *Der "Fall Saller" und die Rassenhygiene*, 88.

28. Ibid., 95.

29. Ibid., 95–98.

30. Quoted in Klee, *Deutsche Medizin im Dritten Reich*, 372.

31. Ibid., 286–89; Simpson, *War Crimes of the Deutsche Bank and the Dresdner Bank*. My own experience has been to find inexplicable "holes" in document files in a vast variety of personal and government records.

32. Personal conversation with David Marsden, director of the BDC, Aug. 7, 1991.

33. This censorship is also discussed in Klee, *Deutsche Medizin im Dritten Reich*, 378.

34. Later, in an e-mail, she disavowed having made this statement. Margit Berner to author, Apr. 19, 2002.

35. Routil, "Das Erscheinungsbild gefangener Polen aus dem Weltkrieg," 129–43.

36. Akademischer Senat der Universität Wien, *Untersuchungen*, 2.

37. Ibid., 4–13. This is by no means an exhaustive list but rather an example of the kinds of materials collected and the indeterminate nature of the inventory.

38. Hirte, "Die anthropologische Untersuchung im Stadium," 22.

39. Hossfeld, "Vom Antlitz zur Maske," 372.

40. Quoted in Hirte, "Die anthropologische Untersuchung im Stadium," 27. The statement by Grünberg begins in the first person but moves quickly to the third person, depersonalizing, or placing in a larger context, the horrible experience of the Holocaust.

41. Berner e-mail, Apr. 19, 2002 (see note 34).

42. Quoted in Aly, Chroust, and Pross, *Cleansing the Fatherland*, 141.

43. The plaque is a result of the campaigning of people who worked in the postwar years in the Max Planck Society. It was erected in 1985 after a struggle with the then president of the Free University of Berlin, who did not want it placed on the building on Ihne Strasse.

44. Quoted in Klee, *Deutsche Medizin im Dritten Reich*, 362.

45. Quoted in ibid., 365.

46. Ibid., 368.

47. MPGA, I Abt., Rep. 1A, Nr. 2400/1, Bl. 159–70, S.1.

48. Magnussen, *Rassen- und bevölkerungspolitisches Rüstzeug*, 54.

49. See Verschuer, "Das ehemalige Kaiser-Wilhelm-Institut für Anthropologie, menschliche Erblehre und Eugenik."

50. Jacobeit, "Die Auseinandersetzung mit der NS-Zeit in der DDR-Volkskunde," 303.

51. Quoted in ibid.

52. Rösing and Schwidetzky, *Maus und Schlange,* 92.

53. Schwidetzky, *Rassen und Rassenbildung beim Menschen,* 112.

54. Hossfeld and John, "Die Universität Jena im 'Dritten Reich,'" 20.

55. Hossfeld, "Von der Sozialanthropologie zur Humangenetik," 82.

56. Quoted in Schafft, "Civic Denial and the Memory of War," 267.

57. Quoted in Müller-Hill, *Murderous Science,* 117.

58. Lewis, "Passion of Franz Boas," 455–56.

59. Bose, "Interaction of Waist-Hip Ratio and Conicity Index with Subcutaneous Adiposity in Two Ethnic Groups," 281.

Epilogue

Goals and Values

Nazi anthropology had one overriding goal: to assist the government in making the German Reich a rational, unified, homogeneous state with the most optimal gene pool that science could provide. What one could call "the ideology of excellent uniformity" was familiar to the German and Austrian anthropologists through years of discussions within their organizations and the published work of their colleagues.

Anthropologists and other perpetrators seem to have had a bifurcated value system. On the one hand, they endorsed the instrumental values—those that would make their long-term goals possible—of progress, career success, and modernity. These justified any actions that would take them to their goal. The other values, those that one could identify as stabilizing values, such as empathy, inner-directedness, and a feeling of shared humanity, were reserved for those closest to them by virtue of kinship or friendship. On the personal level, they might be devoted to family, friends, nature, animals; but on the professional level, they experienced a total disconnect from human involvement with those deemed outsiders to the Reich. We have hints, through the correspondence of Kahlich and Fliethmann (chapter 1), that this separation of instrumental and stabilizing value systems was not always easy. Kahlich was affected by the crying of Jews in her office, and Fliethmann was capable, after the war, of viewing the Nazi period from a new perspective that she gained through her marriage and, perhaps, personal reflection.

What we should not forget is that opposing ideas and values existed at every stage of the history of German anthropology. It took the enormous two-pronged push of Gleichschaltung and ruthless totalitarianism to narrow the field of ideas to the single voice from which anthropologists in the Third

Reich spoke. If the fascist regime had not taken power in 1933, certainly the competition of ideas and beliefs would have gone on without leading to the annihilation of unprecedented numbers of people and groups.

Linkages between Thought and Action

To what extent can we blame the *ideologies* so rigidly disseminated throughout the Reich for the *actions* that took place? Learning of, or even accepting, the racial valuations assigned to each group does not mean that one is prepared to define some of them as unworthy of life. Where are the linkages between thought and action in this case?

Perhaps Ulrich Herbert says it best in speaking of the Einsatzgruppen. Their ability to relate their mass murders to an established ideological principle not only gave them political cover against authorities who may have been inclined to intervene but also enabled them to justify their crimes—to themselves and to their comrades. Their deeds were part of many actions that were "necessary" in order to reach a higher end: the purification of the Reich. This justification was so internalized that it no longer needed to be a matter of reflection.[1]

Too often, when authors discuss the period and the racialization of German society, it is the theories and written materials that draw their attention. From the beginning, however, even before the Third Reich, at least some of the discipline's leaders were engaging in *actions* that dehumanized others, created great pain and suffering, and contributed to murder. Zimmerman writes of the anthropologists' role in exhibiting "exotic" people in public zoolike circumstances while "studying" their physical, cognitive, social, and spiritual selves.[2] Several died from exposure to the cold and wet weather of Berlin. With the financial support of the Rockefeller Foundation, twins were exposed to chemical substances and possibly disease at a prominent Berlin hospital in experiments led by those who would later be linked to similar experiments in Auschwitz. Anthropologists like Hans Günther were widely read and their works widely distributed long before Hitler, spreading ideas of racial hierarchies and fear of the "other."

Knowledge and Shame

The notion that the anthropologists did not know the implications of what they did is now discredited. By 1941, those involved with the movement of people—and that included to some extent almost all the anthropologists—were aware of the concentration camps, mass shootings, and deportations throughout the Reich.[3] Many different arms of the Nazi bureaucracy were working toward the same goals and often in competition with one another. Probably none who were involved in the German expansion avoided coming into contact with some arm of Himmler's operations. Yet, after the war, it became useful to have a cover that one's work was merely academic or scientific rather than tied to the political structure of a discredited regime. There were many bureaucracies within the Reich of anthropological interest, but a single book can only address a few of them. Rosenberg's *Osterministerium* (East Ministry), Himmler's *Ahnenerbe,* and the organizations that sponsored colonization of Germans in the east, for example, are all worthy of more attention.

For these respected academicians and laboratory scientists, shame could never have been far from the surface. The subject of the shame of perpetrators rarely has been explored in the Holocaust literature. In looking at the vocabulary used, one is struck by the care perpetrators used in describing their actions. This was certainly for their own protection, but it also could have been used to mitigate the tremendous guilt that they must have suffered. "Resettlement" often meant the expulsion of people from their homes, with only a dim future ahead. "Evacuation" often meant sending people on forced treks, with purposeful exhaustion and undernourishment leading to a preordained death. "Overpopulation" meant the extermination of people who, having long populated an area, were now viewed as causing a drain on resources and should be eliminated. "Racial hygiene" meant the practice of eugenics and euthanasia.

Recently, information has become available about the importance of the area of Galicia in occupied Poland and the development of the "Final Solution." The hypothesis has been put forth that this area served as a middle ground between the Altreich and the newly conquered region in the east. Using the initiative of police battalions and the Einsatzgruppen, early extermination of isolated groups could be a test for reaction from the public and the international community. Only later, when it was clear there was no significant reaction, did the orders come from Berlin to continue with total annihilation of unwanted populations. Does not this hesitation also indicate an element of shame and discomfort for what the perpetrators were doing?

There was, at the same time, concern among commanders of battalions moving eastward that their troops could turn into beasts if they continued the mass executions in forests and city squares. The report of one SS officer indicates this anxiety. He ordered Ukrainian troops to do the actual mass shooting of Jewish children that he described thus: "I went out to the woods alone. The Wehrmacht had already dug a grave. The children were brought along in a tractor. I had nothing to do with this technical procedure. The Ukrainians did not aim at any particular part of the body. They fell into the grave. The wailing was indescribable. I shall never forget the scene throughout my life."[4]

Blut und Boden, the ideology that was intended finally to create the racialization of geographic space, could only be achieved by moving thousands of people from one place to another. When this could not be accomplished according to plan, individual initiative was fostered. Thus, Herbert Grohmann, the anthropologist from the KWIA who served as the public health director of Łódź, prepared to house the "repatriated" Germans coming to settle in the eastern region in a hospital. In order to make room for these "settlers," he ordered 540 patients murdered in mobile gas chambers.[5] Thus, the beginning of the Final Solution was in acts taking place outside of the Altreich, away from the direct confrontation with stabilizing forces, such as family and friends, that might have made such atrocities less likely.

Certainly, the stress of the resettlement program, the shortage of food, the losses at the front, and the increasing risk of epidemics all contributed to the liquidation of millions of people. The economic value of the goods that could be taken from the victims diminished over time, and instead of a cipher on the positive side of the balance sheet, there was one on the negative. Getting rid of the "overpopulation" then conformed to the ideology of racial hygiene that anthropologists had propagated so carefully. Perhaps, the ideology also mitigated shame and guilt by providing a rationale for the individual acts that made up an otherwise unthinkable genocide. Regardless, the descriptions in most documents remain euphemistic.

Anthropologists as Perpetrators

There is sufficient evidence to place anthropologists in the German Third Reich squarely within the category of perpetrators. In every way, they prepared the German population for the Holocaust and helped it almost to succeed.

It is clear that the records needed to make this case are difficult to find, to access, and to analyze. Documents that would make a clear connection between various active institutions and the activities of the Nazi anthropologists have been purged. Even if all the documents had survived in the archives, we would not have found much incriminating language. Specific content of courses given to doctors, teachers, and clergy by the anthropologists was not retained for our perusal. The involvement of anthropologists in various government commissions and agencies is also difficult to find. Each author who works seriously with this material tries to add to the work of others in exposing this history. Each adds documents that he or she has found and makes them available for use by others in putting together this huge puzzle. Informants are not easy to find, nor are they always forthcoming. People with information generally keep it to themselves. It is undoubtedly difficult, and perhaps impossible, for an American to understand the depth of personal and national shame, guilt, and fear that makes this behavior so common in Germany and Austria.

Responsible Anthropology and Responsible Science

On the other hand, there has been no particular inquiry from anthropological professional organizations to explore this area in depth. Professional pride and the urge to support the field of anthropology make many in our discipline nervous when the topic is raised. Anthropology is a field that straddles many others. It has never been totally secure in its own authority. Some anthropologists have told me that airing such dirty linen cannot help us today to maintain our professional credibility.

However, even those who would like to protect our discipline from historical criticism find it possible to address larger ethical issues without hesitation. These issues, such as the responsibility of science and the candid foreclosure of any disregard for the sanctity of human life, are virtually universally held today. The public is very anxious to know of any failures in these areas, which, after all, may affect the lives of themselves or their families.

Where does the responsibility within any science lie? The individual scientist embodies accountability for his or her individual work, but in this study, we have seen that the funding agencies also carry a heavy burden of responsibility. The burden of guilt for promoting racist thinking and disregarding the context in which studies were being done was shared during the Third Reich first by the Rockefeller Foundation and then more seriously by the German research foundations. They funded science at the expense of human values and human life.

When the Rockefeller Foundation had the chance to alert the world to the nature of German science and the racist folly that was occurring even before Hitler, they did nothing. One can only wonder what reward they thought they would gain by disregarding the early elimination of Jews and liberals from the KWI, as if it had no particular meaning. Where are the inquiries about the nature of the human research they were funding? Where are the research reports that came to them? These archives, too, are strangely empty.

The state that requests the research or fails to put limits on it has itself to blame for the misuse of science. However, in the case of the Third Reich, the state had the willing assistance of its best minds, who wanted their ideas to gain recognition and be turned into active programs. The more the state needed their assistance, the more their scientism met the challenge.

Recently, interesting work has been done on the American bison exhibit of the late 1800s, which remained in the Smithsonian Institution for fifty years.[6] William T. Hornby, taxidermist, preservationist, park director, and prolific writer, was the person who mounted the exhibit as an expiation for the decimation of a species. He called the American buffalo a "vanishing race." German anthropologists dealing with human life were not as sentimental. They collected body parts, bones, and measurements of a people they were helping to eliminate, believing that such memorabilia would have "a rare value" when the work was done, the annihilation complete.

Today, we are on the brink of a new era of genetic and human biological research and human manipulation. There are no clear guidelines, nor can a single country create and develop them. In a global environment, what is outlawed in one country easily can be shipped into another, whether in the form of ideas, technology, or practice. Stem cell research is just one example of work that could lead to cures for scourges that are still among us. It could also lead to unthinkable reproduction of genetically engineered humans. Who should decide how we proceed and on what basis?

The denial of professional responsibility in the past is a sign of the coming difficulties in facing these issues in the future. It is our *attitude* toward science that is most important. There is a critical need for heightened sensitivity to the issues of ethics in science and in social science. The public must take responsibility, too, for the questions that scientists are posing. We must be educated enough to know what the critical issues are in scientific investigation and feel enough involvement to *care* about the ethical issues that define life as we know it. That is the only way that oversight, both national and international, has a chance of succeeding.

Responsible Representation of the Third Reich and the Holocaust

In a recent review of an art exhibit that many thought trivialized the Holocaust through "pop" images, the writer said that, in the final analysis, what people really want is for Germany to say, in the words of artist Bruce Nauman, "'We are sorry for what we did, and we promise not to do it again.'"[7] But that is not the case. This has been expressed already many times and in many ways.

Rather, what is needed is an outcry against any attempt to trivialize, relativize, or hide the history of the Third Reich. Anthropology is a profession that has had every opportunity to know, understand, and value diversity in human life and its cultures, peoples, and habits; yet, in the case of the Nazi anthropologists, it turned against that opportunity. Instead, it measured the value of human beings by fictitious standards of *pseudo*natural science and *pseudo*social science, causing the obliteration of rich cultural traditions, as well as death, and destruction to unfathomable numbers of human beings.

The German Democratic Republic (GDR), the former communist East Germany, spent many of its resources exposing former members of the Nazi regime who continued to find acceptance, jobs, and prestige in the Federal Republic (FRG) or the United States. Communist survivors of the Third Reich were well-represented in the GDR and sought justice through these denunciations. This effort also was designed to legitimize the GDR's existence as the true antifascist German state and to draw attention away from the annihilation of Jews and its own curtailments of human rights and civil liberties. This was a major theme of the GDR for the fifty years of its existence.

At least one historian believes that the group of prolific and tireless writers who are not university-based but who have worked over the last twenty years to expose the Nazi past are politicizing history as they, in the process, expose the continuing careers of many perpetrators. There is a suspicion that the attempts to tie the Nazi period to activities of former Nazis in the postwar period could be used to promote a left-leaning agenda by implying that nothing has changed in Germany from the Nazi era. In other words, such exposés could continue the former GDR agenda of ideological anticapitalist criticism.[8]

However, there is another way to look at the exposure of the postwar careers of those perpetrators who were never brought before the courts or even confronted by their own professions. The only agenda this exposure needs to serve is that of justice and admonition. Of course, there are continuities between one time frame and another, even when political systems radically change. People remain. Their personal and political cultures adjust to the new circumstances, but the past remains, in whole or in part, as a source of ideas, values, and identities.

For this author, it was important just to set the record straight. What did anthropologists do? What did they know about the human costs of their work? Where did they get their support, both psychological and financial, for their travels down the genocidal path? What alternatives were available to them that they did not take? And finally—yes—what were the consequences that they faced when the "Thousand-year Reich" reached its end in its thirteenth year?

Authors have identified themselves and their positions on grave theoretical issues of the Holocaust and the Third Reich. Was the Holocaust the result of deep-seated ideologies, even an eliminationist anti-Semitism, or was it the result of a technocratic system that ran out of control? Were events centrally planned, or were they the result of actions on the periphery, almost experiments that then became endorsed in Berlin as generalized policy? Was antihumanism the result of a turn toward modernism and away from the traditional values and structures of the church?

The questions and the theoretical positions are important, but we cannot allow them to structure, a priori, how we approach the documentation, insights, personal testimonies, and experiences with the material that we are privileged to obtain. This book has tried to show the roots of genocide over time and the support of these roots, at least in the beginning stages, across national boundaries, without adhering to a particular defined Holocaust or Third Reich theoretical framework. Being open to all the diversity that the subject matter brings to us is important if we are to be worthy of dealing with it. For any study of the events of this period is an objectification of the reality that once was and, for many people still is, a nightmare.

As I am finishing this book, I am thinking of Hans Gasparitsch, a "graduate" of Dachau and Buchenwald. Hans was a young teenager when he and a group of his friends decided to make a stand against Hitler shortly after he was elected chancellor.[9] They printed flyers and distributed them around Stuttgart and pasted some on public buildings and kiosks. The group met regularly for long hikes and discussions in the woods that surrounded the city. One of their members kept a diary.

When the police searched their rooms in their separate homes on a tip, they found nothing except the diary. It was sufficient to place all the group under arrest. They were kept in the city prison for almost a year. There, the young woman in the group went mad. The others lived in fear of what would come next. For Hans, it was a transfer at age sixteen to Buchenwald, a notorious concentration camp near Weimar.

Hans's political ideas were just forming in 1935. He was immediately influenced by the organization of the communists in the camp and joined them as a runner. He carried messages, slipping from building to building, person to person. Toward the end of the war, he had seen all the brutality that one could imagine but had been spared some of the worst horrors himself. He was then transferred to Dachau, where he was far less protected.

By the end of the war, he was almost thirty, and his youth had been spent in prison and in concentration camps. He decided to study journalism in

Leipzig, in communist East Germany. With his wife and small child, he lived among the believers, but somewhere along the line he gave up any orthodoxy in favor of a humanistic and pacifist stance. He lived the rest of his life in Stuttgart with his many friends, most veterans of those times.

Hans was not invited to the commemorations of various milestones in the liberation of the city from the Nazi yoke. He was too outspoken about the real history that he had experienced. He knew of the guillotine that had been used in the city courthouse, and he criticized the modern structure of three huge blocks that was meant to commemorate the war but was used as a public toilet by the homeless. He was aware of the former Nazis who continued in their businesses even though they could no longer use slave labor.[10]

Unacknowledged as he was throughout his life, at the end he was award-ed the *Bundesverdienstkreuz* (Meritorious Cross), one of Germany's top cit-izen honors for his work with students and with memorial sites. He was hap-py to accept it in his last year of life, still fighting for a recognition of truth about Germany's past and compensation for those who had suffered. His family was happy too for his honor, but it in no way made up for their pain in watching his physical and psychological traumas increase with age.

And for those of us who study the times in which the victims lived, we must remember that each of them, those who are now dead and those who remain, are still individuals, each with a separate fate. The perpetrators too were in-dividuals and should be known as thoroughly as the victims. If we do not keep this in mind as we research and write our works, we have not learned from the careerists who earlier placed all human concern for their subject matter to one side. Placing our thoughts in boxes and our studies in theo-retical molds serves the real history of the Third Reich poorly. The victims often knew only a fragmented share of their real truth, for unlike Hans Gas-paritsch, many did not have the stomach to seek out the truth of their own history after the war. It is up to those of us who can study this period to rec-ognize and respect a real diversity of knowledge, ideas, and approaches to studying and interpreting the Third Reich. As we strive to bring more infor-mation into the light, we recognize and respect the variability of human nature found in those victims and perpetrators who lived this history and realize that we are required, in the interest of truth, to be open to all the in-formation we can gather.*

---

*No, we didn't have misgivings. It was science, after all.
—Irmgard Haase, Verschuer's medical technician, 1988

Notes

1. Herbert, "Extermination Policy," 27.
2. See Zimmerman, *Anthropology and Antihumanism in Imperial Germany.*
3. Herbert, "Extermination Policy," 39.
4. Quoted in Klee, Dresser, and Riess, *"Good Old Days,"* 154.
5. Aly, *Endlösung,* 124.
6. Shell, *Extermination of the American Bison,* viii–xxii.
7. Schjeldahl, "The Hitler Show," 87.
8. Burleigh, *Ethics and Extermination,* 170–71.
9. See Kaspar, *Hanna, Kolka, Ast und Andere.* This fictionalized account by Gasparitsch under a pen name is supplemented here by numerous conversations between him and the author between 1994 and 2001.
10. Schafft, "Civic Denial and the Memory of War," 263–65.

Appendix 1:
Anthropologists' Activities in the Third Reich

These are examples only, not complete listings.

Creating racial divisions
    Claiming inferiority of the Jews
    Claiming Nordic racial superiority
Engaging in "negative" eugenics
    Aiding sterilization
    Identifying "Life unworthy of life"
Engaging in "positive" eugenics
    Encouraging Lebensborn program
Participating in policy formation
    Serving on policy commissions
    Serving in SS academic elite
    Lawmaking
Engaging in government activities proactively
    Training SS doctors in "hereditary hygiene"
    Training SS doctors in "racial studies"
    Training Nazi teachers, doctors, clergy
    Expelling colleagues from jobs
    Certifying racial status
    Measuring Jews and other groups for racial identification
    Serving on racial courts
    Naming victim groups
    Aiding in resettlement schemes
Disrespecting human remains
    Collecting and using body parts, embryos, and neonates from Jews and
        European "races"
    Robbing graves
Torture, maiming, and death
    Ordering specific types of human remains from death camps
    Designing human experiments
    Murdering (or ordering the murder of) victims for "scientific purposes"

Appendix 2:
Chronology of the Third Reich

This chronology is based in part on the even more comprehensive chronology in Martin Weinmann's *Das nationalsozialistische Lagersystem*, lxxxix–cxxxiv.

January 1933   President of the German Reich, Paul von Hindenburg, appoints Adolf Hitler, leader of the Nazi Party, to be chancellor on January 30.

February 1933   The Weimar Constitution is disavowed, and there is a call for new elections.

Group of major industrialists give Hitler significant financial backing.

Hermann Göring uses existing SA, SS, and Stahlhelm troops to form a paramilitary force.

The Reichstag (parliament) fire on February 27 occasions the Order for the Protection of People and State (*Verordnung zum Schutz von Volk und Staat*) suspending civil liberties and removing the rights of free expression, free press, and free assembly.

Approximately 100,000 people are incarcerated and placed in "wild" concentration camps.

March 1933   A wave of arrests takes place before the election.

Göring institutes the Gestapo, and an additional 25,000 people in Prussia alone are arrested and sent to "wild" concentration camps.

The Nazis get 44 percent of the vote, and all 81 Communists elected members of the Reichstag are annulled.

Forty-six unions and associations are taken over by the police or the SA.

Heinrich Himmler, head of the SS and chief of the political police in Bavaria, orders the construction of Dachau, the first concentration camp under the SS.

April 1933	Boycott of Jewish stores and professional people is ordered.
	Employers are authorized to fire employees on suspicion of being against the state.
	Civil servants who are either Jewish or Marxists are ordered to be fired.
	Jewish doctors are denied right to claim insurance for their patients.
May 1933	Trade union offices are occupied by SA troops, and all unions are forbidden and replaced by the German Labor Front, a Nazi organization.
	Public book burning of books by Jewish and Marxist authors takes place on May 10.
July 1933	The Law for the Prevention of Congenitally Ill Progeny (*Gesetz zur Verhütung erbkranken Nachwuchses*) allowing forced sterilization is announced.
	Law is passed allowing confiscation of Jewish property.
	There are at this time 26,789 people in "protective custody" (*Schutzhaft*).
	Concordat is signed with the Catholic Church.
August 1933	A list of banished Jewish and Marxist authors is made public on August 25.
September 1933	Jews are removed from cultural life, and there is a *Gleichschaltung* (forcible standardization) of cultural events.
	It is ordered that farmers only be recognized if they can prove that they have no Jewish ancestry since 1800.
November 1933	First women's concentration camp is established at Moringen, Germany.
	The first nonpolitical prisoners are taken to concentration camps from work houses—charged with being "asocial."
January 1934	The German-Polish nonaggression pact is signed on January 26.
February 1934	The Reich defense department begins economic preparation for war.
April 1934	Heinrich Himmler becomes chief of the Gestapo and appoints Reinhard Heydrich the Gestapo chief of Prussia on April 20.
June 1934	Hitler orders the murder of Ernst Roehm, his followers in the SA, and others considered politically untrustworthy.
August 1934	Law combines posts of chancellor and president on August 1, and Hitler becomes the single head of state.
February 1935	The open production of fighter planes begins.
	The Saarland is annexed.

May 1935	A secret law allows for rearmament under the direction of Dr. Hjalmar Schacht, president of the Reichsbank.
June 1935	All men between the ages of 18 and 25 are required to serve in the work corps (*Reichsarbeitsdienst*) for 6 months.
July 1935	Only "Aryans" are allowed to be students or soldiers.
September 1935	The Nuremberg Laws define "German Jews" and redefine their citizenship rights.
October 1935	Law to protect society from "unworthy life," interpreted as people with handicaps, marks the beginning of extermination policy.
December 1935	*Lebensborn* program is started under the SS.
March 1936	German Army (*Wehrmacht*) marches into the Rhineland, a demilitarized zone since the armistice of World War I, on March 7.
July 1936	German Air Force (*Luftwaffe*) is sent to Spain to support Franco. About 5,000 Germans volunteer to fight on the side of the antifascists in the International Brigades.
August 1936	Universal draft is extended to two years' duration.
November 1936	The Nobel Peace Prize is given to Carl Ossietzky, an antimilitarist and writer, while in Esterwegen Concentration Camp.
	Pact between Japan and Germany (the *Antikominternpakt*) is signed on November 25.
February 1937	Two thousand "habitual criminals" are arrested at one time and sent to concentration camps.
April 1937	Guernica, Spain, is the first civilian center destroyed in a German air attack.
July 1937	Buchenwald is built as a major concentration camp housing primarily political prisoners in preparation for Jewish arrests.
November 1937	Hitler plans the annexation of Austria, and Britain concurs.
	Propaganda Minister Goebbels opens the "Eternal Jew" exhibit in Munich.
February 1938	All single women under the age of 25 are ordered to perform farm or domestic labor for a year.
March 1938	Austria is occupied by the German Army and becomes known as that part of the Reich called the *Ostmark*.
	The SS begins its first industry, "the German Earth and Stone Works," using concentration camp labor to produce building materials.
	Thousands of arrests are made in Austria, and prisoners are sent to German concentration camps.

	The category of "asocial" is adopted, and unemployed are imprisoned in Buchenwald.
April 1938	The systematic takeover of all Jewish property and the "aryanization" of businesses begins.
June 1938	Jews are ordered to carry identity cards. Massive arrests of Roma as "asocials" occur.
August 1938	Jews are ordered to take "Sara" or "Israel" as a first name.
September 1938	Hitler meets with Chamberlain, the prime minister of Great Britain, Mussolini, and Daladier on September 29 in Munich to sign pact giving the Czechoslovakian Sudetenland to Germany.
October 1938	Germany occupies the Sudetenland on October 1. Seventeen thousand Jews of Polish nationality are deported from Germany following the shooting by a young Jew of Ernst von Rath, a German diplomat, in Paris.
November 1938	*Reichskristallnacht,* the plundering of synagogues, homes, and businesses and almost 100 murders, marks the mass arrest of Jews; 35,000 Jews are sent to Buchenwald, Sachsenhausen, and Dachau. Concentration camps at this time reach a population of 60,000. The Nazi administration demands a "compensation contribution" from Jews in the amount of 1 billion RM.
January 1939	Hitler predicts the "destruction of the Jewish race" in the coming war. Anthropologists meet in Munich to discuss the racial certification process and racial hygiene.
February 1939	Jewish emigration is handled under the Gestapo, and Jews are told they should leave Germany, leaving almost all their belongings to the German state; other countries take measures to prevent massive Jewish immigration.
March 1939	The German Army occupies the rest of former Czechoslovakia, and Czechs are sent to work as forced labor in Germany. Czech territory is annexed as a *Protektorat* of the Reich, a kind of colony. Hitler declares his intention to build the *Autobahn* through the "corridor to the sea" in what had been Poland. The Spanish Civil War ends; Spain becomes fascist.
April 1939	According to Gestapo figures, there are at this time 162,734 "protective custody" prisoners, 27,396 accused political activists, and 112,432 political criminals in custody.

May 1939	The foreign ministers of Germany and Italy sign a military pact. Japan attacks Mongolia.
June 1939	Children with disabilities become subject to euthanasia.
July 1939	Euthanasia planning staff meets with Hitler; it is decided that all mentally ill will be killed to make room in hospitals for the wounded from the coming war; doctors are protected from legal action.
August 1939	Midwives and doctors are required to report all births of malformed children. A German-Soviet nonaggression treaty is signed on August 23, and many political prisoners are released from concentration camps.
September 1939	The German Army invades Poland on September 1. England and France declare war on Germany on September 3. The Soviet Army marches into eastern Poland on September 17. The central organ combining the secret police functions of the state with the security police functions of the party is formed as the Reich Main Security Office (*Reichssicherheitshauptamt,* or RSHA), under the command of Reinhard Heydrich. Jews are placed under curfew and must give up their radios. Women who have relationships with foreigners are ordered to have their heads shaved and be put into concentration camps. Any statement against the Reich is declared punishable by death. Many worker privileges are revoked, and virtually all women and girls in the Reich are ordered to work. Heydrich orders all Polish Jews into restricted areas.
October 1939	The German Army advances on the west. One hundred thousand Poles are forced to labor in German agriculture. Those without work are ordered to be put in concentration camps. The first Jews are transported from Austria and Czechoslovakia to Poland. An order is given that those in "protective custody" will not be released during the course of the war. Forced labor is ordered for Jews and "Aryan" Poles, without exception. The first Jewish ghetto is established by the Nazis in the area of occupied Poland's *Generalgouvernement* (GG).
November 1939	Jews are ordered to wear armbands with a yellow star throughout the area controlled by Germany.

December 1939   The first euthanasia center is established near Berlin.

January 1940   The first attempt at using gas to kill victims is made at the euthanasia center near Berlin.

February 1940   Youth are incarcerated for rebellious acts.

March 1940   Workcamps are set up for Poles who do not fulfill work quotas or who are rebellious to German authority.

April 1940   First group of 2,500 Roma is transported to Polish ghettos.
Action T4 begins; euthanasia is widened.
The Institute for German Work in the East (*Institut für Deutsche Ostarbeit*) is founded in Kraków on April 20.
Denmark and Norway are invaded and overtaken by Germany.
All Polish youth, ages 15–25, are ordered to serve in Germany as workers.

May 1940   Germany attacks Holland, Belgium, Luxembourg, France, and the British Isles.
People from occupied lands are sent to work in German factories and mines and in support of all German industry.

June 1940   Auschwitz is built by 728 Polish prisoners.
German U-boats are sent to the Atlantic, Pacific, and Indian Oceans.
German troops march into Paris, and the Vichy government in France is set up.

July 1940   At this point, 14,000 patients have been killed in euthanasia centers.

August 1940   Germany attacks England by air, especially armament factories.
German firms are ordered to pay for the use of Polish prisoners.
First youth concentration camp is established at Moringen.

September 1940   German air attacks lasting 65 days aim to demoralize the civilian population in England; Coventry, Liverpool, and Manchester are demolished.
Systematic murder of Jewish patients under Action T4 continues.
Forced laborers from France and the Low Countries are added to the labor force and kept in camps.
Axis powers (Germany, Italy, and Japan) form an alliance pact on September 27.

October 1940   Some 1.2 million prisoners of war, many of whom are French, are put into slave labor.
The Warsaw Ghetto is established.

November 1940   All "foreign Volk" in captured lands are ordered to be educated only to the fourth grade.

December 1940	The Reich Commissar for the Strengthening of the German Volk (*Reichskommissar für die Festigung deutschen Volkstums,* or RKF) begins the massive task of moving people throughout eastern and southeastern Europe.
January 1941	German troops are sent to North Africa.
March 1941	Alfred Rosenberg, chief Nazi race theoretician, founds the Institute for Research on the Jewish Question and opens the Foreign Office of Higher Education on March 26. Five thousand Roma are sent to the Łódź Ghetto in Poland, where 300,000 Jews are already housed.
April 1941	Large ghettos in Lublin and Radom are established. First mass arrests of Jews in Paris take place.
June 1941	Invasion of the Soviet Union begins on June 22; Germany retrieves all Polish territory. Roosevelt offers help to Stalin. Plans are made to execute all Jews, Communists, and partisans through the use of special troops (*Einsatzgruppen*); over 1 million are murdered before March 1942.
July 1941	Göring tells Heydrich to plan to address the total "Jewish question" in all of Europe; the Holocaust begins in earnest.
August 1941	America sends materials to the U.S.S.R. under the Lend Lease Act. The bishop of Münster, Graf von Galen, speaks out against euthanasia and distributes thousands of leaflets in protest on August 3. The so-called stop to euthanasia is declared, but it continues more carefully; by this time, there have been 70,273 murders of patients and others. Euthanasia is transferred to concentration camps under Action 14f13, in which psychologically distressed prisoners and civilians are put to death as "useless eaters."
September 1941	German troops begin the blockade of Leningrad, which will last until January of 1943. Some 2.6 million jobs become vacant in Germany, .5 million of them in agriculture. Killing by gas begins in Auschwitz.
October 1941	There are now 2,139,553 foreign workers in Germany, about half of whom are Polish. Jews are forbidden to leave the country; at this time 169,869 Jews are left in Germany.

The Gestapo arrest 15,160 persons in this month alone, ten times as many as were arrested in the year 1935–36.

About 300,000 Jews and 50,000 other Soviet people are murdered by the Einsatzgruppen, special German troops, in the Soviet Union.

December 1941	Japan attacks Pearl Harbor on December 7, and America declares war on Japan. Germany and Italy declare war on America on December 11. The death camp at Chelmno begins operation. Action 14f13 begins operation in earnest.
January 1942	The Red Army begins its counteroffensive. The Wannsee Conference decides on January 20 how the annihilation of Jews will be coordinated. The number of living Jews in Polish ghettos reaches 1.5 million.
March 1942	The British start blanket bombing of German cities. Fritz Sauckel takes over the coordination of foreign labor. By the end of the war 14 million have been in impressed labor for the Reich. Sobibór, another death camp, is built; first massive transports of Jews arrive at death camps. Some 100,000 prisoners are in concentration camps and are put to work primarily for the armaments industry.
April 1942	Rations for the Germans are cut; German citizens demand that rations for foreign laborers be reduced. Sauckel removes the work requirement for German women, who are now replaced with foreign labor. The IDO conducts research on Jews of the Tarnów Ghetto.
May 1942	Reinhard Heydrich is assassinated, and the Czech town of Lidice is annihilated in retaliation. Selections begin in Auschwitz for gassings; Treblinka is built as a death camp. Aleš Hrdlička meets with President Roosevelt to discuss postwar immigration policy.
July 1942	All remaining Jews must leave the Reich; mass transports begin from Germany, Holland, and other countries to Auschwitz. Himmler orders that all Jews in the GG should be killed by the end of 1942; annihilation is accelerated.
August 1942	Germans attack Stalingrad. Bormann, henchman of Hitler, begins a surveillance of German women to see that they do not have relations with foreign workers, the beginning of the spy system on German citizens.

October 1942	Jews receive no ration cards for meat or milk; eggs had been forbidden earlier.
	Verschuer takes over from Fischer as head of the KWIA.
November 1942	The German Army is encircled at Stalingrad.
	All Jews remaining in concentration camps are ordered to be removed from the Reich for death camps in occupied Poland; those in Germany receive no ration cards.
December 1942	Individual industries build concentration camps next to their plants.
	The "Gypsy camp" is established at Auschwitz-Birkenau.
January 1943	Representatives of the armaments industry state that it needs 800,000 workers.
	All German women and youth become subject to military duty.
	All nonessential businesses are closed.
	A concentration camp for children is established in Łódź (Litzmannstadt) for Polish children ages 8–16 and later for children 2–16.
	Concentration camps multiply as all major camps establish outer camps.
February 1943	The German Army capitulates in Stalingrad on February 2 after a loss of 250,000 troops.
	Some 1,622,000 prisoners of war and 4,121,000 foreign workers work in Germany at this time.
March 1943	It is determined that pregnancies of Polish women in forced labor in Germany should be terminated; "racially worthy" children are to be "sustained in pregnancy" among foreign workers and at birth placed in the Lebensborn program.
	Greek Jews are transported to Auschwitz.
	The SS takes over private industry in the eastern lands.
	The 2,000th transport of forced laborers to Germany takes place from Poland; the millionth prisoner is freed as a joke.
April 1943	Warsaw Ghetto Uprising occurs.
	Concentration camps Bergen-Belsen and Lublin-Majdanek are created. Majdanek is the center of the SS-East Industry Work (*SS-Ostindustrie GmbH*).
May 1943	Germans capitulate in North Africa.
	Mengele arrives at Auschwitz.
	The United States and England decide to develop nuclear weapons.
	To cover up deaths in concentration camps, prisoners are no longer given consecutive numbers.

June 1943   English and American pilots engage in massive bombardment of German cities.

All problems with foreign laborers are turned over to the Gestapo.

First gassings start in Stutthof of Poles and "White Russians."

July 1943   Mussolini is overthrown; General Badoglio forms a new government.

Transports from the Netherlands arrive in Sobibór, and of these 34,000 persons, only 19 survive.

August 1943   The British bomb Peenemünde, delaying the German development of the V-weapons (rockets).

Almost 3,000 Roma men, women, and children from the "Gypsy camp" in Auschwitz-Birkenau are gassed.

Prisoners revolt in Treblinka, where 700,000–800,000 have already died.

September 1943   Hostilities end in southern Italy as it is liberated by the Allies.

Italian troops are captured by the German Army in the north, the south of France, Yugoslavia, and Greece.

The SS recapture Mussolini, who starts a new fascist government in the occupied part of Italy.

There are 388,000 arrests by the Gestapo in the first nine months of the year, of which 260,000 are foreign impressed laborers.

Albert Speer takes over war production.

October 1943   Some 200,000 partisans are active in Italy.

Prisoners are taken from original camps, and at least 200,000 are placed in armaments factories; there are now 500 outer camps associated directly with industries.

The eastern Ukraine is liberated.

Three death camps are abandoned, but transports from Italy reach Auschwitz.

About 7,500 Jews are saved in Denmark, while 220 fall into the hands of the Gestapo.

Prisoners revolt in Sobibór and destroy the camp where 250,000 had already been murdered.

November 1943   Britain begins an air offensive over Berlin.

At a conference in Teheran, Churchill, Roosevelt, and Stalin decide on a second front.

December 1943   Mussolini orders all Italian Jews to concentration camps.

Three million foreign workers are now in slave labor in the Reich.

February 1944   Tarnów Ghetto is emptied of the last Jews who have not already been murdered.

March 1944	The Soviet Army reaches Rumania and Czechoslovakia. All efforts are directed toward airplane fuel production; underground factories proliferate.
April 1944	Jews are deported from Greece and Hungary. It is ordered that all sabotage by prisoners will result in hanging.
May 1944	Allies bomb all hydroelectric works and fuel depots systematically. Hungarian Jews are deported to Auschwitz. Deaths in Auschwitz reach their peak. Hitler decides to put all able-bodied Jews in weapons production. By this date, 5 million Soviet soldiers have been imprisoned in German concentration camps; by the end of the war, 5.7 million will have been imprisoned, of whom less than 1 million survive.
June 1944	The Normandy Invasion brings the Allies onto the European continent. V-1 rockets land on London. Of the 8,000 rockets fired, only 29 percent of them reach their targets.
July 1944	The Breton Woods Conference takes place among the Allies to plan for the postwar period. Von Stauffenberg's attempt on Hitler's life fails and is followed by massive arrests. Majdanek Concentration Camp is freed by the Soviet Army.
August 1944	The Warsaw Uprising begins on August 1 and lasts until October. Allies land in the south of France, and troops reach Paris. The Dumbarton Oaks Conference creates the United Nations. Sixty-hour work weeks are ordered for German civilians, with no holidays, as total war is declared. There are now 7,615,970 foreign impressed laborers in the Reich and 379,167 men and 145,119 women in concentration camps.
September 1944	Brussels and Antwerp are freed, as are Finland, Hungary, Yugoslavia, and parts of Czechoslovakia. The first V-2 rockets hit London. In the first half of the year, 181,764 prisoners die in the building of tunnels for underground armaments factories.
October 1944	Aachen is the first major city in Germany occupied by the Americans. Black-marketing and plundering occur in German cities. *Mischlinge*, mixed Jewish-gentile offspring, are ordered to report for impressed labor. More than 2.8 million people from the Soviet Union are working in the Reich.

A revolt in the Auschwitz crematorium causes its destruction.

Previously "privileged Jews" married to Aryans are deported to death camps.

November 1944   The last of the IDO is moved out of Poland and into Bavaria.

December 1944   German communities begin to "evacuate" foreign laborers to the east.

The crematoria in Auschwitz-Birkenau are blown up on Himmler's orders.

Gassings stop in euthanasia centers in the Reich.

January 1945   Warsaw is freed by the Soviet Army and the First Polish Army.

Hitler holds his last radio speech.

Evacuation of Auschwitz and outer commandos begins before they are freed.

Women prisoners of Ravensbrück who can no longer work are systematically murdered in the neighboring youth camp of Uckermark.

February 1945   The city of Dresden is destroyed in British-American raids.

German women are called to military service to protect their communities.

March 1945   The Allies cross the Rhine at Remagen.

Hitler declares that all of Germany must be destroyed so that the Allies get nothing.

Death marches are begun in which one-third of the surviving concentration camp prisoners die.

April 1945   Twenty-one German divisions are captured by the western Allies.

The Red army begins its offensive on Berlin and captures the city after massive losses on both sides.

American and Russian troops meet at the Elbe.

The German Italian Army surrenders, and Mussolini is killed.

May 1945   The German Army surrenders at Reims and in Berlin.

Concentration camps are freed.

At the end of the war, there are still 6 million foreign workers, 2 million prisoners of war, and 750,000 concentration camp prisoners on German territory.

Bibliography

Akademischer Senat der Universität Wien. *Untersuchungen zur Anatomischen Wissenschaft in Wien 1938–1945.* Wien: Universität Wien, 1999.

Allen, Michael Thad. *The Business of Genocide: The SS, Slave Labor, and the Concentration Camps.* Chapel Hill: University of North Carolina Press, 2002.

Aly, Götz. *Endlösung: Völkerverschiebung und der Mord an den europäischen Juden.* Frankfurt am Main: Fischer Taschenbuch Verlag, 1995.

———. "Medicine against the Useless." In *Cleansing the Fatherland: Nazi Medicine and Racial Hygiene.* Ed. Götz Aly, Peter Chroust, and Christian Pross. 22–98. Baltimore: Johns Hopkins University Press, 1994.

Aly, Götz, Peter Chroust, and Christian Pross, eds. *Cleansing the Fatherland: Nazi Medicine and Racial Hygiene.* Baltimore: Johns Hopkins University Press, 1994.

Aly, Götz, and Suzanna Heim. *Vordenker der Vernichtung.* Frankfurt am Main: Fischer Taschenbuch Verlag, 1997.

Ammon, Otto. *Gesellschaftsordnung und ihre natürlichen Grundlagen: Entwurf einer Sozial-Anthropologie zum Gebrauch für alle Gebildeten, die sich mit sozialen Fragen befassen.* Jena: Gustav Fischer Verlag, 1900.

Annas, George J., and Michael A. Grodin. *The Nazi Doctors and the Nuremberg Code: Human Rights and Human Experimentation.* New York: Oxford University Press, 1992.

Arad, Yitzhak, Shmuel Krakowski, and Shmuel Spector, eds. *Einsatzgruppen Reports.* New York: Holocaust Library, 1989.

Arendt, Hannah. *Eichmann in Jerusalem: A Report on the Banality of Evil.* New York: Viking Press, 1963.

Arnold, Bettina. "Justifying Genocide." In *Annihilating Difference: The Anthropology of Genocide.* Ed. Alexander Hinton. 95–116. Berkeley: University of California Press, 2002.

———. "The Past as Propaganda." *Antiquity* 84 (1990): 464–78.

Baader, Gerhard, Johannes Cramer, and Bettina Winter. *Verlegt nach Hadamar.* Kassel: Landeswohlfahrtsverband Hessen, 1994.

Barkan, Elazar. *The Retreat from Scientific Racism: Changing Concepts of Race in Britain and the U.S. between the World Wars.* Cambridge: Cambridge University Press, 1992.

Bartosz, Adam. *Tarnowskie Judaica.* Warsaw: Wydawnictwo Pttk "Kraj," 1992.

Bauer, Yehuda. *A History of the Holocaust.* Danbury, Conn.: Franklin Watts, 1982.

Bauer, Yehuda, and Nathan Rotenstreich, eds. *The Holocaust as a Historical Experience.* New York: Holmes and Meier, 1981.

Bauman, Zygmunt. *Modernity and the Holocaust.* Cambridge: Polity Press, 1989.

Baur, Erwin, Eugen Fischer, and Fritz Lenz. *Menschliche Erblichkeitslehre.* Berlin: J. F. Lehmann Verlag, 1923.

———. *Menschliche Erblichkeitslehre und Rassenhygiene.* Berlin: J. F. Lehmann Verlag, 1927.

Benz, Wolfgang. *Feindbild und Vorurteil.* München: Deutscher Taschenbuch Verlag, 1996.

———. "Realität und Illusion: Die deutschen Juden und der Nationalsozialismus." In *Herrschaft und Gesellschaft im nationalsozialistischen Staat.* 119–20. Frankfurt am Main: Fischer Taschenbuch Verlag, 1990.

Béon, Yves. *The Planet Dora.* Boulder, Colo.: Westview, 1997.

"Bericht über die 2. Internationale Tagung für anthropologische und ethnologische Wissenschaften in Kopenhagen." *Rasse* 5:12 (1939): 471–72.

Black, Edwin. *IBM and the Holocaust.* New York: Crown, 2001.

Blaich, Fritz. *Wirtschaft und Rüstung im Dritten Reich.* Dusseldorf: Schwann, 1987.

Borkin, Joseph. *The Crime and Punishment of I. G. Farben.* New York: MacMillan, 1978.

Bose, Kaushik. "The Interaction of Waist-Hip Ratio and Conicity Index with Subcutaneous Adiposity in Two Ethnic Groups: Native British and Migrant Pakistani Men." *Anthropologischer Anzeiger* 59:3 (2001): 275–82.

Botting, Douglas, and the Editors of Time-Life Books. *The Aftermath: Europe.* Alexandria, Va.: Time-Life Books, 1983.

Brace, C. Loring. "The Concept of Race in Physical Anthropology." In *Physical Anthropology: Original Readings in Method and Practice.* Ed. Peter N. Peregine, Carol R. Ember, and Melvin Ember. 239–53. Upper Saddle River, N.J: Prentice Hall, 2000.

Breitman, Richard. *The Architect of Genocide: Himmler and the Final Solution.* Hanover, N.H.: Brandeis University Press, 1991.

Bridgman, Jon. *The End of the Holocaust: The Liberation of the Camps.* Portland, Ore.: Areopagitica Press, 1990.

Brömer, Rainer, Uwe Hossfeld, and Nicolaas A. Rupke. *Evolutionsbiologie von Darwin bis heute.* Berlin: Verlag für Wissenschaft und Bildung, 2000.

Broszat, Martin. *Nationalsozialistische Polenpolitik, 1939–1945.* Stuttgart: Deutsche Verlags-Anstalt, 1961.

Broszat, Martin, and Norbert Frei. *Das Dritte Reich im Überblick: Chronik, Ereignisse, Zusammenhänge.* München: Piper, 1989.

"Bund der 'Euthanasie': Geschädigten und Zwangssterilisierten e.V." *Ich Klage an* (1989): 22–25 and 31–32.

Burleigh, Michael. *Ethics and Extermination: Reflections on Nazi Genocide.* Cambridge: Cambridge University Press, 1997.

———. *Germany Turns Eastward.* New York: Cambridge University Press, 1988.

———. *The Third Reich.* New York: Hill and Wang, 2000.

Cohen, Elie A. *Human Behavior in Concentration Camps.* London: Free Association Books, 1988.

Comas, Juan. *Manual of Physical Anthropology.* Springfield, Ill.: Charles C. Thomas, 1960.

Daum, Monika, and Hans-Ulrich Deppe. *Zwangssterilisation in Frankfurt am Main, 1933–1945.* Frankfurt: Campus Verlag, 1991.

Distel, Barbara, and Ruth Jakusch. *Concentration Camp Dachau, 1933–1945.* Brussels: Comite International de Dachau, 1978.

Dobzhansky, Theodosis. "Dobzhansky Comments." In *Physical Anthropology and Archaeology: Selected Readings.* Ed. Peter B. Hammond. 182. New York: MacMillan, 1964. Reprinted from *Current Anthropology* 3 (1962): 279–80.

Drobisch, Klaus, and Gunther Wieland. *System der NS-Konzentrationslager, 1933–1939.* Berlin: Akademie Verlag, 1993.

Elon, Amos. *The Pity of It All: A History of Jews in Germany, 1743–1933.* New York: Metropolitan, 2002.

Ferenz, Benjamin. *Less than Slaves.* Cambridge, Mass.: Harvard University Press, 1979.

Fest, Joachim C. *Hitler.* New York: Harcourt, Brace, 1974.

Fischer, Eugen. "Anthropologische Erforschung der deutschen Bevölkerung." Anthropological Archives no. 4816. Vienna: Museum of Natural History, n.d.

———. "Die Bedeutung der menschlichen Erblehre." *Sonderdruck aus der Zeitschrift des Reichsbundes der höheren Beamten,* no. 11 (November 1933).

———. "Die Rassenmerkmale des Menschen als Domesticationserscheinungen." Freiburg Anatomisches Institut, Zeitschrift für Morphologische Anthropologie 1914, (18).

Fischer, Hans. *Völkerkunde im Nationalsozialismus: Aspekte der Anpassung, Affinität und Behauptung einer wissenschaftlichen Disziplin.* Berlin: Reimer Verlag, 1990.

Fish, Jefferson M. "What Anthropologists Can Do for Psychology: Facing Physics Envy, Ethnocentrism, and a Belief in 'Race.'" *American Anthropologist* 102:3 (2000): 552–63.

Fliethmann, Elfriede. "Vorläufiger Bericht über anthropologische Aufnahmen an Judenfamilien in Tarnów." *Deutsche Forschung im Osten* 2:3 (1942): 92–111.

———. "Bericht über anthropologisch-ethnologische Untersuchungen in Szaflary und Witow, zwei Goralenorte im Kreise Neumarkt." *Deutsche Forschung im Osten* 2:7 (1942): 272–76.

Frank, Anne. *The Diary of Anne Frank.* London: Heron Books, 1973.

Frank, Hans. "Das Führerprinzip in der Verwaltung." *Die Burg* 4 (1943): 213–20.

Frankel, Neftali. *I Survived Hell.* New York: Vantage Press, 1991.

Frei, Norbert. "Die Juden im NS-Staat." In *Das Dritte Reich im Überblick: Chronik, Ereignisse, Zusammenhänge.* Ed. Martin Broszat and Norbert Frei. 124–36. München: Piper, 1989.

Freud, Sigmund. *Civilization and Its Discontents.* New York: Norton, 1961.

Friedlander, Henry. *The Origins of Nazi Genocide: From Euthanasia to the Final Solution*. Chapel Hill: University of North Carolina Press, 1995.

Fröbe, Rainer. *Deutsche Wirtschaft: Zwangsarbeit von KZ-Häftlingen für Industrie und Behörden*. Hamburg: VSA Verlag, 1991.

Fromm, Erich. *Beyond the Chains of Illusion*. New York: Touchstone, 1971.

Garbe, Heinrich. "Von Spengler zu Gobineau. Weg und Ziel der rassischen Geschichtswertung." *Rasse* 8:2 (1942): 443–59.

Gernt, Helge. *Volkskunde und Nationalsozialismus*. München: Vereinigung für Volkskunde, 1987.

Gillis, J. R., ed. *Commemorations*. Princeton, N.J.: Princeton University Press, 1994.

Goguel, Rudi. "Über die Mitwirkung deutscher Wissenschaftler am Okkupationsregime in Polen im Zweiten Weltkrieg, untersucht an drei Institutionen der deutschen Ostforschung." Ph.D. diss., Humboldt University, Berlin, 1964.

Goldberg, David Theo. *Racial Subjects*. New York: Routledge, 1997.

Goldhagen, Daniel. *Hitler's Willing Executioners: Ordinary Germans and the Holocaust*. New York: Alfred A. Knopf, 1996.

Gottong, Heinrich. "Bedeutung und Aufgaben der Sektion Rassen und Volkstumsforschung." *Deutsche Forschung im Osten* 1:6 (1941): 28–40.

Gravlee, Clarence C., H. Russell Bernard, and William R. Leonard. "Heredity, Environment, and Cranial Form: A Reanalysis of Boas' Immigrant Data." *American Anthropologist* 105:1 (2003): 125–38.

Grebing, Helga. *History of the German Labour Movement: A Survey*. Dover, N.H.: Berg, 1985.

Gumkowski, Jan. *Poland under Occupation*. Warsaw: Polonia Publishing House, 1961.

Günther, Hans. "Berichte. Zum Tode des Verlegers J. F. Lehmann, Dr. e.h. zweier deutscher Universitäten." In *Rasse: Monatsschrift der Nordischen Bewegung* 2 (1935): 155.

Gutman, Israel, ed. *Encyclopedia of the Holocaust*. New York: MacMillan, 1990.

Gutman, Yisrael, and Shmuel Krakowski. *Unequal Victims: Poles and Jews during World War II*. New York: Holocaust Library, 1986.

Gütt, Arthur, Ernst Rüdin, and Falk Ruttke. *Zur Verhütung erbkranken Nachwuches: Gesetz und Erläuterungen*. München: J. F. Lehmann Verlag, 1935.

Haar, Ingo. "'Ostforschung' und 'Lebensraum'-Politik." In *Geschichte der Kaiser-Wilhelm-Gesellschaft im Nationalsozialismus*. Ed. Doris Kaufmann. Vol. 2. 437–67. Göttingen: Wallstein Verlag, 2000.

Harwood, Jonathan. "The Rise of the Party-Political Professor." In *Geschichte der Kaiser-Wilhelm Gesellschaft im Nationalsozialismus*. Ed. Doris Kaufmann. Vol. 1. 21–45. Göttingen: Wallstein Verlag, 2000.

Hauschild, Thomas. Review of *L'quete de la race: Une anthropologie du Nazaisme*, by Edouard Conte and Cornelia Essner. *American Anthropologist* 95 (1966): 894–95.

Hebel, Walter, Hrsg. *Wer ist Wer?* Berlin: Arani Verlag, 1970.

Herbert, Ulrich. "Extermination Policy: New Answers and Questions about the History of the 'Holocaust' in German Historiography." In *National Socialist Exter-

mination Policies: Contemporary German Perspectives and Controversies. Ed. Ulrich Herbert. 1–52. New York: Berghahn Books, 2000.

———. *A History of Foreign Labor, 1880–1980: Seasonal Workers/Forced Laborers/Guest Workers*. Ann Arbor: University of Michigan Press, 1990.

Herf, Jeffrey. *Reactionary Modernism*. New York: Cambridge University Press, 1984.

Hilberg, Raul. *The Destruction of the European Jews*. New York: Holmes and Meier, 1985.

Hinton, Alexander. *The Annihilation of Difference*. Berkeley: University of California Press, 2002.

Hirsch, Rudolf, and Rosemarie Schuder. *Der Gelbe Fleck: Wurzeln und Wirkungen des Judenhasses in der deutschen Geschichte*. Berlin: Rütten and Loening, 1987.

Hirte, Ronald. "Die anthropologische Untersuchung im Stadium." In *Vom Antlitz zur Maske*. Ed. Volkhard Knigge and Jürgen Seifert. 20–25. Weimar: Stiftung Gedenkstätte Buchenwald und Mittelbau-Dora, 1999.

Hitler, Adolf. *Mein Kampf*. Trans. Ralph Manheim. Boston: Houghton Mifflin, 1971.

Hohmann, Joachim. *Der "Euthanasie" Prozess Dresden 1947*. Frankfurt am Main: Peter Lang, 1993.

Homze, Edward. *Foreign Labor in Nazi Germany*. Princeton, N.J.: Princeton University Press, 1967.

Hossfeld, Uwe. "Vom Antlitz zur Maske—Gedanken zu einer auch 'anthropologischen' Gedenkausstellung." *Anthropologischer Anzeiger* 57:4 (1999): 371–73.

———. "Von der Sozialanthropologie zur Humangenetik." In *Zwischen Wissenschaft und Politik. Studien zur Jenaer Universität im 20. Jahrhundert*. 67–92. Jena: Verlag Dr. Bussert and Stadeler, 2000.

Hossfeld, Uwe, and Jürgen John. "Die Universität Jena im 'Dritten Reich.'" *Uni-Journal Jena* (November 1998): 20–21.

International Military Tribunal. *Trial of the Major War Criminals before the International Military Tribunal*. Documents and Other Material in Evidence. Vols. 27 and 29. Nuremberg: IMT, 1948.

Jacobeit, Wolfgang. "Die Auseinandersetzung mit der NS-Zeit in der DDR-Volkskunde." In *Volkskunde und Nationalsozialismus*. Ed. Helge Gernt. 301–18. München: Vereinigung für Volkskunde, 1987.

Jacobsen, Hans-Adolf. "The Structure of Nazi Foreign Policy 1933–1945." In *The Third Reich*. Ed. Christian Lietz. 54–93. Oxford: Blackwell, 1999.

Jensch, Hugo. *Euthanasie—Aktion "T4": Verbrechen in den Jahren 1940 und 1941 auf dem Sonnenstein in Pirna*. Pirna: Abteilung Kultur, 1990.

Jochheim, Gernot. *Frauenprotest in der Rosenstrasse*. Berlin: Edition Hentrich, 1993.

Junker, Thomas, and Uwe Hossfeld. *Die Entdeckung der Evolution: Eine revolutionäre Theorie und ihre Geschichte*. Darmstadt: Wissenschaftliche Buchgesellschaft, 2001.

Kaienburg, Hermann. *Vernichtung durch Arbeit: Der Fall Neuengamme*. Bonn: J. H. W. Dietz Nachf., 1990.

Kaspar, Fritz. *Hanna, Kolka, Ast und Andere*. Tübingen and Stuttgart: Silberburg-Verlag, Titus Häussermann GmbH, 1994.

Kater, Michael. *Doctors under Hitler.* Chapel Hill: University of North Carolina Press, 1989.

Katz, Steven T. *The Holocaust in Historical Context.* Vol. 1. New York: Oxford University Press, 1994.

Kaufmann, Doris. *Geschichte der Kaiser-Wilhelm-Gesellschaft im Nationalsozialismus.* Göttingen: Wallstein Verlag, 2000.

Kelly, Alfred. *The Descent of Darwinism: The Popularization of Darwinism in Germany, 1860–1914.* Chapel Hill: University of North Carolina Press, 1981.

Kershaw, Ian. *Hitler.* 2d ed. New York: Longman, 2001.

———. *The Nazi Dictatorship: Problems and Perspectives of Interpretation.* 2d ed. London. Edward Arnold, 1989.

———. *The Nazi Dictatorship: Problems and Perspectives of Interpretation.* 3d ed. London: Edward Arnold, 1993.

Kettenacker, Lothar. "Die Behandlung der Kriegsverbrecher als anglo-amerikanisches Rechtsproblem." In *Der Nationalsozialismus vor Gericht: Die alliierten Prozesse gegen Kriegsverbrecher und Soldaten, 1943–1952.* Ed. Gerd R. Ueberschär. 17–31. Frankfurt am Main: Fischer Verlag, 1999.

Klee, Ernst. *Auschwitz, die NS Medizin und ihre Opfer.* Frankfurt am Main: S. Fischer Verlag, 1997.

———. *Deutsche Medizin im Dritten Reich: Karrieren vor und nach 1945.* Frankfurt am Main: S. Fischer Verlag, 2001.

———. *Dokumente zur "Euthanasie."* Frankfurt am Main: Fischer Taschenbuch Verlag, 1992.

Klee, Ernst, Willi Dresser, and Volker Riess. *"The Good Old Days."* New York: Konecky and Konecky, 1988.

Klemperer, Victor. *I Will Bear Witness.* 2 vols. New York: Random House, 1998.

———. *Language of the Third Reich: LTI, Linguistic Tertii Imperii.* London: Athlone Press, 2000.

Klessmann, Christoph. *Die Selbstbehauptung einer Nation.* Düsseldorf: Bertelsmann Universitätsverlag, 1971.

Klingemann, Carsten, ed. *Rassenmythos und Sozialwissenschaft in Deutschland.* Opladen: Westdeutscher Verlag, 1987.

Knigge, Volkhard, and Jürgen Seifert, eds. *Vom Antlitz zur Maske.* Wien/Weimar: Stiftung Gedenkstätten Buchenwald und Mittelbau-Dora, 1999.

Kogon, Eugen, Herbert Longbein, and Adelbert Rückerl. *Die nationalsozialistischen Massentötungen durch Giftgas: Eine Dokumentation.* Frankfurt am Main: Fischer Verlag, 1983.

Kornbluth, William. *Sentenced to Remember.* Bethlehem, Pa.: Lehigh University Press, 1994.

Kretschmar, Georg, ed. *Dokumente zur Kirchenpolitik des Dritten Reiches.* Vol. 1, *Das Jahr 1933.* München: Christian-Kaiser-Verlag, 1970.

Kühl, Stefan. *The Nazi Connection: Eugenics, American Racism, and German Socialism.* New York: Oxford University Press, 1994.

Kühnl, Reinhard. *Der deutsche Faschismus in Quellen und Dokumenten*. Köln: Pahl-Rugenstein, 1987.

Kühnrich, Heinz. *Der KZ-Staat: Die faschistischen Konzentrationslager, 1933–1945*. Berlin: Dietz Verlag, 1983.

Kühnrich, Heinz, and Eugen Kogan. *Der SS Staat: Das System der deutschen Konzentrationslager*. 3d ed. München: Kindler-Verlag GmbH, 1976.

Kundt, Ernst. "Entstehung, Probleme, Grundsätze und Form der Verwaltung des Generalgouvernements." *Die Burg* 5 (1944): 47–67.

Landau, Misia. "A People's History of Human Biodiversity." *American Anthropologist* 99 (1997): 392.

Lehmann, Melanie. *J. F. Lehmann, ein Leben im Kampf für Deutschland*. München: J. F. Lehmann Verlag, 1935.

Levi, Neil, and Michael Rothberg. *The Holocaust: Theoretical Readings*. Piscataway, N.J.: Rutgers University Press, 2003.

Lewis, Herbert. "The Passion of Franz Boas." *American Anthropologist* 103 (2001): 447–67.

Lewy, Guenther. *Nazi Persecution of the Gypsies*. Oxford: Oxford University Press, 2000.

Lifton, Robert. *The Nazi Doctors: Medical Killing and the Psychology of Genocide*. New York: Basic Books, 1986.

Linenthal, Edward T. *Preserving Memory*. New York: Viking, 1995.

Linimayr, Peter. *Wiener Völkerkunde im Nationalsozialismus: Ansätze zu einer NS-Wissenschaft*. Frankfurt am Main: P. Lang, 1994.

Linke, Uli. *German Bodies: Race and Representation after Hitler*. New York: Routledge, 1999.

Livingstone, Frank. "On the Nonexistence of Human Races." In *Physical Anthropology and Archaeology: Selected Readings*. Ed. Peter B. Hammond. 180–84. New York: Macmillian, 1964. Reprinted from *Current Anthropology* 3 (1962): 279–83.

Lord Russell of Liverpool. *The Scourge of the Swastika*. New York: Philosophical Library, 1954.

Lösch, Niels C. *Rasse als Konstrukt: Leben und Werk Eugen Fischers*. Frankfurt am Main: Peter Lang, 1997.

Lüddecke, Andreas. *Der "Fall Saller" und die Rassenhygiene: Eine Göttinger Fallstudie zu den Widersprüchen sozialbiologistischer Ideologiebildung*. Marburg: Tectum Verlag, 1995.

Lukas, Richard. *The Forgotten Holocaust*. Lexington: University Press of Kentucky, 1986.

Luschan, F.v. *Völker, Rassen, Sprachen. Anthropologische Betrachtungen*. Berlin: Deutsche Buch-Gesellschaft, 1927.

Magnussen, Karin. *Rassen- und bevölkerungspolitisches Rüstzeug. Statistik, Gesetzgebung und Kriegsaufgaben*. München: J. F. Lehmann Verlag, 1943.

Marks, Jonathan. *Evolutionary Anthropology*. Fort Worth, Tex.: Harcourt Brace Jovanovich, 1991.

Marrus, Michael. *The Holocaust in History.* Hanover, N.H.: University Press of New England, 1987.

Massin, Benoit. "From Virchow to Fischer." In *Volksgeist as Method and Ethic: Essays on Boasian Ethnography and the German Anthropological Tradition.* Ed. George W. Stocking Jr. 79–153. Madison: University of Wisconsin Press, 1996.

Matalon Lagnado, Lucette. *Children of the Flames: Dr. Mengele and the Untold Story of the Twins of Auschwitz.* New York: Marrow, 1991.

Meinhold, Helmut. "Die Arbeitsreserven des Generalgouvernements." *Die Burg* 2 (1943): 273–91.

Mitscherlich, Alexander, and Margarete Mitscherlich. *Die Unfähigkeit zu trauern.* München: R. Piper and Co. Verlag, 1977.

Mogilanski, Roman, ed. *Encyclopedia Judaica.* Los Angeles: American Congress of Jews from Poland and Survivors of Concentration Camps and Nazi Victims of Piotrkow Trybunalski, 1985.

———, ed. *The Ghetto Anthology.* New York: American Congress of Jews from Poland and Survivors of Concentration Camps and Nazi Victims of Piotrkow Trybunalski, 1985.

Mommsen, Hans. *From Weimar to Auschwitz.* Princeton, N.J.: Princeton University Press, 1991.

Montagu, Ashley. *Man's Most Dangerous Myth: The Fallacy of Race.* Walnut Hill, Calif.: Alta Mira Press, 1942.

Montgomery, Robert Lynn. *Register to the Papers of Aleš Hrdlička: Finding Aids to the National Anthropological Archives.* Washington, D.C.: Smithsonian Institution, 1996.

Mosen, Markus. *Der koloniale Traum: Angewandte Ethnologie im Nationalsozialismus.* Bonn: Holos, 1991.

Müller-Hill, Benno. *Murderous Science.* Oxford: Oxford University Press, 1988.

Noakes, J., and G. Pridham, eds. *Nazism: A History in Documents and Eyewitness Accounts, 1919–1945.* 2 vols. New York: Schocken Books, 1984.

Neufeld, Michael. "Introduction: Mittelbau-Dora-Secret Weapons and Slave Labor." In *Planet Dora,* by Yves Beon. Boulder, Colo.: Westview, 1997.

———. *The Rocket and the Reich.* Cambridge: Harvard University Press, 1996.

Nicholas, Lynn H. *The Rape of Europa.* New York: Alfred A. Knopf, 1994.

Nixdorff, Heide, and Thomas Hauschild. *Europäische Ethnologie.* Berlin: Dietrich Roemer Verlag, 1982.

Payne, Robert. *The Life and Death of Adolf Hitler.* New York: Praeger, 1973.

Penny, Glenn H., III. "Cosmopolitan Visions and Municipal Displays: Museums, Markets and the Ethnographic Project in Germany, 1868–1914." Ph.D. diss., University of Illinois, 1999.

Persico, Joseph. *Roosevelt's Secret War.* New York: Random House, 2002.

Planck, Max. *25 Jahre Kaiser-Wilhelm-Gesellschaft: Erster Band Handbuch.* Berlin: Springer Verlag, 1936.

Ploetz, Alfred, ed. *Archiv für Rassen- und Gesellschaftsbiologie* 24 (1930).

Plügel, Anton. "Das Rassenbild des Vorfeldes im deutschen Osten." *Das Vorfeld* 2:6 (1941): 6–15.

Plum, Günther. "Übernahme und Sicherung der Macht 1933/34." In *Nationalsozialistische Polenpolitik 1939–1945*. Ed. Martin Broszat. 34–37. Stuttgart: Deutsche Verlags-Anstalt, 1961.

Pohl, Dieter. "The Murder of Jews in the General Government." In *National Socialist Extermination Policies: Contemporary German Perspectives and Controversies*. Ed. Ulrich Herbert. 83–103. New York: Berghahn Books, 2000.

———. *Nationalsozialistische Judenverfolgung in Ostgalizien 1941–1944*. München: Oldenbourg Verlag, 1997.

Poliakov, Leon, and Josef Wulf. *Das Dritte Reich und die Juden: Dokumente und Aufsätze*. Berlin Grunewald: Arani Verlag, 1975.

Pollak, Michael. *Rassenwahn und Wissenschaft*. Meisenheim: Anton Hain, 1990.

Posner, Gerald. "Secrets of the Files." *New Yorker*, March 14, 1994, 39–47.

Posner, Gerald L., and John Ware. *Mengele: The Complete Story*. New York: McGraw Hill, 1986.

Proctor, Robert. "From Anthropologie to Rassenkunde." In *Bones, Bodies, Behavior: Essays on Biological Anthropology*. Ed. George Stocking. 138–79. Madison: University of Wisconsin Press, 1988.

———. *Racial Hygiene: Medicine under the Nazis*. Cambridge: Harvard University Press, 1988.

Rasch, Manfred. "Forschung zwischen Staat und Industrie." In *Geschichte der Kaiser-Wilhelm-Gesellchaft im Nationalsozialismus*. Ed. Doris Kaufmann. 373–97. Göttingen: Wallstein Verlag, 2000.

Reiss, Johanna. *The Upstairs Room*. New York: Harper Collins, 1972.

Rich, Norman. *Hitler's War Aims*. New York: Norton, 1973.

Riemann, Erhard. *Preussisches Wörterbuch*. Mainz: Akademie der Wissenschaften und Literatur, 1959.

Rohrlich, Ruby, ed. *Resisting the Holocaust*. New York: Berg, 1998.

Rose, Romani. *"Den Rauch hatten wir täglich vor Augen": Der nationalsozialistische Völkermord an den Sinti und Roma*. Heidelberg: Wunderhorn, 1999.

Rosenbaum, Alan S. *Prosecuting Nazi War Criminals*. Boulder, Colo.: Westview, 1993.

Rösing, Ina, and Ilse Schwidetzky. *Maus und Schlange: Untersuchungen zur Lage der deutschen Anthropologie*. München und Wien: R. Oldenbourg Verlag, 1982.

Routil, Robert. "Das Erscheinungsbild gefangener Polen aus dem Weltkrieg." *Mitteilungsblatt der anthropologischen Gesellschaft Wien* 70 (1940): 129–43.

Saller, Karl Felix. *Die Rassenlehre des Nationalsozialismus in Wissenschaft und Propaganda*. Darmstadt: Progress-Verlag, 1961.

———. "Eugenische Rundschau." *Archiv für soziale Hygiene und Demographie* 3 (1928): 272–89.

Sandkühler, Thomas. "Anti-Jewish Policy and the Murder of the Jews in the District of Galicia, 1941–43." In *National Socialist Extermination Policies: Contemporary*

German Perspectives and Controversies. Ed. Ulrich Herbert. 104–27. New York: Berghahn Books, 2000.

Schafft, Gretchen. "Civic Denial and the Memory of War." *Journal of the American Academy of Psychoanalysis* 26 (1998): 255–72.

Schafft, Gretchen, and Gerhard Zeidler. "'Antropologia' Trzeciej Rzeszy: Z dziejow Instytutu Niemickiej Pracy na Wschodzie (Institut für Deutsche Ostarbeit)." *Alma Mater: Miesiecznik Uniwersytetu Jagiellonskiego* 47 (2003): 12–15.

———. *Die KZ-Mahn- und Gedenkstätten in Deutschland.* Berlin: Dietz Verlag, 1996.

———. *Register to the Materials of the Institut für Deutsche Ostarbeit.* Washington, D.C.: National Anthropological Archives, 1998.

Scheidt, Walter. *Rassenbiologie und Kulturpolitik.* Leipzig: Verlag von P. Reclam jun. 1930.

Schjeldahl, Peter. "The Hitler Show." *New Yorker,* April 1, 2002, 87.

Schubert, Helmut. "Mitteilungen zur Rassenpflege- und Bevölkerungspolitik." *Rasse: Monatsschrift für den nordischen Gedanken* 6 (1939): 24–26.

———. "Zur Praxis der Volkstumspolitik." *Volk und Rasse* 17 (1942): 103–8.

Schwarz, Gisela. *Kinder, die nicht zählten: Ostarbeiterinnen und ihre Kinder im Zweiten Weltkrieg.* Essen: Klartext Verlag, 1997.

Schwarz, Gudrun. *Die nationalsozialistischen Lager.* Frankfurt am Main: Fischer Taschenbuch Verlag, 1996.

Schwidetzky, Ilse. *Rassen und Rassenbildung beim Menschen: Typen—Bevölkerungen—Geographische Variabilität.* Stuttgart: Gustav Fischer Verlag, 1979.

Segal, Lilli. *Die Hohen Priester der Vernichtung.* Berlin: Dietz Verlag, 1991.

Seidler, H., and A. Soritsch. *Rassen und Minderheiten.* Wien: Literas Verlag, 1983.

Seidler, Horst, and Andreas Rett. *Rassenhygiene.* München: Jugend und Volk, 1988.

Seraphim, P. H. "Die Judenfrage im Generalgouvernement als Bevölkerungsproblem." *Die Burg* 1 (1940): 56–63.

Shell, Hanna Rose. "Introduction: Finding the Soul in the Skin." In *The Extermination of the American Bison,* by William Temple Hornaday. Washington, D.C.: Smithsonian Institution Press, 2002.

Simpson, Christopher. *The Splendid Blond Beast: Money, Law, and Genocide in the Twentieth Century.* New York: Grove Press, 1993.

———. *War Crimes of the Deutsche Bank and the Dresdner Bank.* New York: Holmes and Meier, 2002.

Sofsky, Wolfgang. *The Order of Terror: The Concentration Camp.* Princeton, N.J.: Princeton University Press, 1997.

Sokal, Alan, and Jean Bricmont. *Fashionable Nonsense: Postmodern Intellectuals' Abuse of Science.* New York: Picador, 1998.

Sommerfeldt, Josef. "Das Schicksal der jüdischen Bauernkolonisation Josefs II in Galizien." *Die Burg* 2 (1941): 29–41.

———. "Die Aufgaben des Referats Judenforschung." *Deutsche Forschung im Osten* 1 (1941): 29–35.

———. "Die Entwicklung der Geschichtsschreibung über die Juden in Polen." *Die Burg* 1 (1940): 64–79.

———. "Die Juden in den polnischen Sprichwörtern und sprichwörtlichen Redensarten." *Die Burg* 3 (1942): 313–29.

———. "Galizien und die ersten russisch-jüdischen Auswanderungswellen nach Amerika." *Die Burg* 4 (1943): 187–96.

———. "Judenstaatsprojekte in der polnischen Publizistik des 19. Jahrhunderts." *Die Burg* 5 (1944): 14–26.

Sparks, Corey S., and Richard L. Jantz. "A Reassessment of Human Cranial Plasticity: Boas Revisited." *Proceedings of the National Academy of Sciences* 99:23 (2002): 14636–39.

Spencer, Frank. *History of Physical Anthropology.* New York: Garland, 1997.

Stadtmuseum Gardelegen/Abteilung Gedenkstätte. *Tage im April.* Gardelegen: Stadtmuseum, 1995.

Steinbach, Peter. "Der Nürnberger Prozess gegen die Hauptkriegsverbrecher." In *Der Nationalsozialismus vor Gericht: Die alliierten Prozesse gegen Kriegsverbrecher und Soldaten 1943–1952.* Ed. Gerd R. Ueberschär. 32–44. Frankfurt am Main: Fischer Verlag, 1999.

Steinbacher, Sybille. "In the Shadow of Auschwitz: The Murder of the Jews of East Upper Silesia." In *National Socialist Extermination Policies: Contemporary German Perspectives and Controversies.* Ed. Ulrich Herbert. 276–305. New York: Berghahn Books, 2000.

Stern, Fritz. *Einstein's German World.* Princeton, N.J.: Princeton University Press, 1999.

Stocking, George, ed. *Bones, Bodies, Behavior: Essays on Biological Anthropology.* Madison: University of Wisconsin Press, 1988.

Stokesbury, James L. *A Short History of World War II.* New York: William Morrow, 1980.

Stoltfus, Nathan. "Protest and Silence." In *Resisting the Holocaust.* Ed. Ruby Rohrlich. 151–78. New York: Berg, 1998.

Stölting, Erhard. "Die anthroposoziologische Schule." In *Rassenmythos und Sozialwissenschaft in Deutschland.* Ed. Carsten Klingemann. 130–68. Opladen: Westdeutscher Verlag, 1987.

Stone, Norman. *Hitler.* Boston: Little, Brown, 1980.

Strzelecka, Irena, and Piotr Setkiewicz. "The Construction, Expansion and Development of the Camp and Its Branches." In *Auschwitz, 1940–1945.* Ed. Henryk Swiebecki. Vol. 1. 63–136. Oświęcim: Auschwitz-Birkenau State Museum, 2000.

Stürmer, Michael. *The German Empire.* New York: Modern Library, 2002.

Styron, William. *Sophie's Choice.* New York: Random House, 1979.

Suttinger, Günter. "Zwillingslager Norderney." In *Rasse: Monatsschrift der Nordischen Bewegung* 5 (1938): 23–25.

Suzuki, D. T., Erich Fromm, and Richard De Martino. *Zen Buddhism and Psychoanalysis.* New York: Harper and Row, 1960.

Swiebecki, Henryk, ed. *Auschwitz, 1940–1945*. Vol. 1. Oświęcim: Auschwitz-Birkenau State Museum, 2000.

Szöllösi-Janze, Margit. "Der Wissenschaftler als Experte." In *Geschichte der Kaiser-Wilhelm-Gesellschaft im Nationalsozialismus*. Ed. Doris Kaufmann. 46–64. Göttingen: Wallstein Verlag, 2000.

Taylor, James, and Warren Shaw. *The Third Reich Almanac*. New York: Pharos Books, 1987.

Tierny, Patrick. "The Fierce Anthropologist." *New Yorker,* October 9, 2000.

Tolstoy, Nicholas. *Victims of Yalta*. London: Holder and Staughton. 1977.

Tuppa, K. "Dora Maria Kahlich-Koenner, 25.12.1905–28.3.1970." *Anthropologischer Anzeiger* 32:3–4 (1970): 291–92.

Tyrell, Albrecht. "Das Scheitern der Weimarer Republik und der Aufstieg der NSDAP." In *Das Dritte Reich im Überblick. Chronik, Ereignisse, Zusammenhänge*. Ed. Martin Broszat and Norbert Frei. 20–33. München: R. Piper GmbH, 1989.

———. "Towards Dictatorship: Germany 1930 to 1934." In *The Third Reich*. Ed. Christian Leitz. 29–48. Oxford: Blackwell, 1999.

United States Holocaust Memorial Museum. *Historical Atlas of the Holocaust*. New York: MacMillan, 1996.

Verschuer, Otmar Freiherr von. "Anomalien der Körperform." In *Menschliche Erblehre und Rassenhygiene*. Vol. 1, no. 2. *Hälfte, Erbpathologie*. Ed. Erwin Baur, Eugen Fischer, and Fritz Lenz. 100–193. München: J. F. Lehmann Verlag, 1940.

———. "Das ehemalige Kaiser-Wilhelm-Institut für Anthropologie, menschliche Erblehre und Eugenik. Bericht über die wissenschaftliche Forschung, 1927–1945." *Morphologie und Anthropologie* 55 (1964): 127–74.

———. "Rassenhygiene als Wissenschaft und Staatsaufgabe." *Der Erbarzt* 2 (1936): 17–19.

———. "Vom Umfang der erblichen Belastung am deutschen Volke." *Archiv für Rassen- und Gesellschaftsbiologie* 24 (1930): 238–67.

Vetulani-Belfoure, Krystyna Ewa. *In einem deutschen Städtchen: Erinnerungen einer polnischen Zwangsarbeiterin, 1942–1945*. Bremen: Donat Verlag, 2000.

Vossen, Rüdiger. "Die Entwicklung der Europa-Abteilung am Hamburgischen Museum für Völkerkunde." In *Europäische Ethnologie*. Ed. Heide Nixdorff and Thomas Hauschild. 73–75. Berlin: Dietrich Reimer Verlag, 1982.

Walker, Mark. *Nazi Science: Myth, Truth, and the German Atomic Bomb*. New York: Plenum Press, 1995.

Waltemath, Kuno. "Deutsches Blut im polnischen Volke." *Volk und Rasse* 7 (1940): 91–92.

Weindling, Paul. "Tales from Nuremberg: The Kaiser Wilhelm Institute for Anthropology and Allied Medical War Crimes Policy." In *Geschichte der Kaiser-Wilhelm-Gesellschaft im Nationalsozialismus*. Ed. Doris Kaufmann. 635–52. Göttingen: Wallstein Verlag, 2000.

Weinmann, Martin. *Das nationalsozialistische Lagersystem*. Frankfurt am Main: Zweitausendeins, 1990.

Weiss, Hermann. *Biographisches Lexikon zum Dritten Reich.* Frankfurt am Main: Fischer Taschenbuch Verlag, 1999.

Wieland, Günther. *System der NS-Konzentrationslager, 1933–1945.* Berlin: Akademie Verlag, 1993.

Williams, Vernon. *Rethinking Race: Franz Boas and His Contemporaries.* Lexington: University Press of Kentucky, 1996.

Wysocki, Gerd. *Arbeit für den Krieg.* Braunschweig: Steinweg Verlag, 1992.

Ziegelmayer, Gerfried. *100 Jahre Anthropologie in München.* Würzburg, 1987.

Zimmerman, Andrew. *Anthropology and Antihumanism in Imperial Germany.* Chicago: University of Chicago Press, 2001.

Zimmermann, Michael. *Rassenutopie und Genozid: Die nationalsozialistische "Lösung der Zigeurnerfrage."* Hamburg: Christians, 1996.

Index

GRETCHEN E. SCHAFFT is an applied anthropologist-in-residence at the American University in Washington, D.C., and the author of numerous articles on various aspects of her research.

The University of Illinois Press
is a founding member of the
Association of American University Presses.

Composed in 10.5/13 Minion
with Helvetica Neue Condensed display
by Celia Shapland
for the University of Illinois Press
Designed by Dennis Roberts
Manufactured by Thomson-Shore, Inc.

University of Illinois Press
1325 South Oak Street
Champaign, IL 61820-6903
www.press.uillinois.edu

OSPREY AIRCRAFT OF THE ACES 117

ACES OF THE 325th FIGHTER GROUP

SERIES EDITOR: TONY HOLMES

OSPREY AIRCRAFT OF THE ACES 117

ACES OF THE 325th FIGHTER GROUP

Thomas G Ivie

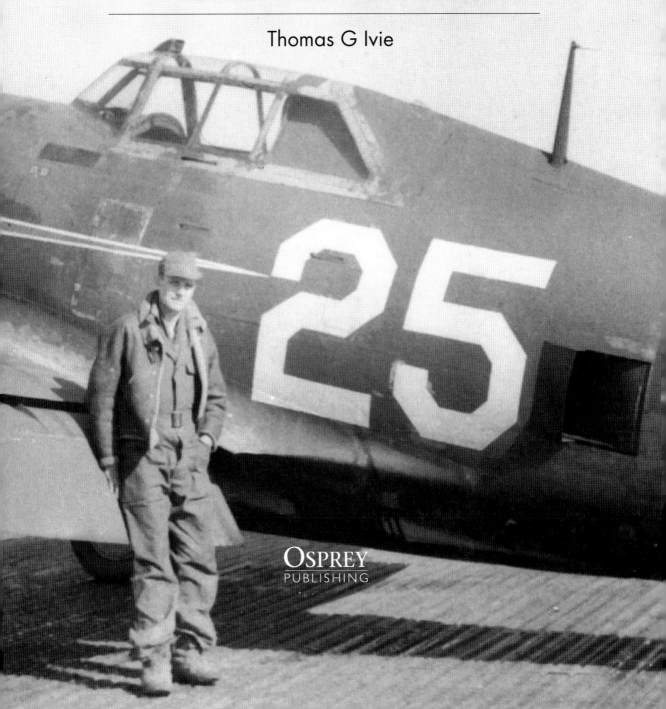

OSPREY
PUBLISHING

Front Cover
On 14 March 1945 the 325th FG escorted bombers from the Fifteenth Air Force on a raid against the railway marshalling yards in the Hungarian town of Nové Zámky. The 'Checkertail Clan' had taken off at 1020 hrs and accompanied the bombers to the target. No one could have anticipated the turn of events after an uneventful escort to Nové Zámky. The action commenced when one of the returning Mustang pilots experienced problems with his oxygen supply and dived to a lower altitude. As he broke through the undercast, he saw four Fw 190s and radioed for help. When the remainder of his flight dropped down to assist him they ran into a large gaggle of enemy aircraft and a major dogfight ensued. During the next 15 minutes seven Fw 190s were shot down, five of them by Lt Gordon McDaniel.

By now the action had dropped to a lower altitude, and Capt Harry Parker (flying P-51D-5 44-14400) entered the fray and attacked a Fw 190 at 6000 ft. The enemy aircraft dived for the deck, and Parker followed. He opened fire at a distance of 1500 ft and closed to 50 ft, dead astern. His gunfire ripped pieces from the fuselage and wings, and as the Fw 190 started to go out of control its pilot bailed out, but his parachute did not open. Immediately after this kill Parker attacked another Fw 190 at 5000 ft, opening fire from 4500 ft and again closing to within 50 ft of his opponent. Parker noted, 'I saw hits enter the wings and fuselage of the enemy aircraft, which went out of control and crashed to earth'. With these two victories Capt Harry Parker, who had recently returned from leave in the US, raised his victory tally to 13. He was now the 'Checkertail Clan's' second-ranking ace.

By the time the dogfight had ended the pilots of the 325th had claimed 20 Fw 190s destroyed (these aircraft were almost certainly from the Hungarian Royal Air Force's 102. *Csatarepülő* Osztály) for the loss of two Mustangs.

Sadly, Capt Parker's victories would be his last, for he disappeared on 2 April 1945 after going down to investigate an enemy aircraft. No trace of him or his aircraft were ever found (*Cover artwork by Mark Postlethwaite*)

First published in Great Britain in 2014 by Osprey Publishing
PO Box 883, Oxford, OX1 9PL, UK
PO Box 3985, New York, NY 10185-3985, USA

E-mail: info@ospreypublishing.com

Osprey Publishing is part of the Osprey Group

© 2014 Osprey Publishing Limited

A CIP catalogue record for this book is available from the British Library

ISBN: 978 1 78096 301 3
PDF e-book ISBN: 9781780963020
ePub ISBN: 9781780963037

Edited by Tony Holmes
Cover Artwork by Mark Postlethwaite
Aircraft Profiles by Chris Davey
Index by Sharon Redmayne
Originated by PDQ Digital Media Solutions, UK
Printed in China through Asia Pacific Offset Limited

14 15 16 17 18   10 9 8 7 6 5 4 3 2 1

Osprey Publishing is supporting the Woodland Trust, the UK's leading woodland conservation charity, by funding the dedication of trees.

www.ospreypublishing.com

CONTENTS

DEDICATION

This book is dedicated to the memory of the late Dwayne Tabatt, who worked so diligently in his position as the 325th FG Association's photo archivist. His efforts insured that a very large number of images of the group's personnel and aircraft would be available for researchers to use for many years. As such, he gave me numerous photographs to use should I be able to get a book contract and tell the story of the 'Checkertails'. After his death the remainder of his collection was given to my colleague, and fellow Osprey author, Carl Molesworth for safekeeping. Virtually all of the images used in this book are due to Dwayne's generosity and dedication to the telling of the 325th FG history.

The author would also like to thank the following individuals for their generous help in the preparation of this book. My old friend, and fellow Osprey author, William N Hess, provided all of the 325th's mission summaries and numerous letters and documents received from former 'Checkertail' pilots that were extremely important in the preparation of this book. The microfilm of the 'Checkertail Clan's' encounter reports, provided by Frank Olynyk, was invaluable in preparing this history. Carl Molesworth supplied numerous photographs from the Tabatt collection, as well as 325th FG documentation that augmented the narrative of this book. Other photographs came from the late Lt Col Lewis W Chick, the late Col Chester Sluder and from the National Museum of the US Air Force. Finally, thanks to my friend Sam Sox for using his 'magic' to enhance the quality of several images published in this volume.

Finally, thank you to my wife, Mary, for proofreading the manuscript and offering suggestions on how it could be improved.

Tom Ivie
Taylor Mill
Kentucky, USA
July 2013

ACTIVATION, TRAINING AND INTO COMBAT

Probably one of the most feared symbols an Axis pilot in the Mediterranean Theatre of Operations (MTO) could see in the air were the bright yellow and black 'checkerboard tails' of the 325th FG. There was a good reason for this concern, as the 'Checkertail Clan' was one of the deadliest fighter groups in the MTO. Indeed, by war's end its pilots had downed 534 Axis aircraft in aerial combat, making the 325th the second highest scoring unit (behind the 82nd FG – see *Osprey Aircraft of the Aces 108 – P-38 Lightning Aces of the 82nd Fighter Group* for further details) in the Fifteenth Air Force. The 325th produced a total of 28 aces during its combat tour, which began in April 1943 in the skies over North Africa and ended in Italy two years later.

General Order 50, dated 30 June 1942, issued by Headquarters First Air Force, Eastern Defense Command, activated the 325th FG. The order authorised the detaching of officers and enlisted men from the 79th FG under the command of Maj Leonard C Lydon as a cadre around which the 325th FG was to be formed. The new group was composed of the 317th, 318th and 319th Fighter Squadrons. Initially, HQ 325th FG and the 317th Fighter Squadron (FS) were sent to Theodore Green Field at Hillsgrove, Rhode Island, while the 318th and 319th FSs set up shop at Grenier Field in Manchester, New Hampshire.

As the units settled in at their respective bases the training of both flying and ground personnel began in earnest. We will take a look at the training period through the eyes of the 317th FS, which was activated

In January 1943 P-40Fs of the 325th FG were loaded aboard USS *Ranger* (CV-4) and shipped across the treacherous waters of the Atlantic to North Africa (*National Museum of the USAF*)

7

on 3 August 1942 with 1Lt James E Tucker as its first commanding officer. During the next several days personnel began rolling in and the unit began its organisational setup. Operational training began shortly thereafter when the 317th received 12 P-40Es from the 86th FS. The squadron history noted that;

'Intense, vigorous training missions were scheduled in interception, ground gunnery tactics, dive-bombing and simulated dogfights. P-40s were idle only when bogged down by weather, flying from dawn to dusk and frequently at night. On 7 October Capt Jack C West was appointed squadron commander, relieving Lt Tucker who was transferred to Headquarters, 325th FG. On 13 October SSgt Watkins Mayo was killed when his aeroplane crashed at Norwood, Massachusetts. On 23 December Lt Bart Judge failed to return from a routine training mission, and it was not until several months later that the squadron learned he had crashed to his death'.

A change of command occurred on 10 December 1942 when Lt Col Gordon H Austin replaced Maj Leonard Lydon as commanding officer of the 325th FG. By now the group had nearly reached its authorised strength, and during the remainder of December Lt Col Austin quickly brought the 325th up to combat readiness.

The new year started on a positive note for the group as it received orders to move to Langley Field, Virginia, on 1 January 1943. The pilots headed for their new home by train the following day, and upon their arrival they found that they had been equipped with mostly brand new P-40Fs. It was whilst at Langley Field that the pilots learned that they and their aircraft would be shipped to North Africa aboard the aircraft carrier USS *Ranger* (CV-4). Having reached their destination, the Warhawk pilots would have to fly their P-40s off the vessel as the carrier sailed in open waters. For the next few days the squadrons spent time practising takeoffs from a simulated carrier deck. This training ended on 6 January, and 24 hours later the P-40s were flown to Norfolk Naval Yard, where they were loaded aboard *Ranger*. On 8 January the carrier and its screening ships sailed for the combat zone of North Africa.

After a virtually uneventful voyage *Ranger* arrived at the point of takeoff and pilots were ordered to man their aeroplanes. The carrier takeoffs and flight to Casablanca were performed without incident, and soon the group was safely ashore at Cazes airfield, in French Morocco. The air and ground echelons left the US a few days after the pilots and their aeroplanes, and by 1 March 1943 the entire 325th FG had finally been reunited at Tafaraoui airfield, about 30 miles from Oran.

During February 1943 the group had to turn over some of its P-40s to the veteran 33rd FG, which needed replacement aircraft to continue supporting the ground forces in western Tunisia. As a result of this the 325th retained

On 19 January 1943 *Ranger* reached the launching point off North Africa and the 325th's pilots flew their P-40s off the carrier and headed for Cazes airfield near Casablanca, in French Morocco. All arrived safely (*National Museum of the USAF*)

Future ace Lt Frank 'Spot' Collins shot down a Bf 109 on 6 May 1943 for his first kill. He ended his tour of duty with a total of nine victories, as well as one probable and one damaged (*Dwayne Tabatt collection via Carl Molesworth*)

only 38 Warhawks when its final operational training began in March. This shortage of aircraft meant that when the group was declared combat ready in early April, only two of its squadrons could be sent to the 325th's new base at Montesquieu, in Algeria. The squadrons drew straws to see which one would have to remain behind, and the 317th FS lost. The 318th and 319th FSs moved to their new base during the first two weeks of April, and by the 15th they were settled in and ready for combat operations.

The 325th FG's first mission took place two days later, escorting bombers attacking the airfield at Mateur. Enemy aircraft were encountered over the target area, and during a brief engagement with two Bf 109s, Flt Off Howard Cook of the 318th FS destroyed one of them before he was himself shot down by another Messerschmitt. He bailed out and was later picked up by British forces. No bombers were lost – this was the first of 59 straight escort missions where no bombers were lost to enemy fighters.

During the next 30 days the 325th flew 24 missions that saw its pilots perform bomber escort, dive-bombing and strafing. The fast faltering Luftwaffe was encountered just once, on 6 May 1943. On that date the 318th and 319th FSs flew a sea sweep between Cap Bon and Cap Serrat, and left several vessels burning after they were bombed.

Following these attacks, Lts Frank Collins and Harmon E Burns and Flt Offs Richard Catlin and Edmund Parent became separated from the rest of the formation and headed back to base. On their homeward flight they spotted a Luftwaffe airfield packed with 20 Ju 52/3ms, so they strafed them. As they pulled up a number of the tri-motor transports were observed burning on the field. Future ace Lt 'Spot' Collins then saw a Bf 109 in the landing pattern, and with a few bursts from his 0.50-cal machine guns he sent it crashing to earth in flames. At about the same time Lt Burns spotted a Ju 52/3m flying nearby at an altitude of 1000 ft and quickly shot it down too, the transport crashing into the sea.

One week later the campaign in North Africa ended with the surrender of Generaloberst Hans-Jürgen von Arnim, commander of the *Afrika Korps*.

The 325th FG would now be flying missions against Axis-held islands in the Mediterranean. The first such target was Sardinia, with the group undertaking a combination escort/dive-bombing mission against Porto Ponte Romano. The Luftwaffe was not encountered, but the 325th's dive-bombing resulted in severe damage in the harbour area.

By mid-May the 317th FS was at last up to full strength, and it joined the remainder of the group. The unit flew its first mission on 19 May, escorting bombers sent to attack Decimomannu airfield on Sardinia.

Future ace Herschel H Green recalled the day's events, which remained firmly entrenched in his memory decades later;

'The "old timers" who had been flying combat for only a few weeks told us that we were lucky to have joined them at that time because there had been little action on the escort missions, and we would have the chance to break into combat slowly. WRONG.'

The target was obscured by heavy clouds, and the results of the bombing were questionable. There was no question about the ferocity of the resistance offered by defending Axis fighters, however. In the first of a series of encounters three Bf 109s were shot down over Cagliari, two more southwest of Cap Frasca and one 15 miles east of Cap Frasca. Individual credits of one victory each went to Maj Bob Baseler (a future ace), 1Lts Joseph Bloomer Jr, Herschel H 'Herky' Green and Lawrence Ritter and Flt Offs John Smallsreed and Ebert W Smith. 'Herky' Green described his first mission, and victory, as follows;

'We flew into Sardinia and my section of four aeroplanes was attacked just as we crossed the coastline. In short order we became separated, and I found myself tangling with six or eight Me 109s, and was fast losing control of the situation. They were attacking me from both sides, so no matter which way I turned I just set myself up for somebody else. After a few minutes of this – it seemed like a lifetime – I realised that there was no way I could live in this environment for more than a few seconds. Our P-40s could out-turn the Me 109s, but that was all we could do. We couldn't out-run them.

'While attempting to evade a bunch of tracers that were trying to occupy the same area as I was I spun out and went into an undercast over which we had drifted by this time.

Some of the battle damage to Herschel H 'Herky' Green's P-40F '13', after his narrow escape during the aerial battle of 19 May 1943. Although Green scored his first kill during this dogfight, he was fortunate to escape with his life during an action that saw him chased by six to eight Bf 109s (*Dwayne Tabatt collection via Tom Ivie*)

This was my salvation as I recovered and headed home, staying in the clouds as long as I could. Although my aeroplane was riddled and most of my instruments and radio were shot away I managed to get back to North Africa without further incident. During the melee I had shot down one Me 109, but at the time it seemed hardly worth it.'

'Herky's' victory was scored during a head-on pass, and it was confirmed by Capt W R Reed, who witnessed the engagement.

Lt Green's P-40, side number '13', had been shot so full of holes that it was consigned to the scrapyard, and as far as Green was concerned so was the number '13'. After this hair-raising ordeal he switched to side number '11', which he had applied to all of his remaining assigned aircraft. Two P-40s were lost in these

dogfights, Lt Charles Housel bailing out and Lt D R Brown crashing to his death.

Since the accuracy of the bombing on 19 May had left something to be desired, a second mission against Decimomannu was ordered for the following day. This time the bombing results were excellent. As the 325th FG went down to strafe the few remaining targets on the airfield, 16 enemy fighters arrived on the scene and a dogfight quickly ensued. During the engagement the 325th downed six enemy aircraft, and claimed a seventh as a probable. Frank 'Spot' Collins, with his second victory, reported;

'At 1155 hrs I shot down one Me 109 from about 7000 ft in a diving attack just west of Decimomannu landing ground. The Me 109 came in from the east, and I saw it crash into the ground just west of Siligna. The pilot did not bail out.'

The other kills were scored by Capt Everett Howe and Lts Harold Crossley, William Lott and Arthur McDaniel. Lt Thomas Johnson was hit and made a forced landing in the sea.

A second flight led by Col Austin spotted a flight of seven huge Me 323 transports and shot them all down. Col Austin, Lts John Tuchson and John Grove and Flt Offs David McCampbell, Archie McKeithen and John Smallsreed each claimed one of the six-engined giants.

The 325th FG returned to Decimomannu on 21 May and claimed four more kills, although it suffered two losses in the process. The first two victories were scored by Lts Grove and Frank Hamilton, but they were both, in turn, bounced and shot down by more enemy fighters. The final two kills were claimed by Capt William Reed and Lt John Palmer.

Lt Col Robert Baseler poses with USO stalwarts Frances Langford and Bob Hope in front of Baseler's P-40F 41-20006 *STUD/Mortimer SNERD* at Mateur, in Tunisia, during August 1943. The aircraft bore the number '88' on its fuselage (*Dwayne Tabatt collection via Carl Molesworth*)

These victories ended the 325th's scoring for a few days. During the next week the group turned its attention to targets on the island of Pantelleria. It attacked airfields, harbour defences and port facilities, all of which were thoroughly worked over with machine gun fire and bombs. Several small vessels were damaged or sunk in the harbour and a number of freighters were damaged during the attacks, but at the cost of two pilots.

All squadrons were up and escorting B-26s to Decimomannu on 27 May when a mixed force of 35 German and Italian fighters attacked the bombers. Maj Bob Baseler led his flight down to break up the attack, and during a spirited dogfight he and his men downed six enemy fighters – four Bf 109s and two Italian Macchi C.202s. Maj Baseler and newly promoted Maj E B Howe each downed a C.202 and the four Bf 109s were credited to 'Spot' Collins, John Smallsreed, Dick Catlin and Mark Boone. Lt Collins, apparently a man of few words, described his third kill in the following encounter report;

'At 1850 hrs I shot down a Me 109 from about 3000 ft over the sea at a point about four miles east of Cape Spartivento. The effective hits were fired into the enemy aircraft at a quarterly angle as it was in combat with another P-40. The pilot of the Me 109 evidently was not aware of my approach from above and in the rear of him. The Me 109 dove into the sea and the pilot did not get out.'

Lt Bill Hemphill was hit during the dogfight and he had to ditch in the sea. Flt Off Catlin saw him, dropped a life raft and radioed for Air-Sea Rescue. Hemphill was picked up by an RAF Walrus, which, tragically, crashed on takeoff and all aboard were killed.

Mission 44 for the 325th on 28 May 1943 was another bomber escort, this time to Trapani-Milo airfield on the island of Sicily. 'Herky' Green reported that Bf 109s attacked the bomber formation east of the target and continued the fight out to sea;

'Ten miles off the coast, at 9000 ft, I saw a Me 109 far below me. I rolled over and went after him, firing on the way down. As the range shortened, he pulled up and I did likewise, firing into him. I then went over him and climbed, before rolling over and diving after him again, shooting on the way. To keep from hitting the water I pulled up and climbed to 9000 ft again, blacking out for a moment. When I looked for the Me 109 again I could find no trace of him.'

At the interrogation after this mission it was reported by Maj Howe that he and several other pilots saw a Bf 109 plunge into the water at the point described. Victory number two was confirmed for Green. Two other pilots, Lt Rayburn Lancaster and Flt Off Bruce Cunningham, added to the day's total, with each of them destroying a Bf 109. Sadly, the 325th lost a talented pilot and potential ace during the mission when Flt Off John Smallsreed, who had scored his third victory only the day before, was listed as missing in action (MIA) – no one had seen what had happened to him.

On 29 and 31 May the 325th returned to Pantelleria to attack gun emplacements by dive-bombing with 500-lb bombs. On the second of these missions, while escorting B-26s and carrying 1000-lb bombs, the group targeted an oil dump and several gun emplacements. It should be mentioned here that the 325th FG was the first P-40 outfit in the MTO to deliver 1000 'pounders' on enemy targets.

1 June 1943 found 36 P-40s from the group heading for Sicily in an early morning strafing attack on Stagnone seaplane anchorage. 325th records stated;

'The group, attacking in flights, came in down on the deck over the seawall protecting the anchorage from the open sea. The early hour caught the enemy completely by surprise. Twelve seaplanes were destroyed and six others left burning. These seaplanes were used to ferry supplies from the mainland to Sicily. Maj Bob Baseler, who was credited with destroying two of them, later commented, "We just snuck in on them before anyone was moving around and were out before they really knew what had hit them". While hitting other targets on the island of Sicily flak downed the P-40 flown by Lt Thomas Johnson, who was killed when his aircraft exploded.'

The next opportunity for engaging the Luftwaffe occurred on 6 June 1943 during a dive-bombing mission to Pantelleria. Five P-40s carried 1000-lb bombs while 18 others provided escort. As the dive-bombers were attacking targets on the ground 25 Bf 109s intercepted them, apparently not noticing the top cover. In the ensuing dogfight six Bf 109s went down under the guns of the 325th pilots. One of the kills was scored by Flt Off Charles Engle, who later reported;

'I had a bird's eye view of the whole business. They didn't seem to notice our high cover, and about 12 of them started down after the P-40s on the deck. My flight turned and dove after them. I lined up on one, gave him a little lead and he flew right through my burst. His aeroplane seemed to stand still, roll over and plunge straight down into the sea.'

Between 7 and 10 June 12 escort missions were flown to Pantelleria. Six of these were undertaken on the 10th, and during the last two on this date enemy aircraft were encountered. The fifth mission had taken off at 1400 hrs to escort B-26s of the 320th Bomb Group (BG) and dive-bomb assigned positions on Pantelleria. Over the island the B-26s were targeted by a mixed force of about 25 Italian and German fighters, and the 325th's P-40s dived into the fray to break up the Axis attack. In the following dogfight three Bf 109s were shot down by Lts Herbert Andridge, Lawrence Ritter and Kenneth Rusher for the loss of Flt Off Jim Dunlap, who did not return to base. Four other Bf 109s were claimed as damaged during the dogfight.

The sixth mission of the day took off at 1440 hrs, and this time the 325th was escorting B-26s of the 319th BG. Again, the P-40s would dive-bomb assigned targets on Pantelleria. Over the target, 14 Bf 109s were seen approaching the bombers and they were bounced by the 325th. Two of the Bf 109s were downed by Capt Ralph 'Zack' Taylor and a third was destroyed by 'friendly flak'. Future ace Capt Taylor described his dogfight actions as follows;

'The group was dive-bombing gun positions on Pantelleria, and also escorting B-26s of the 319th BG that were level bombing the same targets. Flying rear cover, I was

Capt Ralph 'Zack' Taylor is seen relaxing on the wing of his P-40L-1 42-10436 '13' before the name *Duchess of Durham IV* and pin-up nose art had been added to its cowling. Taylor would score five of his six confirmed victories in this aircraft (*Dwayne Tabatt collection via Carl Molesworth*)

on the left when my flight was attacked simultaneously by three Me 109s from the side and two Me 109s diving from the rear. Lt Crawford and his wingman turned to meet the three coming from the side while I turned into those diving from the rear. I shot at one of the Me 109s and saw him start smoking, then crash into the water at a point two miles due west of the island.

'In the dogfight off the Pantellerian coast, after seeing the first Me 109 crash I pulled behind another Me 109 that did not see me coming. Firing from dead astern, I saw him roll over and start downward toward the water at a point three miles west of the westernmost tip of Pantelleria.'

One of the 325th's pilots, Lt R D Clark, was shot down by an enemy aircraft, but he was subsequently located in a hospital in Sousse, in Tunisia, and returned to duty shortly thereafter.

No enemy aircraft were encountered during the next five missions, but things changed on 15 June when all three squadrons escorted B-26s of the 17th BG to De Pizzo, on Sicily. As the bombers hit the target and set off an immense explosion, Bf 109s engaged the formation. In the running air battle that ensued, two Messerschmitts were shot down. One was claimed by Lt R D Clark, who after his short hospital stay got sweet revenge with his first victory. The other Bf 109 was downed by Lt Harmon E Burns for this third, and last, kill. During the skirmish Flt Off Jim Beck's P-40 was heavily damaged by enemy gunfire, and he was last seen bailing out.

Three days later, in action over Sardinia, Lt Warren Penny destroyed a Bf 109 and Lt Robert Rogers claimed a Fi 156 Storch – he damaged a second Fieseler liaison aircraft in the same engagement. During this sweep the 325th also destroyed a Me 323 and damaged two Ju 52/3ms on the ground, and all pilots returned safely to base.

In addition to the flurry of aerial victories scored while the 325th was flying out of its bases at Montesquieu and Souk el Khemis, another important milestone occurred – the adoption of the group's bright yellow and black checkerboard markings on its P-40s' vertical and horizontal tails. The 325th FG was the first unit in the MTO to be allowed to decorate its aircraft with distinct unit markings.

On 19 June the group moved to a new airfield at Mateur, in Tunisia. Its first mission from here, on 24 June, was a diversionary sweep over Sardinia that saw the 325th claim five more kills at a cost of four of its own. Individual victories were credited to Capt Bunn Hearn, Flt Offs Bill Slattery and Mark Boone, Lt Rayburn Lancaster and future ace Lt Roy Hogg. The latter was also a man of few words, as his encounter report revealed;

'Fired head-on at a Me 109 doing same with cannon. Me 109 burst into a stream of smoke and Lt Boone saw it crash.'

Lost to enemy action were Lt Blifford, whose P-40 was badly shot up and he was forced to crash land in the target area, and Lt Rappman, his aircraft being hit by flak and crashing into the sea. Lts Bollich and Cutter failed to return to base and were listed as MIA.

The next encounter with enemy aircraft occurred on 28 June when the 325th escorted B-26s of the 17th BG once again, this time to Decimomannu. The results of the bombing were undetermined as the formation was attacked by a gaggle of Bf 109s. The enemy pilots

Herschel H 'Herky' Green, who would finish the war as the 325th FG's leading ace with 18 victories, one probable and six damaged to his name (*Dwayne Tabatt collection via Tom Ivie*)

Lt 'Herky' Green and his groundcrew pose with their new P-40F-5 41-14512 at Mateur during the late summer of 1943. When Green was assigned this Warhawk it was coded '28', but he soon had this changed to his customary '11' (*Dwayne Tabatt collection via Tom Ivie*)

suffered serious losses as they attempted to defend their airfield, with four Bf 109s being shot down and a fifth listed as a probable. In addition to these claims, a sixth Bf 109, two C.202s and a C.200 were damaged during the engagement. The kills were credited to Lt Col Gordon Austin, Capt 'Herky' Green and Flg Offs Clifford Huntington and Archie McKeithen. 'Herky' Green's kill, his third, occurred five miles west of the targeted airfield. He described his victory as follows;

'On an escort mission over Decimomannu airdrome the formation was jumped by enemy fighters before reaching the target. Some minutes after the fight started I encountered a Me 109. He turned sharply to avoid me, and I cut inside his turn and fired a stream of bullets, which he flew through. He straightened out and I continued to fire directly into him. Grey smoke began pouring from the fuselage and he flipped over and dove.'

Green's kill was confirmed by bomber crews that saw the Bf 109 crash. One P-40 and its pilot were lost as Lt Mierizejewski failed to return. He was last seen over the target area.

During the next nine missions no enemy aircraft were encountered, but on 3 July a tragic accident occurred during a strafing mission to Sardinia. Whilst making his pass at the target Lt Keith Bryant pulled up sharply in front of another P-40 and its propeller ripped off the tail section of his Warhawk. Bryant perished in the subsequent crash. The pilot of the second P-40 made it back to Mateur, where he crash-landed.

The Luftwaffe next made an appearance on 7 July during an escort mission to Trapani-Milo airfield on Sicily. Charged with protecting 25 Baltimore IIIA bombers of the Royal Air Force's No 323 Sqn, the 325th engaged 12 Bf 109s and C.202s that attempted to attack the bombers as they approached the target area. Again, the Axis fighters took a beating at the hands of the 'Checkertails', with six aircraft being claimed as destroyed for the loss of one P-40. Single Bf 109s were credited to Lts Hank Brundydge and future ace Walter Walker and Flt Offs Bill Brookbank (his second), Clifford Huntington (his second)

and Bruce Cunningham. The sixth kill, a C.202, was credited to Lt Warren Penny, raising his total to two. Lt Donald Castelberry was shot down in flames by an enemy fighter during the dogfights. Lt Clifford Huntington tried to save Lt Castleberry but failed, stating;

'Flt Off Castelberry and I fell behind the formation as it approached the target. A Me 109 got behind Lt Castelberry, who turned left, with the Me 109 following. I was on Castelberry's left, turning right as I passed him and shot a burst at the Me 109. After a diving turn to the right I came upon the tail of the Me 109, which was still after Castelberry. Shooting again, I saw the canopy come off and smoke pour from the enemy aircraft. The pilot started to spin and I lost sight of him. That both the Me 109 and the P-40 of Lt Castelberry crashed was witnessed by the bombers and confirmed by telephone with Sqn Ldr Hood, RAF, of the Tactical Air Force.'

Lt Walker described his first kill as follows;

'A Me 109 and I met in a head-on attack, but both of us missed, and I turned to meet him. We were both going fast as I approached his tail, but when he did a climbing slow roll he lost most of his speed. I whipped past him and we both dove. Coming out of the dive I blacked out, and when I came to I was in a climbing turn with the Me 109 on my tail. I was turning too tight for his guns to bear, however.

'As I turned inside him he went past me, only to be attacked by another P-40. He avoided this attack by another climbing slow roll, but I was watching him and got on his tail. He dove as I followed, firing at about 200 yards. He pulled up, with me after him, and I fired again as he fell off to the left. We were then at about 2500 ft. He dove, and I expected him to come up beneath me. I tilted up my left wingtip just in time to see him bail out at 200 ft or less and plummet into the sea not ten yards from his aeroplane, which knifed in, making almost no splash.'

Lt Brundydge's victory involved much less dogfighting than Walker's, but the end result was the same;

'The Me 109 came down from the top, about 500 yards behind and to my left. I was alone, so I went after him and caught up with him at about 4000 ft still going straight down. Squeezed a burst into him and he pulled straight up. Followed him up, got off one more burst and we both fell off to the side. He went straight down again and I circled to catch him when he came back up, but when he didn't come back up I looked down and saw him just as he hit the water. The pilot did not leave the aeroplane, nor did it smoke.'

The invasion of Sicily began during the night of 9-10 July 1943, and the 325th FG was kept very busy covering the action. The first of these missions was a sweep over the southern coast on the 9th, pre-invasion. No enemy aircraft were encountered on this mission, but on 10 July it was a different story. While escorting B-25s sent to attack an airfield on Sicily contact was made with the Luftwaffe and three Bf 109s were destroyed for the loss of two P-40s. Single victories went to Lts Joe Bloomer (his third) and Dudley Clark (his second) and Flt Off Otis Prevatt (his second). On the debit side Lt Rogers spun in and crashed on the island and Lt Bill Russell bailed out over the sea and was rescued by an invasion barge.

The second mission of 10 July took off at 1630 hrs, with pilots from the group escorting B-25s of the 321st BG that again targeted airfields

The right side of 'Zack' Taylor's P-40 carried the name *My Gal Sal*. Note the replacement lower portion of the cowling (*Dwayne Tabatt collection via Tom Ivie*)

Capt Ralph 'Zack' Taylor's P-40L-1 41-10436 as it appeared after he scored three kills on 20 July 1943 to raise his total to six victories. At this time the fighter bore the names *Duchess of Durham IV* on the left and *My Gal Sal* on the right side of the cowling, but the artwork on the lower cowling and the group's 'checkerboard' on the tail surfaces were still to be applied (*Dwayne Tabatt collection via Tom Ivie*)

on Sicily. More Bf 109s were encountered in the target area, and once again three of them were shot down. This time the victories went to future aces Capt 'Zack' Taylor (his third) and Lts Walter Walker (his second) and 'Spot' Collins (his fourth). The latter pilot's encounter report stated;

'While flying an escort mission with the 321st BG over Trapani-Milo airdrome I destroyed a Me 109. Just as the formation was making a turn to the left, coming from the north, I saw the Me 109 making a dive from out of the sun to attack the bombers. I turned into him and fired into his engine during a head-on pass. The Me 109 rolled over to the right and went down, flames and white smoke coming from the aeroplane as it descended.'

Two P-40s were also shot down, but both pilots survived. Further action over Sicily on 12 and 13 July added three more victories to the 325th's growing scoreboard. On the 12th Flt Off Mark Boone shot down a Bf 109 for his third, and last, victory, and on the 13th Lt Donald Dove and Flt Off Paul M Hesler Jr each claimed a Messerschmitt. Tactical missions were then flown for the next few days, and no enemy aircraft were encountered during the dive-bombing and strafing attacks undertaken by the group against targets on both Sardinia and Sicily.

On 20 July the 325th FG again headed to Sardinia to dive-bomb several targets on the island, and this time the Luftwaffe was there to greet the group. The action began with a strafing attack on an airfield, where five Bf 109s and two Ju 52/3ms were shot up on the ground along with ten trucks and about 300 German soldiers that were caught in the open. At this point a flight of 12 Bf 109s arrived on the scene and immediately engaged the P-40s, shooting down Flt Off George Dickas. It was a short-lived victory for the mixed force of German and Italian fighters, however, with the hunters quickly becoming the hunted. Capt 'Zack' Taylor led a furious counterattack on the enemy formation, and seven Axis fighters were quickly shot down.

Capt Taylor led the scoring by downing two C.202s and a Bf 109, thus raising his score to six to become the 325th's first ace. Taylor reported;

'While flying south toward Monserrato I saw three enemy aeroplanes dead ahead and one off to the left. I fired directly into one of the 202s. There was a dogfight with several sharp turns. He was finally hit by some of my bursts, and I saw him crash-land in a cloud of dust in an orchard just north of Monserrato airdrome.

'In a dogfight with several other 202s and some other P-40s, I engaged a 202 and was turning left tightly enough to fire into him when he flipped over to turn right. I let go a long burst that hit him squarely. He went down, crashing on the northwest corner of Monserrato airdrome. A huge burst of flame and smoke indicated complete destruction.

'In a running combat with a Me 109 and three 202s, the Me 109 overran a turn and I fired a long burst at him from completely astern. We were headed east at the time. I saw the flash of flame under my left wing as he crashed.'

The remaining victories were credited to future ace Lt George Novotny (a C.202), Capt Warden (a Bf 109) and Flt Offs Jones (a Bf 109) and Brundydge (a C.202).

On the 22nd the 325th headed to the island of Sardinia at 0805 hrs for an early fighter sweep, and it turned

Lt Walter B Walker (in the centre) became an ace in his P-40F-15 41-19896 on 30 July 1943 by downing three enemy aircraft over Sardinia, thus raising his total to five victories (*Dwayne Tabatt collection via Carl Molesworth*)

out to be quite a day for the group. After strafing a number of targets on the island the P-40s ran into a swarm of 25-30 enemy aircraft, the bulk of which were Italian C.202s. In the dogfight that followed no fewer than 17 victories were claimed for the loss of two pilots from the 325th. Two of the kills (both C.202s) were credited to Bob Baseler, and these raised his total to four confirmed victories. Five other pilots from the group scored double kills on this mission, namely Maj Everett Howe, Lt Gilbert Gerken and Flt Offs Archie McKeithen, Al Moon and Ebert Smith. Single victories were credited to Lt Richard Copsey and Flt Offs John Gonda, Otis Prevatt and Bill Slattery. The 17th aircraft destroyed was a Ju 52/3m that had been attacked on the ground during the earlier strafing runs.

The 'Checkertails' resumed their scoring spree on 26 July during another fighter sweep to Sardinia – the group's 100th mission. As the 325th passed over southern Sardinia a mixed flight of ten C.202s and two Bf 109s tried to intercept the P-40s, and they paid heavily for their effort. Maj Baseler became the group's second ace when he shot a C.202 down for his fifth victory. Three other Macchi fighters were downed by Capt Watkins, Lt Whiteside and Flt Off Maret, and the fifth, and final, kill of the day was a Bf 109 claimed by Flt Off Charlie Brown.

Two more victories were added to the 325th's scoreboard on 28 July over Sardinia when Flt Off Bill Slattery destroyed a C.202 for this third, and final, victory, and a second Macchi was claimed by future ace Lt Roy Hogg. This skirmish turned out to be minuscule compared to what happened over southern Sardinia two days later. The 317th FS was attacked by 25 to 30 Bf 109s just north of Alghero, and shortly thereafter an additional eight to twelve Messerschmitt fighters and C.202s joined in the attack. Ultimately, this proved to be an ill-fated decision for the Axis pilots, because when the air battle finally ended some 21 Bf 109s had been destroyed at the cost of one P-40 – its pilot, Bob Sederberg, survived as a prisoner of war.

Lt Walter B Walker Jr led the scoring with three kills, raising his total to five to make him the group's third ace. Walker downed his first two Bf 109s within two minutes, but in the process his P-40 sustained some damage and ran out of ammunition. Nevertheless, he engaged a third Bf 109;

'I was flying about 50 ft above the water when the Me 109 turned down and into me. I turned sharply to the left. He tried to pull in too tight, stalled viciously, flipped over and went straight down into the water. I didn't fire a shot at him because I had used up all my ammunition before the attack.'

Three other pilots scored doubles in the action, namely Capt D E Warden, Lt H E Eyerley and Flt Off Clifford Huntington. Future aces Capt Richard Dunkin and Lt Cecil Dean also downed a Bf 109 apiece for their first victories, while future ace Lt George Novotny claimed his second kill in this massive engagement. Capt Dunkin reported;

'The squadron was flying a fighter sweep over northern Sardinia when we were attacked by about 30 Me 109s. In the ensuing fight I was flying on my flight leader's wing when I saw a Me 109 climbing on the tail of a P-40 about 500 ft above me. I turned into the Me 109, shooting from a deflection angle of about 45 degrees. My tracers appeared to hit the aeroplane. When he noticed that I was shooting at him he tightened his turn and nosed down. I turned inside of him and got on his tail, firing a good burst from dead astern. The aeroplane burst into flame and nosed down, then I saw the explosion as he struck the ground.'

Lt George Novotny recalled;

'We were attacked by 12 Me 109s just as we turned south on a fighter sweep down the valley. The fight was about eight minutes old when a Me 109 came down on me from the rear. He passed over me and pulled up in a half roll and waited upside down. At this time I pulled up and fired a long burst into the aeroplane. There was a flash and the aeroplane started to smoke. The pilot bailed out on the left side of his ship and dropped about 2000 ft before he opened his 'chute.'

Lt Dean scored his first victory as he was heading home from the raid;

'While returning from a fighter scramble south of Sassari a Me 109 jumped me and started firing. I had to make a right turn, flying through a barrage set up by the Me 109 – two shells hit my aeroplane. I pulled up and rolled and then pulled down to the left, firing a ten-degree deflection shot at close range at the Me 109. My bullets riddled his fuselage and pieces flew off the aeroplane in all directions. The aeroplane took a dive and headed straight down toward the earth, where it was seen to crash.'

The remaining kills were scored by Capts W R Reed and B Hearn, Lts N C Carroll, R H Mock, G C Staley, R S Sederberg and G C Hamilton and Flt Offs W T Tudor and A D Donovan. It had been a big day for the 'Checkertails', with 21 confirmed victories, but they were to learn much later that in the heat of battle they had actually under-claimed! In September 1943, following the signature of the armistice with Italy, future group CO Col Chet Sluder learned from Italian pilots that the 325th had engaged a new and inexperienced German unit (possibly III./JG 77) on 30 July and downed between 30 and 35 Bf 109s during the ensuing action. Lt Sederberg, who had been shot down during the clash, later found out that he should have been credited with downing four or five enemy fighters per the testimony of several other 325th FG pilots, instead of just the one he was officially credited with. Unfortunately for him the USAAF never changed the official record. The 325th FG received a Distinguished Unit Citation (DUC) for this action, and the survivors of the German unit were sent home the next day for retraining.

The mission of 2 August cost the 325th FG a potential ace when Flt Off Archie McKeithen suffered a mid-air collision with an Axis seaplane that was marked with red crosses. McKeithen had scored four aerial victories prior to this unfortunate accident. A search mission was flown that day, but no traces of the downed pilot were found.

On 5 August the P-40s of the 325th found and destroyed a target of a totally different type during an escort mission to Sardinia. While returning to base three pilots of the 319th FS saw a U-boat on the surface of the Mediterranean Sea and attacked. Lt William R Elliott made the first pass, the burst from his machine guns causing an explosion in the conning tower. Following Elliott's attack Lts Ritter and Hartley targeted the submarine with some long bursts from their guns, and the stern of the vessel was seen to lift into the air before it went straight down, leaving a large oil slick in its wake. Initially the U-boat was reported as damaged, but the pilots later received credit for the destruction of the vessel.

A mixed gaggle of Bf 109s and C.202s was encountered by the 325th during a fighter sweep over Sardinia on 7 August. Engaged just east of Oristano, two of the enemy fighters were shot down by Capt Joe Bloomer and Flt Off Paul Maret of the 318th FS. With these two kills the group's grand total now reached 128 victories, for the loss of 33 aircraft in combat.

With the battle of Sicily winding down, the attacks on Sardinia increased as that was where most of the Axis airfields that remained operational were located. In what was to become its final month of flying the P-40, the 325th flew numerous missions to Sardinia to help disrupt the Luftwaffe's bombing of Allied seaports in North Africa, and to lessen its ability to launch air assaults against the upcoming landings at Salerno, in Italy. The 325th FG became so heavily involved in this aerial assault against Sardinia that the group gained the nickname of the 'Sardinian Air Force'.

During much of this period the 325th's pilots bombed and strafed many targets throughout Sardinia without any opposition from the Luftwaffe. Finally, on 28 August, the Luftwaffe decided to show its face and partially disrupt the group's attack on industrial sites across the island. Twenty-six Bf 109s attacked, but the P-40 pilots were more than up to the task of defending themselves and duly claimed seven of the Axis fighters shot down – these proved to be the last aerial victories claimed by the 325th FG in the P-40.

Leading the counterattack was Capt John A Watkins, who was later awarded the Distinguished Flying Cross (DFC) for his actions. The 325th's public relations officer described the mission as follows;

The *Duchess of Durham IV/My Gal Sal* is seen here in its final scheme while assigned to Capt 'Zack' Taylor. After the 325th FG's conversion to P-47 Thunderbolts, this aircraft was transferred to the 324th FG. It soldiered on with the group as Capt Bruce Hunt's '11' (*Dwayne Tabatt collection via Tom Ivie*)

'On 28 August 1943, while on a fighter-bomber mission over southwestern Sardinia, Capt Watkins had dropped his bombs on the target when he looked back and saw that a squadron of P-40s was being attacked by approximately 30 Me 109s. He left his flight and turned back to aid the outnumbered squadron. He attacked two Me 109s that were diving on a flight of four P-40s, destroying one and damaging the other so severely that it broke off and went into a glide toward the ground. A few minutes later he saw two Me 109s making a surprise attack on a flight of P-40s. Capt Watkins called a warning to the P-40s, then turned into the enemy aircraft and opened fire. He shot one of them down in flames and severely damaged the second. He then attacked a fifth enemy fighter, firing four bursts into it.'

Another Bf 109 was shot down by Lt 'Spot' Collins, raising his total to five and thereby making him the 325th's fourth ace. Future ace George Novotny also claimed a Messerschmitt for his third victory, reporting;

'We were attacked from the rear by two Me 109s and immediately went into a Lufbery. My leader got on the tail of a Me 109 going straight up and I made a turn to the right, finding two Me 109s slightly below me. I attacked them from a 90-degree approach and closed on the last aeroplane. I saw my tracers hit his engine and fuselage and observed flame and smoke coming out of the aeroplane. Then the aeroplane started spinning and crashed in flames on the coast.'

The remaining three Bf 109s were credited to Lts Henry Brundydge and Daniel Owen and Flt Off John Palmer. Two of the P-40s were damaged in the skirmish but both pilots made it back safely.

During the remainder of August and until its final P-40 mission on 22 September 1943, the 325th continued carrying out bombing and strafing attacks against targets in Sardinia. This final offensive against the island was ordered by Gen Jimmy Doolittle, commander of the Northwest African Strategic Air Force (NASAF). Indeed, he told Lt Col Bob Baseler (now CO of the 325th FG) that Sardinia was the group's prime target, and that only the 325th would be attacking it. Missions continued to be flown against Axis forces until they finally surrendered Sardinia on 22 September.

The P-40 era had now come to a close for the 325th FG, and it was soon withdrawn from combat in order to be re-equipped with Republic P-47 Thunderbolts. While flying Warhawks the 325th had completed 128 missions totalling 3990 sorties, claimed 135 aerial victories and dropped 328,820 lbs of bombs. It had in turn lost 35 pilots in combat.

THUNDERBOLT AND THE FIFTEENTH AIR FORCE

The 325th FG commenced its transition to the P-47 on 22 September 1943. This would be a major change for the unit, as not only would it be receiving a new aircraft, it would also be using the big Republic fighter to perform missions that were entirely different to those the group had previously flown with the P-40.

On this date Mateur airfield received a number of important visitors in the form of civilian technical representatives from Republic. With their arrival pilots and groundcrew commenced the intensive training that would be needed to allow the 325th to operate the P-47s effectively. The first appearance of the group's new fighter was on 11 October 1943 when Lt Col Bob Baseler picked up a P-47 from the aircraft assembly area at Bizerte, in Tunisia, and flew it to Mateur. Shortly thereafter the rainy season hit the training area and the 325th moved to Soliman, also in Tunisia, on 4 November, where it resumed training from a better facility that boasted paved runways.

Armed with a new aircraft that was far superior to the P-40, the 325th FG was now given a major change of assignment, to the newly formed Fifteenth Air Force. During this training period the group provided a fighter escort for the transport aircraft that was carrying President Franklin D Roosevelt and his party to the Tehran Conference. This assignment was proof positive that the 325th's outstanding record in the bomber escort role had been recognised by senior staff officers in the USAAF.

In order to assist with the group's P-47 training, Wing Headquarters thought it would be beneficial to bring in some experienced Thunderbolt pilots from the Eighth Air Force to assist – Lewis W 'Bill' Chick, Bill Madole and Archie Hill duly arrived at Soliman on 3 December. Probably the most experienced of the three was Maj Bill Chick, who had flown Spitfire Vs and the Thunderbolt

Lt Col Lewis W Chick, CO of the 317th FS, poses in his P-47D 42-76021 *Rocky* shortly after becoming an ace on 14 February 1944. Chick closed out his tour of duty with a total of six aerial victories to his name (*Lewis W Chick via Tom Ivie*)

as a member of the 4th FG before being transferred to VIII Fighter Command's Combat Operations Section. A man of action, Chick was unhappy in this staff position and soon transferred to the 355th FG so that he could see further combat in P-47 missions. From here he joined the 325th FG.

Maj Chick, who would soon become the CO of the 317th FS and an ace with the 325th, was an outspoken character who had expressed his dissatisfaction with the Eighth Air Force's fighter tactics. Upon joining the group in Tunisia he was greatly cheered by Gen Doolittle's support for the implementation of new fighter tactics over Italy. Chick noted in a letter to the author;

'I was sent to Italy, where Gen Doolittle said to stay with the bombers until enemy fighters are sighted and then go after them. He wanted us to destroy the enemy fighters whenever we saw them so that we wouldn't have to engage them again tomorrow.'

Chick loved the P-47 as a combat aircraft, and he explained why – in a typically colourful way – in a comparison between the Mustang and the Thunderbolt in his letter of 17 June 1975;

'The Mustang was a lady, and as long as you treated her like a lady she was fine, but if you abused her she would let you down. The "Jug" was an old whore. The more you kicked her around, the more she loved you. She used up all of your money [fuel] in a hurry, but she would still give you a hell of a ride even if the cops [enemy aircraft] were knocking at the door. Not the kind of gal that you wanted to take home and introduce to your mother, but always fascinating and fast.'

The groundcrew began their move to Italy, and the new base at Foggia Main, between 1 and 3 December, with the pilots following them on the 9th. Although the group was still short of its complete complement of maintainers, it began P-47 operations from Italy on 14 December 1943 with an escort mission to Greece. It turned out to be a 'milk run', as did the next five, but on mission four two of the 'Checkertail Clan's' pilots did get a chance to fire their guns at targets on the ground. 'Spot' Collins strafed and destroyed a Ju 52/3m on the airfield at Ancona and Maj Chick strafed a 200 ft vessel moored at Rozzeto di Abrizi, receiving a hail of flak in return.

The mission scheduled for Christmas Day ended tragically when bad weather swept in and three of the 325th's pilots were killed when they flew into a mountain in overcast conditions.

By 30 December Foggia Main had become so overcrowded that the 325th was transferred to a nearby airfield referred to as Foggia 1. In spite of the move, the group still flew a mission that day – withdrawal support for B-17s bombing Verona. A number of Bf 109s were encountered during the operation and three of them were shot down. Two of the kills were claimed by Flt Off Richard Catlin, and the third fighter was downed by Lt Clarence Greene of the 319th FS.

The New Year would see the 325th FG increasingly involved in the Fifteenth Air Force's strategic plan to isolate the battle for Italy from Germany. The group's primary role was to escort the heavy bombers to targets throughout Italy, Austria and some of the Balkan countries. It would also fly fighter sweeps against the Luftwaffe's fighter forces in an attempt to draw them into combat, thereby reducing the number of enemy aircraft available to intercept Allied bombers.

Between 4 and 10 January the 325th flew unopposed escort missions to targets in Italy, Austria and Bulgaria. The only loss during this period was Lt Miller, who failed to return from the 10 January mission in unknown circumstances.

The absence of enemy aircraft ended on the mission of 13 January when the 325th provided withdrawal support for bombers that had attacked German airfields in the Rome area. The group intercepted a flight of approximately 25 Bf 109s over the target area and shot down three of them. One of the kills was scored by the newly promoted Capt 'Spot' Collins (his seventh victory), while the other two were claimed by Maj James Toner and Lt John M Forrest. The P-47 of Lt Fallons was damaged in the melee but he returned safely to base.

The next five missions were again uneventful, but on the second mission of 19 January the 325th ran into some Bf 109s in the Rome area and two of them went down under the guns of future aces Maj Chick and Flt Off Edsel Paulk. The encounter took place just after the B-17s had bombed Contocello airfield, the two enemy fighters being spotted attempting to attack the Fortresses from the rear. Maj Chick, who led his section after them, initially attacked the leader of the pair, hitting him with a burst before losing both fighters momentarily at 10,000 ft. Chick subsequently reported;

'I pulled up from my dive and fired at the wingman from about 50 yards. The shots were telling, as he burst into flames and started down. I followed him down from about 8000 ft to 4000 ft and watched him crash.'

Edsel Paulk, who destroyed the other Bf 109, noted;

'There were four of us and two of them, so it was a question as to who would get to them first. We all shot at them. After Maj Chick got the first one, the second one tried to get away, but I was able to make a quick turn and keep on his tail until I saw the aeroplane smoking and the pilot bail out.'

The next encounter with the Luftwaffe took place on 21 January during a fighter sweep over the Florence area, and this time the foes were Fw 190s. The group engaged the German fighters about 20 miles southeast of Florence and claimed four Focke-Wulfs destroyed. They were credited

P-47D *Little Sir Echo* was the mount of Lt Edsel Paulk of the 317th FS. He served in the 317th FS from June 1943 through to July 1944, and scored at least one of his five victories in this P-47. Paulk's encounter reports did not note if he was flying this aircraft when he claimed his first four kills (*Dwayne Tabatt collection via Carl Molesworth*)

Capt Raymond Hartley served with the 319th FS from December 1943 through to August 1944, commanding the squadron from March to June 1944. He scored two victories and one damaged with the 'Checkertails', and later became an ace by scoring three more kills as a member of the 353rd FG (*Dwayne Tabatt collection via Carl Molesworth*)

Lt Robert M Barkey served in the 319th FS from December 1943 through to mid-June 1944, scoring six victories during his tour of duty. Five of his kills were claimed in the P-47, while his final victory, on 6 June 1944, was scored in his P-51B-15 43-24857 *Dorothy-II* (*Dwayne Tabatt collection via Carl Molesworth*)

to Capt Raymond Hartley Jr and Lts Harry Carroll, William Elliott and Fielder Smith. Future ace Capt Hartley gave a long and detailed report of his trials and tribulations before scoring his first victory;

'We were at 15,000 ft about six minutes south of Florence when, at 1225 hrs, Lt Elliott called out "bogies at 11 o'clock". Maj Tirk, leading the squadron, instructed Lt Elliott to go after them – I led my flight down with Elliott's. The aeroplanes were FW 190s, painted dark blue on top and light blue underneath. There were five or six flying south in a line abreast formation at about 10,000 ft, and we peeled off after them when they were almost directly beneath us. Lt Elliott's flight went after the left-hand three and I led my flight after the right-hand two. I selected the one on the left as my target.

'Elliott's flight, being ahead of us, opened fire, and the FW 190s started split-essing. I saw one roll over and up trailing smoke and fire, and moments later a 'chute opened. My FW did a split-s and then a half roll, and I was able to follow him through both manoeuvres despite the fact that my fighter was still carrying its wing tanks. I finally released my wing tanks as we pulled out of a dive at 2000 ft. I then forgot to switch to my main tank, and momentarily lost speed when the engine was briefly starved of fuel. Another P-47 now got out in front of me in pursuit of the FW.

'We chased the enemy fighter down to the deck and quite a way south. The lead P-47 fired several bursts and I thought I observed several explosions along the wing of the FW, although I was well behind and it was hazy. Then the lead P-47 broke off the chase, banking away to the left despite me calling him to keep going. I continued the chase.

Although the FW pilot was weaving as if to look behind him, I apparently took my opponent by surprise when I fired from close range. I scored hits along the left wing and bottom of the fuselage. The FW started a long climbing turn to the right, and I adjusted my lead and observed hits on top of the fuselage. The FW then rolled slowly onto its back and a large sheet of flame came out of its belly at the wing root. The pilot then split-essed into the ground from about 100 ft. This was between 1230 and 1235 hrs. Just before the crash I had to pull back on my throttle to keep from overrunning the FW.'

This mission was followed up by another fighter sweep on 22 January, this time to Rome and the invasion area around Anzio. The 325th dodged flak and groundfire throughout the operation, and it also encountered 12-15 Bf 109s south of Rome – five of these aircraft were shot down. Capt 'Spot' Collins flamed two of them for his seventh and eighth victories, while future ace Lt Robert Barkey claimed his first victory. He reported;

'Two of us were over Guidonia airdrome, near Rome, when we spotted about 12 Me 109s below us, so we dove on them. We were less than 30 ft from the ground and travelling at about 400 mph. When I was about 50 ft behind a Me 109 I got a good burst into his tail. I could see pieces fly off, he rolled over and crashed.'

The remaining two kills were credited to Maj Chick and Lt Elliott. Sadly, two of the 325th's pilots were reported missing following this mission.

Additional victories were scored on 23 and 27 January by Lts Steacy Rogers and George Hamilton, but for the most part the ten missions from 23 through to 29 January were uneventful. This would all change on the 30th, however.

Throughout the previous several weeks USAAF intelligence had been closely listening in on Luftwaffe radio traffic. From this clandestine eavesdropping it had been determined that the Germans scrambled their fighters about 15 minutes before the USAAF heavy bombers arrived over their targets. Armed with this knowledge, Fifteenth Air Force mission planners decided to despatch 61 P-47s (one of which aborted) from the 325th on a fighter sweep against five enemy airfields in the Villaorba and Udine areas. The 'Checkertail Clan' was instructed to attack enemy aircraft as they were taking off and forming up to meet the oncoming bomber formations.

The 325th departed at 0945 hrs and headed across the Adriatic Sea at a height of just 50 ft in order to escape German radar. The fighters then climbed to altitude over the Gulf of Venice. Reaching Villaorba at 1145 hrs and stacked from 15,000 ft up to 19,000 ft, the group observed 60 German fighters scrambling into the sky. In addition to these fighters, a number of other types of Axis aircraft were

A smiling Capt 'Herky' Green after returning to base on 30 January 1944. Flying Bunn Hearn's Thunderbolt *The Star of Altoona* on that date instead of his assigned P-47 '11', Capt Green destroyed six enemy aircraft to become the 'Checkertail Clan's' first 'ace-in-a-day' (*Dwayne Tabatt collection via Tom Ivie*)

Capt Bunn Hearn poses in the cockpit of his P-47 *The Star of Altoona*, the serial of which remains unknown. The two swastikas represent victories Hearn scored while flying the P-40 (*Dwayne Tabatt collection via Tom Ivie*)

Lt Cecil Dean's P-47D-6 42-74957 was adorned with one of the most aggressive bits of nose art seen on a fighter of the 317th FS – a black panther with a Bf 109 in its mouth. Dean scored three of his six kills in P-47s (*Dwayne Tabatt collection via Carl Molesworth*)

fleeing the airfields so as to avoid the upcoming bombing. The stage was now set and the massacre of enemy aircraft was about to begin. When it was all over no fewer than 37 Axis aircraft had fallen to the guns of the 325th, with a further seven claimed as probables, against two losses. 'A' Flight of the 317th claimed 15 of the confirmed kills, with Capt 'Herky' Green showing the way by shooting down four Ju 52/3ms, a C.202 and a Do 217. His mission report read as follows;

'Immediately upon reaching the target area we began to encounter isolated enemy aeroplanes, and several fights started. I peeled off with a section of four and went down to attack a bunch of transports we could see approaching at an altitude of about 1000 ft. There were 11 Ju 52/3ms and they were strung out in a loose in-trail formation. We came out of the sun at high speed and went right down the line. I got four on one pass, and three other pilots, Lt Novotny and Flt Offs Dean and Paulk, destroyed the remaining seven.'

Shortly afterwards Capt Green downed his fifth victim – a C.202 – at treetop level. After destroying the Macchi he found himself alone, so he started a climbing turn to the south in the direction of home. As he was crossing the coastline at 15,000 ft he saw a Do 217 at about 5000 ft, so he dived after the bomber and quickly set it on fire with several bursts. Green then watched as the aircraft exploded in flames when it hit the ground – victory number six! With these six kills Capt Green tied with Capt 'Spot' Collins (who also scored a victory on this mission) as the 325th FG's leading ace with nine victories. Collins reported;

'I was circling at 11,000 ft, heading north over a railway line ten miles east of Villaorba airdrome, when I observed a Me 109 attacking two P-47s at about 3000 ft below me. I rolled over and dove straight toward the Me 109 and gave it a burst from the rear and above, but saw no hits.

The enemy aeroplane saw me, then turned to the right and then levelled out, evidently trying to outrun me. I closed to firing range and continued firing until I had almost overrun him. I broke off, peeled up and looked back. Flames were coming from the Me 109's fuselage, and the aeroplane was obviously out of control. It spiralled in from about 6000 ft and crashed.'

Lt George Novotny downed two of the Ju 52/3ms, followed by an Hs 126, to raise his total to six and thus become the 'Clan's' newest ace. Future ace Flt Off Cecil Dean nailed three Ju 52/3ms, raising his

score to four. Not to be outdone, fellow future ace Flt Off Edsel Paulk shot down a Bf 109 and two Ju 52/3ms, which also raised his total to four.

Maj Chick's flight of four 317th FS Thunderbolts, meanwhile, was attacked head on by six Bf 109s. In the ensuing combat Chick scored two kills within ten minutes when he shot a pair of enemy fighters off the tail of a lone P-47, thus raising his score to four kills. Two other future aces also claimed victories in this engagement, Lt Roy Hogg downing a Fw 190 as his fourth kill and Lt Eugene Emmons being credited with his first two successes (a Bf 109 and a C.202). Lt Hogg reported;

'I saw a MC 202 pressing an attack against a P-47 [Lt P E Suehle] in a fight slightly below me. I immediately turned into the Macchi, fired a short burst and saw the enemy aircraft blow up in mid-air, hit the ground and burn.'

A few minutes later Lt Col Bob Baseler downed a Ju 88 for his sixth, and final, victory. He said in his encounter report;

'Saw a Ju 88 being attacked by four P-47s. The Ju 88 turned into the attackers and they overshot. I slowed up, slid in behind him and gave him two short bursts. He pulled straight up, stalled, flame belched forth from both engines and he crashed and burned on the west side of the town of Palmaniva, Italy.'

The remaining kills were claimed by Lts Neil Carroll, James Jones, Noel Kitchen and Phillip Whiteside, with each pilot being credited with two apiece. Single kills were awarded to Lts John Brower, J C Dorety, Gerald Edwards, Walter Dahl, Donald Kerns and P E Suehle.

P-47D-10 42-75008 *BIG STUD* was probably the best known of the various fighters flown by Lt Col Robert Baseler during his long tenure as CO of the 325th FG – he led the group from 5 April 1943 to 1 April 1944. Baseler scored his sixth, and final, victory in this Thunderbolt on 30 January 1944 (*Dwayne Tabatt collection via Carl Molesworth*)

For his leadership and aggressiveness in planning and leading this record-breaking assault on the Axis air forces in Italy, Lt Col Baseler was immediately awarded the Silver Star after the group returned home. The 325th also received its second DUC for this daring mission.

The assault on Axis aircraft continued the next day during an escort mission to Udine, in Italy. Whilst over the target area the group encountered a mixed bag of enemy aircraft. The first of these was a group of six Fw 190s that attempted to attack the B-17s being escorted by the 325th. The German pilots broke off their interception and fled when the P-47s turned into them. Four Bf 109s then tried to engage the bombers, but they too were driven off. This time two enemy aircraft were shot down by Lts William Rynne and Ferdinand Suehle, the former noting in his encounter report;

'I dove through flak after a Me 109. The enemy aeroplane split-essed and I followed, firing as I closed in. I then saw the canopy open and the pilot bail out. The aeroplane spun in and crashed. Other pilots saw a parachute in the combat area.'

Moments later five SM.82 transports were seen flying far below, and future aces Lts Richard Dunkin, Cullen Hoffman and William Rynne pulled in behind them on the deck and quickly shot down three of the Savoia-Marchetti tri-motors.

The month of February 1944 got off to a slow and sad start for the 'Checkertail Clan', as the first six missions were flown without any encounters with enemy fighters. The unit suffered a fatality, however, when Lt Phillip Whiteside apparently became disorientated in a heavy overcast and spun into the ground.

The mission of 14 February at last saw the heavy bombers – targeting Verona's railway marshalling yards – engaged by Axis fighter units once again. After rendezvousing with the bombers, 47 Thunderbolts had shepherded the 'heavies' to within ten miles of the target when they were challenged by a mixed force of 25 Bf 109s and five C.202s. Thirty-two of the P-47s peeled off and went after the enemy aeroplanes, and in the 30-minute dogfight that ensued seven Axis fighters were shot down and three more were claimed as probables. Future ace Lt Eugene Emmons brought down both a Bf 109 and a C.202 for his third and fourth kills and Maj Bill Chick flamed a Messerschmitt for his fifth victory – the 'Clan' had another new ace. His wingman, Lt Rynne, downed the wingman of Maj Chick's kill shortly thereafter for his third victory. The report stated;

'Maj Chick, with Lt Rynne on his wing, chased a lone Me 109 about 50 miles, then returned to the combat and saw two Me 109s and pursued them to the southeast through a long dive from 30,000 ft to 13,000 ft, steadily closing in on them. About 15 miles northwest of Ferrara, Chick and Rynne each chose a target and fired at their respective Me 109s. Maj Chick shot one of them down in flames and Lt Rynne observed it.'

Moments later Lt Rynne knocked the other Bf 109 out of the sky and Maj Chick confirmed it. In other actions Lts Mock, Malloy and Clark each claimed a Bf 109 destroyed to round out the day's score. Weather then became the enemy and only five more missions were flown during the remainder of February, with Lt Soper failing to return from the 22 February mission, cause unknown. Another pilot, Lt Clifford White, was killed three days later when his engine failed on takeoff and he crashed into Lake Lesina.

The first mission of March 1944 turned out to be a milk run when the 325th escorted B-17s attacking German troop concentrations in the Anzio beachhead area. However, on the next mission, flown on 3 March, the Luftwaffe was up in force, and it was an experienced gaggle of German fighters that tangled with the 'Checkertail Clan' that day. The group was escorting B-24s attacking airfields in the Rome area when the bombers were hit over the target from both sides and from the rear by 20 Bf 109s and 12 Fw 190s in a well executed attack. The 325th FG quickly swung into action, and in a swirling series of dogfights the 'Clan' managed to claim six fighters destroyed, two probables and six damaged, but at a cost of four pilots shot down.

Lt Col Lewis W 'Bill' Chick's P-47D 42-76021 was named *Rocky*, and he scored at least two of his six kills in this Thunderbolt. Chick served as commanding officer of the 317th FS from January to March 1944 (*Lewis W Chick via Tom Ivie*)

P-47D 42-75929 *Ginger* was assigned to Capt William A Rynne of the 317th FS, and he put it to good use scoring five victories and one probable with it. In March 1944 he transferred to the 319th FS, serving as its CO from 20 to 28 March, when he was shot down. Rynne has been mistakenly reported as having been killed in action in several documents, but he survived the war after spending several months as a PoW (*Dwayne Tabatt collection via Tom Ivie*)

'Herky' Green's famous P-47D '11', the serial number of which remains unknown, is seen here at Lesina shortly after he scored his 13th victory on 7 April 1944. Maj Green, CO of the 317th FS from 25 March to 23 September, claimed three of his ten P-47 kills in this aircraft (*Dwayne Tabatt collection via Tom Ivie*)

Future ace Lt Richard Deakins was the top scorer for the day with a Bf 109 and a Fw 190 destroyed. Newly promoted Lt Col Bill Chick claimed his sixth, and final, victory of his tour with the 317th FS by downing a Bf 109. He noted;

'I spotted a lone Me 109 at about 16,000 ft flying towards Rome. I dived on the Me 109 and chased him down to 8000 ft, at which point I fired a few bursts from directly behind the enemy aircraft. The Me 109 caught on fire as it entered a cloud, and when the aeroplane came out on the far side of the cloud the pilot was seen to bail out. The remainder of my flight confirmed the victory.'

Two other Bf 109s were shot down by Flt Off Gerald Storts and Lt Winston Vaught, while the final kill of the day was a Fw 190 destroyed by Lt S E Brown. Lts Walker, Been, Ridgeway and Eastman failed to return to base, however.

The fierce fighting on the ground continued as Allied forces tried to break out from the Anzio beachhead. Their efforts were supported from the air by continual attacks on German positions, supply lines and airfields. As expected, Axis fighter units were up in strength in an attempt to meet the threat of Allied air power. The 'Checkertail Clan' experienced this for themselves on the escort mission of 11 March. The target was the Padua railway marshalling yards, and the bombers were met by a force of 65 enemy aircraft in the target area.

Dogfighting broke out when the lead and centre sections of the bomber formation were jumped by 15 Bf 109s. Simultaneously, the straggling rear section was also engaged by a gaggle of 50 enemy aeroplanes. The 325th saw the attacks as they materialised and immediately bounced the German formations. A series of individual encounters then took place in the skies over Padua, and when they were all over 'Clan' pilots claimed a total of ten enemy aircraft destroyed, four as probables and one damaged, at the cost of three of their own. Maj 'Herky' Green reported;

'My wingman and I dove into a concentration of about 40 enemy aircraft. During the scramble I was able to get behind a Me 109, and at first my gunfire did not have any effect as I was being bounced around by the prop wash from the enemy aeroplane. Later, while still in a dive, I hit the Me 109 – I observed explosions in and around the cockpit. Then the Me 109 caught fire and went out of control.'

Green's tenth kill was confirmed by Lt Hogg.

Capt William Rynne chipped in by destroying two Bf 109s for his fourth and fifth kills, thus becoming the 'Clan's' newest ace. The remaining kills were credited to Lts Frank Butler, Robert Clark, Robert Barkey, Robert Chesney, James Jones, Lynn Kern and William Carswell. All of the downed enemy aircraft were Bf 109s except for Carswell's, which was a C.202. The 'Clan's' three losses were especially tragic as Lt James Jones was accidently shot down and killed by one of his fellow pilots, while Lt Col Anthony Tirk Jr, CO of the 319th FS, was lost after he led his flight of four P-47s in an attempt to break up the attack by 50 enemy aircraft on the rear bomber formation. Tirk's flight succeeded in disrupting the Axis fighters, but his P-47 was shot up in the process and he bailed out. Tirk's parachute caught fire as he jumped from his blazing fighter and he fell to his death. The final casualty of the day was Flt Off Knox, who was also shot down during the aerial battle.

The next three missions – two fighter sweeps and a bomber escort – were uneventful as the Axis air forces were nowhere in sight. The mission of 18 March (an escort fighter sweep to the Villaorba/Udine area) did, however, stir up the Luftwaffe. Some 30 enemy fighters attacked the bomber formation, and without hesitation the 325th engaged them in what was described in the mission summary 'as a turning fight of chiefly deflection shots and at a higher altitude than usual'. The deflection shooting was apparently quite good, as nine enemy aircraft (seven Bf 109s and two C.205s) fell to the guns of the 325th's P-47s. Double ace Maj 'Herky' Green flamed a Bf 109 for his 11th kill, while Lt George Novotny destroyed another Messerschmitt for his seventh victory. Maj Green's encounter report stated;

After Lt George Novotny's departure from the 317th FS his P-47D 42-75971 *Ruthless Ruthie/Lady Janie VI* was reassigned to future ace Lt John Simmons. These individuals are, from left to right, John Kerr, Pete Vitale, John Simmons, J Bramer and Ira Grandel (*Dwayne Tabatt collection via Tom Ivie*)

P-47D *Shimmy II* was flown by Lt Col Chester 'Chet' Sluder, CO of the 325th FG from 1 April 1944 until 11 September 1944. Sluder scored the first of his two kills in this aircraft (*Col Chester Sluder via Tom Ivie*)

A close up of the personal markings on Capt William Rynne's P-47D 42-??877 *Ginger* at Lesina, in Italy, during March 1944 (*Dwayne Tabatt collection via Tom Ivie*)

'After about ten minutes of fighter scrambles I observed a Me 109F on my left making a pass at a P-47. I broke left into the Me 109 and he pushed over and headed for the deck. I saw the Me 109 under me and did a double reverse and ended up on his tail. I fired while in a dive, and observed flashes all over its wings and fuselage. As I pulled up the enemy aeroplane was totally out of control and totally enveloped in flames.'

Future ace Robert Barkey downed a Me 109 for his third victory, and the remaining kills were credited to Lts Noel Kitchen, Frank Walker, Lynn Kern, Charles House, Robert Chesney and Harold Clinge. Two P-47s and their pilots, Lts Daniel Davis and Walter Hallet, were lost during the swirling dogfight.

After three uneventful missions flown on the 19th, 22nd and 25th, the 325th FG headed to Verona on 28 March to provide escort for B-17s attacking the city's railway marshalling yards. Near Ferrara the 'Clan' encountered, and engaged, a formation of 40 Bf 109s, and in a 15-minute duel seven of the enemy fighters were destroyed at a cost of three P-47s. Lt Col Chet Sluder and Lts Joseph Folkes and A O Jones each shot down a Bf 109, but the most unusual claim of the day was when Lt John Booth of the 319th FS destroyed four Messerschmitts in a matter of seconds. The event was reported by HQ 325th FG as follows;

'Lt John R Booth set two Me 109s afire and was in the act of turning into more when his wing tip collided with the right wing of a Me 109. The enemy aeroplane's wing was torn off and it twisted away, only to crash into another Me 109 and both were destroyed. Lt Booth had to crash-land his P-47 when he returned to base due to the mid-air collision, but he emerged safely. When his combat film was developed, it was discovered that the two Me 109s he had fired on before the collision were destroyed, thus giving Lt Booth the record of five seconds of combat and four Me 109s destroyed.'

These victories were costly though, as the 319th FS lost its CO, Capt William Rynne, and Lts A O Jones and Hudson.

The last days of March saw the 325th FG move to its new base at Lesina, which was the most forward location of all of the Fifteenth Air Force bases in Italy. The group's first mission from its new base was flown on 29 March, when bombers were escorted to Steyr, in Austria. As the formation approached the target three enemy aircraft were sighted

33

making passes at the bombers. It was a futile effort on their part as none of the German fighters survived after their attempt to disrupt the mission. The aeroplanes destroyed by the group, which were described in the mission summary as 'FW 290s', were almost certainly standard Fw 190s or Bf 109s, as the Fw 190D long-nose did not reach frontline units until late 1944. Whatever the fighters were, they were sent crashing to earth by Maj 'Herky' Green (his 12th kill) and Lts Frank Butler and John Forrest. Maj Green described his kill as follows;

'While I was covering some straggling bombers I observed a FW 290 below me closing on one of the bombers. I rolled over and came down close behind the enemy aircraft. I gave the FW 290 a burst of fire and saw hits along the fuselage and at the wing roots. At this time black and white smoke began pouring out of the enemy aeroplane. Because of my low altitude I had to pull up, and did not see it crash.'

Lt Penny, however, witnessed Maj Green's attack, and saw the enemy aeroplane trailing smoke and then crashing to earth.

On the final mission of March 1944 Lt George Hamilton destroyed a C.205 over Sofia, Bulgaria.

Lt Col Bob Baseler turned over command of the 325th FG to Lt Col Chester L 'Chet' Sluder on 1 April 1944 and then headed to his new assignment in the 306th Fighter Wing Headquarters. Combat resumed on 2 April with an escort for bombers returning to Steyr, and resulted in three more victories for the 325th FG. Two of the kills were scored by future aces Lts Richard Dunkin and Cullen Hoffman, and a third Bf 109 was shot down by Lt Richard Mock. It was the second victory for Dunkin and Hoffman, and Mock raised his total to three. No P-47s were lost in this skirmish with a gaggle of 20 Bf 109s.

On 6 April the 'Checkertail Clan' headed to an airfield near

An early photograph of Lt Eugene Emmons' P-47D 42-75737 *Hun Hunter*. At this time the fighter is devoid of any victory markings or the group's distinctive 'checkertail', but that would change in short order. Emmons scored his first two kills on 30 January 1944 and became an ace on 6 April that same year. His final count was nine destroyed and one damaged – at least four of these kills were scored in this aircraft (*Dwayne Tabatt collection via Tom Ivie*)

Unknown, Lt Cullen Hoffman and Sgt Buford Pasley pose with their P-47D '39' after Hoffman's third kill on 6 April 1944. He claimed at least three of his victories in this aircraft (*Dwayne Tabatt collection via Carl Molesworth*)

Lt Cullen Hoffman chose a bright red lightning bolt as the personal marking for his P-47D (*Dwayne Tabatt collection via Carl Molesworth***)**

Zagreb, in Yugoslavia, as escorts for a mixed force of B-17s and B-24s. They were met by 40 Bf 109s, C.202s and C.205s about 60 miles southwest of the target. The 325th broke up the Axis fighter formation and commenced an aerial battle that lasted more than 30 minutes. Predictably, the results came out entirely in the 'Clan's' favour, with ten enemy aircraft being shot down, again for no losses. During the course of the dogfight Lt Novotny downed a C.205 for his eighth, and final, victory, and Lt Eugene Emmons flamed a Bf 109 for his fifth kill, thus becoming the 325th's newest ace. Future ace Cullen Hoffman also downed a Messerschmitt to raise his total to three. Lt Jim Oxner was the high scorer during the far-ranging clash, as he destroyed two C.205s. Lts Hamilton, Dorety, Storts, Mock and Penny disposed of the remaining five enemy aircraft downed that day.

Several pilots were decorated for their part in rebuffing the Axis attack. Two of the pilots receiving DFCs for their courage and skill in breaking up the attack were Lts Warren Penny and James Dorety of the 317th FS. Penny's citation said in part;

'Realising the imminent danger, and with complete disregard for overwhelming odds, Lt Penny attacked the hostile formation and in the ensuing battle destroyed one enemy fighter. Returning to his formation, he assisted in beating off persistent attacks, enabling the bombers to complete a highly successful bomb run and return to base without loss.'

The following day the 325th FG took off for a special fighter sweep of the Udine area but found the Axis air forces conspicuous by their absence. During the 30-minute sweep of the area only one enemy aeroplane was spotted in the air, and Maj Green made quick work of it. He was about 20 miles east of Venice when he saw a Bf 110 and dived to attack it. Green later noted in his encounter report;

'I came in close behind the enemy aeroplane, and after firing a few bursts its left engine exploded and the aeroplane started to spin. I then pulled up and around to get into position for another firing pass, and noted that even though the fuselage was burning the pilot had righted his aeroplane. I gave the Me 110 another burst, and a few seconds later the enemy aeroplane crashed and cart-wheeled in a ball of flames.'

With victory number 13 in the bag 'Herky' Green was now the top scoring active pilot in the MTO.

Having a break from operations between 8-11 April, the group returned to the fray on the 12th when it provided withdrawal support for B-24s attacking an aircraft factory in Wiener Neustadt. Just after rendezvousing with the bombers in the target area a large gaggle of 57 enemy aircraft were encountered. Six Bf 109s were shot down and another was claimed as a probable, Lt Edsel Paulk flaming one for his fifth victory – another ace was added to the 325th's growing list. Future ace Lt Richard Dunkin also downed a Bf 109 to raise his total to four, his success on this mission earning him a DFC. Dunkin's leadership was particularly praised, as he had engaged a considerably larger formation and shot down its leader. This in turn caused the enemy fighters to break off their attack on the bombers.

The remaining kills were credited to another future ace, Capt Raymond Hartley Jr (his second kill) and Lts G W Gerken, J R Strain and R Malloy. The 325th almost lost future ace Lt Harry Parker when an overzealous P-38 pilot shot up his P-47, forcing him to bail out. Parker was rescued and returned to base.

Lt Edsel Paulk claimed his fifth kill on 12 April 1944 and posed with his groundcrew for a photograph on their P-47D *Little Sir Echo* to mark the occasion (*Dwayne Tabatt collection via Carl Molesworth*)

The following day (13th) the 325th escorted B-24s when they targeted Budapest airfield. The group discovered a number of enemy aircraft in the target area and immediately engaged them. They were a mixed bag of German and Italian aircraft, and some of them represented new adversaries for the 'Clan'. Lt Eugene Emmons, for example, downed a Reggiane Re.2001 for his sixth kill. Future ace Richard Deakins sent a Bf 109 down in flames for his third success, while Lts A E Aho and J L Brower each destroyed a Me 410. The final victory, a Bf 109, was claimed by Lt R Garcia. Unfortunately, the 325th did not leave the encounter unscathed as Lts Richard Malloy and Richard Mock were lost in this action.

The missions of 15 and 16 April saw no enemy action, but the 'Clan' lost two of its own on the latter date apparently to engine problems. The first to go down was Flt Off J W Barrett, who was forced to ditch into the sea. Later in the flight Lt J R Booth, who had scored four kills in a matter of seconds on 28 March, also ditched in the sea. Both pilots were seen floating in their Mae Wests. but neither was ever recovered and both were entered into the MIA list.

Matters improved on 17 April when the 325th escorted B-24s attacking targets in Belgrade and Sofia, in Yugoslavia. The mission assignment had been to Belgrade, but there was a mix up at the rendezvous point and one squadron continued on to the Yugoslavian capital while the other two units headed to Sofia with the 'wrong' B-24s. The latter group subsequently engaged eight Bf 109s and shot four of them down in flames during a brief action. Ace Eugene Emmons accounted for two of the fighters, raising his score to eight, while Flt Off P J Kastner and Lt Gerald B Edwards destroyed the remaining two Messerschmitts. Lt H C Wolfe claimed a fifth Bf 109 as a probable, and no P-47s were lost or damaged in the skirmish. Lt Edwards' actions in this engagement earned him a DFC, the citation accompanying the medal noting that;

'Near the target Lt Edwards saw eight enemy fighters preparing to attack the bombers. Reacting immediately, he dove after the hostile aircraft and through his aggressiveness and combat proficiency destroyed one enemy fighter and aided in the dispersal of the others.'

The scoreboard on Lt Eugene Emmons' P-47D 42-75737 reflects his new total after his double victory on 17 April 1944 (*Dwayne Tabatt collection via Tom Ivie*)

Action continued on 18 April during a fighter sweep to the Udine area, where the group found a mixed bag of 11 Bf 109s and Fw 190s. Two of the latter and one Messerschmitt went down under the gunfire of Lts Paul Dowd, Steacy Rogers and Sam Brown, but this time at a cost, as Lt John Gonda was listed as MIA.

During the remainder of April, except for the mission on the 25th, the Axis air forces were nowhere to be seen. On 25 April the 'Clan' escorted B-24s whose target was an aircraft factory in the Italian city of Turin. This time enemy aeroplanes were spotted twice during the course of the mission. The first encounter was with a formation of 16-20 Bf 109s and C.202s, but as 24 P-47s turned to meet their attack, the enemy fighters broke away and fled rather than face the oncoming Thunderbolts. The remaining 17 P-47s continued with the bombers, and over the target a covey of seven Fiat G.55s tried to attack. Pilots of the 318th FS blunted their attempt, however, and future ace Benjamin Emmert Jr destroyed one of them for his first kill. A second G.55 went down under the guns of Lt Donald MacDonald, while Lt Harper claimed a third Fiat fighter as a probable. All the 318th pilots emerged from the dogfight unscathed.

On 5 May, during the 325th's second mission of the new month, Axis air forces again made their presence known when the group escorted bombers to Turnul Severin railway marshalling yards in Rumania. The mission summary noted that the 325th escorted the B-24s to the target area, where they were forced to turn back due to low fuel. 'Fifteen P-47s were intercepted by approximately 25 FW 190s, MC 205s and Me 109s 40 miles east of the rendezvous point, and by ten Me 109s in the target area. Enemy aircraft attacked in twos and threes from above and then pulled back up. The pilots of the enemy aeroplanes were aggressive and seemed experienced'. Nevertheless, the 325th was able to down four of the Bf 109s against the loss of Lt Arthur Fitch. Individual claims were made by Lts Warren Penny, Ferdinand Suehle, Harold Wolfe and Robert Clark.

Tragedy struck the 'Checkertail Clan' on 12 May, and once again the culprit was bad weather. The group had been tasked with escorting bombers to Bologna, in Italy, but it encountered heavy cloud that extended to an altitude of 28,000 ft in the target area and prevented the fighters from rendezvousing with the 'heavies'. While feeling their way through this nightmarish overcast, five P-47 pilots spun out and disappeared. Lts John Brower, Joseph Folkes, John Forrest, Edward Nuniveller and Richard Scott were all listed as MIA.

Enemy aircraft were next encountered on 13 May during a fighter sweep over Ferrara, Verona and Lake Garda. As 47 Thunderbolts of the 325th patrolled the target area at altitudes ranging from 24,000 ft up to 28,000 ft, a formation of 20-25 enemy aircraft was observed flying at the same height. The 'Checkertails' quickly engaged the enemy machines, the mission summary stating that 'during 25 minutes of intense combat two Me 109s were destroyed and two others damaged'. One of the kills was credited to Lt Eugene Emmons as his ninth, and final, victory and Lt Frank Butler claimed the other Bf 109 for his third, and final, kill.

The 'Checkertail Clan's' brief, but highly successful, association with the Thunderbolt was now nearing its end, and during the group's final five missions in the P-47 enemy aircraft were encountered only once – on the last mission flown with the Republic fighter, on 25 May 1944. The 325th was providing penetration escort for bombers attacking the airfield at Wöllersdorf, in Austria, when, shortly after rendezvousing with the bombers, a flight of 15 enemy aircraft bounced the formation northwest of Zagreb. They were in turn bounced by the 'Checkertails', who shot down six Bf 109s. Lt Don Kerns led the scoring by downing two of them for his second and third kills. He was also awarded the DFC for leadership and aggressiveness in this action, the medal citation stating in part;

'He broke up the enemy formation and drove them from the area. During the aerial battle he successfully destroyed two enemy fighters, and saved a fellow pilot from two aggressive enemy fighters. Under his protective cover the bombers were thus enabled to complete a highly successful bombing mission unmolested.'

Another of the Bf 109s was destroyed by Lt Robert Barkey for his fifth kill, making him the 325th's newest ace. The final three victories were claimed by Lts Hiawatha Mohawk, Robert Rausch and Robert Bass. All of the 'Clan's' P-47s returned safely to base.

Thus ended the group's short Thunderbolt era. The rugged P-47 had seen the 'Clan' through some tough combat, and provided pilots with much needed experience for their endeavour in the P-51 Mustang. During the six months that the 325th had been equipped with the Thunderbolt it had flown 97 combat missions, scored 153 victories and suffered 38 losses. Of the latter, only seven were at the hands of enemy aircraft – five P-47s also fell to flak. The remaining losses were attributed to weather, mechanical problems, etc. Six of the 'Clan' became aces while flying the Thunderbolt, namely Maj Herschel 'Herky' Green with ten victories (plus three in the P-40), Lt Eugene Emmons with nine, Maj Lewis W Chick with six victories, Lt George Novotny with five victories (and three in the P-40), Capt William A Rynne with five and Lt Edsel Paulk with five. Five other pilots scored four kills in the Thunderbolt. During this period 66 of the 325th's pilots scored one or more kills in the P-47.

MUSTANG ERA

With the arrival of the P-51 pilots of the 325th FG again found themselves flying an aircraft powered by a liquid-cooled engine, but this time it was a fighter with an unmatched range that could take them much deeper into enemy territory. The Mustang would in turn produce a whole new crop of aces.

The conversion to the North American fighter was completed quickly, and on 27 May the 'Checkertail Clan' flew its first mission in the P-51 – an escort to southern France, where the bombers hit several railway marshalling yards. Enemy aircraft were nowhere to be seen, and the absence of Axis air power continued during the 325th's next two missions to Turin and Wöllersdorf. These three milk runs were just a break-in period for a big adventure that would begin on 2 June 1944.

The 'Checkertail Clan' would now be putting its long-ranged mount to a spectacular new test by undertaking the first Shuttle Mission to the USSR. This mission was classified top secret, and Lt Col 'Chet' Sluder, group CO, only informed four of his HQ staff officers on what was going on so that they could help him with preparations for this historic operation. Sixty-four of the 325th's P-51s were slated for the mission, and numerous members of the group's groundcrew would fly in the escorted B-17s as gunners. Prior to the mission commencing the groundcrew accompanying the fighters were provided with brand new uniforms, which immediately fuelled the 'guard-house' rumours that they were either going home or to England. On the following morning the excitement was quickly quashed as they found themselves being loaded onto B-17s for their trip to Russia.

The outbound trip consisted of escorting the bombers to targets in Debreczen, Hungary, and onward into Russia to Pyriatin. The last leg the was most difficult as 'Chet' Sluder was unable to acquire decent maps

Lt Col 'Chet' Sluder led the first Shuttle Mission to the USSR in his new P-51C 42-103867 *Shimmy III* (*Col Chester L Sluder via Tom Ivie*)

of Russia, and there was a solid undercast at about 2000 ft that complicated his navigation. Finally, after initially overshooting Pyriatin, he realised his error and led his flock of Mustangs to their assigned landing field. After arrival the 325th FG was welcomed by both the American contingent and its Russian hosts, and wined and dined for the next four days.

On 6 June 42 of the 'Clan's' Mustangs escorted B-17s attacking targets in Galati, Rumania, and this time the Luftwaffe was waiting. Sixteen enemy fighters were encountered in the target area, 'Chet' Sluder noting, 'I clobbered a FW 190 and Capt Roy Hogg nearly got himself killed shoving six more of them off of my tail'. In spite of the attempts on his life Capt Hogg managed to out-duel two Fw 190s and send them both down in flames for his fifth and sixth kills – the 'Clan' now had another new ace. Not to be outdone, Lt Cullen Hoffman also became an ace when he shot a lone Ju 88 down in flames for his fifth kill. The third man to achieve acedom that day was Lt Robert Barkey, who despatched a Bf 109. Future ace Lt Wayne Lowry also downed a Messerschmitt for his first victory. Unfortunately, these victories were not without cost as Lts Mumford and MacDonald failed to return.

Lt Ed Strauss of the 318th FS participated in this mission;

'On the trip out we ran into two lone aeroplanes. One was Russian and the other was a Ju 88, which was immediately shot down [by Cullen Hoffman, who became the first American pilot to shoot down an enemy aircraft while flying from a Russian base]. We picked up the bombers over the target. Bombing results looked to be excellent. Flak over the target was very inaccurate. Just as we left the target Me 109s and FW 190s tried to get at the bombers. I saw enemy fighters all around, but every one of them had

When Lt Cullen Hoffman downed a Ju 88 during the air battle over Galati on 6 June 1944 he became the third 'Checkertail' pilot to make ace on that date (*Dwayne Tabatt collection via Tom Ivie*)

Lt Wayne Lowry was one of the 'Clan's' most aggressive pilots, claiming 11 kills and two probables between 18 March and 7 August 1944. Frustratingly for him, the opportunity to score more victories ended on 7 October when he became a guest of the Germans after running short of fuel and having to bail out east of Treviso, in Italy (*Dwayne Tabatt collection via Tom Ivie*)

at least two P-51s on its tail. Our section had to stay on top for target cover. I landed [at Pyriatin] with plenty of gas.'

The 'Clan' would not take to the air again until 11 June, when the group escorted bombers attacking Fosconi airfield, before flying home to their bases in Italy. The takeoff was not without incident, as one Mustang crashed and eight others had to abort and return to Pyriatin, leaving 52 fighters for the long escort. The P-51 pilots had to deal with 12 Bf 109s that were lining up behind a straggling B-17 over Fosconi, the 'Clan' breaking up the attack by diving directly at the enemy aircraft. Lt Strauss recalled;

'We picked up the bombers near the Rumanian border and subsequently met moderate inaccurate flak over the target. As we left we encountered a few Me 109s, but they would split-s as soon as we approached, and our orders were not to follow them. The 318th ran into quite a few of them, and shot down three. We had a small rat race when an olive drab P-51 of the 31st FG jumped us. We left the bombers over Nis, in Yugoslavia.'

The three Bf 109s were claimed by future aces Benjamin Emmert (his second kill) and Richard Deakins (his fourth), while the third Messerschmitt was downed by Ferdinand Suehle. This proved to be his third, and last, victory. Maj 'Herky' Green also managed to damage a Fw 190.

Upon returning to its base at Lesina, the 325th stood down for a day in order to rest the pilots and have their Mustangs checked over. The 'Clan's' next mission was flown on 13 June, and it began rather ominously. Two Mustangs crashed on takeoff and as the remaining fighters were forming up two others were involved in a mid-air collision that killed Lt Kidder. The other pilot was able to safely land his aircraft. As the rest of the group headed for escort duties over Munich, no fewer than 11 Mustangs returned to base due to mechanical problems, leaving only 34 to escort the B-24s to the target area.

Once over Munich 23 enemy fighters were encountered, with two of them being shot down by Lts Wayne Lowry and Paul Tatman. The former later described his second victory;

'I was so sure of my new found power in the P-51 that I actually trapped a Me 109 at 30,000 ft while I was at 20,000 ft. He kept trying to get away and I kept cutting him off. I must have stalled out 50 times trying to get to his altitude. The Mustang was really screaming over such treatment, as I relaxed full power only momentarily to boot her out of the notion of flipping. I suppose there were moments when I could have been clobbered, but somewhere around 28,000 ft the German pilot lost his nerve and attempted to dive by me. That was his mistake, and it led to a one way trip to Valhalla for him.'

Somehow Maj 'Herky' Green got separated from his squadron during

Maj Herschel Green readies for
a mission in his P-51C 42-103324.
Although this is one of his better
known aircraft, Green only managed
one damaged claim – a Fw 190 on
11 June 1944 – while flying it
(*Dwayne Tabatt collection
via Tom Ivie*)

the dogfight and headed back to base alone. Upon reaching the Udine area, he came across a flight of six C.202s at 32,000 ft. He chased the Macchis for four minutes before finally catching up with them about 20 miles northeast of Venice. As he closed in from 'six o'clock', three of the enemy aircraft rolled over and headed for the deck. The remaining three, obviously unaware of his presence, continued to fly straight and level. Green opened fire on the last aeroplane in the formation, and as it staggered under the impact of his gunfire the other two C.202 pilots split-essed and dove away. His target suffered many hits in the fuselage, causing an explosion that started a fire. Moments later Maj Green saw his 14th victim crash, after which the ace continued on to Lesina. All 34 participating Mustangs made it safely back to base.

On 15 June the 325th FG, along with four other Fifteenth Air Force fighter groups, was sent on a massive strafing mission along the coast of southern France. The bad luck that had affected the group two days earlier struck again on the 15th. The 'Clan' took off and went into a line abreast formation as it crossed the Tyrrhenian Sea. As they approached the target area, the P-51 pilots noticed that their assigned airfields had already been attacked, so they searched for targets of opportunity.

The first mishap occurred when Lt Lott's air scoop hit the water and he bounced over his wingman and crashed into the sea. As the 319th FS dived on a railway marshalling yard Lts Reed and Rosar both hit high-tension wires. Rosar's fighter lost a wing and he died when the Mustang exploded upon hitting the ground. Reed, however, bailed out at 1000 ft. After the strafing began in earnest, Lt Starck was shot down by a Bf 109 whilst attacking an airfield. Lt Rausch also fell to Bf 109s, two of which got onto his tail as he flew over the French coast. The final loss of the day was Maj Woods, whose Mustang had been hit by flak over the target area and then burst into flames over the sea as he headed for home. Seen to bail out, he was listed as MIA.

On a more positive note Lt Hiawatha Mohawk shot down a Bf 109 and destroyed a Ju 88 on the ground. Other pilots from the 325th also successfully strafed several railway targets and a coal mine(!), but these claims in no way compensated for the heavy losses suffered by the 'Checkertail Clan' on this ill-fated mission.

On 16 June the Fifteenth Air Force began directing its attention to targets in eastern Europe, with a special emphasis on Axis oil supplies. On that date the 325th FG escorted B-24s to the Nova oil refinery at Schwechat, in Austria. The group encountered 11 enemy aircraft just north of Lake Balaton and destroyed four of them, Lt Richard Deakins ripping into the formation and quickly downing a Bf 109 for his fifth kill to make ace. At about the same time future ace Lt Wayne Lowry scored his third kill in ten days by adding another Bf 109 to his list of victims. The scoring was rounded out by Lts Paul Jensen and John Reynolds with a Bf 109 each, and single probables were claimed by Lts Don Kerns and W A Murphy. All P-51s returned safely home.

After an uneventful escort mission to railway targets in Italy on 22 June, the 'Clan' was directed to escort B-17s to a real hot spot – the oil fields at Ploesti, in Rumania – the following day. The Luftwaffe, as expected, was up in force to meet the attack, and at least 35 enemy aircraft were engaged by the 'Checkertails' near the target. When the air battle ended the outcome was a virtual draw, the 325th having downed four fighters for the loss of three of its own. One of the successful pilots was Maj 'Herky' Green, who sent a Bf 109 down in flames for his 15th kill and damaged another. He reported;

'I saw three Me 109s below us turning toward the bombers. I dived after them and came in on the tail of the last Me 109 and fired a long burst. I saw hits all along the fuselage and engine, and it burst into flame before spinning to earth completely out of control.'

Lt Cecil Dean flamed a Fw 190 for his fifth kill and future ace John Simmons destroyed another Focke-Wulf for his first victory. He had been leading a flight at 27,000 ft when he observed two Fw 190s coming in from '12 o'clock high'. Another flight chased one of them and Simmons led his flight down after the second Focke-Wulf. The German pilot saw him and executed a split-s in an attempt to get away, but Simmons followed. When the Fw 190 pulled out of its manoeuvre at 15,000 ft Lt Simmons fired several short bursts. The enemy fighter took numerous hits in the tail section, left wing and in the cockpit before large pieces began flying off and the Fw 190 went into a spin and crashed. Lt P J Kastner closed out the scoring by blasting another Fw 190 out of the sky. On the debit side, Lts E L Mueller, P C Osterhaus and D C Hanson all had to take to their parachutes over the target area.

The 325th FG returned to Ploesti on 24 June, and this time it was met by a mixed force of German and Rumanian fighters consisting of Bf 109s, Fw 190s and Rumanian IAR 80s and 81s. The air battle that followed also turned out to be an ace maker, for Lt Wayne Lowry scored a double for his fourth and fifth kills – he despatched a Bf 109 and a Fw 190. Two other aces increased their respective scores to six

Lt Cecil Dean claimed six destroyed and two damaged during his tour with the 317th FS (*Dwayne Tabatt collection via Carl Molesworth*)

43

as Cecil Dean downed an IAR 80 and Richard Deakins flamed a Fw 190. Two more Bf 109s and an IAR 80 were also claimed as probables. Lt J W Harper was shot down, however, his Mustang last being seen with six Bf 109s on its tail.

A second mission was flown that afternoon, when ten of the 'Clan's' P-51s escorted a PBY Catalina on a search and rescue mission over Lake Lesina. Another pilot was lost in the process, Lt H F Welch apparently flying too close to enemy flak positions near Pescara and being shot down into the water.

On 26 June the 325th participated in the second Shuttle Mission to Russia, escorting Eighth Air Force B-17s targeting the Debreczen railway marshalling yards in Hungary. The group rendezvoused with the Fortresses near the target area and covered the B-17s all the way to Italy, where the bombers completed their second leg of the shuttle. This mission was followed up the next day with a fighter sweep over the Budapest area, which was for the most part uneventful. Only three enemy aircraft were observed, and Lt Cecil Dean managed to damage two of them (Bf 110s) before departing the scene when his fuel ran low.

Lt Robert H Brown was assigned to the 318th FS in late April 1944 and began his scoring run on 28 June. By 24 August 1944 he had raised his tally to seven destroyed, one probable and one damaged to become an ace (*Dwayne Tabatt collection via Tom Ivie*)

On 28 June the 325th flew another fighter sweep, this time to Bucharest, in Rumania. The Mustangs stirred up a hornets' nest over the Rumanian capital, with 47 enemy aircraft engaging the 40 'Clan' machines as they swept over the area from 29,000 ft down to the deck for an hour between 0930-1030 hrs. In a series of running dogfights the 325th racked up no fewer than 17 kills for no losses. Several future aces contributed to this lopsided victory, with the top scorer being Flt Off Robert Brown with three Bf 109s destroyed and a fourth as a probable. Next was Lt Arthur Fiedler with two Bf 109s destroyed, Lt Barrie Davis with a Fw 190, Lt John Simmons with a Bf 109 (his second victory in five days) and Flt Off Philip Sangermano with an IAR 80. Finally, ace Lt Wayne Lowry also destroyed a Fw 190 for his sixth victory. John Simmons reported;

'I observed four enemy aircraft heading toward my formation at "ten o'clock" and led my flight into a turn to the left and closed on the enemy aircraft from astern. I fired several short bursts from 1000 ft down to 200 ft, and saw hits on the tail, cockpit and base of both wings of the Me 109, which then exploded.'

Five minutes later Simmons' wingman, Lt Paul Kastner, shot down another of the Bf 109s for his third, and last, victory. The remaining kills were credited to Lt L J Stacey, who downed two Bf 109s, while Lts William Pomerantz, George Sweeney, W A Murphy and Henry Greve claimed one Messerschmitt each. Lt Paul Jensen added to the day's total by flaming an IAR 80.

During this period the 325th FG played host to the 334th FS/4th FG of the Eighth Air Force, as the latter squadron was still performing Shuttle Mission sorties. Throughout their stay at Lesina the pilots of the 334th displayed a somewhat condescending attitude towards the 325th in particular and the Fifteenth Air Force in general, insinuating that they were playing a support role in the war and facing only weak and inexperienced Axis units. This superior attitude greatly annoyed the pilots of the 325th, who knew damn well that they were facing some tough opponents in the air. Even Col Sluder noticed what was going on, and noted, 'They obviously felt that we were in the bush leagues and treated us with bored tolerance. The next morning they were scheduled to go on a mission with us, and leisurely drifted into the S-2 hut for the briefing, gazing vacantly out the door while the mission was briefed'.

On 2 July the pilots from the 334th FS would learn the hard way that they had been very much mistaken in their outlook about operations in the MTO. The mission was a massive fighter sweep ahead of B-24s attacking rail and petroleum targets in and around Budapest, the combined forces of the 325th, 52nd and 4th FGs providing the fighter screen. The enemy was also up in force, and all three USAAF fighter groups met stiff opposition. The 325th encountered 40 Axis aircraft, the 52nd engaged 60+ and the 4th found itself overwhelmed by 75-80 enemy fighters.

All three groups scored victories during the swirling air battles over Hungary. For the 325th it was a bittersweet day as its pilots destroyed two Bf 109s and claimed another as a probable, but the group lost ace Cecil Dean and Lt J A Murphy in a mid-air collision. Dean was fortunate

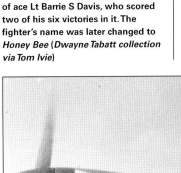

P-51D 44-13451 *Bee* was the aircraft of ace Lt Barrie S Davis, who scored two of his six victories in it. The fighter's name was later changed to *Honey Bee* (*Dwayne Tabatt collection via Tom Ivie*)

45

enough to bail out and became a PoW, but Murphy died in his aircraft. Both of the Bf 109s were downed by future ace Barrie Davis, who later described his second and third victories to the 'Clan's' public relations officer;

'I'll never forget the day that I remained behind to escort some cripples home. We were jumped, but somehow only a single Me 109 remained to press the attack. I got in behind him finally and, unable to shake me, he rolled over and headed straight for the deck. We started the dive at about 25,000 ft, and with everything bent past the firewall we were travelling at well past 550 mph as we dived through 20,000 ft. My guns were spraying the sky, but not a damned thing was happening to the Me 109. Finally, at about 15,000 ft, bits of his aeroplane began coming off. First a bit of the wing tip, then what looked like cowling, then other parts. They streaked past my fuselage, scaring the devil out of me in the process. I couldn't lay a gun on the guy though and I was shooting from sheer fright now.

'Finally, we must have been below 10,000 ft when the German jettisoned his canopy, struggled upward, pushed outward twice and finally bailed out. His 'chute was ripped to pieces as he sailed past me. I felt right sick about it – I guess nobody gets hardened to death.

'I blacked out when I hauled back on the stick to pull out of the dive. When I came to my aeroplane was flying upward through 18,000 ft and still climbing.

'Up ahead I saw a flak burst and then I began to wonder what 20 mm flak was doing at 20,000 ft. I broke, right or left – I don't remember – and sitting behind me popping out cannon shells was another Me 109! I finally tacked onto his tail, and this time my shooting was a bit improved. I knocked out his oil coolers and set him afire. The oil dumped all over my aeroplane and wrapped up the windshield and wings, and I flew blind all the way back to Lesina.'

The 4th FG met some aggressive enemy aircraft in its area, and while the group was able to claim eight enemy aircraft destroyed, it lost five of its own pilots, including high-scoring ace Lt Ralph 'The Kidd' Hofer. In addition to the losses its squadron leader, Capt Howard 'Deacon' Hively, and Lt Grover Siems both returned to Lesina badly wounded in aircraft that looked like sieves. After this mission the surviving members of the 334th were somewhat chastened, and had to admit that they were wrong in their earlier assessment of aerial combat in the MTO. In addition to the combined kills by the 325th and 4th FGs, the 52nd FG destroyed eight enemy aircraft on 2 July.

The 'Clan' escorted B-24s attacking oil storage facilities at Giurgiu, in Rumania, the following day, and the raid was again opposed by a large number of enemy fighters. Forty-one were engaged in the target area and five were sent down in flames by the gunfire of Lts Jack Houghton, Bruce Cobb, S E Myers, L J Stacey and R S Bass. All were Bf 109s except Houghton's, which was a Fw 190. Maj J S Perry claimed another Bf 109 as a probable and Lts D J Schmerbeck and W R Hinton damaged two more. All of the 325th's aircraft returned safely.

The 'Clan' was back over Rumania again on 4 July, but this time the enemy chose not to challenge the group. Only six Axis fighters were observed, and they stayed a safe distance away from the Mustangs.

Two days later the 325th escorted B-17s targeting the railway marshalling yards in Verona, and this time a small mixed formation of German and Italian fighters attempted to attack the bombers. In the brief dogfight that ensued, Lt Jack Houghton destroyed a Bf 109 and Lt Leland Stacey damaged a C.205. Lt Kenneth Ostrum was lost in return, however, his fighter last being seen performing a diving attack on enemy aircraft. He was later reported as MIA.

Oil production was again the target for Fifteenth Air Force B-17s on 7 July, and this time the 'Clan' escorted them to the Blechhammer oil refinery in Germany. Only 13 Bf 109s were sent up against the bombers, and the 'Clan' shot two of them down and damaged two others. The kills were awarded to Lts Bruce C Cobb and Jack H Bond, while the two damaged Bf 109s were shot up by Maj 'Herky' Green. Unfortunately, the elation of adding two more kills to the 325th's ever growing scoreboard was quickly silenced when the Mustang flown by Lt Frank Soltesz inexplicably blew up in mid-air without any warning, killing him instantly. The mission report narrative speculated that the explosion was caused by a mechanical failure.

On 8 July the 325th travelled to Austria while escorting B-17s that were to bomb the airfield at Zwölfaxing, the 'Clan' providing penetration, target and withdrawal support for the bombers. During the flight 11 unidentified twin-engined enemy aircraft were observed, but not engaged. Then a dogfight broke out with a gaggle of 13 Bf 109s that had used cloud cover to sneak in and bounce some of the Fortresses. One B-17 was seen to explode, another dropped out of formation in flames in the target area and a third bomber crashed during the flight home. In spite of the 325th's late arrival on the scene, Lt Wayne Lowry destroyed one of the Bf 109s for his seventh victory and probably destroyed another before the remaining German fighters fled for home.

In a further attempt to cleanse as many enemy fighters from the air as possible, the following day the 'Clan' travelled to the Bucharest-Ploesti area on a fighter sweep ahead of oncoming bomber formations. The enemy was not totally cooperative, however, as only 11 Axis fighters were encountered in two separate dogfights that resulted in the destruction of one Bf 109 – two others were damaged.

The day's solitary kill was scored by Maj 'Herky' Green in an aerial battle that took place 20 miles southeast of Ploesti. Having led his 317th FS on an uneventful sweep of the area, he engaged German fighters after hearing a call for help from the bombers. Making a 90-degree turn and diving from 28,000 ft, Maj Green closed to within 600 ft of a Bf 109 and damaged it, before breaking off to bounce another Messerschmitt that was on the tail of a P-51. Apparently, the German pilot of the latter machine had forgotten the fighter pilot's cardinal rule to 'check six', because Maj Green slipped in behind him completely unnoticed and opened fire. After firing several short bursts Green saw large chunks of the fuselage fly off and the Bf 109 began smoking. As he closed for the second time and opened fire on the crippled fighter, its pilot bailed out. Maj Green had just scored his 16th victory.

Future ace Lt Harry Parker damaged another Bf 109 for his first claim. By month-end his tally would stand at eight Messerschmitts destroyed and seven damaged.

The missions of 12 and 13 July turned out to be milk runs, and in both cases no enemy aircraft were observed throughout the missions. The Luftwaffe finally showed its face again during an escort to the Porto Marghera oil storage facility in Italy, although cloud cover limited any encounters. Once the target had been successfully attacked Maj 'Herky' Green led his 317th FS on a fighter sweep of the Ferrara area, and he soon spotted a flight of 20 enemy aircraft shadowing a flight of medium bombers.

As the Mustangs of the 317th started to dive on the Bf 109s, the enemy pilots spotted them and all bar one broke for cloud cover. The German that did not follow his comrades paid for his mistake with his life. As he belatedly attempted to dive away from Green's oncoming Mustang, the 325th's ranking ace opened fire at 700 ft. Four short bursts scored numerous hits in the left wing and the cockpit area. The Bf 109 staggered from the impact, shed a large portion of its fuselage skinning and then exploded. A second Messerschmitt was hunted down and damaged by Maj C E Caple to end the day's scoring.

P-51D 44-13642 was Capt Harry Parker's first D-model Mustang, and he used the fighter to claim eight victories. He also damaged a further six enemy aircraft while flying it (*Dwayne Tabatt collection via Tom Ivie*)

Maj Herschel H Green's P-51D 44-13498 was photographed in July 1944 after his 17th kill, which occurred on the 14th of that month (*Dwayne Tabatt collection via Tom Ivie*)

Rumanian oil was again the target on 15 July when the 325th FG escorted B-24s to Ploesti, although no enemy fighters were observed. After being released from its escort duties the group found five B-17s heading home alone, so it formed up around them. Shortly thereafter the 'Clan' had to fend off an attack by P-38s whose pilots clearly needed a little more work on their aircraft identification skills. Fortunately, no damage was done, and all the Mustangs made it safely back to base.

After two straight escort missions to petroleum targets the 325th flew a fighter sweep on 16 July to Vienna. During the sweep, which lasted from 1000 hrs to 1105 hrs, the 'Clan' encountered a large formation of Bf 110s for the first time. About half of the German force quickly showed its reluctance to engage Mustangs by retreating into a large cloud bank. The remaining gaggle of 15-20 Messerschmitts did not escape, however, and in a matter of minutes four of them had been shot down – two by Lt Robert Black and one each by Lt Col Ernest Beverly and Lt Bruce Cobb.

In addition to these kills the 'Clan' claimed three more Bf 110s without firing a shot. As Lts Stanley DeGrear, Horace Self Jr and Edwin R Williams dived to attack three more of the twin-engined fighters that were approaching the bomber formations, the pilot of the Bf 110 in the centre of the three enemy aeroplanes saw them coming and panicked. He attempted to evade the attack by quickly flipping over and heading down between the other two Bf 110s, but in doing so his wings hit both of his wingmen and all three enemy aircraft went out of control and crashed almost simultaneously. Williams later commented, 'His wingtips struck those aeroplanes and all three crashed together. The air was filled with a mass of motors, wings and tails'. Per the mission report for 16 July 1944, these kills were credited as a 'Group claim', rather than individual credit being awarded to the three pilots that forced the mid-air collision.

The 'Clan' travelled to Friedrichshafen, in Germany, on 18 July, escorting bombers attacking fuel facilities. This turned out to be a milk run, as no enemy aircraft attempted to block the approach of the B-24s. The 325th FG returned to Germany the following day, this time to Munich, and again met with only minimal opposition in the form of five Bf 109s – three of which were promptly shot down by Lts J R Oxner, S E Myers and D J Schmerbeck.

During the next four missions (all escorting bombers to oil production facilities) not a single enemy fighter rose to challenge the attacks, and the 'Clan' had to turn to strafing ground targets on its way home. On 23 July pilots from the 325th strafed targets in the Yugoslavian cities of Prizren and Dakovica, scoring numerous hits on vehicles and buildings in Prizren and shooting up the telephone exchange in the latter city. Lt Austin Watkins was lost during this mission, however.

On 24 July the 325th FG escorted bombers heading southwest rather than northeast, with the airfield at Chanoines, in France, being attacked. Forty-one of the 'Clan's' Mustangs rendezvoused with the bombers as they neared the target area at 1200 hrs, and escorted them for the next 50 minutes. Two Bf 109 pilots made a foolhardy attempt to attack the bombers, and one of them was shot down for his efforts. Lt Wayne Lowry saw the attack and described his encounter with the luckless fighter;

'On our escort mission to Chanoines airdrome I observed a Me 109 break away from four P-51s. My wingman and I continued the attack, and after a few tight turns, wingovers and chandelles I closed on him and got a few hits. Then I closed to 500 ft and saw many hits in the engine, lower fuselage and some in the cockpit area. After receiving these hits the pilot bailed out, and a few moments later his Me 109 exploded in mid-air.'

Lt Art Fiedler confirmed Lowry's ninth victory.

The next day the 'Clan' returned to more familiar territory when it escorted B-17s targeting the Herman Göring tank works in Linz, Austria. As the formations approached the target area the 325th was again met with a feeble effort by the Luftwaffe. Seven Bf 109s were encountered as

'Art' Fiedler poses with his P-51D *Helen* after his second victory, which occurred over Bucharest on 28 June 1944 (*Dwayne Tabatt collection via Carl Molesworth*)

they attempted a head-on attack on the bombers, P-51s following the enemy fighters and making quick work of four of them. Two of the Messerschmitts gave Lt Harry Parker his first kills, the rising star of the 325th reporting that Bf 109s had dived through the bomber formation, and he had followed two of them;

'I dived astern of the rearmost Me 109 and fired from 1200 yards down to 20 yards. I saw many hits all over the Me 109, and it seemed to fall apart at 8000 ft. After destroying this enemy aircraft I was so close that I had to dive under it, before pulling up astern of the second Me 109. I fired a long burst at this enemy aircraft from 100 yards, closing to 50 yards. Many hits were seen entering the fuselage and wings, and shortly thereafter there were several explosions. During this action the Me 109 was smoking profusely, and I saw pieces coming off the aeroplane as it headed earthward.'

Parker's wingman, Lt Benjamin Emmert, confirmed both kills. The remaining two kills were credited to Lts Harold Wolfe and Henry Greve. Capt Richard Dunkin added to the count by claiming another Bf 109 as a probable.

Zwölfaxing airfield was targeted yet again on 26 July, and this time the Luftwaffe was up in strength to meet the bomber formations. The 325th received a distress call from a group of unescorted B-17s shortly before rendezvousing with the B-24s, and 22 of the 'Clan's' 36 Mustangs rushed to their rescue. Upon reaching the Fortresses, the P-51 pilots quickly noticed that the bombers were taking a real pounding. They immediately went after the enemy force, breaking up their latest attack. Eight of the Mustangs were led by Lt Wayne Lowry, who reported;

'Forty enemy aircraft were attacking the B-17s and I led my flight after them. During our attack I saw three FW 190s on the tail of my wingman [Lt Henry Greve]. I latched onto them and then followed the one that broke off from the others as they dived away. I followed the FW 190 down and fired a few ineffective bursts, but when he went into a tight turn on the deck I was able to close to 500 ft and hit him with a telling burst.

Wayne Lowry is seen here in his P-51D *My Gal Sal* in August 1944, the fighter's scoreboard now reflecting his full score of 11 victories (*Dwayne Tabatt collection via Tom Ivie*)

Capt 'Art' Fiedler's P-51D *Helen* was photographed in late 1944 displaying a score of seven victories. Fiedler would later add one more kill marking, indicating his final victory over a Fw 190 near Regensburg on 20 January 1945 (*Dwayne Tabatt collection via Tom Ivie*)

I saw hits on the engine and cockpit, and at about 300 ft the FW 190 burst into flame and exploded.'

This was victory number ten for Lt Lowry.

Future ace Lt Art Fiedler picks up the action;

'On the mission to Zwölfaxing airdrome my section encountered approximately 40 enemy aircraft at 22,000 ft and we went into action. As I was manoeuvring after a FW 190 I saw two other enemy aircraft and turned into them. This manoeuvre led to a fight to the deck with one of the FW 190s. While chasing him I saw another FW 190 below at "seven o'clock" and turned after him. I closed from "three o'clock" and fired a burst from 200 yards and hit him in the cockpit. Shortly afterwards the FW 190 straightened out from a turn, rolled over and from about 50 ft headed down and crashed and exploded.'

Another future ace, Capt Richard Dunkin, joined in the action, noting;

'I observed 40 enemy aircraft preparing to attack the bombers. I led my flight down from 27,000 ft to 24,000 ft, where we scattered the enemy aircraft. Then I closed on a FW 190 from dead astern and opened fire at 275 yards, closing to about 100 yards. Blue smoke began pouring from the fuselage below the cockpit and the enemy aircraft went into a spin at 21,000 ft and was seen to explode when it crashed. I then observed a Me 109 at 21,000 ft and dove after him, opening fire from 250 yards from "six o'clock" as he made a gentle turn to the left. Direct hits were scored on the fuselage in front of, and around, the cockpit, and the Me 109, smoking profusely, was seen to crash and burn.'

Both kills were confirmed by Lt Roper. These were Capt Dunkin's fifth and sixth victories, making him the 'Clan's' newest ace. He did not enjoy that accolade for long, however, as a few minutes later Lt Art Fiedler downed a Bf 109 for his fifth victory;

'On the way home from the mission to Zwölfaxing airdrome, while flying at 11,000 ft, my leader, Lt Wayne Lowry, and I saw a Me 109 on the deck and we went after it. Lt Lowry opened fire but quickly ran out of ammo, so he told me to go after the Me 109. I closed in and opened fire, and the enemy aircraft started smoking immediately and went into a gentle turn. I closed to 75 yards and fired again, observing hits on its wings and fuselage. Shortly afterwards the Me 109 exploded, spraying oil all over my windshield and left wing. The pilot was seen to bail out at 50 ft, but his 'chute did not open.'

By the time the aerial battles had ended 13 enemy fighters had been destroyed and another was listed as a probable. The remaining eight aircraft were downed by Maj John Peery, Capt Sheldon Farnham and Lts John Kinney, Jack Bond, Paul Tatman, W P Hinton, E T Strauss and V A Woodman. Capt Farnham also claimed a Bf 109 as a probable, while Lt H C Wolfe damaged four other Messerschmitts. Lt Henry Greve and Lt H M Self were lost in return. During the initial attack by Lt Lowry's section, Lt Greve had become separated from the formation whilst flying as 'tail end Charlie'. He bravely fought off any enemy aircraft trying to come in behind his section, damaging four or five of them before he was shot down with severe wounds. Greve ended up in a PoW camp, and six months later he was reunited with Lt Lowry after he too was captured.

On 27 July the 'Clan' escorted B-24s sent to attack the Manfred Weiss armament works in Budapest, and engaged enemy fighters several times during the mission. Five Bf 109s were destroyed and two damaged in these clashes, with two future aces adding to their respective tallies. Lt Robert Brown reported his fourth kill as follows;

'I observed two Me 109s from 24,000 ft, and when one of them peeled off to the left I followed him down and opened fire at 300 yards with 60 degrees of deflection. I then closed to 50 ft and fired again. Many hits were seen to enter the enemy aircraft's tail and right wing. As a result of these hits the enemy aircraft's tail broke off and the crash was observed by Lts Woodson and Roper.'

Harry Parker's second victory was a similar story;

'I was flying at 25,000 ft when I observed a Me 109 at "three o'clock" and I closed and opened fire at 400 yards with 90 degrees deflection. I then closed again to 50 yards and opened fire with 70 degrees deflection. I saw many hits on the enemy aircraft's fuselage and tail. He pulled up quickly and his tail broke off, sending him crashing to earth. Lt Gaston confirmed.'

Lts Jack Houghton, John Conant and Sam Brown accounted for the remaining three Bf 109s (text continues on page 65).

P-51C 42-103562 *Little Bastard,* **displaying three of Lt Robert Brown's victories, rests between missions at Lesina during the summer of 1944 (***Dwayne Tabatt collection via Carl Molesworth***)**

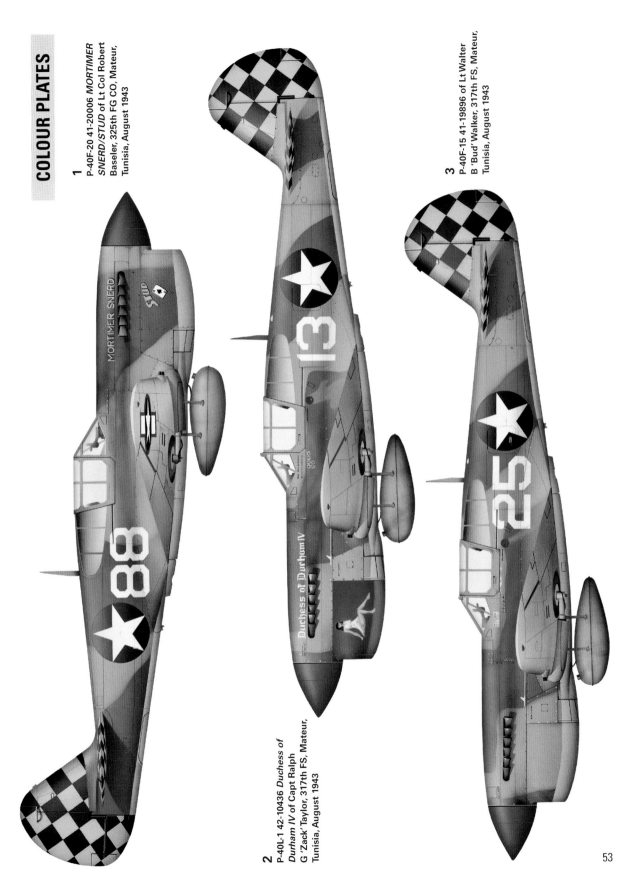

1
P-40F-20 41-20006 *MORTIMER SNERD/STUD* of Lt Col Robert Baseler, 325th FG CO, Mateur, Tunisia, August 1943

2
P-40L-1 42-10436 *Duchess of Durham IV* of Capt Ralph G 'Zack' Taylor, 317th FS, Mateur, Tunisia, August 1943

3
P-40F-15 41-19896 of Lt Walter B 'Bud' Walker, 317th FS, Mateur, Tunisia, August 1943

53

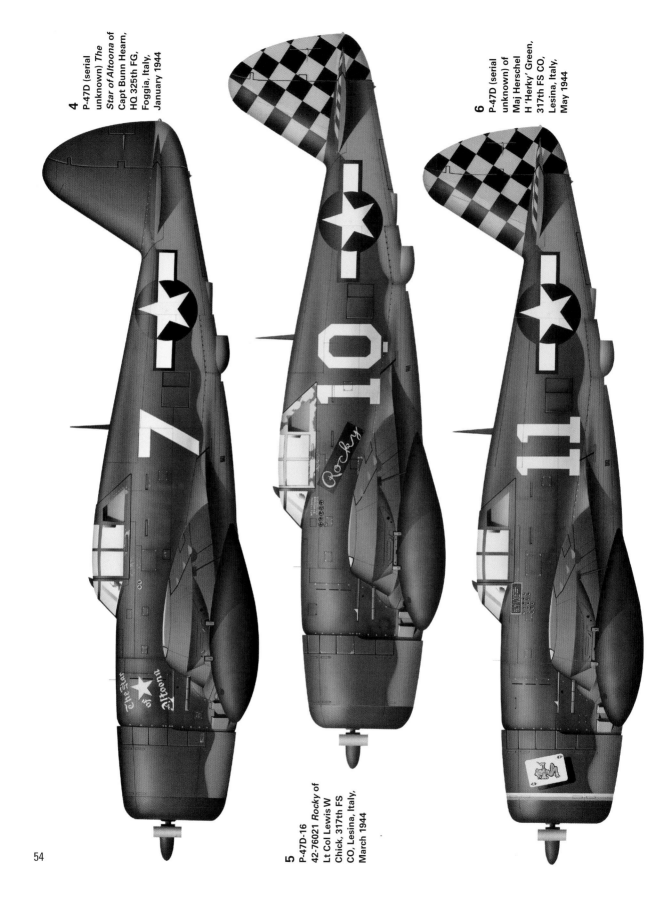

4
P-47D (serial
unknown) *The
Star of Altoona* of
Capt Bunn Hearn,
HQ 325th FG,
Foggia, Italy,
January 1944

6
P-47D (serial
unknown) of
Maj Herschel
H 'Herky' Green,
317th FS CO,
Lesina, Italy,
May 1944

5
P-47D-16
42-76021 *Rocky* of
Lt Col Lewis W
Chick, 317th FS
CO, Lesina, Italy,
March 1944

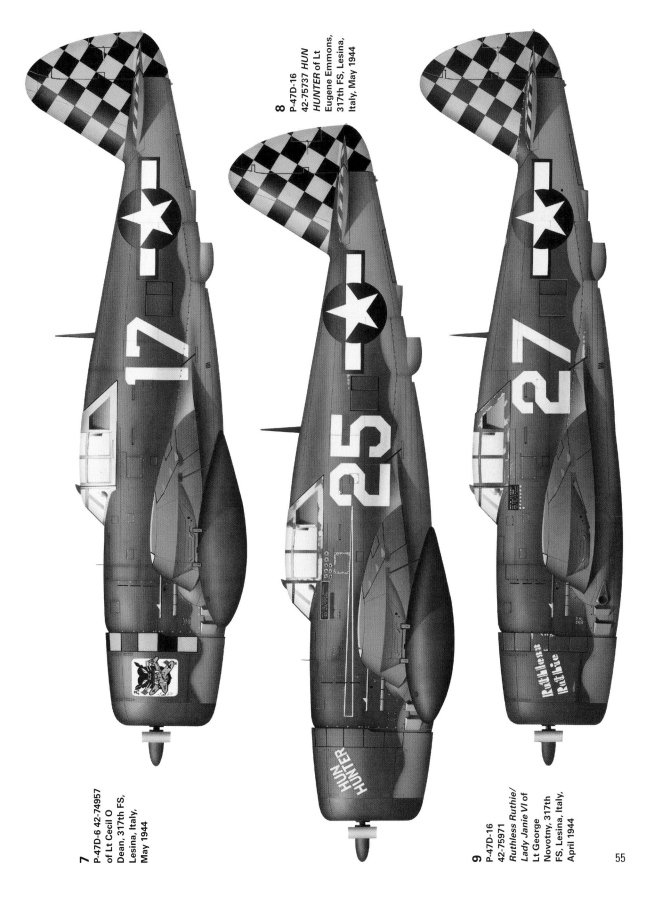

7
P-47D-6 42-74957
of Lt Cecil O
Dean, 317th FS,
Lesina, Italy,
May 1944

8
P-47D-16
42-75737 *HUN
HUNTER* of Lt
Eugene Emmons,
317th FS, Lesina,
Italy, May 1944

9
P-47D-16
42-75971
*Ruthless Ruthie/
Lady Janie VI* of
Lt George
Novotny, 317th
FS, Lesina, Italy,
April 1944

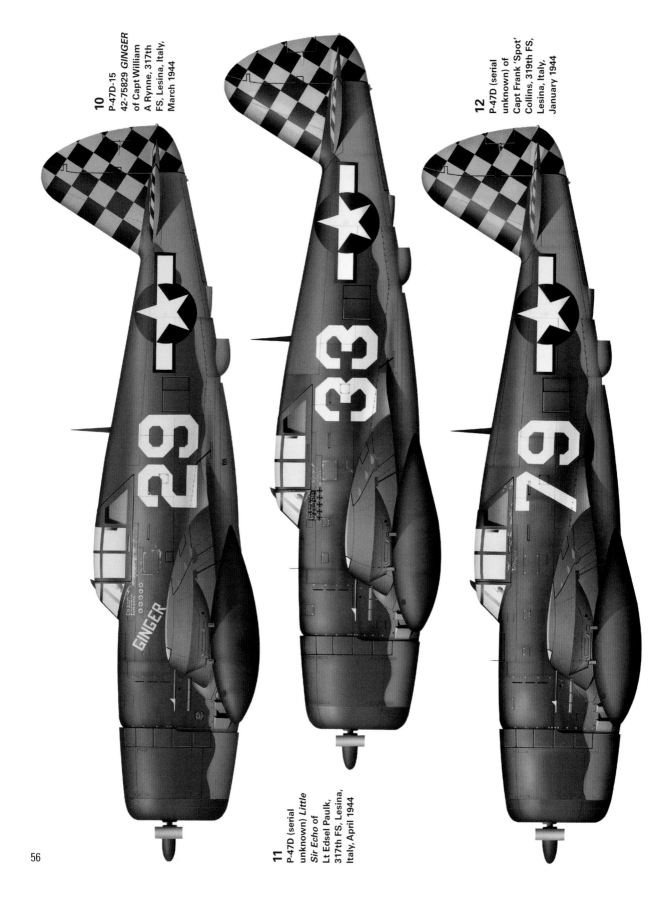

10
P-47D-15
42-75829 *GINGER*
of Capt William
A Rynne, 317th
FS, Lesina, Italy,
March 1944

11
P-47D (serial
unknown) *Little
Sir Echo* of
Lt Edsel Paulk,
317th FS, Lesina,
Italy, April 1944

12
P-47D (serial
unknown) of
Capt Frank 'Spot'
Collins, 319th FS,
Lesina, Italy,
January 1944

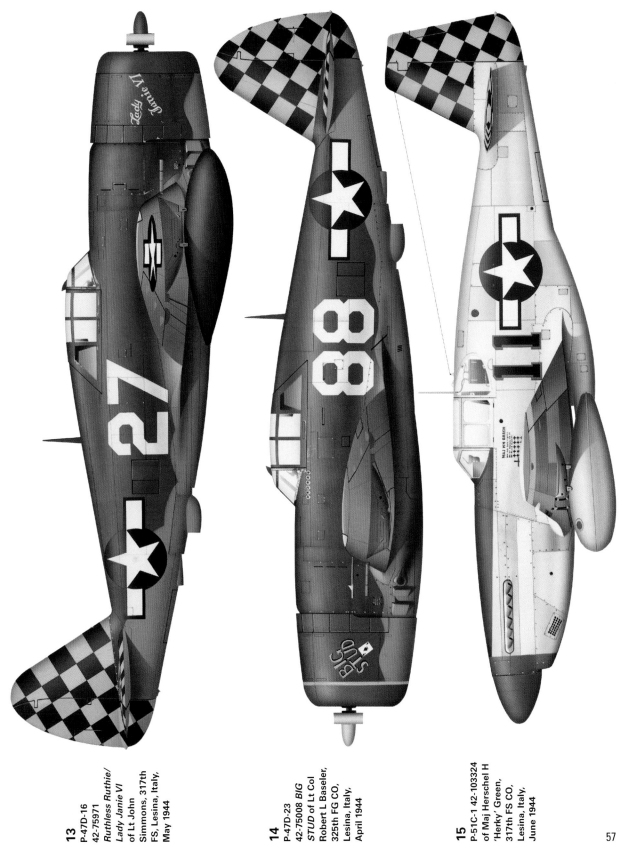

13
P-47D-16
42-75971
Ruthless Ruthie/
Lady Janie VI
of Lt John
Simmons, 317th
FS, Lesina, Italy,
May 1944

14
P-47D-23
42-75008 *BIG*
STUD of Lt Col
Robert L Baseler,
325th FG CO,
Lesina, Italy,
April 1944

15
P-51C-1 42-103324
of Maj Herschel H
'Herky' Green,
317th FS CO,
Lesina, Italy,
June 1944

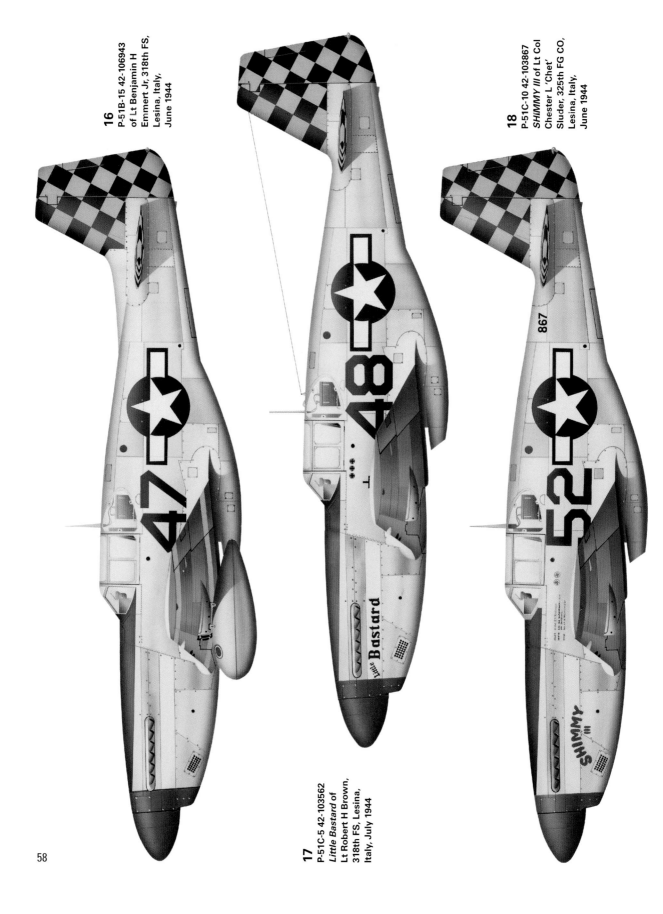

16
P-51B-15 42-106943
of Lt Benjamin H
Emmert Jr, 318th FS,
Lesina, Italy,
June 1944

18
P-51C-10 42-103867
SHIMMY III of Lt Col
Chester L 'Chet'
Sluder, 325th FG CO,
Lesina, Italy,
June 1944

17
P-51C-5 42-103562
Little Bastard of
Lt Robert H Brown,
318th FS, Lesina,
Italy, July 1944

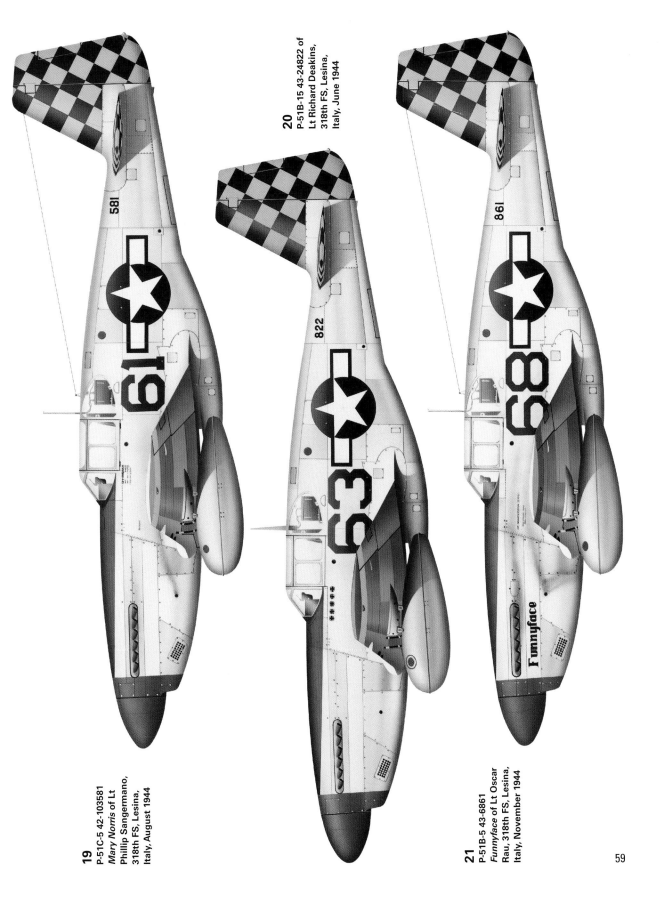

19
P-51C-5 42-103581
Mary Norris of Lt
Phillip Sangermano,
318th FS, Lesina,
Italy, August 1944

20
P-51B-15 43-24822 of
Lt Richard Deakins,
318th FS, Lesina,
Italy, June 1944

21
P-51B-5 43-6861
Funnyface of Lt Oscar
Rau, 318th FS, Lesina,
Italy, November 1944

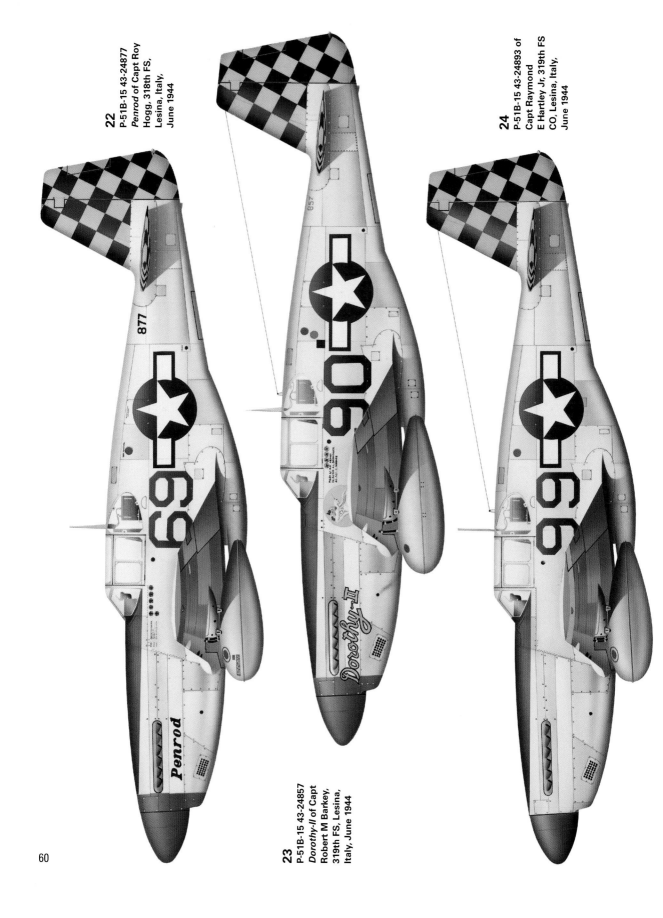

22
P-51B-15 43-24877
Penrod of Capt Roy
Hogg, 318th FS,
Lesina, Italy,
June 1944

24
P-51B-15 43-24893 of
Capt Raymond
E Hartley Jr, 319th FS
CO, Lesina, Italy,
June 1944

23
P-51B-15 43-24857
Dorothy-II of Capt
Robert M Barkey,
319th FS, Lesina,
Italy, June 1944

60

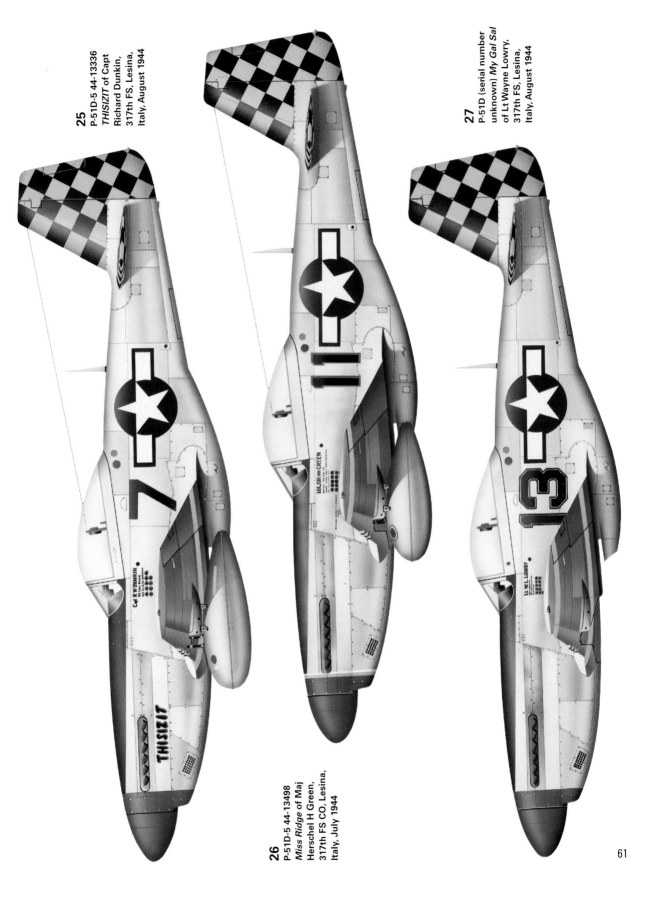

25
P-51D-5 44-13336
THISIZIT of Capt
Richard Dunkin,
317th FS, Lesina,
Italy, August 1944

26
P-51D-5 44-13498
Miss Ridge of Maj
Herschel H Green,
317th FS CO, Lesina,
Italy, July 1944

27
P-51D (serial number
unknown) *My Gal Sal*
of Lt Wayne Lowry,
317th FS, Lesina,
Italy, August 1944

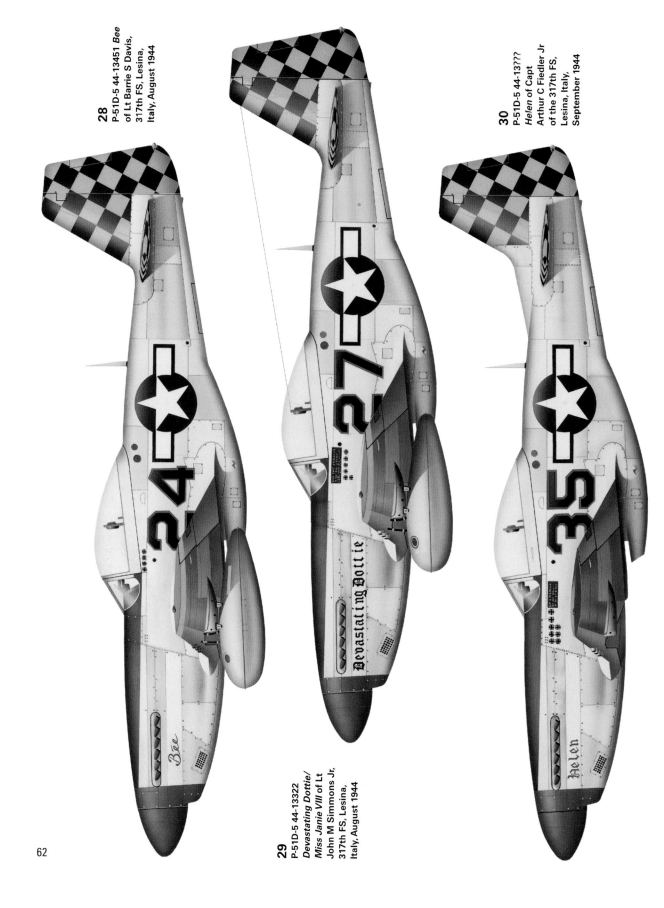

28
P-51D-5 44-13451 *Bee*
of Lt Barrie S Davis,
317th FS, Lesina,
Italy, August 1944

30
P-51D-5 44-13???
Helen of Capt
Arthur C Fiedler Jr
of the 317th FS,
Lesina, Italy,
September 1944

29
P-51D-5 44-13322
*Devastating Dottie/
Miss Janie VIII* of Lt
John M Simmons Jr,
317th FS, Lesina,
Italy, August 1944

62

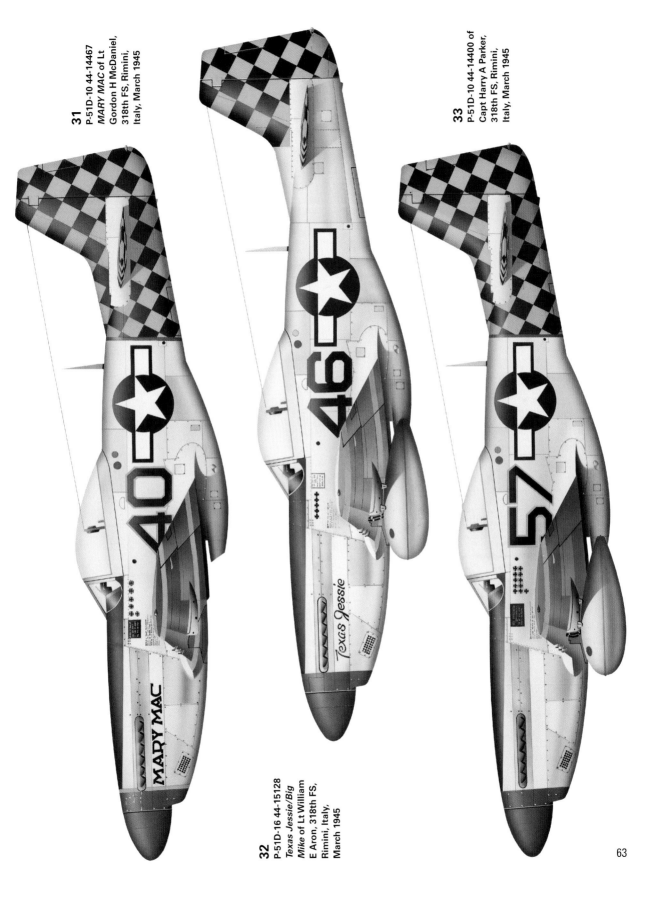

31
P-51D-10 44-14467
MARY MAC of Lt
Gordon H McDaniel,
318th FS, Rimini,
Italy, March 1945

33
P-51D-10 44-14400 of
Capt Harry A Parker,
318th FS, Rimini,
Italy, March 1945

32
P-51D-16 44-15128
*Texas Jessie/Big
Mike* of Lt William
E Aron, 318th FS,
Rimini, Italy,
March 1945

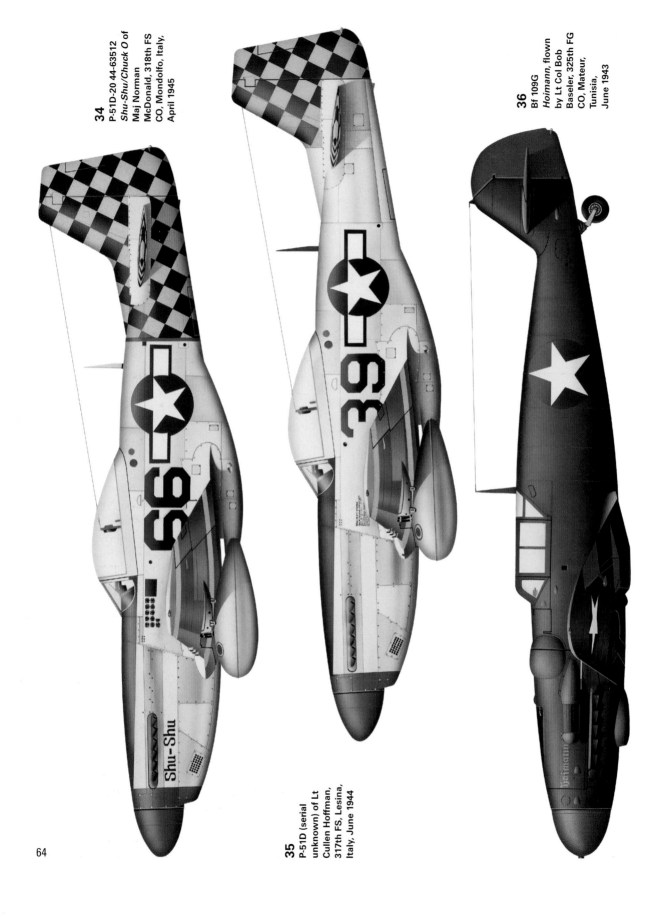

34
P-51D-20 44-63512
Shu-Shu/Chuck O of
Maj Norman
McDonald, 318th FS
CO, Mondolfo, Italy,
April 1945

35
P-51D (serial
unknown) of Lt
Cullen Hoffman,
317th FS, Lesina,
Italy, June 1944

36
Bf 109G
Hoimann, flown
by Lt Col Bob
Baseler, 325th FG
CO, Mateur,
Tunisia,
June 1943

Lt Harry Parker continued his scoring streak when the 325th FG flew to Ploesti once again on 28 July, the group escorting B-24s that were tasked with attacking the Standard Oil and Astra Romano refineries. As the bombers came away from the target a gaggle of 30 Bf 109s and Fw 190s was seen circling and waiting to bounce the bombers. The P-51 pilots dived on the Axis fighters, breaking up the formation and then individually dogfighting with their opponents. By the time this clash was over three Bf 109s and Fw 190s had gone down in flames, two of them under the guns of future aces Harry Parker and Ben Emmert.

Lt Parker's fourth victory in the past 72 hours was yet another Bf 109, which he swooped down on and then showered with many hits as he closed to within 150 yards of his foe. The Messerschmitt exploded in mid air. Lt Emmert's fourth kill was also a Bf 109, as he recalled in his encounter report;

'I dove on a flight of three or four Me 109s and they immediately headed for the deck, and I followed one of them. I opened fire from 250 yards directly astern of him and closed to about 30 yards, noticing numerous hits in the tail and on the fuselage, after which he crash-landed. Lt Woodson confirmed.'

Lt Gerald Edwards destroyed a Fw 190 and Lt Paul Jensen flamed a Bf 109 to round out the scoring. Lt John Roper, however, was forced to bail out after suffering engine trouble deep in enemy territory.

Action then shifted on 30 July to Budapest, when B-24s attacked the airfield near the city. It turned out to be a quiet mission, for only 12 enemy aircraft were observed and they quickly turned away from the bombers so as to avoid combat with the 'Clan's' Mustangs. Shortly afterwards, however, Lt Wayne Lowry spotted a light grey Bf 109 and quickly shot it down for his tenth victory.

Oil facilities were again the target on 31 July when the 325th travelled to Bucharest. The target on this occasion was the Mogosaia oil storage facility, which proved to be heavily defended by Axis fighters. The 'Clan' spotted 40 Bf 109s and five Fw 190s at 27,000 ft, and when the group began its climb towards the gaggle of German fighters, the enemy aircraft formed a large Lufbery circle and stayed in it as they slowly lost altitude. This defensive tactic failed to protect the enemy machines, as the 'Clan' tore the formation apart. Lt Parker had his best day with four kills, and he damaged six others before he finished. He reported;

'I climbed to attack approximately 40 Me 109s that were at 27,000 ft. The enemy aircraft went into a tight Lufbery and I came in on one of the Me 109s from "six o'clock" and opened fire from 300 yards with 60-degree deflection. I then closed in dead astern of the enemy aircraft and fired from about 20 yards. I observed many hits all over the aeroplane and its right wing fell off. The enemy aircraft went straight down, and its crash was confirmed by Lt Emmert.

'After destroying this Me 109 I turned into another at 22,000 ft and fired from 300 yards down to 200 yards with 60 to 30 degrees deflection. I observed a few hits on the wings and fuselage of the enemy aircraft, then the pilot bailed out and his 'chute did not open.

'With the Me 109s that I attacked still in a Lufbery, I attacked a third Me 109 in a tight turn. I fired from 300 yards with 60 degrees deflection and closed to 200 yards, firing with 20 degrees deflection. I saw a few hits on the wings and fuselage before the pilot bailed out and the Me 109 went down trailing smoke. I now attacked a fourth Me 109 at 4000 ft and the enemy aircraft started turning and skidding. I fired first from 400 yards with 60 degrees deflection and then manoeuvred into a position directly behind the Me 109, closing to 20 ft, and fired. The enemy aircraft, hit in the wings and fuselage, crashed into the ground.'

With these four kills Harry Parker's score now stood at eight, making him the 'Clan's' newest ace. Such was the level of combat that day two more pilots from the 325th also achieved this much sought after status later in the mission. The first of these individuals was Lt Ben Emmert when he destroyed three Bf 109s. He reported;

'I climbed to attack 40 enemy aircraft at 27,000 ft and overtook a Me 109 that broke into a tight Lufbery with the rest of the enemy aeroplanes. I started firing from 300 yards astern, closing to 75 yards, and observed many hits on the wings and fuselage, which started burning as the enemy aeroplane lost height. Lt Walker saw the fighter hit the ground and explode. I then went after another Me 109 at 10,000 ft, firing at it from 200 yards at 20 degrees deflection. I saw many hits about the cockpit of the enemy aircraft, and the pilot bailed out as his aeroplane started burning at about 1200 ft. I then climbed to 1500 ft and turned into a third Me 109. I pulled up astern of the enemy aircraft and opened fire at 250 yards with 20 degrees of deflection, then closed to 100 yards and fired again with ten degrees of deflection. I saw a few hits on the fuselage of the Me 109, which split-essed at 1000 ft and crashed into the ground.'

Lt Phil Crookham and very casually dressed ace Lt Ben Emmert pose for the camera at Lesina during the summer of 1944. Lt Emmert reached acedom when he downed three Bf 109s and damaged five others on 31 July 1944, boosting his overall tally to six destroyed, one probable and five damaged. He was in turn downed by flak on 1 September 1944, spending the rest of the war as a PoW (*Dwayne Tabatt collection via Carl Molesworth*)

Eight-victory ace Lt Phillip Sangermano and his crew chief pose with their P-51C 42-103581 *Mary Norris* at Lesina. Sangermano succumbed to wounds after being shot down during a local test flight in P-51C 42-103410 on 9 December 1944 (*Dwayne Tabatt collection via Tom Ivie*)

Lt Johnson confirmed Emmert's second and third victories, taking his overall tally to six.

The third pilot to reach ace status on this mission was Lt Phillip Sangermano, who also chipped in with three victories. He reported;

'I led my flight down and attacked approximately 35 Me 109s and FW 190s that were at about 20,000 ft. I closed astern and above one of the Me 109s and it tried to turn inside of me. He was unsuccessful in this manoeuvre and I pulled up to within 150 yards of him, firing at 15 degrees deflection and closing to 50 yards. The Me 109 was badly hit in the cockpit and wings and started to burn. It started down and crashed into the ground.

'After destroying this Me 109 I turned into a second one. The enemy aircraft tried to evade by wildly turning in all directions, but I stayed right with him and opened fire from 150 yards with 45 degrees deflection. Then I moved in to within 25 ft of the Bf 109 and fired. I saw many hits in the cockpit area of the enemy aircraft and it went into an immediate spin and crashed. I then encountered a third Me 109 at 5000 ft, out-turned him and closed from above and astern, firing from 150 yards down to 50 yards. I saw many hits on the fuselage and cockpit before the Me 109 went into a spin and crashed.'

The 'Clan's' newest ace now had six kills to his name. Three other pilots from the group scored doubles during this 'turkey shoot' – Lts John Reynolds, William Pomerantz and V A Woodman. The remaining victories were scored by Lt Henry Southern and Flt Off Wesley Terry. All in all the 'Clan's' score for the day was 18 kills, one probable and 12 damaged.

After a milk run to Avignon, in France, on 2 August the 325th headed to Germany the following day when it escorted B-24s heading to Friedrichshafen to bomb Dornier's Manzell aircraft factory. Shortly after the bombers hit the target three Bf 109s were engaged and one of them was shot down by future ace Lt John Simmons. He reported;

'I observed a Me 109 at 16,000 ft flying straight and level. Using the cloud cover for concealment I was able to surprise the enemy aircraft, and I came in from the rear at "six o'clock" and began firing at 500 yards, closing to 50 yards. Hits were observed to enter the cockpit and the left wing, and shortly afterwards the enemy aircraft exploded and spun in. Flt Off Victor Ames witnessed the combat and confirmed the victory.'

At about the same time as this combat was taking place other 325th Mustangs encountered 14 Bf 109s and 20 Fw 190s that had come up through the clouds and bounced the trailing group of bombers, shooting five of them down. A running battle over 50 miles duly ensued as the USAAF fighter pilots worked hard to keep the enemy aircraft from the surviving bombers, which according to the mission summary were not in proper formation. In doing so the 325th claimed nine more kills, including a Bf 109 for Lt Harry Parker for his ninth victory in ten days. Parker's kill was a quick one, as he stated in his report;

'I attacked three Me 109s at 24,000 ft, singling out one of them, who saw me and dived away. I followed and fired from 300 yards to 150 yards, and saw many hits on the left wing and fuselage of the enemy aircraft. The Me 109 began burning and the pilot bailed out.'

Another Bf 109 was blown out of the air by Lt Robert H Brown for his fifth victory, making him the 'Clan's' latest ace. Brown reported;

'I attacked a Me 109 that was in a steep climb at 12,000 ft. At that point the enemy pilot saw me and turned sharply, but I fired from 200 yards with 60 degrees deflection, before moving in directly astern of him. I closed to about 20 ft, fired a burst and saw hits on the tail and wing of the enemy aircraft, which split-essed and crashed into the side of a mountain.'

The top scorer for the day was Lt Col J V Toner who downed two of the Fw 190s, while four other Focke-Wulfs were destroyed by Lt Col E H Beverly and Lts J R Bond, E T Strauss and H R Loftus. The remaining kill – a Bf 109 – was credited to Lt A J Fitch. All 325th FG Mustangs returned safely to base.

The 'Clan' headed to France again on 6 August, and it was an uneventful mission with only two Fw 190s seen – they immediately fled upon spotting the P-51s. Oil targets in Germany were attacked the following day when the 325th escorted bombers striking production facilities in Blechhammer. This time the Luftwaffe showed up, with 14 aircraft being encountered in the target area – 13 Bf 109s and a He 111(!). Two engagements followed, allowing three aces to add to their scores and one near ace to get closer to his goal.

In the first clash five Bf 109s attempted to bounce the bombers just as they left the target area, but they dived away when the Mustang pilots challenged them. Lt Paul Tatman shot one of them down in flames at 1110 hrs. Thirty minutes later eight more Bf 109s attempted a pass at the bombers but they too were intercepted and split-essed away. Two of them were attacked and destroyed at 1140 hrs by Lt Henry Wolfe and ace Capt Richard Dunkin, who scored his seventh victory. He reported;

'I saw a group of enemy fighters getting ready to bounce the bombers. Diving from 28,000 ft, I came in behind one of the Me 109s and started firing from "six o'clock", observing many hits on the fuselage. I continued to fire in a turning fight and closed to 150 ft, seeing parts come off of the enemy aircraft. Shortly afterwards I saw it emitting smoke and the propeller wind-milling. The pilot jettisoned his canopy, rolled over and bailed out, but his 'chute did not open.'

P-51D *My Gal Sal,* **with Lt Wayne Lowry at the controls, taxies out at Lesina at the start of another mission in August 1944 (***Dwayne Tabatt collection via Tom Ivie***)**

Ten minutes later ace Lt Wayne Lowry and near ace Lt Barrie Davis chose their victims, and two more Bf 109s met their fate. Lt Lowry's encounter report read as follows;

'I was a section leader on an escort mission to Blechhammer when I observed eight enemy aircraft preparing to attack the Allied bombers from "five o'clock low". I executed a 90-degree turn and closed on the extreme right Me 109, closing to 800 ft and firing a short burst. I continued firing from 500 ft dead astern. Hits were observed in the fuselage, around the cockpit and in the engine as the enemy aircraft went into a spin and the pilot bailed out.'

Lt Davis noted in his report;

'Leading my section on an escort mission to Blechhammer, I saw eight Me 109s 5000 ft below me preparing to attack our bombers. Executing a diving turn, I led my flight down to 20,000 ft and closed on the No 2 positioned enemy aircraft in the leading flight. I fired a short burst from "six o'clock" with no apparent results. I continued firing short bursts as I closed in from dead astern, and from 100 yards I saw hits in the fuselage near the base of the wings. Coolant began pouring from the Me 109, followed by a stream of smoke as the enemy aircraft went into a steep dive and exploded as it hit the ground.'

Lt Lowry's victory was his 11th, and last, victory, and it was Lt Davis' fourth. The last victory of the day was claimed by future ace Lt John Simmons, who downed the He 111 for his fourth victory.

No enemy aircraft were encountered on the mission of 9 August and only one showed up during an escort mission to Ploesti the following day. This was quickly despatched by Capt Richard Dunkin;

'On an escort mission to Ploesti, and after leaving the bombers, I noticed a lone Me 109 at 15,000 ft making a pass at a forward flight of P-51s. I dove after the Me 109 and closed in, starting firing from "six o'clock" from 300 yards and closing again to 225 yards and firing again. I saw many strikes on the fuselage and followed the Me 109 down to 1000 ft, where I watched the enemy aircraft split-S and head for the ground. A faulty 'chute was seen trailing the Me 109, and I believe the enemy pilot, when jumping, fell out of his 'chute.'

Over the next several days the 'Clan' flew softening up missions in southern France in preparation for the upcoming invasion. On some of these missions the 325th FG attacked heavy gun emplacements and radar stations in the planned invasion area, and on others escorted B-24s bombing German positions in the area. The 'Clan's' final mission in support of Operation *Dragoon* (the invasion of southern France) was to escort transport aircraft and gliders carrying paratroopers to Draguignan, France.

On 17 August the group flew the first of three straight missions to Ploesti, and to the surprise of all participants met no opposition from German or Rumanian aircraft. Three days later the 325th escorted B-24s to oil facilities in Poland, and again the Axis air forces were nowhere to be seen. The enemy continued to be absent in the air when the 'Clan' escorted bombers attacking Hajdúböszörmény airfield in Hungary on 21 August. On this occasion, since the enemy would not come up, the 325th went down and thoroughly strafed the airfield, claiming 37 enemy aircraft destroyed, 13 probably destroyed and 17 damaged.

Having thoroughly worked over the target area, Lt Robert Brown noticed a Bf 109 at 11,000 ft and after a brief chase shot it down for his sixth victory.

As the B-17s began their return to base after attacking the oil refinery in Edertal, Germany, on 22 August, Axis fighters began attacking some of the straggling Fortresses. The enemy aircraft were in turn bounced by pilots from the 325th, and after a series of dogfights four German fighters fell to earth. Lt Barrie Davis bagged two of them for his fifth and sixth victories, making him an ace. He reported the action as follows;

'I was escorting a B-24 straggler home when I heard a call for help from a B-17. I turned 180 degrees and headed north. About 15 miles west of Lake Balaton I saw six FW 190s making attacks on a B-17 at 17,000 ft. Just as I arrived at the scene the bomber went down in flames. I quickly bounced the enemy aircraft, firing several short bursts at two of them and then tacking onto a third FW 190. I fired short bursts from 300 yards down to 50 yards, dead astern, and saw many strikes around the cockpit area of the fuselage. The enemy pilot went into a spin at 12,000 ft and I followed him down to 1000 ft, where I was forced to break off because of the FW 190 following me down. Lt John Conant saw the enemy aircraft crash and confirmed my claim.

'I then heard bombers calling for help over Lake Balaton, and after turning north I observed six Me 109s making passes at a B-17 and a B-24, which were both straggling. As I approached the Me 109s scattered, and I followed one of them down to 3000 ft before breaking off my attack and heading back to the bombers. At this time I saw another Me 109 on my tail so I broke left. After three or four turns I closed in on the enemy aircraft from "six o'clock" and opened fire from 300 yards. Hits were scored on the fuselage as the Me 109 rolled and headed for the deck. I followed him and fired short bursts from dead astern. Smoke began streaming from the Me 109 as a result of many hits in the fuselage and the pilot bailed out at 2000 ft.'

Maj Herschel Green's P-51D 44-13498 is seen at Lesina in late August 1944 with its full victory tally of 18 kills under the canopy and a newly added fin strake (*Dwayne Tabatt collection via Tom Ivie*)

P-51C 42-103581, seen at Lesina during the summer of 1944, was assigned to Lt Phil Sangermano. He scored five of his eight victories in this machine (*Dwayne Tabatt via Tom Ivie*)

The remaining kills, both Bf 109s, were credited to Lts William Hinton and Larry Ritter. One P-51 was lost due to mechanical failure, but Lt James Lintz was able to bail out successfully over enemy territory.

A major air battle took place on 23 August during the 'Clan's' escort mission to Markersdorf airfield in Austria. Eighteen of the group's Mustangs stayed with the bombers over the target while 31 others engaged in a big dogfight with a mixed bag of 45 Bf 109s and Fw 190s. The enemy aircraft had been spotted at 'nine o'clock' to the bombers when the formation was about 20 miles southwest of Wiener-Neustadt, and Maj 'Herky' Green immediately led his 317th FS down to attack the Axis fighters. Four Fw 190s and a Bf 109 were destroyed during the encounter, one of the Focke-Wulfs providing Maj Green with his 18th, and final, victory;

'Upon hearing distress calls from the bombers I led my squadron in a diving turn to the right, passed under the bombers and attacked the enemy aircraft from "six o'clock". I picked out a FW 190 and opened fire from 300 yards down to 175 yards. The FW 190 took a barrage of hits in the fuselage around the cockpit and then a small explosion occurred. The enemy aircraft made a right turn at 22,000 ft, then split-essed and the pilot bailed out after a second explosion shook his FW 190.'

Lt Harry Parker continued his fast paced assault on the Luftwaffe by downing a Fw 190 for his tenth victory, the double ace reporting;

'I attacked a FW 190 at 25,000 ft and the enemy aircraft dove into the clouds and I followed. I overtook the FW 190 at 20,000 ft and opened fire from 300 yards and six degrees deflection and closed to 150 yards with no deflection. I got many hits in the tail and fuselage of the FW 190 and the pilot bailed out as his aeroplane went down smoking badly.'

Lt John M Simmons of the 317th FS, seated in his P-51B 42-106891. He finished the war with a total of seven victories to his name (*Dwayne Tabatt collection via Carl Molesworth*)

Lt Phillip Sangermano raised his total to eight by downing two Fw 190s in short order, the ace describing his victories as follows;

'I attacked a FW 190 that had just made a pass at the bombers. The enemy aircraft started spiralling down at a steep angle, and I overtook him at 15,000 ft and commenced firing from 250 yards with 15-45 degrees deflection. I then closed to within 50 yards dead astern and fired. I observed many hits in the wings, engine and cockpit of the FW 190, which exploded and went down enveloped in flames. After destroying this FW 190 I attacked a second FW 190 at 500 ft. The enemy aircraft attempted to evade by turning sharply but I followed, firing from astern with 15-45 degrees deflection and closing to 75 ft with no deflection. I saw many hits in the cockpit of the FW 190, which crashed into the ground and burned.'

Lt John Simmons also downed two Fw 190s during the melee to raise his total to six, and thus become the 'Clan's' latest ace. His first kill came after he observed 15 Fw 190s attacking the rearmost box of bombers. Diving to break up the enemy formation, Simmons made a pass at the gaggle of Focke-Wulfs and then picked out one of them, which he shot down at a height of 5000 ft. After this victory Simmons climbed back up to 10,000 ft and then spotted two more Fw 190s flying on the deck. Diving after them, he closed on the trailing fighter until the two machines split-essed. Simmons followed the leader, opening fire at 1000 ft and closing to within 50 ft of his quarry, at which time the Fw 190 burst into flames and crashed into the side of a mountain.

Seven other Fw 190s were destroyed by Maj J E Peery, Capt S W Farnham, Lts J Bond, W Pomerantz and L Schacheur and Flt Offs F G Johnson and W D Terry. Lts Woodman and Bass closed out the scoring with a Bf 109 apiece. A total of 15 enemy aircraft had gone down under the guns of the 'Clan' for the loss of Lt Donald Hawkins.

Aerial action continued on 24 August when the 325th escorted a raid on oil refineries in the Czech city of Pardubice. The USAAF formation

Capt Richard Dunkin of the 317th FS flew P-51D 44-13336 during his second tour of duty with the 'Checkertail Clan' and scored three victories in it to raise his final tally to nine destroyed and one probable (*Dwayne Tabatt collection via Tom Ivie*)

endured very heavy flak as it approached the target, and two P-51s were hit. Both were able to return to base, however, as was a third Mustang crippled by mechanical failure. Over the target area a Bf 109 made a diving attack on the bombers. It was followed down by Capt Richard Dunkin, who reported;

'I was leading my section over the target area when I observed a single Me 109 making a pass at the B-24s. I was at 29,000 ft when I made a diving turn and chased the enemy aircraft to the deck. The Me 109 made a gentle turn to the left, then straightened out as I closed from 275 yards to 150 yards and fired several short bursts from dead astern. I observed strikes in the cockpit as the pilot jettisoned the canopy and the aeroplane crashed into the ground.'

This was Lt Dunkin's ninth, and final, victory.

Moments later a force of 20 Bf 109s and 20 Fw 190s bounced the bombers and shot down seven of them before the 'Clan' could intervene. Additionally, several pilots from the 325th FG reported seeing a captured P-51, painted black with yellow wing stripes, flying with the German fighters. Stung into action by the falling bombers, the 'Clan' bounced the German formations and exacted a small measure of revenge by downing three fighters. Lt Harry Parker reported;

'I attacked a Me 109 at 15,000 ft and fired a short burst from 300 yards, before turning away after my guns quit working. The pilot of the Me 109, however, rolled over and bailed out. My wingman, Lt Gaston, observed the action and confirmed my victory.'

With his 11th kill Harry Parker had now tied with Wayne Lowry as the second-highest scorer in the 325th FG.

Another of the 'Clan's' aces, Lt Robert H Brown, clobbered a Fw 190 for his seventh, and final, kill;

'I attacked a FW 190 at 15,000 ft and he dived away, but I caught up with him at 10,000 ft. I opened fire from 100 yards astern with 40 degrees deflection and closed to 20 ft with no deflection. Many hits were observed on the wings and fuselage of the FW 190 and it burst into flames and crashed into the ground.'

The remaining victory of the day was recorded by Lt P H Whipperfurth.

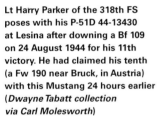

Lt Harry Parker of the 318th FS poses with his P-51D 44-13430 at Lesina after downing a Bf 109 on 24 August 1944 for his 11th victory. He had claimed his tenth (a Fw 190 near Bruck, in Austria) with this Mustang 24 hours earlier (*Dwayne Tabatt collection via Carl Molesworth*)

WHERE IS THE LUFTWAFFE?

After the mission of 24 August the Luftwaffe seemed to vanish from the skies. Indeed, between 25 and 29 August not one enemy aeroplane was seen during escort missions that travelled to Czechoslovakia, Rumania, Austria and Germany. On 31 August the 325th returned to Ploesti when it escorted B-17s that were not carrying bombs, but were instead flying a mission of mercy. Soviet troops had overrun the area and numerous American PoWs had been freed from their Rumanian camps and would now be flown back to Italy in the B-17s. More than 1000 Allied airmen were successfully evacuated during the course of the day.

With the continued absence of the Axis air forces in the sky the 'Clan' received orders to carry out a strafing attack on Debreczen airfield in Hungary on 1 September. The plan called for 11 Mustangs to fly cover for the strafing P-51s, which would attack the airfield from three different directions. The first section would hit the target from west to east, the second section from north to south and the third section from east to west. The three-pronged attack was a complete success, with the 'Clan' destroying 59 aircraft, several transports and four locomotives at the cost of two Mustangs and their pilots. One of the lost airmen was ace Lt Benjamin Emmert, who was downed by flak after destroying five aircraft on the ground. He managed to bail out and became a PoW. The other loss was Lt. Lowell Steere.

The strafing was not the day's only action, as Lt Col Ernest Beverly shot a Me 410 down and Lts Bruce Cobb and David Schmerbeck combined to destroy three Ju 52/3ms. Two of the tri-motor transports were credited to Lt Schmerbeck.

Strafing was also the order of the day on 2 September after the 325th was released from its escort duties in Yugoslavia. Railways became the 'Clan's' target, with pilots strafing the marshalling yards at Nis. The group returned to Yugoslavia the following day, and again it targeted rail traffic between Nis and Belgrade. From 1350 hrs to 1500 hrs 37 of the 'Clan's' Mustangs strafed rail targets and achieved the following results – 13 locomotives destroyed and 25 damaged; 12 freight wagons destroyed and 73 damaged; ten oil wagons destroyed and 15 damaged; 12 trucks destroyed and six damaged; two armoured vehicles destroyed; two coal wagons destroyed and 15 damaged; eight flat wagons with 15 motor vehicles damaged; one house damaged; one railway repair workshop damaged. After the strafing attack was completed Lt Don Terry caught a lone Ju 52/3m in the air and promptly shot it down.

On 4 and 5 September the 'Clan' escorted bombers striking railway infrastructure in Italy and Hungary, and destroyed one more enemy aircraft and several other targets during a strafing run on Bački Brestovac airfield in Yugoslavia. After an uneventful escort mission on 6 September, the group took off for another strafing raid two days later. The target on this occasion was Ecke airfield, again in Yugoslavia. From 1000 hrs 35 of the 'Clan's' Mustangs made between five and eight passes on the deck from the south to the north. The strafing attack destroyed 22 Ju 52/3ms, seven Fw 190s, four Fi 156s, 19 Ju 88s, two Me 210s and a single Bf 109, Hs 126, Bf 110 and Hs 129. One section from the 325th also made a pass at nearby Petrovgrad airfield, where three Ju 52/3ms were destroyed. One P-51 was lost, Flt Off Thomas Rogers last being seen on the first pass over Ecke when his aeroplane pulled up at 500 ft trailing smoke.

A later photo-reconnaissance sortie over Ecke confirmed that all the aircraft on the airfield had indeed been destroyed. Brig Gen Dean Strother, Commanding General of Fifteenth Fighter Command, stated that 'This is the most thoroughly effective strafing attack I have ever known in terms of the completeness of the destruction accomplished'.

The Luftwaffe was still staying on the ground when the 'Clan' escorted bombers to Lobau and Schwechat oil refineries in Austria on 10 September, so one of the 325th's sections looked for targets on the ground during the trip back to Lesina. Me 410s were observed on the airfield at Papa, and after a strafing run nine of them were left in flames.

These recent strafing runs dramatically boosted the 325th FG's score of enemy aircraft destroyed, but unfortunately for the pilots involved these victories did not count towards acedom as was the case in the Eighth Air Force. Nevertheless, they would continue risking their lives by flying these dangerous missions, which further reduced Germany's ability to defend itself against the oncoming Allied forces.

11 September saw a change of command at Lesina when Lt Col Ernest Beverly replaced Lt Col 'Chet' Sluder as CO of the 325th FG – no missions were flown that day. The next two missions were uneventful, but when the 'Clan' travelled to Greece on 15 September two German aircraft were actually seen in the air. The Ju 52/3ms were spotted circling above Megara airfield, and Lts Art Fiedler and John Simmons wasted no time in shooting the 'sitting ducks' down. Lt Simmons reported;

'I was flying over Megara airdrome, in Greece, at 14,000 ft when I saw two Ju 52s in the traffic pattern at "one o'clock". I executed a 180-degree turn and closed on the leading Ju 52 from "seven o'clock". I opened fire

P-51D 44-13322 *Devastating Dottie/ Miss Janie VIII* **was flown by Lt John Simmons, and it is seen here displaying its pilot's final score of seven confirmed kills. Simmons' seventh, and final, victory was a Ju 52/3m that he shot down over Megara airfield, in Greece, on 11 September 1944 (***Dwayne Tabatt collection via Tom Ivie***)**

with a series of short bursts from 1000 ft down to 50 ft and scored hits on the left wing base and front section of the fuselage. The enemy aircraft exploded as I broke away from my attack, then hit the ground enveloped in flames.'

This was John Simmons seventh, and final, victory with the 325th FG. 'Art' Fiedler then took over and blasted the other Ju 52/3m out of the sky for his sixth victory.

While these attacks were taking place two flights of 'Clan' fighters strafed Megara and Eleusis airfields, destroying eight enemy aircraft and damaging four others. Strafing claimed another of the group's pilots when Lt John Lynch's Mustang was hit by flak and he crashed on Eleusis airfield.

During the remainder of September the 'Clan' flew 12 more missions and the Luftwaffe was nowhere to be seen. Two P-51s and their pilots, Lts R A Trautt and G N Strait, went missing probably due to weather over Hungary on 21 September. During early October the Luftwaffe was still absent from the skies, but on the 4th the 325th lost another of its aces when Lt Wayne Lowry was forced to bail out due to mechanical problems on a mission to Munich. He too became a PoW.

Finally, on 12 October, the pilots of the 'Clan' got to fire their guns again during a strafing mission to Budapest and Vienna. The primary targets of the day were railways and their rolling stock, the 'Clan's' pilots claiming 33 steam locomotives, one electric locomotive, eight trucks, two civilian vehicles, 20 oil wagons, one powerplant and one oil barge destroyed, before turning their attention to airfields. Four P-51s strafed Csákvár airfield, destroying five Ju 52/3ms, one Ju 88, one He 111 and two unidentified twin-engined aircraft. A further two Ju 52/3ms and four

A smiling 'Art' Fiedler poses with his Mustang *Helen* after destroying a He 111 on 12 October 1944 for his seventh victory. He finished the war with a total of eight kills and one probable – four of the victories were scored while flying this aircraft (*Dwayne Tabatt collection via Carl Molesworth*)

Go 242 gliders were damaged. Four other Mustangs strafed Győr airfield, destroying four Ju 52/3ms (and damaging two more), a Fi 156 and a Ju 88. Meanwhile, Lt 'Art' Fiedler reported;

'While on a strafing mission between Budapest and Vienna I observed a He 111 at "seven o'clock" at approximately 1000 ft. I closed to about 300 yards and decided to pull out to the side so that I could further identify the enemy aircraft. When the He 111 started firing I turned into it and fired from 75 yards. Many hits were seen to enter the wings, motors and cockpit of the enemy aircraft. At this time the He 111 began burning and started down in a left turn. As I followed it down I fired a few bursts and saw parts flying off of the enemy plane. The burning enemy aircraft continued on down and crashed and exploded.'

Lt Fiedler had just scored his seventh victory. The action in the air did not end with Lt Fiedler's kill, as Lt J V Heimback found and shot down another He 111. Lts H L Long and C C Whitmire closed out the day's scoring by destroying a Fi 156 and an unidentified twin-engined aircraft, respectively.

13 October found the 325th FG escorting B-17s that were attacking the oil refineries at Blechhammer. Again, no aerial opposition was met, and after they were released from close escort the 'Clan' pilots turned their attention to targets on the ground. Two P-51s strafed Csákvár airfield, destroying a pair of Ju 52/3ms, a Fw 189 and an unidentified twin-engined aircraft. All of the Mustangs returned safely to Lesina. The 'Clan' returned to Blechhammer the following day, hitting rail targets on the way home – six locomotives and three oil wagons were destroyed, but at the cost of one Mustang and its pilot, Lt J Houghton.

The group's missions on 16 October were two-fold. One was to provide fighter escort for a 'cloak and dagger' operation involving a PBY carrying British agents whose job it was to foment unrest and encourage sabotage against the German occupiers of Greece, while the second mission was a standard escort to Brux, in Czechoslovakia.

In total contrast to what 'Clan' pilots had been experiencing in recent weeks, 48 enemy aircraft were encountered between Brux and Dresden. A single flight of four Mustangs intercepted the attacking fighters. Leading the USAAF machines was Lt Sheldon K Anderson, who had yet to engage the Luftwaffe in aerial combat despite this being his 31st mission. Anderson's story was related by the 'Clan's' public relations officer;

'Anderson and his wingman, Lt Vernon Kahl, swooped down for positive identification. About half of the enemy formation saw them, dropped their tanks and started to climb. Five minutes later, the youthful flyer who had not done too well in pilot training (by his own admission) had shot down five enemy aeroplanes. Number one – "My wingman and I hit the tail-end flight of the box. The one I went after blew up right in front of my prop".

'The speed of their dive carried them through to the next flight. Number two – "Again I thought I was going to hit him, but the explosion of his aeroplane came just in time. I flew right through the smoke of his explosion".

'Number three – "The formation was scattering out now, but we still had enough speed to keep going after them. The one I got this time seemed to fall apart, there was no explosion".

'Number four – "I went in and got on one's tail. I chased him around a couple of turns, firing all the time. He began to smoke and started going down". The second of two enemies who sought to ambush Anderson was now on his tail, "so I cut the throttle and slowed down".

'Number five – Anderson suddenly twisted his Mustang to the left and then he was on the enemy's tail. He started firing as soon as he came in range. "Only one gun was working. It sounded like a B-B. All of a sudden the Jerry aeroplane went limp, like a rag, as if it didn't have a pilot. It went into a stall and headed down". After that Anderson really did get started for home.'

After a review of his claims Lt Anderson was officially credited with three destroyed (two Bf 109s and one Fw 190) and two probables. His wingman, Lt Kahl destroyed one Fw 190 and probably destroyed a Bf 109. Lt L D Voss closed out the day's scoring by destroying two Bf 109s. No losses were incurred by the 325th FG.

The next four missions – two bomber escorts, one C-47 escort and the escort of a reconnaissance Mosquito – were performed without incident. The periodic escort of reconnaissance F-5 Lightnings or Mosquitos, which started at around this time, came about following the appearance of the Me 262 jet fighter. Prior to its arrival on the scene, the unarmed reconnaissance aircraft, flying at high speed at a very high altitude, had been able to perform their missions without interference.

In an effort to again take the fight to the enemy the 'Clan', on 21 October, headed out for a far-ranging strafing mission that would cover territory between Vienna and Budapest. The targets were the airfields at Szombathely and Seregélyes and rail traffic in the area. The results of this mission were quite spectacular, with 37 enemy aircraft, six locomotives and four tank wagons being destroyed and 20 enemy aircraft, one locomotive and two freight wagons being damaged. In addition to the strafing claims, Lt John Gaia found a Ju 88 in the air;

'While on a strafing mission to Szombathely airdrome I observed a Ju 88 ten miles northeast of the target, coming head-on at me at "nine o'clock" at about 1500 ft. I made a diving turn and came in dead astern of the enemy aircraft. I opened fire at 400 yards and closed to 50 yards. Hits were seen in the cockpit, fuselage and left engine of the enemy aircraft. At this time the left engine caught fire and the enemy aircraft went into a shallow dive. Other members of the flight got hits on the fuselage and right

Lt Oscar 'Ockie' Rau's big day occurred on 5 November 1944 when he led his flight into an attack on eight Bf 109s near Lake Balaton. When the skirmish was over 20 minutes later six of the Messerschmitts had been downed, four of them by Lt Rau (*Dwayne Tabatt collection via Tom Ivie*)

Lt Rau scored his four kills on 5 November 1944 in his P-51B 43-6861 *Funnyface* (*Dwayne Tabatt collection via Tom Ivie*)

When Maj Norman McDonald joined the 325th FG's 318th FS as its new CO in October 1944 he was already an ace with 7.5 victories to his name following a tour of duty with the 52nd FG in 1942-43. He destroyed four more enemy aircraft during his second tour, giving McDonald a total of 11.5 victories, two probable and four damaged (*Tom Ivie collection*)

engine. Shortly afterwards the enemy aircraft crashed and burst into flames.'

Lt Gaia was given full credit for the victory.

One pilot, Lt F Johnson, had to bail out after his Mustang was hit by small arms fire whilst strafing. He was seen to have landed safely on the ground.

Between 23 October and 4 November the 'Clan' flew four escort missions, and again the Luftwaffe was not interested in engaging the bomber formations. However, on 5 November, during an escort to Vienna, the 325th finally engaged a small and reluctant force of eight Bf 109s and shot down six of them. The enemy aircraft were spotted flying northeast at the south edge of Lake Balaton, and Lt Oscar Rau and his flight went after them. By the time this brief, one-sided clash was over Lt Rau had personally downed four of the Bf 109s. He reported;

'I saw three Me 109s flying on the deck and dived down to attack the rear enemy aircraft, opening fire at 250 yards with 20 degrees deflection. Closing to 200 yards, I saw many hits on the wings and fuselage. The Me 109 burst into flames and the right wing fell off, the fighter crashing to the ground. I then pulled up behind another Me 109 and opened fire at 250 yards, closing to 200 yards where I saw numerous hits on the fuselage. The Me 109 immediately pulled up to 800 ft, where the pilot bailed out.

'I next saw a Me 109 trying to pull in behind my wingman. I made a very tight turn and fired a short burst from 90 degrees deflection at the Me 109. My burst missed the enemy aircraft, but in his attempt to evade he tried making a very tight turn and spun into the ground and burst into flames.

'After this Me 109 crashed I was flying at 100 ft when I spotted two Me 109s attempting to land. I chose my target and told my wingman to attack the other enemy aircraft. I closed to 200 yards and opened fire, then closed to 150 yards and saw my gunfire score many hits on the fuselage and cockpit.

The enemy aircraft immediately spun into the ground, where it burst into flames.'

The second of these Bf 109s went down shortly thereafter, having been hit by gunfire from Lt Robert Newell's Mustang.

The sixth kill of the day was scored by Maj Norman McDonald who had recently transferred to the 325th FG from the 52nd FG to take command of the 318th FS. McDonald, who was already an ace with 7.5 victories, downed a Bf 109.

Two missions were flown on 6 November. The first was undertaken by the 318th, which escorted B-24s sent to attack troop movements in Yugoslavia. The Mustang pilots then turned their attention to targets on the ground, four passes being made on motor transport on the road between Mitrovica and Donje Stanovce – 19 trucks were destroyed. Rail targets were also struck, with one locomotive being destroyed and four wagons damaged. During the second mission aircraft from all three squadrons escorted B-24s attacking an ordnance plant in

Ace Lt Richard Deakins scored six victories – three in P-47s and three in P-51s – while serving with the 318th FS. He was killed in a flying accident in a P-47 on 24 November 1944 (*Dwayne Tabatt collection via Tom Ivie*)

Vienna. A solitary Fw 190 was encountered and shot down, its demise being credited to Lt J E Fehsenfeld. However, the Mustang piloted by Lt A K Rebb was lost due to unknown reasons.

Worsening weather was now beginning to have an adverse effect on the group's mission effectiveness. For example, on 11 November, 14 of the 'Clan's' Mustangs were forced to land at various friendly bases in Italy because of weather-related issues on the return trip from Brux. One week later, on the 18th, the Mustangs flown by Lts R A Fischer and R D Dowiatt crashed in the vicinity of Lesina due to poor visibility caused by thick cloud.

Neither the weather nor the Luftwaffe caused the group any issues during a run of seven bomber escort missions in mid November. Finally, on 21 November, in a change of pace, the 'Clan' returned to strafing. It was tasked with patrolling the road between the Yugoslavian towns of Prijepolje and Rogatica, as well as nearby rail facilities, and destroy any moving targets the group encountered. During 45 minutes of strafing the 325th destroyed 51 trucks, a locomotive, three staff cars, three ammunition trucks, a German jeep and 12 horse-drawn carts. It also killed 49 German soldiers. In addition to these claims, another 23 trucks, ten flat cars and six horse-drawn carts were damaged. Two Mustangs were downed by flak during the strafing runs, but both pilots, Lts D C Haertel and C C Whitmire, were seen to bail out and land safely.

Several of the missions flown in late November and in the first few days of December saw Mustangs escorting reconnaissance aircraft over enemy territory. During the third such operation, on 2 December, pilots from the 'Clan' encountered a Me 262 for the first time. The flight had arrived at a point about 50 miles north of Augsburg, in Germany, when a Me 262 flashed through the undercast. One of the P-51 pilots succeeded in hitting it with a few rounds as it shot on past in the direction of the F-5 Lightning that the group was protecting. The jet fired at the reconnaissance aircraft but missed. Its pilot then turned and made a head-on pass at the lead

'Checkerboards' on the tail surfaces were not enough for Lt John Perry and his groundcrew. They duly decorated *Linda Joyce*'s flaps with another display of the 'checkerboard' marking synonymous with the 325th FG, making this fighter one of the most colourful Mustangs in-theatre (*Dwayne Tabatt collection via Tom Ivie*)

P-51, flown by Lt Billy Hinton. Hinton was able to score a few more hits on the jet before the German pilot disengaged and headed east. Lt Hinton was officially credited with damaging the Me 262.

Twelve more uneventful missions were flown between 9 and 17 December. However, on the first mission of the 17th, when the 'Clan' escorted B-17s to Blechhammer, four Fw 190s were encountered south of the target. In an attempt to positively identify the 'bogies' a flight of Mustangs overran the Fw 190s, but fired at them before doing so – Lt C A Morey claimed a probable. The Fw 190s evaded the attack by diving to the deck. Soon after this encounter two Bf 109s were spotted, but they escaped by diving into the clouds. The Mustang of Lt L E Schackner failed to return, his aircraft last being seen headed south across Lake Balaton trailing black smoke.

Fifteen of the 'Clan's' next 20 missions were as escorts for reconnaissance aircraft, with the remaining five being in support of heavy bombers. As per usual the Luftwaffe failed to make an appearance. One P-51 was lost on a bomber escort mission on Christmas Day, although its pilot, Lt L R Merrifield, was returned safely to Lesina. The remaining three missions flown on 25 December were photo-reconnaissance escorts (one to Pilsen, in Czechoslovakia, and two to Munich), and all aircraft returned safely.

Three more missions were flown the following day, two of which were photo-reconnaissance escorts. The third operation was a bomber escort mission, which took the group to the oil refineries of Blechhammer once again. During the approach to the target one of the 'Clan's' Mustangs was hit by flak and had to be escorted back to base. Bombs were released at 1340 hrs, and some 20 minutes later, during the return trip home, Lt David Ambrose spotted a single Bf 109 below him;

'I was at 22,000 ft when I observed a Me 109 flying at 18,000 ft heading toward Linz and dived down to identify it. The enemy pilot firewalled his engine upon observing our P-51s and climbed to 24,000 ft. I closed in and

Mustangs of the 319th FS at rest at Lesina in late 1944. In the foreground is Lt Robert Storey's P-51D *Dottie* (*Dwayne Tabatt collection via Tom Ivie*)

fired a short burst at a ten-degree deflection and saw many hits on the wing. The enemy pilot then split-essed and executed violent turns toward the deck, before levelling off at 10,000 ft. From dead astern I fired a long burst from 1000 ft to 500 ft and observed many hits in the fuselage around the cockpit. The enemy pilot then executed another split-S, levelled out at 3000 ft, jettisoned his canopy and went into a dive, his fighter bursting into flames as it hit the ground. Confirmed by Lt Hosford.'

Five minutes later Lt Fred Wulf claimed another kill;

'I was flying at 26,000 ft when I observed a Ju 88 ahead of me at about 24,000 ft. I attacked from 700 yards, at which point the enemy aircraft turned away and started to climb, firing back at me. I closed to 200 yards dead astern, fired again and observed many hits entering the wings, engines and fuselage. The Ju 88 rolled over, went into a spin and burst into flames. Lts Woodson and Margetts observed and confirmed the destruction of this enemy aircraft.'

The 'Clan' split its forces on 27 December to cover two different groups of bombers attacking the railway marshalling yards in Maribor, Yugoslavia. The bombing ripped the target apart, but again no Luftwaffe fighters rose to defend their territory against the Fifteenth Air Force. The next day the 'Clan' flew to Czechoslovakia to provide penetration escort for B-24s of the 304th Bomb Wing (BW) that were attacking targets in Kolin and Pardubice. The Mustangs were released from escort duty as soon as the bomb run had been completed, and 32 of the 325th's 51 fighters dived down to the decks to carry out strafing attacks on two airfields and numerous road and rail targets.

During 45 minutes of strafing the 'Clan' destroyed four Me 323s, a He 111, a Ju 52/3m, a Fw 190, 26 locomotives, one freight wagon and two vehicles. This success cost the group the P-51 of Lt W C Margetts, who failed to return from the mission.

1944 was then brought to a close with an escort mission to the Brenner Pass in northern Italy, where bombers of the 47th BW attacked bridges and rail targets, and a photo-reconnaissance escort for an aircraft covering future targets in Augsburg.

SWANSONG OF THE LUFTWAFFE

The new year of 1945 began the same way as the old year had ended, with missions being limited by bad weather over Europe. Indeed, only eight missions were flown between 3 and 18 January, and Axis aircraft were not to be seen during bomber escort missions to northern Italy, Germany, Yugoslavia and Austria.

These missions were followed up on 19 January by a fighter sweep over Zagreb and Szombathely, and this time the 'Clan's' pilots found a number of enemy aircraft in the air. Six had been destroyed by the time the group headed for home. The action began when Lt David Ambrose bounced a Ju 52/3m and shot it down north of Zagreb at 1005 hrs. Ten minutes later Lt Robert Reid encountered another Junkers tri-motor southeast of Vienna;

'While participating in a fighter sweep in the Zagreb and Szombathely areas I covered my leader as he made a pass on a Ju 52 flying due east at an altitude of 1000 ft. Because of his excessive speed my leader overshot, and I closed on the enemy aircraft, opened fire with short bursts at 1000 ft and broke off at 500 ft. Direct hits were seen at the wing roots and in the front section of the fuselage as the enemy aircraft went into a spiral and crashed with the left wing enveloped in flames.'

The next German aircraft fell at 1025 hrs under the gunfire of future ace Lt Gordon H McDaniel, and he reported his first kill as follows;

'I was leading a section of eight P-51s at 1000 ft and observed a FW 190 at "five o'clock" at our altitude. I overtook the enemy aircraft, opened fired from 1000 ft with ten degrees deflection and scored many hits on the fuselage and tail. The tail of the FW 190 broke off and the enemy aircraft went straight down, crashing into the ground. Witnessed and confirmed by Lts Wulf, Anodro and Raymond.'

P-51D *Watch On The Rhine* **was assigned to Lt Leland Stacey of the 317th FS, and he used it to claim the last of his three victories (***Dwayne Tabatt collection via Tom Ivie***)**

Ten minutes later at 1035 hrs, Lt Robert Reid claimed his second kill of the day, reporting;

'I was flying at 9000 ft and observed a Me 109 at "one o'clock", 8000 ft below me. I executed a diving turn and closed on the Me 109. I closed throttle, dropped flaps and fired a series of short bursts from 1500 ft to 800 ft from "six o'clock high". Direct hits were seen in the fuselage around the cockpit and the Me 109 dropped a wing and went directly into the ground. Capt Burr observed and confirmed.'

About 30 minutes later Lt Robert W Bean closed out the day's scoring when he shot down an enemy aircraft that he reported as a 'Me 309' (possibly a Fw 190D?). A P-51 was lost due to engine failure, although Lt D Aiken bailed out successfully.

The 325th returned to escort duty on 20 January when it travelled to Regensburg, in Germany. Three groups of B-17s targeted the city's oil storage facilities, and this time the 'Clan' met some resistance from the Luftwaffe. Forty Fw 190s were spotted by a flight from the 317th FS as they were attempting to attack the last box of B-17s. The flight, led by Capt 'Art' Fiedler, charged into the enemy formation, broke up the attack and destroyed four of the Fw 190s – one Mustang was lost in return. The first of the four kills was claimed by Capt 'Art' Fiedler, giving him his eighth, and final, victory of his tour of duty. Fiedler reported;

'While on an escort mission to Regensburg I observed 40 FW 190s just east of the target, approaching from a northeasterly direction at 34,000 ft. We were at 32,000 ft, and I led my flight in a climbing turn after them. I was able to get on the tail of two of the FW 190s and closed on the rearmost enemy aircraft. I opened fire at 200 yards from "seven o'clock". I continued closing to 50 yards and fired again. Many hits were seen to enter the bottom left side of the fuselage, and shortly thereafter the FW 190 burst into flames and exploded in the air.'

The leading scorer of the day, however, was one of the 'Clan's' younger pilots, Lt Edward L Miller, who shot down three Fw 190s;

'While escorting B-17s attacking Regensburg my flight observed 40 enemy aircraft attempting to attack the B-17s and we intercepted the FW 190s. The Germans went into a Lufbery at 33,000 ft and I closed on one of the FW 190s and fired a long burst with 20 down to 5 degrees deflection from 300 down to 150 yards. I saw many hits in the fuselage around the cockpit and base of the wings, and the FW 190 executed a snap roll and the pilot bailed out.

'After this encounter I observed another FW 190 on the tail of a P-51. I dove after the FW 190 and closed from "seven o'clock high", firing a long burst from 300 yards with 25 down to 10 degrees deflection. I saw hits on the base of the wings and the front section of the fuselage. The enemy aircraft executed a modified split-S, began burning and smoking profusely and was last seen spinning into an overcast at 10,000 ft. I then saw an enemy aircraft below the Lufbery and pursued it, opening fire at 400 yards, closing to 150 yards for my last burst. I observed hits on the wings and fuselage, and shortly afterwards the engine quit and the propeller started wind-milling. I followed the FW 190 down and saw it crash-land. I noticed large pieces of it flying off as it crash-landed.'

After two straight days of aerial engagements it was beginning to appear that the Luftwaffe was possibly re-entering the fight, but that proved not to be the case. Indeed, a further 18 missions were flown before another enemy aircraft was sighted and destroyed by a member of the 'Clan'. That event took place on 16 February during an escort mission to Neuburg airfield and the Rosenheim railway marshalling yard in Germany. The engagement took place at 1340 hrs while the 325th was escorting Liberators on the homeward bound leg of the mission. Lt Walter Selenger reported;

'I observed a lone B-24 being attacked by a FW 190 and immediately dived after it. I opened fire at 300 yards directly astern and closed to 160 yards, firing with no deflection. I saw many hits entering the engine, fuselage, cockpit and wings of the FW 190. Black smoke poured from the enemy aircraft, its wheels fell down and the pilot bailed out. Both aeroplane and pilot, whose 'chute did not open, went into the sea.'

The next three missions were all uneventful, but on 19 February the 'Clan' discovered numerous strafing targets in the Vienna-Linz area of Austria. The mission summary stated;

'Seventeen P-51s strafed from St Polten to Amstettin, destroying four locomotives, one tank car, 13 M/T [Motor Transports] and 15 men. Eighteen P-51s strafed between Ybbs and Enns, destroying 18 locomotives, five tank cars and one M/T and damaging 92 freight cars and three barges. Sixteen P-51s strafed between Vienna and St Polten, destroying 19 locomotives, two freight cars, ten tank cars and three M/T and damaging three barges. All strafing was accomplished between 1130-1215 hrs. Four P-51s strafed Markersdorf airdrome at 1145 hrs, destroying one Do 217 and two FW 190s. Two P-51s were lost due to flak in the target area. Forty-eight P-51s down at base at 1415 hrs.'

The next five missions – all bomber or photo-reconnaissance escorts – were completed with the notation 'Mission completed without incident'. On 22 February the 'Clan' returned to strafing, attacking rail targets in the Munich area. The weather, however, was not totally cooperative due to heavy cloud cover, and the strafing was limited to targets in Salzburg, Austria. Here, 12 of the group's Mustangs found a hole in the clouds and succeeded in damaging an electric locomotive, 14 freight wagons and six passenger carriages, as well as a power station and motorised transport. Lt M J Wasser's Mustang was hit by flak during the strafing and he was forced to bail out, while Lt W H Taylor lost the coolant in his engine and crash-landed his fighter. Both pilots appeared to be safe, however.

The next 14 missions (again a mixture of escorts for photo-reconnaissance aircraft and bombers) were uneventful and without loss to the 325th FG. On 28 February the 'Clan' headed out for a strafing mission against rail targets between the Austrian cities of Innsbruck and Salzburg. This turned out to be only a partially successful mission, as just a single locomotive was destroyed. Two more were damaged, as were nine oil tank wagons and 13 box cars, but at the cost of one pilot and his aircraft.

March 1945 began with a move to Rimini airfield near Miramare, in Italy, and a much more successful mission. On 1 March the 'Clan' escorted B-24s to Moosbierbaum, in Austria. After the bomb run was completed the group left the Liberators near Lake Balaton to engage six enemy fighters at 22,000 ft. Before the 'smoke had cleared' five of the German fighters were confirmed as destroyed and the sixth was listed

as probably destroyed. The first victory of the day was claimed by Lt Carl Morey, who stated;

'I attacked a Me 109 from the rear and opened fire from 350 yards with 20 degrees deflection and closed to within 250 yards, firing with no deflection. I saw many hits enter the wings and fuselage of the enemy aircraft, which burst into flames and started spinning down.'

At about the same time Lt Robert Newell bounced a Fw 190, reporting;

'At an altitude of 10,000 ft I attacked a FW 190 from the rear and opened fire from 400 yards with 20 degrees deflection. I closed to 250 yards dead astern, opened fire and saw hits on the tail and fuselage of the FW 190, which burst into flames and crashed into the ground.'

At virtually the same time as the two previous kills Flt Off Bland M Barnes Jr latched onto the tail of another Fw 190. He described his victory in a more formal fashion;

'While participating in a bomber escort to Moosbierbaum oil refineries, I, a wingman in a flight of four P-51s, turned to attack four Me 109s and two FW 190s coming in from the east at "0530 o'clock". A Lufbery then evolved and I got on the tail of a FW 190 and closed to about 300 yards, firing short bursts. Many hits were seen entering the wings and fuselage of the enemy aircraft. The FW 190 split-essed from about 1500 ft, struck the ground and exploded.'

Fifteen minutes later Lt Morey added a second kill of the day to his scoreboard by closing on and destroying a Bf 109. The final victory of the mission was claimed by future ace William Aron, who reported his first victory as follows;

'I was pursuing a FW 190 from an altitude of 400 ft and opened fire from 850 yards with 20 degrees deflection and closed to within 500 yards with no deflection. I saw a number of hits on the wing and the enemy aircraft chandelled up and the pilot bailed out. Lt Newell photographed the bail out and crash of the enemy aeroplane.'

The final claim was a probable scored by Lt G T Barnett over a Bf 109. All of the 'Clan's' P-51s returned safely to base.

Following the Moosbierbaum engagements the Luftwaffe disappeared again during the next 16 missions (1 through 12 March). Since there was no action for the 'Clan' in the skies during this period, the mission for 13 March saw Mustangs sent to strafe railway-related targets in the Munich-Regensburg and Linz areas. However, when the pilots arrived in the target area an overcast prevented strafing. Not content to abort

Lt Bill Aron taxies P-51D 44-15128 *Texas Jessie/Big Mike* **out for another mission in this undated photograph, possibly taken at Rimini. Aron claimed five victories and one damaged, all in this Mustang, between 1 March and 10 April 1945 before being shot down by flak in it on 22 April 1945 (***Dwayne Tabatt collection via Tom Ivie***)**

the mission, nine pilots searched until they found an opening in the cloud cover and strafed railway targets in the Munich, Landshut and Ingolstadt areas. Fourteen more located railway targets in Wiener-Neustadt. The combined totals of the strafing were 26 locomotives destroyed and 33 damaged, 29 freight wagons destroyed and 15 damaged, five passenger carriages damaged, 26 oil

Lt Gordon McDaniel's P-51D 44-14467 was photographed at Mondolfo, in Italy, shortly after its pilot's ace-in-a-day experience on 14 March 1945. As seen here, the aircraft is partially decorated with six kill markings and new red wingtips, but the name *MARY MAC* has yet to be added. Unfortunately, after the name was added to the fighter McDaniel was only able to use it a few more times before the Mustang was lost with Lt Paul Murphy at the controls on 2 April 1945 (*Dwayne Tabatt collection via Carl Molesworth*)

tank wagons destroyed and 16 damaged, one power-house destroyed and one switch house damaged. A Bf 109 loaded on a flat wagon was also destroyed. One of the 'Clan's' pilots was seen to bail out of his crippled fighter during the strafing runs.

When the 325th took off at 1020 hrs on 14 March to escort B-24s attacking the railway marshalling yards at Nové Zámky, in Hungary, no one could have predicted the massive turn of events that would take place on the return trip. It all began when one of the 'Clan's' Mustangs developed trouble with its oxygen supply, forcing the pilot to dive down to a lower altitude. As he came out below the overcast he saw four Fw 190s and radioed for help. When the remainder of his flight dropped down to assist him they ran into a big gaggle of enemy aircraft.

A major dogfight began at around 19,000 ft, and Lt Robert Burns began the massacre of the Axis aircraft by quickly downing a Fw 190 (these fighters were almost certainly from the Hungarian Royal Air Force's 102. *Csatarepülő Osztály*). Next, Lt Gordon McDaniel came in behind a flight of eight or nine Fw 190s flying in a trail formation and took full advantage of the situation. Starting with the last fighter in the formation, he began shooting. Before the hapless pilots even realised what was happening Lt McDaniel had shot down five of them, thus raising his total to six.

Capt Harry Parker, who had only recently returned from leave, found two more Fw 190s at a lower altitude and recorded his 12th and 13th kills. He reported;

'When I attacked a FW 190 at 6000 ft it dived for the deck. I followed it down and opened fire from 1500 ft at 60 degrees deflection and closed to 50 ft dead astern. Many hits entered the fuselage and wings of the enemy aircraft, pieces of which fell off. The enemy aircraft went out of control and the pilot bailed out, but his 'chute failed to open. After downing this FW 190 I attacked another one at 5000 ft. I opened fire from about 4500 ft with 30 degrees deflection and closed to within 50 ft, using no deflection. I saw hits enter the wing roots and fuselage of the enemy aircraft, which went out of control and crashed to earth.'

With 13 victories Capt Parker was now in second place in the 325th's list of aces. Future ace Lt William Aron raised his total to three by downing two Fw 190s at about the same time that Capt Parker claimed his victories. Lt T M Bevan ripped into the remaining Fw 190s, destroying three of them for his first victories of his tour of duty. These kills only describe one half of the destruction suffered by the enemy during this mission. Capt D L

Voss and Lt J S Sutherland each destroyed a Bf 109, and single Fw 190s fell to Lts J B Henry, J G Pace, W K Selenger, R C Burns, P J Murphy and J W Barton. Two other enemy aircraft were claimed as probables and one as damaged. It was a tremendous victory for the 'Clan', whose total for the day was 20 victories, two probables and one damaged at a cost of two P-51s.

This air battle turned out to be the last large-scale dogfight of the war for the 325th.

Capt Harry Parker of the 318th FS scored his 13th, and final, victory on 14 March 1945, and his P-51D 44-14400 displays his final tally. Sadly, three weeks later Capt Parker (the 325th FG's second ranking ace) was killed in action over Austria (*Dwayne Tabatt collection via Tom Ivie*)

Nevertheless, during the last weeks of the conflict enemy aircraft were encountered in smaller numbers on a few occasions, thus allowing the 'Clan' to continue to raise its victory count.

The first of these engagements came on 16 March when Lt J R Dytrych downed a Me 410 during a photo-reconnaissance escort mission to Ruhland, in Germany. Later that day both Capt G Smith and Lt T M Bevan downed a Bf 109. Two more were claimed on 20 March when Lts J C Wilkens and C W Morby downed a Fw 190 and a Bf 109 near Wels, in Czechoslovakia. On 26 March the 'Clan' headed into Czechoslovakia and Austria on a massive strafing mission and destroyed 31 locomotives, along with numerous other rolling stock. But the group paid a high price for this success when three Fw 190s intercepted the Mustangs as they were strafing and Lts R Caudill, V Kahl, J Willhite and L Inks were all shot down. One of the attacking Fw 190s was in turn chased down and destroyed by Flt Off Barnes.

2 April saw the 325th FG moving to its last wartime base at Mondolfo, in Italy, which it would share with the 31st FG. That same day the entire group took off to undertake a broad fighter sweep, the P-51s being broken up into A force, attacking targets from Ljubljana to Celje to Zweiweg to Bruck, and B force, attacking targets from Celje to Maribor to Graz. It turned out to be a mission of both triumph and tragedy for the 'Clan'. The strafing results were minimal, but an encounter with 15 enemy aircraft saw Maj Norman McDonald down two Bf 109s to raise his total to 10.5 kills. A third Bf 109 was sent crashing to earth by Lt G E Amedro. Unfortunately, these victories were dimmed by the disappearance of the group's second ranking ace, Capt Harry Parker. His wingman, Lt Sidney Rosenbloom, reported;

'I was flying as Capt Harry A Parker's wingman on 2 April on a strafing mission in the vicinity of Klagenfurt. Capt Parker observed a "bogie" below and called me, stating that he was going down to investigate. He ordered me to escort Lt Clifford Hill back to home base.' No one knows what happened to Capt Parker, and he is still listed as one of the missing. At the time of his death he had scored 13 victories during 273 missions with the 'Clan'.

Two days later the 325th flew another strafing mission, this time to the Regensburg-Munich-Linz areas, and it was quite successful against targets

The right side of Lt Bill Aron's P-51D 44-15128 before the name *Big Mike* was applied (*Dwayne Tabatt collection via Tom Ivie*)

P-51D 44-63512 *Shu-Shu/Chuck O* was Maj Norman McDonald's last assigned Mustang during his tour of duty with the 318th FS. He scored his final three victories while flying this aircraft (*Dwayne Tabatt collection via Tom Ivie*)

on the ground and in the air. Five locomotives and several other freight wagons and oil tank wagons were destroyed. Upon completion of the strafing runs six Fw 190s were encountered, five of which were promptly shot down. Leading in the scoring was Lt W K Selenger with two of the Fw 190s, which increased his victory tally to four overall (he also had a damaged claim to his name). Lts Bill Aron, J G Howell and L F Seevers accounted for the remaining three kills. For future ace Bill Aron this was his fourth victory, and he also claimed to have damaged the one surviving Fw 190 before it got away.

About 45 minutes later two Me 262s were encountered, and Lt W N Clark shot up one of them sufficiently enough to claim it as a probable. Lt W K Day damaged the second jet before it sped away.

On 6 April the 'Clan' again split into two separate groups to strafe targets in Germany, Austria and Czechoslovakia. It duly destroyed 15 aircraft on the ground, nine locomotives and numerous other railway wagons, including four flat wagons carrying aircraft wing assemblies.

The next time the 'Clan' got to fire its guns was on 10 April during another strafing mission to the Regensburg, Munich and Passau areas. After destroying six locomotives and damaging a radio station, the Mustang pilots turned for home, whereupon they encountered nine enemy aircraft southeast of Linz. During the ensuing dogfight five Fw 190s were destroyed in the initial encounter and, ten minutes later, a Ju 88 was sent down in flames. Maj Norman McDonald destroyed one of the Fw 190s to raise his final score to 11.5 victories. The remaining four Focke-Wulfs were credited to Lts R D Christian, W W Forsyth, J E Mason and

Lt William E Aron of the 318th FS. Downed by flak near Padua, in the Po River Valley, on 22 April whilst flying this aircraft, Aron was reportedly taken alive by local villagers and escorted away. No further information was ever given to his family about his fate, and his body was never recovered. It is believed that Aron was murdered in reprisal for the constant strafing attacks in the Po Valley (*Dwayne Tabatt collection via Carl Molesworth*)

J A Leonard. Lt Bill Aron became the 'Clan's' last ace when he destroyed a Ju 88 for his fifth, and final, victory. He reported his success as follows;

'I observed a Ju 88 flying at 8000 ft, and when I began my attack it went into a dive. I followed it down and opened fire from 1000 ft with 30 degrees deflection. Closing to 600 ft dead astern, I again opened fire. Many strikes were seen in the wing roots before the pilot bellied the Ju 88 in and it burst into flames.'

The 'Clan's' guns remained silent until 18 April, when Maj Ralph Johnson destroyed a Me 262 during a freelance mission into the Regensburg-Munich area. More action followed the following day, when the 325th destroyed seven enemy aircraft. The first kill was credited to Lt Gertin, who had taken off on a test hop to slow time his Mustang's new engine. Whilst flying near Florence a single Fw 190 made a pass at him. Gertin turned into the attack and chased the fighter back to its airfield near Verona, whereupon he shot it down during its landing approach. Later in the day the 317th FS escorted the B-25s of the 340th BG in an attack on the Ora bridge in Italy. On the return trip eight Mustangs tangled with a gaggle of Bf 109s and sent six of them down in flames. Lt W F Baldwin downed two of the Messerschmitts, with the remaining Bf 109s being credited to Lts F W Schaefer, W B Bagley, J Barrett and F M Bolek.

Subsequent missions flown by the 'Clan' were reported as uneventful, but that did not mean without loss. On 22 April the group's final ace, Lt William Aron, was shot down by flak. He bailed out successfully but was murdered by hostile Italian civilians.

The victories of 19 April 1945 closed out the scoring for the 325th FG. During the Mustang era the group had flown 342 missions and scored 246 aerial victories for the loss of 75 fighters in combat. By war's end the 'Checkertail Clan's' final tally stood at 534 aerial victories. An additional 52 enemy aircraft were claimed as probable victories and another 281 aircraft were destroyed on the ground. Strafing victories also included 264 locomotives destroyed and 137 listed as probables. The 325th's 28 aces accounted for 201 of the aerial victories. The group lost 148 pilots during the course of 567 missions.

APPENDICES

Aces of the 325th FG

Rank and Name	Squadron	Official Aerial Credits
Maj Herschel H Green	317th FS	18
Capt Harry A Parker	318th FS	13*
Maj Norman L McDonald	318th FS	11.5 (1)
Capt Wayne L Lowry	317th FS	11
Capt Frank J Collins	319th FS	9
Capt Richard W Dunkin	317th FS	9
Lt Eugene H Emmons	317th FS	9
Capt Arthur C Fiedler Jr	317th FS	8
Lt George P Novotny	317th FS	8
Lt Phillip Sangermano	318th FS	8*
Lt Robert H Brown	318th FS	7
Capt John M Simmons	317th FS	7
Lt Col Robert L Baseler	HQ and 325th FG	6
Lt Col Lewis W Chick	317th FS	6
Lt Barrie S Davis	317th FS	6
Lt Cecil O Dean	317th FS	6
Lt Benjamin H Emmert Jr	318th FS	6
Capt Roy B Hogg	318th FS	6
Lt Gordon H McDaniel	318th FS	6
Capt Ralph G Taylor Jr	317th FS	6
Lt William E Aron	318th FS	5*
Capt Robert M Barkey	319th FS	5
Lt Richard S Deakins	318th FS	5*
Capt Raymond E Hartley Jr	319th FS	5 (2)
Lt Cullen J Hoffman	317th FS	5
Lt Edsel Paulk	317th FS	5
Capt William A Rynne	319th FS	5
Capt Walter B Walker	317th FS	5

Key

* Killed in Action

(1) Maj McDonald scored 7.5 victories with the 52nd FG

(2) Capt Hartley scored three victories with the 353rd FG

1

P-40F-20 41-20006 *MORTIMER SNERD/STUD* **of Lt Col Robert Baseler, 325th FG CO, Mateur, Tunisia, August 1943**
Baseler scored five of his victories in this aircraft. It was later damaged, repaired and repainted black with red trim and modified by removing two of its guns, radio and other items in an attempt to increase its chances of reaching high-flying Axis aircraft.

2

P-40L-1 42-10436 *Duchess of Durham IV* **of Capt Ralph G 'Zack' Taylor, 317th FS, Mateur, Tunisia, August 1943**
Capt Taylor, who served as Operations Officer for the 317th FS, became the 'Checkertail Clan's' first ace when he downed three enemy aircraft on 20 July 1943 to boost his tally to six confirmed victories. Five of the six kills were scored while flying this aircraft, which originally carried number 11 on its fuselage. After being shot up badly in P-40 number 13 Herschel Green wanted no further contact with 'unlucky 13' and Taylor agreed to switch aircraft numbers with him. 42-10436 was passed on to the 324th FG following its service with the 325th FG.

3

P-40F-15 41-19896 of Lt Walter B 'Bud' Walker, 317th FS, Mateur, Tunisia, August 1943
Lt Walker joined the 325th FG in January 1943, and on 30 July that same year he became its third ace. On that date he scored three victories during an aerial battle over Sardinia in this P-40, increasing his overall tally to five. He suffered a wound during the dogfight of 30 July and received a Purple Heart during Bob Hope's USO show at Mateur in August 1943. A few weeks later Walker completed his tour of duty and headed home for a well deserved leave.

4

P-47D (serial unknown) *The Star of Altoona* **of Capt Bunn Hearn, HQ 325th FG, Foggia, Italy, January 1944**
The two kill markings applied to this aircraft denote Capt Hearn's victories in P-40s during June and July 1943. *The Star of Altoona*, however, gained its fame for being the aircraft that 'Herky' Green was using when he scored six victories during a fighter sweep to Villaorba, Italy, on 30 January 1944. On that date he downed four Ju 52/3ms, a C.202 and a Do 217. Green could have probably increased his score if he had known that *The Star of Altoona's* guns had been loaded with 800 rounds per weapon instead of the normal load of 400 rounds that he usually carried in his assigned P-47 '11'.

5

P-47D-16 42-76021 *Rocky* **of Lt Col Lewis W Chick, 317th FS CO, Lesina, Italy, March 1944**
Bill Chick came to the 325th FG as a very experienced P-47 pilot who had flown operationally in England with the 4th and 355th FGs. He was one of three veteran pilots sent from the Eighth Air Force to help with the 325th FG's transition from P-40s to P-47s, and proved to be both an exceptional teacher and leader. While serving as CO of the 317th FS he scored six victories in P-47s, two of them in his *Rocky*.

6

P-47D (serial unknown) of Maj Herschel H 'Herky' Green, 317th FS CO, Lesina, Italy, May 1944
Maj Green, with 18 victories to his name, was the 325th FG's highest scoring ace. He was also a popular and respected leader. Green replaced Bill Chick as CO of the 317th FS, and held this

position for the remainder of his tour of duty with the 'Checkertail Clan'. After barely escaping with his life on his first combat mission, Green took the fight to his Axis counterparts and made them pay a high price for their near victory over him on 19 May 1943. He scored three victories in the P-40, ten in the P-47 and his final five in the P-51 Mustang, making him one of the few USAAF pilots to claim kills in three different types of aircraft.

7

P-47D-6 42-74957 of Lt Cecil O Dean, 317th FS, Lesina, Italy, May 1944
Lt Dean began his flying career as a flying sergeant in September 1942, before becoming a flight officer in December 1942 then joining the 325th FG as one of its original combat pilots. He scored his first victory in the P-40 in July 1943 and his next three in the P-47 on 30 January 1944. Dean received a commission on 2 April 1944 and scored his final two victories in a P-51B. He was involved in a mid-air collision on 2 July 1944 and spent the remainder of the conflict as a PoW.

8

P-47D-16 42-75737 *HUN HUNTER* **of Lt Eugene Emmons, 317th FS, Lesina, Italy, May 1944**
Lt Emmons joined the 317th FS in late July 1943 but remained scoreless while flying the P-40. With the advent of the P-47 he made up for lost time by scoring all nine of his victories between 30 January and 13 May 1944. Four of Emmons' nine kills were scored while flying this aircraft.

9

P-47D-16 42-75971 *Ruthless Ruthie/Lady Janie VI* **of Lt George Novotny, 317th FS, Lesina, Italy, April 1944**
Lt George Novotny was another 317th FS ace that commenced his combat tour flying P-40s, scoring three victories with the Curtiss fighter before converting to the P-47. Novotny's aggressiveness continued into the Thunderbolt era, as he downed five more enemy aircraft before his tour of duty ended. Three of his P-47 victories were scored while flying this aircraft. After Lt Novotny's departure from the 325th FG, future ace Lt John Simmons inherited this aircraft and flew it until the group converted to Mustangs.

10

P-47D-15 42-75829 *GINGER* **of Capt William A Rynne, 317th FS, Lesina, Italy, March 1944**
Capt Rynne joined the 325th FG just prior to its conversion to Thunderbolts, which meant that he had little operational time in the P-40. The big Thunderbolt seemed to be just what he needed, and he scored the first two of his five victories on 31 January 1944. A third followed on 14 February, and Rynne closed out his scoring on 11 March when he downed two Bf 109s and was credited with a probable for a third Messerschmitt. As a result of his aggressiveness and leadership skills, Capt Rynne was given command of the 319th FS on 20 March. His tenure as CO lasted just nine days, however, for he was shot down in a dogfight south of Venice on 29 March 1944 and became a PoW.

11

P-47D (serial unknown) *Little Sir Echo* **of Lt Edsel Paulk, 317th FS, Lesina, Italy, April 1944**
Edsel Paulk reported in to the 325th FS as a flight officer in June 1943, and he was later commissioned as a second lieutenant. His road to becoming an ace began when the 'Checkertail Clan'

converted to P-47s, Lt Paulk scoring all five of his victories with the Thunderbolt between 19 January and 12 April 1944. He completed his tour of duty with the 317th FS in July 1944.

12

P-47D (serial unknown) of Capt Frank 'Spot' Collins, 319th FS, Lesina, Italy, January 1944

Capt Collins scored his first kill on 6 May 1943 during the final days of the Tunisian campaign, and added four more during the fighting over Sardinia, Pantelleria and Sicily. Three of his Warhawk victories were scored while flying P-40F 41-19966. When the 'Clan' converted to P-47s Capt Collins continued his scoring spree by downing four more enemy aircraft (all Bf 109s, and he was also credited with a probable Messerschmitt too), giving him a total of nine kills, one probable and one damaged by the time he finished his tour of duty. This aircraft was allegedly christened *LULU*, but the name was never painted onto the P-47.

13

P-47D-16 42-75971 *Ruthless Ruthie/Lady Janie VI* of Lt John Simmons, 317th FS, Lesina, Italy, May 1944

This aircraft was quite successful during its stay with the 317th FS, with Lt Novotny scoring three of his P-47 kills in it. Future ace Lt Simmons failed to claim a victory with it, however – all seven of his kills would come flying the P-51. When 42-75971 was transferred to the 332nd FG in late May 1944 the P-47 suffered a disastrous fate. Its new pilot, Lt Lloyd 'Scottie' Hathcock, became disoriented during the mission of 29 May and landed it totally intact on an enemy airfield near Rome, where he and his fighter were quickly captured.

14

P-47D-23 42-75008 *BIG STUD* of Lt Col Robert L Baseler, 325th FG CO, Lesina, Italy, April 1944

Lt Col Baseler joined the 325th FG in August 1942 and served as CO of the 319th FS until November of that year, when he became group Executive Officer and Operations Officer. Promoted to group CO in July 1943, he scored the last of six victories (a Ju 88) while flying *BIG STUD*. Baseler's final tally was six destroyed, three probables and three damaged.

15

P-51C-1 42-103324 of Maj Herschel H 'Herky' Green, 317th FS CO, Lesina, Italy, June 1944

Maj Green flew this Mustang on the Shuttle Mission to Russia in June 1944 and several other missions before replacing it with a P-51D in early July 1944. His record while flying the C-model Mustang was two destroyed and two damaged, but he only claimed one of his damaged credits in this particular aircraft. Green's remaining credits while flying the P-51B/C were one kill and one damaged in P-51B '38' and one kill and one damaged in P-51C '31'. His score at this point was 15 kills, one probable and four damaged. 42-103324 was destroyed in a crash on 24 February 1945.

16

P-51B-15 42-106943 of Lt Benjamin H Emmert Jr, 318th FS, Lesina, Italy, June 1944

Prior to his assignment to the 325th FG in January 1944, Lt Emmert had flown a tour in P-39s with the 154th Reconnaissance Squadron. While flying the P-47 Emmert was credited with a G.55 destroyed and a Bf 109 probable. He scored his first Mustang victory in 42-106943 (fitted with a fin leading edge extension) on 11 June 1944. Two weeks later Emmert was assigned P-51D-5 44-13288, and he claimed four more victories with this machine before being shot down by flak on 1 September 1944 and becoming a PoW. 42-106943 had by then been transferred to the 332nd FG. Emmert's final score

in World War 2 was six destroyed, one probable and one damaged, and he claimed another one destroyed and one damaged while flying F-86As in Korea in 1951.

17

P-51C-5 42-103562 *Little Bastard* of Lt Robert H Brown, 318th FS, Lesina, Italy, July 1944

Lt Brown began his scoring in the P-51C in a big way with three kills and a probable over Bucharest on 28 June 1944, but they were claimed in a 'borrowed aircraft'. His only victory in *Little Bastard* came on 27 July when he downed a Bf 109 over Budapest. Brown's next three successes were also scored in 'borrowed aircraft', and his final total was seven kills, one probable and one damaged. Lt Verner Woodman inherited *Little Bastard* from Brown, and he scored one of his four victories in it on 23 August. The aircraft was lost on 17 November with Lt Lawrence Schachner at the controls.

18

P-51C-10 42-103867 *SHIMMY III* of Lt Col Chester L 'Chet' Sluder, 325th FG CO, Lesina, Italy, June 1944

Lt Col Sluder did not qualify as an ace since he was only credited with two aerial victories, but his leadership between 1 April and 23 August 1944 was inspired. Indeed, it was one of the primary reasons why the 'Clan' enjoyed such success against a determined enemy. Sluder led 64 Mustangs on the Shuttle Mission to Russia in this aircraft in a flawless manner on 2 June 1944. He scored his only Mustang victory four days later while leading a mission from the Russian airfield at Pyriatin to Galati, in Rumania. After a five-day delay due to weather, he led his men back to Lesina from Russia on 11 June 1944.

19

P-51C-5 42-103581 *Mary Norris* of Lt Phillip Sangermano, 318th FS, Lesina, Italy, August 1944

Lt Sangermano was assigned to the 318th FS near the end of May 1944, and within two months of his arrival he was already an ace with six victories to his credit. He completed his scoring on 23 August 1944 when he downed two Fw 190s and damaged a third Focke-Wulf during a mission to Austria, raising his totals to eight kills and one damaged. Five of his eight victories were scored while flying this aircraft – it is not known if the name *Mary Norris* was ever actually painted onto the Mustang. Sadly, Lt Sangermano lost his life on 9 December 1944 when he took off in P-51C 42-103410 for a local test flight and disappeared. It was later learned that he was jumped by enemy aircraft and shot down, an Italian family caring for the mortally wounded ace until he passed away.

20

P-51B-15 43-24822 of Lt Richard Deakins, 318th FS, Lesina, Italy, June 1944

Lt Deakins joined the 325th FG at the end of December 1943, and by 13 April 1944 he had scored three victories in his P-47D 42-75824. After the conversion to Mustangs he quickly added two more victories during June 1944, both of which were scored in this aircraft. Deakins died in a flying accident in a P-47 on 24 November 1944.

21

P-51B-5 43-6861 *Funnyface* of Lt Oscar Rau, 318th FS, Lesina, Italy, November 1944

Lt Oscar Rau never became an ace with the 'Checkertail Clan' but he made a determined effort to do so when he downed four Bf 109s within 20 minutes whilst at the controls of this aircraft near Lake Balaton on 5 November 1944.

22

P-51B-15 43-24877 *Penrod* of Capt Roy Hogg, 318th FS, Lesina, Italy, June 1944

Capt Hogg joined the 325th FG in March 1943 and subsequently became one of the few USAAF pilots to score victories in three different types of fighter. He claimed his first two victories in June and July 1943 in P-40s, then added two more in January 1944 in a P-47 and finished his scoring on 6 June 1944 when he destroyed two Fw 190s while flying this particular Mustang.

23

P-51B-15 43-24857 *Dorothy-II* of Capt Robert M Barkey, 319th FS, Lesina, Italy, June 1944

Bob Barkey was assigned to the 325th FG in late 1943 during the unit's conversion from P-40s to P-47s, and he soon found the Thunderbolt to be an excellent mount. Between 22 January and 24 May 1944 he downed four Bf 109s, and later added a probable victory over a C.202 before switching to this Mustang. Barkey claimed the last kill of his war in 43-24857 on 6 June 1944, and two weeks later he was sent home to participate in a War Bond Drive.

24

P-51B-15 43-24893 of Capt Raymond E Hartley Jr, 319th FS CO, Lesina, Italy, June 1944

Capt Hartley was assigned to the 325th FG in December 1943 and commanded the 319th FS from 28 March through to June 1944. During his tour of duty with the squadron he was credited with two kills and one damaged. Hartley left the 'Clan' in August 1944, and following a Stateside leave he flew a second tour with the Eighth Air Force's 353rd FG. On 24 March 1945 he shot down three enemy aircraft and damaged a fourth to take his final tally to five destroyed and two damaged.

25

P-51D-5 44-13336 *THISIZIT* of Capt Richard Dunkin, 317th FS, Lesina, Italy, August 1944

Capt Dunkin flew two tours with the 325th FG. During his first he destroyed four enemy aircraft while flying both the P-40 and the P-47. Upon his return to the 325th in July 1944 Dunkin continued his scoring ways by destroying four Bf 109s (with a fifth as a probable) and a Fw 190. His total stood at nine kills and one probable by the end of his second tour.

26

P-51D-5 44-13498 *Miss Ridge* of Maj Herschel H Green, 317th FS CO, Lesina, Italy, July 1944

Maj Green scored his last three victories in this aircraft (which bore the name *Miss Ridge* on the right side of its nose), destroying two Bf 109s and a Fw 190. At some point between his 17th (14 July) and 18th (23 August) victories a fin strake was added to this aircraft.

27

P-51D (serial number unknown) *My Gal Sal* of Lt Wayne Lowry, 317th FS, Lesina, Italy, August 1944

Although Lt Lowry was assigned to the 325th FG in January 1944, it would be almost six months before his run of victories commenced on 6 June 1944. By 7 August he had amassed a total of 11 aircraft destroyed and two probables, with the last five kills being scored in this aircraft. Lowry became a PoW on 7 October 1944 after running out of fuel during a mission.

28

P-51D-5 44-13451 *Bee* of Lt Barrie S Davis, 317th FS, Lesina, Italy, August 1944

Lt Davis joined the 325th FG in late March 1944, and by 22 August he was an ace with six victories to his credit. Four of his kills were scored in this aircraft. Davis finished his tour of duty and returned to the US in November 1944.

29

P-51D-5 44-13322 *Devastating Dottie/Miss Janie VIII* of Lt John M Simmons Jr, 317th FS, Lesina, Italy, August 1944

Lt Simmons joined the 325th FG in the spring of 1944 and scored the first of his seven victories on 23 June in a 'borrowed' Mustang. His remaining six kills, however, were all scored in 44-13322.

30

P-51D-5 44-13??? *Helen* of Capt Arthur C Fiedler Jr of the 317th FS, Lesina, Italy, September 1944

'Art' Fiedler was assigned to the 325th FG on 20 May 1944, and he scored his first kill on 28 June – he made ace within a month. Between 15 September 1944 and 20 January 1945 he added three more victories, and his final total was eight destroyed and one probable. Four of Fiedler's kills were scored in this aircraft.

31

P-51D-10 44-14467 *MARY MAC* of Lt Gordon H McDaniel, 318th FS, Rimini, Italy, March 1945

Lt McDaniel was assigned to the 325th FG in September 1944 and he scored his first victory on 19 January 1945. After a two month dry spell he quickly became an 'ace-in-a-day' by destroying five Fw 190s on 14 March 1945. All six of McDaniel's victories were scored in this Mustang.

32

P-51D-16 44-15128 *Texas Jessie/Big Mike* of Lt William E Aron, 318th FS, Rimini, Italy, March 1945

Lt Aron began his tour of duty with the 325th in early November 1944, and he would have to wait almost four months to begin his scoring spree. He claimed his first success on 1 March 1945, and by 10 April Aron had raised his total to five destroyed and one damaged, all of which were claimed in this aircraft. Downed by flak near Padua, in the Po River Valley, on 22 April whilst flying 44-15128, Aron was reportedly taken alive by local villagers and escorted away. No further information was ever given to his family about his fate, and his body was never recovered. It is believed that Aron was murdered in reprisal for the constant strafing attacks in the Po Valley.

33

P-51D-10 44-14400 of Capt Harry A Parker, 318th FS, Rimini, Italy, March 1945

This Mustang was the last of three P-51Ds assigned to Capt Parker, and he scored his final two victories with it on 14 March 1945. Parker had joined the 325th in May 1944, and during two tours he became the 'Clan's' second highest scoring ace with 13 victories and seven damaged claims to his name. He was killed on 2 April 1945 during his 237th mission.

34

P-51D-20 44-63512 *Shu-Shu/Chuck O* of Maj Norman McDonald, 318th FS CO, Mondolfo, Italy, April 1945

Maj McDonald was already a 7.5-victory ace (claimed while flying Spitfires with the 52nd FG) by the time he joined the 325th FG during the autumn of 1944. This Mustang was the second of two assigned to him, and he added four more victories to his total while flying 44-63512. His final victory count was 11.5 kills, two probables and four damaged.

35

P-51D (serial unknown) of Lt Cullen Hoffman, 317th FS, Lesina, Italy, June 1944

Lt Hoffman joined the 325th FG in October 1943, and between 31 January and 13 June 1944 he downed five enemy aircraft (and damaged a sixth) in P-47s and P-51Bs. This was his last assigned aircraft, but it never scored a kill with Hoffman at the controls.

36

Bf 109G *Hoimann*, flown by Lt Col Bob Baseler, 325th FG CO, Mateur, Tunisia, June 1943

This aircraft was captured intact and airworthy by the 'Clan' in North Africa and repainted flat black with red trim. After the P-38 Lightning-equipped 14th FG attacked the 325th's P-40 Warhawks by mistake, Lt Col Bob Baseler beat up the airfield of the nearest Lightning group (which was home to the 1st FG) that evening in this fighter in an effort to help with the pilots' Axis aircraft recognition!

INDEX